Praise for *The Monk Within*

"This is a book I have been longing for! Beverly Lanzetta has delved deeply into the wisdom of Christianity and other faith traditions and shares here her study and experience of monasticism. But this book is not satisfied in rehearsing traditional monastic practice. It offers a profound synthesis of ancient sapiential theology with contemporary women's contemplative experience. Dualisms of celibacy and sexuality, solitude and relationship, contemplation and world engagement are beautifully broken down. Here is a spiritual vision for women and men who long for the divine and yet live in the world. Here is a "new monasticism" that will inspire a generation of seekers and lovers of God, humanity, and the world." —Wendy Farley, Professor of Christian Spirituality, San Francisco Theological Seminary and author of *Tragic Vision and Divine Compassion: A Contemporary Theodicy*

"This work is a beautiful reflection on a path that, once upon a time, called seekers to the deserts of Egypt. This book empowers contemporary seekers to find that same desert within their hearts, all while living in the world, confronting structures of violence and oppression, and learning how to help make God all in all. Written from a place of deep prayer, experience, and mystical intuition, it provides invaluable guidance for a world in crisis, inviting people to honor the universal impulse to say yes to God in an authentic way so we can all serve the needs of our time." —Adam Bucko, co-founder of The Reciprocity Foundation and co-author of *Occupy Spirituality: A Radical Vision for a New Generation* and *The New Monasticism: An Interspiritual Manifesto for Contemplative Living*

"*The Monk Within* guides the yearning soul toward the quiet reassurance, devotion to all being, and boundless joy that arise from unmediated engagement with the ever-present Divine. A path of compassionate, integrative, long-seeing faith: the mystic's way of unfolding the Mystery within the ordinary. Read, practice, and find comfort for your restless heart." —Rabbi Raachel Jurovics, President, Association of Rabbis, Cantors, and Rabbinic Pastors for Jewish Renewal and contributing author, *Seeking and Soaring: Jewish Approaches to Spiritual Direction*

"Connection. That is the word that resounds in Beverly Lanzetta's book, *The Monk Within*. Connection with the Holy One, with humanity, and with creation. The new monastic impulse honors the sanctity of creation and the miracle of the spirit, holding the divine presence in one's heart. This book, in a very real way, is a call to the desert as the early monastics journeyed to so long ago. This new desert is not dependent on institution, but embraces mystery, plurality, and openness to the upwelling of God in the soul." —Michael Peterson, OSB, Chairman of the Board, Monastic Interreligious Dialogue and Oblate Director for Saint John's Abbey.

"Beverly's book is a powerful witness that braves the flow and flux of contemporary monastic forms. With insight and passion she identifies the essential elements of the monk's "seeking God" and highlights the paradox of it being both equally for everyone and yet for some in a particular way. As a guide through this often-cloudy time she brings range of vision and sure subtlety of spiritual touch." —Laurence Freeman OSB, director of the World Community of Christian Meditation and author of *Christian Meditation: Your Daily Practice and Light Within: Meditation as Pure Prayer*

"A radiant book, Beverly Lanzetta's latest reminds me why many of us love the Christian mystical tradition but also have trouble finding a home in its wings. The desert calls us, and what we feel there doesn't seem to hold when we try institutions of faith. This is not to say that Lanzetta's take on new monasticism is only for Christians, but for those of us to whom it will speak profoundly, she's a sure guide across the mysteries." —Jon M. Sweeney, publisher of Paraclete Press and coauthor of *Meister Eckhart's Book of the Heart*

"*The Monk Within* is a striking reminder that the truly spiritual life is essentially an inward journey toward a deeper and more penetrating sense of the sacred. Written by one of America's most impressive spiritual figures and writers, this book yields something meaningful for persons of virtually every faith tradition. Her rich tapestry of spiritual wisdom and reflections is really a blessing for these times, when we are witnessing an unprecedented crisis of the sacred. An insightful, inspiring, and moving book!" —Lewis V. Baldwin, Professor Emeritus of Religious Studies, Vanderbilt University and author of *Never to Leave Us Alone: The Prayer Life of Martin Luther King, Jr.*

The Monk Within:

Embracing a Sacred Way of Life

Beverly Lanzetta

BLUE SAPPHIRE BOOKS
SEBASTOPOL

Cover and interior design: Nelson Kane

PUBLISHER'S CATALOGING-IN-PUBLICATION DATA
(Prepared by The Donohue Group, Inc.)

Names: Lanzetta, Beverly.
Title: The monk within : embracing a sacred way of life / Beverly Lanzetta.
Description: Sebastopol, CA : Blue Sapphire Books, [2018] | Includes
     bibliographical references and index.
Identifiers: ISBN 9780984061655 | ISBN 9780984061662 (ebook)
Subjects: LCSH: Spiritual life. | Monastic and religious life. | Feminism-
     -Religious aspects. | Nature--Religious aspects. | Religions--Relations.
Classification: LCC BL624 .L36 2018 (print) | LCC BL624 (ebook) | DDC 204-
     -dc23

Printed in the United States of America

Contents

Wisdom of the Elders

Revisioning Monastic Principles

For my granddaughters, and the next generation, of beautiful monastic hearts:

Sophia

Amira

Isabel

Geneva

Ella

The New Monk

ONE

Longing for Solitude

I IMAGINE THAT FOR MANY OF YOU—as it was for me—the call to be a monk, to seek silence and solitude was in your heart from early childhood. As a nine- or ten-year-old, I loved to be alone in the woods near our home. Here, I experienced Silence. I was free—unbounded—of obligations, interpretations, and identities. I must have sensed that I was being drawn in a direction different than that of my schoolmates.

The joy of being alone and longing for silence caused pain—the extremity of my need was not understood. I had no guidance on how to affirm my quest, or how to establish a self-identity in alignment with this deep call. My childhood experiences of closeness to nature—coupled with my classmates often-cruel behavior toward perceived outsiders—turned me inward, alienating me from family and friends. Yet I could not quell my passion to find what was beyond the everyday.

Because the solace I found in solitude not only was suppressed, but also lacked a language of expression, it remained underneath everything as a feeling state, an aspiration that was never satiated by the multitude of things the world offered.

And perhaps, like many of you, years passed without being able to identify the call.

Looking back, I place awareness of my monastic nature to an evening when I was reading, "Notes for a Philosophy of Solitude," an essay by the Trappist monk Thomas Merton. This was sometime in the 1970s, my children were asleep and, as a recently divorced parent, I had no intrusion into my night rituals. Suddenly, so many aspects of my personality made sense: *I am a monk!* Yet, like other women of my generation, I had pursued the path of marriage and children. How was *I* going to be a monk? I would need time to sort out the implications—marriage, motherhood, and gender roles—of my realization. I would have to explore a spiritual love that was greater than my individual life and personal pain. I would undergo a number of trials before I was able to seize my vocation.

My affinity with monasticism was unformed until one October day in 1976 when a series of revelatory events changed my life and set me on a path of devotion. It was on this day that Divine Mystery broke into my world, transforming my whole being and opening me to a previously unimagined sacred realm. Nothing in my life since compares to the profound changes that took place in my heart and soul that day, which I have described in detail in previous books.[1]

Immediately after this event, I left behind the life I had known. Before long, I was offering classes on contemplation and serving as a spiritual guide to people within and outside religious affiliation. The common denominator in this period was my desire to grow closer to God and to help others embrace the contemplative call. For those who felt disenfranchised by their religion, or who were exploring a renewal of faith, I encouraged them to seek the monk within. Before religion or identity is the capacity for silence and solitude intrinsic to personhood. It is the birthright of everyone.

While my October experience implicitly honored the world's wisdom traditions, it was not a disclosure of these historical religions. It was the unveiling of the Divine—unobstructed by history or theology—whole unto itself. Looking back, it seems as if a new vein of truth was released from the collective storehouse of wisdom, replete with its own language, mysticism, meditative techniques, and vision of ultimate reality. Founded on a unitive consciousness that is nonviolent, merciful, and theologically open, it ushered into my life a new spirituality, perhaps a new way of being human.

I believe that many people have had religious experiences that lack a formal name or association with a divine figure. Increasingly, people self-identify as interfaith, or spiritual but not religious. My sense is that they, too, have tapped into the quickening moment that is pre-religious, before silence becomes word. Perhaps it is akin to the Zen *mu* (absolute nothingness) or what the German mystic Meister Eckhart called the "desert of the Godhead"—and his prayer to God, to free him from "God." The person who has been seized by the Divine Presence and has died to his or her self knows what this is. It is radical openness, flowing in and out of heaven, and direct and unmediated contact with the holy. When the moment comes, when the gift is given, everything in life is seen from a unique vantage point. Faith begins anew. The person becomes a devotee, a disciple of wisdom.

Feb 2015

What I've learned over these years is that the spiritual quest is a fundamental orientation common to the human experience. The commitment to seek the ultimate—Great Spirit, Brahman, Allah, God, etc.—is imprinted in the heart of the world. I also have learned that we live in an era of new visions of the sacred and types of religious expression; the monastic heart resides within all people, regardless of life situation or vocation; and it is a sacred duty to share contemporary spiritual ways of being in a world often lacking healthy models of faith.

Whether or not you belong to a religion, or are uninterested in religion, there is a divine path interior to your being, an organic constellation of wisdom imprinted into your soul. If you have the courage to advance into the mystery of your own solitude, you will discover it for yourself. Composed of its eternal nature, you cannot be lost, abandoned, or forgotten. In the secret teachings of love you will be guided on a spiritual journey that forges a path of holiness in your being and in the world.

New Visions of Monkhood

AS ANCIENT CIVILIZATIONS gave rise to the monastic impulse within a particular religious way of life, our historical period is birthing a new expression of monasticism. It is being shaped by a dynamic, fast-paced global society; by openness to multifaith and interspiritual conversations; by concern for suffering and the ravages of violence; by a desire to prevent further destruction to Earth and its ecosystems. It is fueled by a need for meaning, perhaps nowhere more apparent than in the day-to-day difficulties that beset people today. It is a return to our source, to the visionary, ethereal, awe-inspiring knowledge of those who ventured into the dark regions and came away illumined, transformed.

For centuries, the longing for solitude and closeness to God has engendered rarefied states of consciousness. I hold, as many others do, that the monk is an original essence within each person. Each of us retains a core of silence and solitude that belongs to Mystery alone. An intrinsic part of human nature, the monastic instinct never is extinguished, but expresses its passion for the sacred wherever life is found. Throughout history, monastic communities were established on this desire to become holy, in the process transforming cultures and preserving sacred ways of life. In whatever form—as wandering *sannyasa*, desert abbas, hermits, or cenobites—this primary impulse is present. The monk exists not solely to practice solitude, austerities, vows, obedience, or celibacy. He or she is not solely concerned with community or aloneness or leaving secular society. In the first instance, the desire for monastic solitude arises from passionate and devoted commitment to give one's life to the Divine.

Today we choose to cultivate monastic consciousness beyond the monastic enclosure and even outside of a religious denomination. We draw upon the wisdom of the world's spiritual traditions and the thought of contemplative masters. It is as if the doors of the monastery were flung open and we've been granted access to the collective storehouse of human spiritual possibility.

This development, which offers a monastic way of life for anyone, including the uncloistered and the religiously unattached, grows out of silence itself. For in meditative awareness, we discover the radical emptiness that is more primordial than religious identity—being Christian, Jewish, Buddhist, Hindu, etc. We are called to plant the seeds of a new kind of monastic devotion, one that is open to people of religious, nonreligious, and spiritual orientations.

Of course, the longing for God does not require a monk's robe or ascetic practice or even community. It is imprinted in the soul as its first prayer. It is the quest for the Absolute, which burns like fire in a person's being and will not be quenched until the longing is heeded. And so, the monastic impulse is intrinsic to the human heart. It is imbedded in our spiritual DNA, forming our souls, personalities, and orientations to the world.

The historical monk is a person who publicly vows to spend his or her life seeking the Ultimate. Monks have traditionally been countercultural figures who give up social expectations such as sex, marriage, career, and money—to live singularly devoted to this search. It is the integrity of standing alone, advocating for silence, and developing a spiritually mature outlook that signifies the monk's vocation—the fulcrum or still point around which his or her heart revolves.

As in times past, monks continue to live as hermits, in small traveling groups, and in established residential communities. Yet the size of monastic communities—especially in Western industrialized nations—has diminished, and many of my monastic friends wonder if monasticism will survive in the form it has assumed these past centuries. At the same time, another movement is in play. Across the globe, there is increased interest in monasticism, contemplative prayer, meditation, and silent retreats. Books on these topics (listed in the bibliography)—as well as outreach efforts by monastic orders—have contributed to the formation of new monastic communities, monastic interreligious dialogue, and a universal order of monks. It is a path that celebrates the time-honored wisdom of monastic consciousness—while it simultaneously transposes the role and function of the monk—moving from its traditional focus on ascetic separation from the world, to one of integration with the whole of life's gifts.

If the monastic orders as we know them are in danger of becoming obsolete, the archetype of the monk within us is not.

[handwritten margin note: Contemplation is a protest to rest of life]

What All Persons "Ought to Be"

IN *THE BROTHERS KARAMAZOV*, Father Zossima says that a monk is not a special sort of person, but only what all persons "ought to be." The monk symbolizes one dimension of our natures and the possibility that each of us can reach this dimension. Although not everyone is suited to formal monastic life, we all have a contemplative dimension that is worthy of cultivation. The challenge of being modern, uncloaked monks consists in the attempt to integrate what every person "ought to be" into the wider social and personal circle of our lives. Not aligned with the historical isolation of the monk, or with extreme forms of ascetical renunciation, the contemporary seeker desires to return to the simplicity of the contemplative ideal. As we enter the archives of monastic history, we discover how these ancient resources can assist us in integrating all aspects of contemporary life—work, family, friendship, and sexuality—into the sacred dimension of being.

[handwritten margin note: Monk todo for better entirety life]

Our contemplative nature lives in protest to the complexities of life; while beneath society's competing attractions, the longing for the holy erupts in our souls. The monastic personality finds nourishment in solitude that the relationships of the world cannot provide. Here we contemplate divine things. Here we listen for the whisper of the Beloved, for the truth that can never be captured or diminished or embellished by material goods. Here we are betrothed to solitude, married to silence.

So much of life—even monastic life in its traditional forms—is the pursuit of an already established theology, pattern of consciousness, spiritual practice, or understanding of ultimacy. From the moment we take our first breath until the moment we pass from this world, someone or something is labeling the self. It is the work of the spiritual person to maintain nonviolent resistance to these affronts, and to claim the right to an inner life, and to a solitary encounter with his or her divine source. Often, the monk is a person whose inner nature balks at the norm, who lives in protest to what convention finds significant or meaningful, and who dedicates his or her life to the pursuit. For this reason, the monastic person is often a spiritual revolutionary—not at peace with what fuels and inspires mainstream society.

Monasticism is nothing more than a deconstruction project of continually stripping away unhealthy, false, or degraded identities to encounter the source of life's fullness. We abandon the known for the unknown. Not relying on historical patterns and consensual agreements about how one should practice and live—without rejecting the authentic value and meaning in the world's religions—the new monk is challenged to explore the wild regions, and to find the courage to be an artist for the divine.

naked true self

The desire to pursue the new face of monasticism—to be a universal monk of peace—is a response to the fragileness of the Earth and the alienation of our collective psyche. This call arises from the threat under which much of life, human and planetary, now endures and suffers. It is a call to probe more deeply and profoundly the capacity of the human heart, the efficacy of love as a force of transformation, and the significance of mystical participation in the building up of the world. It inquires: who speaks for the soul today? Is it just the material world? Is it just violence that speaks? The commitment to be a universal monk serves as a counterbalance to the wanton desecration of the spirit in our midst. It is a promise to put our lives in service of the dignity of all beings, and become a friend of the soul.

The new monastic may not be identified with a specific religion or belong to a community. Rather, such a person is staking his or her life on *yes*: the affirmation of love and nonviolence. Being a monk is not attachment to an identity—even to being a monk—but following the call within to honor the sanctity of creation and the miracle of spirit, holding the divine presence in one's heart. It is a commitment to be for the other and not for the self, which yearns to give away all that is petty, constricted, or selfish in one's heart. It is the soul's witness to the tragedies that wound our world, which offers a home for the homeless, a balm of forgiveness for human cruelty and pain.

What is this inner silence that leads us away from the common to the rare, that fosters protest against the way things are, that requires that our wills be harnessed to the divine will, and our feet walk in the footsteps of the saints?

There is no new monasticism without the aspiration of the person who yearns to be free and—in a gesture of faith—surrenders to Mystery.

Returning to Monastic Roots

IT OFTEN REQUIRES TIME and wisdom to heed the inner voice. In my case, the underlying attraction to solitude that I experienced as a child never left me, although many years passed before I formally professed vows as a universal monk of peace. My journey was assisted and witnessed by a small community of women Benedictine monks. Drawing on the eternal call both of and to monasticism, my vows were not made under the auspices of Benedictines or Christianity. Neither were they a rejection of these ancient traditions. Rather, I took monastic vows of commitment to the mystical heart of reality, to that enduring center that precedes and informs religious identification and institutional form. I took vows to love the Divine—and all of creation—and to serve others through love. The ceremonial ritual of monastic profession was spiritually profound, as my consciousness was further re-formed around silence, simplicity, and solitude. Practically, I now assess everything in my environment from this perspective: what brings me closer to the Beloved, what offers peace, great silence?

When people learn I have embraced a monastic form of life, frequently they ask whether the notion of a new kind of monk in the world (especially a re-married woman with grown children) is not stretching the boundaries of monasticism, leading to a dilution of its historical forms. However, I hold that the path that I (and many others) follow today harkens back to the most ancient of expressions—that primordial mystical simplicity, of surrendering oneself to the unknown. I suspect that many monks and hermits—within or outside formal monasteries—eventually abandon the trappings of traditional monastic life, including whatever is institutional, in favor of a more compelling and elusive freedom.

People also question whether there is a genuine spiritual foundation and sacred path for people who identify as multi-religious, spiritual but not religious, nonbelievers, lapsed or dissatisfied members of their denomination, or simply seekers of a new way. Or, is this desire for a new monasticism transitory, or even naïve, superficial, or blasphemous? People want to know: What is the theology or spiritual philosophy that underlies a global monastic path of faith? What spiritual practices and forms of prayer and worship are followed? To which god, master, mystic, or ultimate source does a seeker turn on this path?

Many of these concerns are addressed in the following chapters. Yet, in some primary sense, they arise out of an old paradigm, a collective consciousness formed by the history of discrete religious identities, tribal affiliations, and formal declarations of truth. The answers we seek require a different orientation to the inner life and to the subject of monasticism. We need to dispense with the belief that the only authentic faith is one that is already determined and has a name. We need to recognize with humility that we do not know nor can we control how divine love takes root in a person's heart, and beckons a person to devote his or her life to God.

Of equal significance is that the monasticism of present and future generations may take substantially different expressions than in previous centuries. Evidence of new religious experience is apparent in the varied ways that the sacred is celebrated and practiced today. Human consciousness has entered a period of gestation, as religious life is re-formed and re-born with the heart and spirit of an interdependent world community. We cannot predict where this emerging spiritual consciousness will lead—perhaps to new religions, or to spiritual paths that refuse to take on institutional identity and instead will manifest many varied personal expressions.

Over the course of more than forty years, I have sought the mystical heart of reality, focusing my work on the integration of inner experience with daily life events. I have been grateful to walk this path with women and men from many religious and nonreligious backgrounds, as well as with scholars, clergy, nuns, monks, and hermits. Much of my teaching has taken place in retreat settings, private homes, community churches, monasteries, and lecture halls.

In each of these endeavors, I have been in pursuit of a contemplative experiment, a school for the study of mystical wisdom, and the formation of new monastic community. I have witnessed the tremendous spiritual changes that occur through deep study, personal commitment, and the taking of monastic vows. I have been awed by the effect that mystical wisdom has on the person seeking God or Truth, the efficacy of spiritual development that draws from the inherited knowledge of the world's religions, and from an ever-emerging revelatory disclosure, that is future-oriented and beyond the patriarchal mindset.

Underlying these projects is my advocacy for new visions of the sacred, one that has progressed in four interlocking modes: the **mystical path of the feminine** (which I call *via feminina*)—inspired by the neglected wisdom of women mystics and the founders of female monastic communities; **embodied spirituality** grounded in the sacred web of life and inclusive of divine-soul-body-earth; the **archetype of the monk**, or monastic archetype that is the deep truth of every person and not the exclusive domain of the vowed religious; and the interdependence of the world's wisdom traditions, expressed through **interfaith, interspiritual dialogue**. Of course, embodied spirituality, contemplative dialogue, the divine feminine, and living as a monk in the world are not confined to my experience.

Thus, although this book captures certain essential features of what is loosely termed, the "new monasticism," I do not claim to be speaking for new monasticism in general or for any specific community, practice, or teacher. The monastic journey expressed in these pages is the path I live and the vision I share, but it is not the only or final way.

· ◆ ·

THE MONK WITHIN brings together many of the spiritual talks I have presented on this vibrant and sacred way of life, organized and edited for a reading audience. It is also the first volume of a three-book project, which will include a second volume on spiritual practices and formation, and a third on prayers and liturgies.

If the new monastic way I share in this book can be identified at all, I would say it emerges from intimate contact with a theology of kinship, of a mothering wisdom so vital and yet lacking in our world. It also is nestled in the soil of our collective religious heritage. Yet unlike the many significant acts of historical retrieval and renaming underway in religious circles today, the wisdom of new monasticism flows into us from a future now coming to fruition. In this historic moment of openness, we are participating in the unfolding of new lineages, and a commitment to the expansion of compassion and nonharm.

I am certain that the monastic call is intrinsic to all people and is not confined to religious organizations or orders. It is a free call within the self, one that is born with us into the world and to which we owe allegiance. The years we spend avoiding the monk within, too busy with family and work, and perhaps afraid that it will make us more different or too pious, are empty concerns. Because there is nothing more natural than to affirm one's monastic nature, living in God's time, seeking transformation into the heart of reality, and loving creation with one's whole being.

The monastic archetype will take new forms during this century and those to come. The Great Vocation will evolve, as the human heart grows closer to the Divine Heart.

A Note on Religious Language

Finding words adequate to describe the radiance of our souls and the tender gift of life is always difficult. Too often religious language has been used as a tool of exclusion and pain, sensitizing me to how others hear and read words. For this reason, whenever possible, I alternate between a more generic—Mystery, Divinity, Source, Emptiness, and Creator—and more religion-specific—God, Divine Feminine, Holy Sophia, Allah, and Great Spirit—language when describing ultimacy. All are symbols of an ineffable reality that never will be fully captured in language or experience. These symbolic words open to an infinite horizon, and I employ them interchangeably out of respect for the diversity of divine names used by people around the globe.

Additionally, I use the term "theology" to indicate contemplative reflection on ultimate or spiritual realities. From the Greek, *theos* and *logos*—theology signifies study, rational inquiry, and mystical insight about God. The term isn't strictly applicable to the variety of the world's religions, especially Buddhism that does not focus on a personal god, but it is often used today as shorthand when comparing divinity in multi-religious contexts.

My use of religious language is non-dogmatic and non-absolute in the sense that I keep the door open to dialogue with other theologies and divine realities. To speak about the unspeakable requires symbol, metaphor, parable, and poetry. This approach is not a "what" but a "how"—a process of relating to life that is continually receptive to the coming of an unimaginable gift, which we do not and cannot ever possess.

Thus, the concepts of religion—god-language, theology, spirituality, etc.—point to an ultimately freeing state that travels within every utterance. Viewed in this way, the languages of religions offer a rich tapestry of insight into the sacred dimension of life, which other language structures do not access in quite the same way. It is my hope, as you encounter the various religious symbols used in the pages to follow, that you will be reminded of the many ways the human heart praises the unknown, and of a new silence that flows through all these words.

TWO

The New Monk

R ECENTLY, I had an interesting conversation with a hermit, who remarked, "Monasticism is ancient. It hasn't changed. What's new about it? It's the same—you empty yourself; you sit in your cell." This is the issue, isn't it? Is there really such a thing as the "new" monk?

· ◆ ·

LET ME FIRST SAY that the aspiration to monkhood is intrinsic to human life—a universal quality of being that continually draws us into silence. The concept of the "new monk" includes within its range aspects of this urge, from monks in religious orders to participants without religious affiliation. Some—but by no means exhaustive—examples include the person who chooses to live out a monastic vocation of one religion or a hybrid (Sufi-Hindu, Jewish-Buddhist, Catholic-Quaker) tradition, identifies as an interspiritual monk-in-the-world, or has no formal desire to be a monk, but lives by the universal call to contemplation. In each case, the deep self seeks something more radical and intense from life, and longs to be united with its Source. This is the *monk within*.

Monasticism is not new. Through generations of life on Earth, humans have sought solitude and silence. The monk's journey is the Spirit's fire born with and into us that ignites the pulse of the untamed heart. It is the insistent call to go deeper, to reach higher, and to search more ardently for our original home. And, so, while perhaps we have not been trained to name or recognize the monk within, it has been awake in the center of being all along. We, then, can speak of the new monk as a person who consciously cultivates the interior monkhood, and who lives out an experimental and daily-renewed vocation.

The Universal Archetype of the Monk

IN 1980, RAIMON PANIKKAR—a distinguished scholar, scientist, and theologian of interreligious dialogue—delivered a series of lectures at a conference in Holyoke, Massachusetts, convened by the North American Board for East-West Dialogue. Panikkar's provocative lectures, subsequently published in *Blessed Simplicity: The Monk as Universal Archetype*, were a reflection on the relevance of the monastic archetype, awake in the center of being and intrinsic in human life:

> The thesis I am defending is that the monk is the expression of an archetype which is a *constitutive dimension of human life.* This archetype is a unique quality of each person, which at once needs and shuns institutionalization.... The great monks have always been worried when the monk becomes a well-accepted figure in the world and receives the blessings of society. The monk is highly personal.[1]

An archetype is the original model or pattern from which all things of the same kind are based. In Jungian psychology, an archetype is an idea, pattern of thought, or mental image inherited from the earliest human ancestors and universally present in the collective unconscious. Panikkar qualifies his usage of the archetype of the monk as constitutive of personhood:

> If the monastic dimension exists at least potentially in everybody, the institution of monasticism should be equally open to everybody. We should then distinguish between monkhood and monasticism....

Here appears the consequence of our distinction between the *monk* as archetype, i.e., the monk as a paradigm of religious life, against the *archetype* of the monk, i.e., the human archetype lived out by the monks, but which may also be experienced and lived today in different ways.[2]

Panikkar's subtle distinction between the *monk* as archetype and the *archetype* of the monk amplifies his thesis. In the former, "archetype means a model, a prototypical form (*morphē*).... The monk as archetype may be taken to mean that there is such a thing as an ideal monk, and that monks have incarnated this ideal in different degrees. [Such usage] freezes human creativity inasmuch as it ties us to an almost Platonic and immutable essence of the ideal monk."[3]

The archetype of the monk, however, assumes there is a universal depth common to humanity—monkhood—which is "a product of the different forces and factors," Panikkar writes, "conscious and unconscious, individual and collective, [derived from] an exploration into the very dynamism of the many factors that share human life. Since archetype here does not mean a model, but rather the product of human life itself, this very archetype is thus mutable and dynamic."[4]

While the monk is but one way of realizing the mystical core in every person, "it is in and through this [monastic] way of life," Panikkar contends, "that we may gain access to the universal archetype...and allow ourselves to speak of *the new monk*."[5]

Panikkar's lectures put language to the idea of the "new monk," and to the longing for a deep contemplative orientation outside of institutional forms. He not only situates the locus of the divine quest in the soul, he also returns the historical expression of monasticism to the person. In effect, this removes any hierarchical, authoritative organization, or community from control over the human capacity to strive for union with the Divine, and to experience the fullness of life.

Born in Spain in 1918 to a Hindu father and a Spanish mother, early in life Panikkar was ordained a priest. Later, while traveling to India, he became convinced that solitude not only plays a critical role in the establishment of personhood, but also is the portal of conversion into another worldview. In an article titled, "The New Monk," Panikkar describes three examples of how traditional religious values, East and West, can be reinvigorated by the encounter with the evolving monastic experiment:

Against the Current: the classical *contemptus mundi* [contempt for the world] of the monk, today takes a new and more subtle turn: not abandoning the world (which is practically impossible), but swimming against the current, like living fish in the rivers, without rage or violence, but with poise and elegance, that is, with love and patience.

Truly Myself: the monastic vocation has meant "solitude." But solitude does not mean isolation. On the contrary, solitude demands that I be truly myself so that I may share without encumbrances solidarity with the entire reality: *Buddhakaya*, karma, mystical Body, universal love.

Ever New: The monastic "calling" is ever new. It does not repeat itself, and it has no blueprint; it is not prescribed by any law. It needs to be not just discovered, but created by our cooperation with the very dynamism of reality, by holy "obedience," that is, by attentive listening (*obaudire*) to the "divine" Voice—which is the Hindu name for revelation (*sruti*). It is not enough to "imitate" the Buddha, Christ, God. We have to *become* the Buddha, Christ, God—without asking like Peter, "What about John?" "You follow me" was the answer.[6]

Panikkar's description of the monastic vocation as intrinsic and archetypal challenges the association of monasticism solely with its historical forms. Rather, he underscores that the aspiration to be a monk is the result of some prior mystical experience that convinces the person of a vision of wholeness and human possibility. Francis Tiso in the essay, "Raimundo Panikkar on the Monk as 'Archetype,'" clarifies this point: "Crucial here, especially to the experiential dimension contributed by the 'new monks,' is that monasticism is not described as a set of conditions within which the discovery of transcendence is made."[7]

The new monk—having already experienced something of the unitive goal of life— discovers through his or her single-minded pursuit of the divine, the monastic vocation within. Panikkar writes:

> The monk ultimately becomes monk not by a process of thinking, or merely of desiring, but as the result of an urge, the fruit of an experience that eventually leads him to change and, in the final analysis, break something in his life for the sake of that "thing," which encompasses or transcends everything.... The monk is compelled, as it were, by an experience that can only articulate itself in the praxis of one's life.... It is the existence of such an ontological aspiration in the human being that leads me to speak of monkhood as a constitutive dimension of human life.[8]

Panikkar understood that the monastic archetype is active in people who seek a greater depth of being, including those who are not committed members of a religion. New monasticism attracts people seeking a spiritually open form of life in dialogical relationship with the world's wisdom traditions. "In other words," writes Irish theologian Bernadette Flanagan, "we are in the throes of the birth of a new expression of humanity's transcendent quest. On a wider level, Panikkar is suggesting that monasticism provides a unifying zone for contemplative commitment across religious traditions in an increasingly global world."[9]

It is the contemplative depth of the monastic traditions that appeals to people seeking a new type of spiritual commitment. Panikkar's lectures and the subsequent publication of *Blessed Simplicity* exerted a cathartic influence on seekers, and initiated experiments in alternative monastic communities. Francis Tiso reflects on this history:

> During the 1990s, it is known that there was a dramatic increase in the number of Benedictine oblates in the United States, as if many lay persons began to find their spiritual homes among the monastic communities. Certainly the continuing appeal of the works of Thomas Merton contributed to this tendency.... More broadly, there has been an ecumenical dimension to the "new monk" phenomenon.

Some Christians from the reformation traditions began to see monasticism as a point of departure for living simply, serving the poor, and engaging in social advocacy in both urban and rural environments. Thus, the "new monk" became a social phenomenon reported in both Catholic and Protestant periodicals.[10]

The expansion of interest in the phenomena of the new monk has taken root not only among the contemplative public, but also in traditional monastic communities. My monastic friends welcome the pursuit of monastic formation among lay people through oblate programs and temporary periods of residency in monastic communities. Many actively support new expressions of monasticism, inviting interested seekers to participate in their traditional lifestyle. Some believe that the monastic form of life may be the only religious life that is able to survive the tumult of modern culture. To this idea, Italian monk Fra Mario responds:

> Because it is a perennial form of religious life, [monasticism] seeks the perennial. It does not fade away, it is not meant only for a particular time; it is given for all times.... The person who seeks God and wishes to bear witness to God among people with one's life is always relevant. It is not a charism that passes away the way the times change. This is forever. This desire for God, to seek God, and to stay with God is deep in human nature. It is also a kind of proof—that we come to Him—otherwise our hearts would only be filled with the things of this world.[11]

Critical Response to the New Monk

PANIKKAR'S DEVELOPMENT of the monastic archetype, and the advent of new monastic communities have elicited critical response from monks associated with historical religious orders. They question the validity or viability of the new monk, asserting a distinction between institutional monasticism and these new iterations. Further, there is concern that the new monk may be ungrounded, lack a coherent philosophy or theological orientation, and develop a superficial type of spirituality. Francis Tiso comments:

> There is an inherent tension between living the monastic life and undergoing the spiritual transformations that are the fruit of monastic observance…Moreover, there is a very painful tension between the acquisition of the needed knowledge and personal experience, and the process of becoming a well-balanced person of faith."[12]

This debate continues in private conversations. Some of the reasoning I have heard includes:

The word "new" attached to monasticism is spurious, because the core of monasticism is essentially and always the same.

There may be a new expression of monasticism, but these lay practitioners are not monks.

Monks adhere to a particular schedule of prayers and meditation, and live under obedience to the abbot, prioress, roshi, lama, etc.

The singular and distinguishing feature of monastic life is celibacy. According to Immaculate Heart of Mary sister Sandra M. Schneiders, celibacy is constitutive of religious life and "a free gift, a vocation or call from God to some people. Although singleness or sexual abstinence can be imposed or mandated, celibacy as a charism cannot…it cannot be acquired by one's own efforts or conferred by authority."[13]

In the West, night vigils are definitive of the monk's vocation, and practiced in many Catholic, Orthodox, and Episcopal monasteries. If night vigils are not present, this is not true monasticism.

Traditional vows associated with a religion—poverty, celibacy, obedience, stability, nonharm, etc.—and monastic rules are critical dimensions of every monk's life.

If a person is not connected to one of the established world religions and its monastic community, what theology or philosophy grounds these aspirants, and what is their formation process?

How does one maintain a contemplative focus without the benefit of community or hermitage or shared spiritual experience?

Underlying these debates is the question raised by my hermit friend: Can this contemporary movement still be called monastic? "Should we still speak of monastic values," Panikkar writes, "even though they have changed? Should we still speak of a modern 'monk' when he has abandoned so many of the trappings of the past?"[14]

Why not reserve the historical usage of the word "monk" for the person consecrated to a formal, religious, monastic life? And, instead, use the term "lay contemplative" when referring to people called to some type of alternative, monastic expression? It is true that there is nothing comparable to dedicating one's whole self to the divine quest in a community of like-minded seekers in a physical monastery, often apart from mainstream society, and adhering to a stable religious philosophy and rule of life. From this perspective, it is appropriate that the terminology be different.

My response is that the monk pursues a single-minded and radical quest for the Ultimate, and is the orientation of a person's entire being and life. This ontological imperative and human aspiration is a sacred gift, a vocation initiated by the Divine. It is thus present wherever and whenever the human heart is open to mystery. It cannot be acquired by one's own efforts, nor can institutions or authority deny it. Whether the new monk is drawn into a traditional monastic life form, or an experimental in-the-world monasticism, his or her vocation is a response to a profound spiritual call. Panikkar concurs:

It could be that in the last analysis we would prefer to do away with the word "monk" altogether and find another less overburdened one, but this would not prove that what the contemporary monk intends does not correspond to what the ancients were trying to do. . . . If the modern monks—I mean the new monks, not those of our contemporaries who legitimately repeat the traditions of the past—call themselves monks, there seems no reason to oppose them in this.[15]

For this reason—and to avoid confusion—I reserve the term "contemplative" (as in "John is a contemplative person") to describe a quality of interior solitude, and the word, "contemplation," to refer to deep spiritual practice. Neither derivation of "contemplation" conveys the radical personal and singular commitment of the monk, which both includes and exceeds practice. Panikkar:

> By monk, *monachos*, I understand that person who aspires to reach the ultimate goal of life with all his being by renouncing all that is not necessary to it ... Precisely this single-mindedness ... or rather the exclusivity of the goal ... distinguishes the monastic way from other spiritual endeavors toward perfection or salvation.... If, in a certain sense, everybody is supposed to strive for the ultimate goal of life, the monk is radical and exclusive in this quest.[16]

Members of traditional monastic orders also distinguish between laity and vowed religious, and oppose the conflating of the two ways of life. I avoid using these terms because historically they represent a hierarchy of spiritual purity, with "lay person" almost without dissent assigned lower status in the world's religions. I view the segregation of lay and religious as troubling, not only because of the rejection of domestic wisdom—especially women's experience—but also because religious orders and institutions represent only one historical facet of the interior call to monkhood. In fact, people who had no ecclesiastical status or lacked formal religious authority—female and male hermits, desert elders, mystics, etc.—initiated the earliest expressions of monastic life.

Once again, Panikkar's poignant description of his search to be a different kind of monk is instructive:

> Since my early youth I have seen myself as a monk, but one without a monastery, or at least without walls other than those of the entire planet. And even these, it seemed to me, had to be transcended—

probably by immanence—without a habit, or at least without vestments other than those worn by the human family. Yet even these vestments had to be discarded, because all cultural clothes are only partial revelations of what they conceal: the pure nakedness of total transparency only visible to the simple eye of the pure in heart.[17]

My own experience with monastic communities underscores the significance of the new monk as a catalyst for refounding traditions and for the formation of an emergent religiosity. On the one hundredth anniversary of Merton's birth, I joined Monastic Interreligious Dialogue (MID) at the Trappist Monastery in Gethsemani, Kentucky, where Merton lived for twenty-seven years. I entered into dialogue with Buddhist and Christian monks, as we reflected on the unity and diversity of these two great traditions, and shared prayers and liturgies, honoring each other's respective religious home. Yet, I attended MID as a new monk not associated exclusively with the Catholic tradition into which I was born.

I came away from these gatherings more convinced than ever that it is the marginal status of the new monk—living on the edges of established religions and drawing from the waters of emergent revelatory consciousness—that is such a potent source of creativity and resurgence of the deep self. Tiso agrees:

> Over the years, one of the discoveries that impresses me about these "new monks" is that their very marginality corresponds to the most fundamental discovery of *inner experience*: that material success, name, fame, and outer format count for very little in comparison to the experience of divine, ineffable wholeness...In a very real sense, the world became our monastery, as it did even for Raimundo Panikkar, who concluded his academic career, international televised interviews, and conferences (including the World Parliament of Religions in Barcelona) with a quiet life of reflection in a small village, Tavertet, in his native Catalunya. And here again, Panikkar was right: the inner experience is definitely prior to the subsequent development of career and other commitments, including vows.[18]

A Bit of History

AS FAR BACK AS WE SEARCH in the history of religions, we find shamans, hermits, and other spiritual seekers who practiced various types of asceticism. Yet, the first clear documented account of the monastic impulse is usually traced to the Rig Vedic seers—forest dwellers of ancient India— who sought higher knowledge and pursued various practices of interiority, living singly or with disciples in ashrams.

The religions of India were fertile soil for the development of monasticism: yoga, which was practiced from the earliest times as a means of self-mastery and concentration on the Absolute; Jain monks (eighth century BCE), who evolved a spiritual tradition of detachment and nonviolence; and eventually the Buddhists in the sixth century BCE, who began the great movement of the Sangha, the community of monks. One of the most enduring traditions of monasticism in the world, Buddhist monasticism spread from India into China, Tibet, and Japan.

The inner cultivation lineages of classical Chinese Daoism (circa sixth century BCE) also included hermits and monks, and a range of practices and adherents, "from renunciants living in mountain seclusion," writes Daoist scholar Louis Komjathy, "through married householder priests ministering to local communities to monks and nuns inhabiting hermitages and monasteries."[19] But it was under Buddhist influence—especially from the fifth century CE onward—that Daoist monasticism became more ritualized and systematized, and stable communities of celibate members began to form in China.

In the West, historical records indicate that around 200 BCE an elite group of pious Jews withdrew into the Sinai desert and formed ascetic communities faithful to Mosaic law. One of these communities, described in the Dead Sea Scrolls, belonged to the sect of the Essenes, and lived in the monastery of Qumran.

Another Jewish monastic community—the *Therapeutes*—belonged to the same spiritual group as the Essenes but was not strictly ascetic.

Jewish philosopher Philo of Alexandria (20 BCE–50 CE) provides insight into their practices in his book *De Vita Contemplativa*.

> In each dwelling there was a sacred place called the sanctuary ... Here they practiced the mysteries of their holy life in solitude. They took nothing with them, no food, no drink, but only copies of the laws, the Oracles of the Prophets, hymns and other books, to help them to increase and perfect their devotion and knowledge.[20]

The monks of Qumran and the *Therapeutes* were contemporaries of Christ and the Apostles. It is thought that John the Baptist knew of the Essenes and was, in some way, connected to the community. There is strong speculation that Christian monasticism drew insight and practices from these Jewish communities. However, "there is no direct proof," writes the Benedictine monk Mayeul de Dreuille "of any direct connection between these movements of pious Jews and the disciples of Jesus; but can we suppose that John the Baptist in the desert was completely ignorant of the Qumran community?"[21]

Other accounts indicate that monasticism came to the Christians possibly through Syria and possibly through Greece. The Christian theologian Clement of Alexandria (150–215 CE) specifically wrote that the Greek philosophers borrowed their ideas from India, calling to mind observances of the Hindu *sannyasis* (renunciates). He also documented different categories of Indian gurus—forest ascetics, Brahmins, Jains, and Buddhists—who traveled to the West.[22]

One of the more well-known Christian monastic communities formed in the Egyptian and Syrian deserts around the fourth century CE. It is these desert fathers and mothers (*abbas* and *ammas*) who left wisdom sayings of timeless significance, and mystical depth:

> A certain brother went to Abbot Moses in Scete, and asked him for a good word. And the elder said to him: Go, sit in your cell, and your cell will teach you everything.[23]

Amma Theodora said: "Let us strive to enter by the narrow gate. Just as the trees, if they have not stood before the winter's storms cannot bear fruit, so it is with us; this present age is a storm and it is only through many trials and temptations that we can obtain an inheritance in the kingdom of heaven."[24]

Amma Syncletica said, "There are many who live in the mountains and behave as if they were in town, and they are wasting their time. It is possible to be a solitary in one's mind while living in a crowd, and it is possible for one who is a solitary to live in the crowd of personal thoughts."[25]

They centered their lives on an imitation of Christ, as servants of the divine, in an attitude of love and worship. The development of monasticism in Orthodox and Roman Catholic Christianity was diverse, from loosely associated monks and domestic-based asceticism practiced by males and females, to tightly controlled monasteries under the patronage of bishops, with hierarchical organizational structures beholden to the papacy. Like other religions, the solitary pursuit of truth predates that of formal communities of monks, and wandering hermits and lay monastic men and women—such as the apotactic movement of village ascetics, or the Beguines in Medieval Europe—flourished in the Christian world.[26]

In other religions, formal monasticism is not practiced or became a vestigial remembrance. The Essenes and the Therapeutae, for example, have been absorbed into Judaism's historical archives. And, while mystical Jewish movements and communities continue to flourish, it is an intensely social religion that stresses the sacredness of daily life, and the duty of having children and living in community. Nonetheless, the meditative and contemplative dimension is at the heart of Jewish tradition and there is a growing desire for a type of monastic commitment among the younger generation. "There is a 'tribe' of potential 'Dedicated Jewish Contemplatives,'" writes Norman R. Davies, "within the heart of Israel and most of it is in the closet. I'm out. . . . I became a Jewish monk."

We cleave to God. In doing this, We hope to be redeemed from selfishness; In doing this, We pray for our congregation's members; In doing this, We pray for the Community of Israel; In doing this, We pray for all Creation. We hope that this may be our specific and acceptable Service to God."[27]

Islam also does not have a monastic tradition per se. But, in fact, Islamic religion contains mysticism, ascetic discipline, and a cult of saints, and much of Sufi practice is associated with solitude and silence, bringing the monastic temperament into the world. Frithjof Schuon, in his article "The Universality of Monasticism and Its Relevance in the Modern World," explains why Islam does not adhere to a formal monasticism:

> One of the *raisons d'etre* of Islam is precisely the possibility of a "monastery-society," if the expression is allowable: that is to say that Islam aims to carry the contemplative life into the very framework of society as a whole; ... that permit[s] of contemplative isolation in the very midst of the activities of the world. The famous "no monasticism in Islam" (*la rahbaniyah fi-islam*) really means, not that contemplatives must not withdraw from the world, but on the contrary that the world must not be withdrawn from contemplatives; the intrinsic ideal of monasticism or of eremitism, namely asceticism and the mystical life, is in no way affected.[28]

While an extended study is not the subject of this chapter, suffice it to say that monasticism has evolved in all of its nascent cultures, with new forms supplanting earlier ones over time. Columba Stewart, Benedictine monk and scholar, reflects on the evolution of monasticism:

> Clearly the classic monasticism of many centuries, embedded as it has become in law and custom, isn't nimble enough to meet every challenge.... Even so, we do well to remember that monasticism itself was once the *nouvelle vague* supplanting early forms of asceticism. What will be the next wave? Will it wash away the classic monastic paradigm, or buoy it along to a new destination? I see no clear answer to either question, and history suggests that I shouldn't expect to.[29]

An important contribution to moving the classical monastic paradigm "along to a new destination" is the dialogue between Catholic and Buddhist monks that has been ongoing for over fifty years. This formal "intermonastic" dialogue can be traced to 1960, when the world's Benedictine and Cistercian monasteries created the Alliance for International Monasticism (AIM), which urged monks and nuns to pursue mutual understanding with monastics East and West, especially between Buddhists and Christians. The dialogue of monastics and contemplatives became known as representing one of the most authentic types of interfaith dialogue—the dialogue of religious experience. As monks of different traditions came together they realized that the most significant focus of monastic interreligious dialogue was the sharing of each other's search for God, regardless of their status or religion.

In 1968, AIM sponsored the first Asian East-West Intermonastic conference in Bangkok. It was this conference that brought the Trappist monk Thomas Merton to the East and eventually to his visit with His Holiness the Dalai Lama. It was also at this conference that Merton tragically died soon after giving his speech on the second day. Considered by many to be the founding thinker in the West of intermonastic dialogue, Merton was in the vanguard of a new kind of global mysticism that was working itself out in his encounters with Buddhism, Daoism, Sufism, and other religions. He knew that his monastic vocation, perhaps seen by others to be a parochial or even elite affair, was the leaven that expanded his solitary search for God into a global concern for life itself. Merton realized that deep spiritual experience, and the contemplative vow to seek union with God, was the center point of unity in dialogue with other religions.[30]

During his fateful 1968 trip to Asia, Merton spent three days with His Holiness the Dalai Lama, the exiled Tibetan leader, in Dharamsala, India. Merton and the Dalai Lama developed a close friendship discussing monastic practices, enlightenment, and the role of monks in the world. In *The Asian Journal of Thomas Merton*, Merton recounted that His Holiness the Dalai Lama said "he understood the monk as a person 'for the world,' and Merton, in turn, defined the vocation of monks like themselves in public terms, as a calling to be 'living examples of the freedom and transformation of consciousness which meditation can give.'"[31]

Despite Merton's untimely death, the dynamism of the Bangkok meeting motived the formation of new gatherings to facilitate monastic interreligious dialogue. In 1973, AIM organized a meeting in Bangalore, India, bringing together monastics from Christianity, Buddhism, Hinduism, Shintoism, Islam, Daoism, and other traditions of the East. Shortly thereafter, Cardinal Sergio Pignedoli—Vatican Secretariat for Dialogue with non-Christians—encouraged Catholic monastic orders to assume a leading role in the interreligious dialogue of monastics. In a letter to the Benedictine Abbot Primate, Pignedoli wrote:

Historically, the monk is the outstanding type of *homo religiosus* of all times, and as such, he attracts and serves as a reference point for both Christians and Non-Christians. The existence of monasticism at the heart of the Catholic Church is in itself a bridge connecting all religions. If we are to approach Hinduism and Buddhism, not to mention the others, without the monastic experience we should hardly be considered religious men.[32]

Ten years later, in 1978, AIM created the North American subcommittee—Monastic Interreligious Dialogue (MID), today joined with its European counterpart, *Dialogue Interreligieux Monastique*—to further dialogue between Benedictines and monastics of other religions.[33] The guiding principle that informs these exchanges is a mature contemplative vocation based on purity of heart, for a humble heart is the great equalizer and the bitter medicine necessary to draw out the sweetness of being. For the vow of the monk—and by extension the unspoken oath of every sentient being—is to be for others, to be universal, and not solely for the self.

Whatever role the resurgence of monasticism exerts on society, its form of life historically has been integral to the development and expansion of a religion's spirituality. In the cultures of East and West, monks were formative in the growth of spiritual practices: prayer, meditative techniques, interpretation of scriptural texts, and ascetic rituals. "For many centuries of Christian history," Stewart writes, "monasteries were the laboratories of Christian spirituality.... Virtually all of the famous mystics had monastic ties and the literature shaping the great traditions of Christian spirituality has been remarkably monastic in both origin and orientation."[34] Wisdom sayings and other literature from monastic communities served as direct guidance into the inner life, fostering the maturation of virtues and purity of heart, as they continue to be read and inspire people.

Today, new monastic communities—particularly interfaith or interspiritual ones—are especially tasked with leading the experimental wave into the next evolution of the ancient monastic call.

A New Monastic Orientation

MY PRACTICE of new monasticism is inextricably based on a formative mystical foundation, which is more than a sharing of religious experiences, but a quality of being and consciousness. That is, for myself, the longing to be a monk and its practical expression could be founded on nothing other than an interspiritual and global spirituality, inclusive of but not confined to the wisdom of the world's religions. That is, I am a monk of the tradition of ever-new revelation—that I call *via feminina* (the way of the feminine)—but which is greater than ascription or name. Subsequent chapters develop the relationship of *via feminina* to monastic life in detail.

I use the terms "global spirituality" and "interspirituality" to serve as an umbrella category to capture the emergence of a unique planetary consciousness breaking through traditional religious and disciplinary boundaries, which is affecting all life systems. Wayne Teasdale (1945–2004), a scholar and interreligious monk, introduced the term "interspiritual" to express "the assimilation of insights, values, and spiritual practices from the various religions and their application to one's own inner life and development."[35] Such a person draws from the world's wisdom traditions and belongs to the common spiritual heritage of all humanity. To love and work together toward an ideal greater than our individual or social need is the aspiration of global spirituality.

As the spiritualities of the world's religions often were created and advanced through established monasteries and spiritual lineages, new monastics benefit from the contemplative focus that monasticism provides to express the contours of this new upwelling of the divine in our souls. This advance in humanity's collective religious imagination reveals a spiritual orientation for the entire Earth community.

The new monk also celebrates the creation of new traditions, and affirms both the right and the obligation to be a co-partner with the cosmos, to reach deep within oneself to the source of revelation—listening for the divine voice speaking in our souls. Part of the allure of new monastic life is its emphasis on bringing together both aspects of Panikkar's vision: the monastic archetype and the archetype of the monk. That is, drawing on the wisdom of historical monastic communities, and giving birth to new movements, new religions, even a monastic "mutation or simply another species of religious life altogether."[36] This true birth—which is the result of the confluence and mutual interpenetration of two mystic forces, love and wisdom—grasps life in its potential fullness. We, each, are given the capacity by our Creator to be a creator—in supplication and humility, in prostration and prayer—pulling from our depth what is more holy, what is more compassionate. This is the legacy of authentic wisdom, which is never for the self.

Much like Panikkar, Father Bede Griffiths (1906–1993)—*sannyasi* and leader of the Hindu-Christian ashram community at Santivanam in South India, and another pioneer of interfaith monasticism—eloquently advocated for a monastic order in the world.

> The monk is a layperson... An order of monastics is essentially a lay order. Some monks may live in monasteries, but increasingly the majority will live in their own homes or form small communities—a monastic order in the world. [This would be] one in which communities and individuals live spiritual lives independent of religious organizations or institutions, independent of celibacy and overarching rules and dogmas—free to follow their own conscience and guidance in living a sacred life, yet united in the common cause of building a sacred world.[37]

Bede felt that monks—"new" and "old"—need to maintain an attitude of mature interiority both within oneself and with respect to other religions. The journey toward ultimate reality is premised on a radical interiority, in which the soul integration or unification of divisions between religions is a path of liberation. Bede Griffiths writes:

> It is in prayer or meditation that we communicate with one another at the deepest level of our being. Behind all words and gestures, behind all thoughts and feelings, there is an inner center where we can meet one another in the presence of God. . . . [not because we will or demand it to be, but because we have been seized by the Divine Mystery, and drawn into another dimension of faith] . . . [38]

It is only in this inner depth that we actually experience how evolving expressions of monasticism are intimately connected in a continuum of the same Ultimate Reality. This living faith experience moves beyond dialogue or even mystical awareness of commonalities between religions, to a soul synthesis that forges the convergence of these traditions in the depth of spiritual realization.

New expressions of monasticism are not only authentic, but also offer a vital and necessary counterpoint to secular society. This is especially true because the monk in the world is bound by his or her vocation to be a self-reflective person—one who seeks higher meaning and dedicates his or her life on Earth to its pursuit. It is arduous work to dig deep into one's soul, bringing forth hidden or unconscious motives contrary to a spiritual life. I find that the younger generations are especially drawn to the movement of new monasticism, as many were born with awareness of a new religious sensibility and a global Earth community.

For all of these reasons, this monastic orientation is "new" because it is taking place in the daily routine of a person's life, and not in a monastic setting apart from the world. In addition, the new monastic may or may not be an adherent of one particular religion, has a multiple religious focus (Catholic-Quaker, Jewish-Buddhist-Sufi, Hindu-Muslim, etc.), or identifies as interfaith or interspiritual. Such a person lives an interior experiment, employing various streams of wisdom and emerging theologies in his or her spiritual journey. He or she recognizes that monkhood is not the special preserve of the traditional vowed religious, but the universal heritage of humanity. The more revolutionary of these communities draw authority from a revelatory consciousness and disclosure of divinity that is imprinted in their souls and in the heart of the world.

The challenge of being "new" monks consists in the attempt to expand monastic wisdom into the wider personal and social circle of our lives, while also fiercely protecting the centering point of silence and solitude in our souls. This desire to reclaim holiness as engaged with and intrinsic to life itself—to the flourishing of the human person, sentient beings, Earth, and the global community—is essential for the future of our planet.

The vocation of the monk will always be both immeasurably ancient and new as long as humans are on Earth. For the search for the divine is imbedded in the human heart and is the universal quest of the monk throughout history. The Benedictine monk, Mayeul De Dreuille, on the gift of monasticism:

> Centered on the search for the Absolute, the common role of monastic life in all religions stands as a sign, reminding humankind that the aim of human life is not possession of perishable goods but rather, to become one day, "citizens of heaven," a privilege that all can begin to enjoy, here and now, through an intimate contact with the Divine Presence, which dwells in the depth of the heart.[39]

Traditional Forms of Monastic Life

MONASTICISM HISTORICALLY has developed in a variety of communities and styles of life. People of differing personality types and spiritual inclinations founded monastic lineages and community life forms that resonated with their religious and cultural ethos. While the theology or philosophy behind these monastic expressions is varied, the organization of monastic life can be grouped into five general categories: Hermit, cenobite, mendicant, skete, and *sannyasi*.

Hermit: The word "hermit" is derived from the Latin, *eremita*, "of the desert." The first monks were probably hermits, living in huts, wandering in the deserts, or begging in villages. Many also lived a semi-eremitic life, meeting occasionally for mass or communal rites, and making provision for food or work. Others lived in small groups of two or three. Hermits are found in all cultures, including that of the Indigenous Peoples, Daoist, Theravadan, Tibetan, and Zen Buddhist, as well as Jewish, Christian, and Islamic.

Cenobite: From *cenobium,* Latin for "life in common." Monks live in a stable community, through mutual help in seeking truth more earnestly. Buddha is credited with the formation of the Sanghas, or communities of monks, which endure today across the globe. St. Pachomius (348), St. Benedict (529), and Mar Saba (483) (the latter the mother of all Eastern Orthodox monasteries) are examples of Christian cenobitic founders. Benedictines, in particular, make a vow of stability to a particular monastery in a specific geographical location for the duration of their lives. These monastic community lifestyles function under a rule of life and the leadership of the prior, abbot, lama, roshi, and so forth.

Mendicant: From the Latin, *mendicans,* "begging." Mendicants are members of religious orders that originally, by a vow of poverty, renounce all proprietorship not only individually but also in common; rely on begging for support of their work and for others through charitable donations. Examples include the Dominicans, Friars Minor (Franciscans), Carmelites, Hermits of St. Augustine, Hindu ascetics, some dervishes of Sufism, and monastic orders of Jainism and Buddhism. They don't necessarily live in stable communities.

Skete: A term used by Eastern Orthodox Christians to describe a monastic form usually associated with the northern Egyptian desert, once famous for its many hermitages. As a monastic community it is a mixture of both the eremitical and cenobitic forms, which creates relative isolation for monks, but also allows for communal services and shared resources and protection. Such settlements often consist of a group of small monastic cottages centered around a church, and dependent upon a parent monastery.

Sannyasi: (Sanskrit: "abandoning" or "throwing down") also spelled *sannyasin*. In Hinduism, a religious ascetic who has renounced the world by abandoning all claims to social or family standing. It requires rejection of the household duties and responsibilities of all stages of life, and the rejection of religious beliefs, in exchange for a search to attain *moksha* (enlightenment), that is, release from the cycle of *samsara* (cycle of death and rebirth). A person may enter into this stage of life at any time. Many *sannyasis* become wandering hermits, living without any shelter or possessions, and become holy men, seeking spiritual enlightenment and the wisdom of the cosmos.

· ◆ ·

THE ARCHETYPE OF THE MONK and its various forms of life are part of our spiritual heritage. The ideal of aloneness with the divine is foundational to the deep self. There are times when we are hermits, and others when we need relationship or community. There are times when we are beggars. And each of these monastic forms has a specific spiritual ethos associated with it, a way of approaching life itself. Discovering which form of life resonates with the seeker's personality is a good exercise in consciously identifying how the monastic archetype lives within.

Each monastic expression is focused on one thing: seeking truth, the ultimate. The monk is a person who has committed his or her life to a search for the holy, to encounter reality directly. This radical experiential approach cannot be found in books. It develops from a commitment to silence and solitude, and from recognizing that the tools for transformation exist within each person's depth.

If we desire to live for more than what is external, there is nothing more meaningful than living with and for the divine, and being a monastic presence in the world. What greater gift can we give the Earth, the cosmos, our bodies, and each other than love? Our souls want to grow in love, because that is their nature. Our souls expand in wisdom and magnitude when we abandon self-will and surrender to the divine.

It is a gift to devote our hearts to seeking the Holy. I cannot adequately convey the great blessing of abandoning our lives to the pursuit.

THREE

Contemplation and the New Monk

NOT ALL MONKS ARE CONTEMPLATIVES, and not all contemplatives wish to be monks. A state of being and a quality of consciousness available to every person, contemplation is inherent in human nature, even when it remains unrealized. I feel that the new monk, however, has a special need to be a contemplative, because he or she usually lives in secular society, outside of institutional monasticism, and thus lacks the enclosure of silence and the liturgical resources that a monastery provides.

In particular, the new monk finds his or her inner monastery by cultivating contemplative depth. Stabilized in the center of being—in what the Upanishads calls "the cave of the heart"—the new monk garners the fortitude and wisdom to maintain a steady focus on the Divine in the course of everyday life. The ability to be solitary and seek silence requires exceptional intention and is not a suitable path for every person. But, for those who recognize the value of, and desire to live the new monastic vocation, Spirit already has called them, and guides their way.

In fact, every facet of new monasticism benefits from the integration and practice of contemplation. Without a contemplative foundation, the new monk will not develop the spiritual maturity necessary to stand apart from social demands, belong to a vocation with scant historical precedent, or weather accusations about the naivety or superficiality of a universal monasticism that embraces all genuine religions, and may not exclusively identify with any.

Further, the theology, spirituality, prayers, and rituals associated with authentic new monastic community arise from universal mystical archetypes that are realized in contemplative consciousness. New monasticism is then the fruit of direct religious or mystical experience. In the first instance, it is not the result of combining religious ideas or dialogue among traditions—although these activities are employed along the way—but expresses the unveiling of another, divinely ordained manner of seeking God, devoted to and in service of the holy.

Contemplation is not only an anthropological imperative, it is also an experiential state that underlies and gives rise to the monk. This emphasis on the person's aspiration to seek the divine—rather than on the role of the monk—is especially significant to this new branch of monasticism. The person who attempts to devote his or her life to the pursuit of truth in the midst of daily events needs to harness the mystic within, which is more than a transient occurrence. Rather it is an entire vantage point on reality, the interpretive perspective and starting place of devotion and deed.

For this reason, a profound grasp of the interior life, and awareness of temptations and false motives are crucial to spiritual stability. Without mature guidance or grounding in the contemplative traditions, the new monk risks veering into self-delusion or superficiality. I encourage new monastics to seek spiritual guidance and study in-depth one or more wisdom traditions, learning about the grandeur of the human heart that has pursued the divine creator over the centuries. It is this illuminative, mystical capacity of knowing intrinsic to the person that provides entrance into Mystery, which the world's religions have diligently honored, preserved, expanded, and shared throughout history.

I have enormous respect for religious communities, and for the masters, prophets, mystics, and monks who have reached across the millennia into this transhistorical moment to guide us into the meaning that is born in silence, and flows from the deep vein of wisdom. Mystical awareness, then, is never the rejection or dismissal of religion or authentic wisdom. Rather, the mystically aware person desires to *live in and for* truth, *live out* its highest ideals, *share in and alleviate* the suffering of others, and *work toward* peace and the liberation of the heart.

Inner Monastery

DIONYSIUS THE AREOPAGITE, a fifth-century anonymous Christian author, emphasizes internal unity as the characteristic most descriptive of the monk. In *The Ecclesiastical Hierarchy*, he writes that the devotees, the *therapeute*, are the highest order of the initiated and are called "monks because of their pure service... as well as on account of their undivided and united life, which unifies them by holy combinations of their differences into godlike unity and perfection of divine love."[1] For Dionysius, what characterizes monks above all is not that they live alone, apart from society, or that they live with brothers or sisters in community, together as one, but that they have realized a purely internal unity, that is, singleness of heart and unity with the One.[2]

The contemporary person who seeks a devoted life is especially called to Dionysius' emphasis on internal unity, placing the locus of his or her commitment on the deepening of contemplation. While spiritual reading, scripture, ritual, and liturgy individually or in community are vital elements of monastic spirituality, they are not central. Rather, the aspiration of the new monk rests on the monastic solitude that is purely internal, without division, and found through loss of self. By this, I do not exclude participation in monastic community in its many expressions, but place primary emphasis on the internal state of consciousness of the adherent.

The state of being a monk—from the Greek word *monos*, "alone"—can be practiced in or outside of a monastic setting. The physical monastery or hermitage is transposed to an interior space, and quality of being that resides within the heart. The true monastery is not dependent on the enclosure of walls. It is, rather, an "inner monastery," a state of consciousness that involves a daily commitment to interior solitude, the quest of the alone to the Alone. Fostered by prayer and silence, intimacy between God and the soul is maintained through self-discipline and self-awareness.

Here, in the "inner monastery," a person discovers solitude with the Divine, preserving a sacred space within. Just as the soul in its center is always one with its creator, so does a person who focuses on the inner monastery maintain that centering in all he or she does. This centering of attention performs a spiritual repetition in our world of the intimacy between the soul and the Divine. Thus, the new monastic—through study of wisdom traditions and self-reflection—is called to redefine monastic virtues, among them silence, solitude, poverty, chastity, and obedience, in a contemporary context.

Mystical Foundation of New Monasticism

THE SPIRITUAL PRACTICES of new monasticism derive their strength and unifying vision from the contemplative or mystical heart of all religions. This divine energy is the primary foundation of a new monastic way, and binds together the diverse practices and theologies that nourish the modern disciple. Because monasticism in its historical expressions is held together by a specific religious orientation—Buddhist, Christian, and so forth—and a set of discrete practices, these institutional foundations stabilize the monk's life. Since new monastics often do not belong to a particular religion, or to an organized community that follows a daily set of practices, the impetus for deepening one's path must come from within, from the force of mystical awareness in the soul.

In contemporary usage, contemplation frequently is associated with the practice of silent or passive (receptive) prayer, and mysticism with an immediate consciousness of Divine Presence, but in actual fact the two terms are used interchangeably in many texts—with the implication that all deeply spiritual persons are also mystic-contemplatives. Both terms refer to the quality of being associated with the mature spiritual life, and not just to the heightened, but temporary, altered states of consciousness that are sometimes associated with peak experiences. Each also includes both subjective, personal encounters, and those mediated by text, ritual, relationship, and community. In addition to an emphasis on a state of being, mysticism and contemplation involve various spiritual disciplines and meditative techniques that have been practiced by seekers throughout the long history of human spirituality.

We may imagine mysticism or contemplation to be the privilege of monks and mystics, saints and prophets, and of the cloistered and the devout. But, to this I add: you are made both of and for contemplation. It is the secret longing of your being. And because this is so, each and every one of you contains the seed consciousness and the archetypal reality of its hidden ways. It is in the silent and subtle aspect of your self that a mystical path was imprinted. It is in the wilderness of your heart that you discover a reality beyond every religious form.

In the world's religions, mysticism is variously described as an experience of Divine Presence that is accessible to us in the fully actualized depths of consciousness itself. It is spontaneous awe at the sacredness of life and the infused presence of Mystery in one's inner depth. In fact, mysticism is defined more truly as the intrinsic capacity of each self to touch and be touched by the Source—to know the Source through certitude too deep for words or images. This touching is the mystical heart of the monk, and every aspect of his or her journey is directed toward this inner discovery.

And then living its truth.

Mysticism also refers to a universal and unifying view of the world. One of the quintessential insights of mystics through the centuries is that the entire cosmos is intersubjective—all beings are embedded in webs of relationship that are interconnected, interdependent, and constantly being co-created and reinvented. Today, mystical awareness expands to incorporate our relationships, and also our collective religious and spiritual inheritance, the whole of humanity, creation, and the cosmos. It extends to the suffering of the planet, wounding of the soul, and violence caused by religious superiority, national self-interest, poverty, homelessness, starvation, and war. The theme of oneness is so common in mystical literature that I consider it to be a fundamental attribute of consciousness.

Mysticism, however, is not merely a shift in perception or how one knows. It is not disembodied or relegated to rarefied states of being.

Instead, mystical consciousness affects the whole of one's life by opening the heart to the Divine Presence in all realities. Further—in contemporary thought—mysticism is in service of and the means by which we discover the unification of spirit and matter, male and female, intuition and reason, mercy and justice. It is not a goal to be reached at the endpoint of the religious life. Rather, mystical perception is the *starting* point, the power that un-forms and then reforms knowledge, love, and perception. Unitive consciousness is not something "out there," in the future, but right here, right now.

Mysticism and contemplation are often associated with their sister terms—spirituality and meditation. The world religions have sophisticated vocabularies to describe the subtleties of these paths of realization, which have (over the course of history) developed multiple and contradictory usages and definitions, while some language families do not have corresponding words. Nonetheless, "spirituality" is generally described as the broader term, applicable to the presence of the spirit of life within a tradition—for example, Jewish or Hindu spirituality.

In its various expressions, spirituality signifies the depth or core of the person in touch with the transcendent dimension. Referring to the force of divine breath, we can think of spirituality as the all-pervading divine energies and the seamless matrix of oneness intimate to life itself. Creation is not alone, separate from its source, but deeply and mysteriously imbued with spirit in every aspect of mind, soul, and matter. Today, spirituality has become a kind of universal code word to indicate the human search for meaning and purpose in life—with or without a religious orientation— and as a quest for transcendent truth.

When our natural spirituality becomes more mature and focused, and expands beyond an instinctive activity of the heart to turn toward an intensity of desire for God, it is called mysticism or contemplation. Dionysius the Areopagite introduced the word "*mystica*" into Christianity in the late fifth to early sixth century CE. In his *Mystical Theology*, Dionysius writes, in "mystic contemplation" that the person leaves "the senses and the activities of the intellect and all things that the senses or the intellect can perceive."[3] Mysticism approaches the Divine through various mediums of experience—nature, language, religion, study, liturgy, ritual—but it is also said to be accessible directly through our inner experience in a moment of pure, contentless, or empty consciousness.

Mysticism displays multiple forms and expressions ranging from the highly personal to the communal, finding expression in visionary experiences and illuminative states. It also refers more radically to the divine without image and name, to Buddha's Silence, Dionysius' "superessential ray of divine darkness," and the Zen *mu* (nothing). It was not until the end of the Middle Ages that the term "mysticism" moved toward the highly individual, subjective meaning involving a purely private, inner experience prevalent today. In these various manifestations of the mystical, there are certain shared elements, among them a transforming quality of being, and an experience of union, intimacy, or absorption in the divine. In addition, mystical knowledge is often termed hidden or secret because the Divine is known not by mental effort but is taught through love, a knowing that is "unknowing"—knowledge through direct insight.

The term "contemplation" emerges in the West from the distinction made in the Platonic schools between the "description of the soul's return to God through purification . . . followed by contemplative vision (*theoria*)."[4] In the Christian tradition, meditation (Latin, *meditari*) prepares one for contemplation, often by focused attention on a single theme, symbol, or word. In the Zen schools, meditation is undertaken for the sake of pure consciousness, without content or discursive thought—and holds a similar meaning as the word "contemplation." Whereas certain forms of meditation remain cognitive, contemplation is a direct intuitive seeing or knowing beyond intellect. Richard of St. Victor, a twelfth-century Christian mystic, distinguishes them thus: "in meditation, investigation; in contemplation, wonder."[5]

Contemplation is beyond the normal consciousness of the mind, granting access to the mystery, known only by love. Here, the normal activities of the human personality come to rest, in order to hear what has remained unheard and to see what has been hidden or veiled. The mystics call this kind of knowing "unknowing" insofar as it approaches reality from the spiritual core of the person and not from the mind alone. Far more than a meditative practice or a temporary respite from worldly concerns, contemplation revolutionizes conventional attitudes and roles in order to transform the foundation upon which life is lived. And to illuminate the hidden teaching of love inscribed in our souls. Christian *sannyasi* Bede Griffiths writes about contemplation:

> It is not something that we achieve for ourselves. It is something that comes when we let go. We have to abandon everything—all words, thoughts, hopes, fears, all attachment to ourselves or to any earthly thing, and let the divine mystery take possession of our lives. It feels like death, and it is, in fact, a sort of dying. It is encountering the darkness, the abyss, the void.[6]

Although contemplation and mysticism can invoke rarefied experiences, "the true contemplative," Catholic priest and Zen master Pat Hawk writes, "does not strive for unity of Divine and human only at specific times of prayer, but in all circumstances and conditions of daily life: washing dishes, caring for children, family, work, sleeping."[7] Contemplation refers to an inner monastic attitude, a centering point of one's whole life and being. This centering reference may be taken in solitude or in the marketplace, but it never leaves the ground of its longing for God, turning the person's whole life toward creation, hope, and love. Further, this living, daily prayer breaks through into one's mind and heart, teaching those insights and wisdoms that uplift the soul and lead it toward what Buddhists call *Prajñāpāramitā* ("perfection of wisdom").

Contemplation normally is associated with formal religious institutions, yet it both precedes and exceeds religion itself. New traditions of contemplation—interfaith, interspiritual, intermonastic—pass beyond religious forms into deep states of consciousness that—while remaining part of the enduring wisdom of the world's religions—also are the site of new spiritual traditions and forms of practice. This emergence expresses the timeless qualities of the monastic, contemplative experience outside of denominational institutions and structures. Open to the pluralism of spiritual paths, this search for a spirituality that honors divine manyness is not a reality every fully achieved, a finished theological project, or a final word. Rather it is the struggle to find the openness of heart in which life is embraced and sustained. Its theology emerges out of the metaphorical desert—a place of renunciation or ascetic abandon—because it fosters a spirituality of humility receptive to the voice of the divine speaking in the wilderness of our hearts.[8]

What binds mysticism and its sister terms together is the commitment to disciplined practice that awakens in the seeker a visceral apprehension of universal oneness, and a process of spiritual growth and transformation.[9] Experience of life's interdependence, coupled with deep empathy and compassion, is the quintessential insight of the spiritual-contemplative-meditative soul. These expressions of divine-human communion are variously described as having three degrees or modes: active, passive, and nondual.

Active, Passive, and Nondual Contemplation

CONTEMPLATION unleashes a distinctive mode of consciousness that is more passive than active, more illuminative than intellective, more merciful than just. This is not to say that contemplation shuns activity, mind and reason, or justice. Rather, having opened the vault of a hidden reality, contemplation is the repository of a receptive way of seeing the world with its own set of principles and properties. This distinction between active and passive—sometimes also termed acquired and infused contemplation by Christian mystics—is important in the spiritual life because it highlights the two sides of the person's journey. On the one hand, we must and will struggle toward our own authenticity; on the other hand, there is a point on the path in which only the Divine can lead us to our true self. Although this distinction of active and passive is applicable to all modes of spirituality, the passive dimension is usually associated with higher mystical or contemplative states.

Acquired or active contemplation addresses the ways the person seeks ultimacy: prayer, good works, study, and self-discipline. It employs the faculties of thought, action, and will, involving all the traditional means and practices of the interior life. It functions to awaken and prepare the mind and the heart for the quickening of being and the inflaming of the soul caused by divine touches. Sometimes in this way, the seeker has glimpses of the more intense infused or passive contemplation, but it is fleeting and transient.

Passive contemplation is a supernatural gift and, in some religious texts, it is the precursor of advanced mystical states. As the absence of self-willed activity, passive contemplation refers to the ways in which the Divine seeks us out, works in our souls, and bestows grace upon our hearts. It is a free gift of divinity. It is the consciousness of surrender, vulnerability, and love. It is the ground from which all other activities germinate. It is thus the place of divine rest, of un-doing and un-being. More than five hundred years ago, the Spanish mystic Teresa of Avila articulated one of the more lucid distinctions between the active life of faith and passive, mystical consciousness. While active practices "have their beginning in our own human nature and end in God," what she calls "passive" or mystical contemplations "begin in God and end in ourselves."[10] The entire vocation of the monk is premised on this divesting of "self" in order to participate in the life of the Divine.

Another mystical state—nondual contemplation—ushers in the soul's intimacy, where subject-object distinctions disappear in nonduality, or oneness. Here the soul is described in various mystical texts as "annihilated," "fused," "inebriated," "dissolved," or mystically "one" with the Divine. Lifted above the phenomenal order to its supernatural counterpart, this is the seasoned nirvanic state, the master satori life, the messianic fulfillment and resurrected hope. Where one's being and the divine being are consummated in such a way that the person now radiates simplicity, becoming a source of healing, wisdom, and transformation.

Both passive and nondual contemplation are transcendent states of awareness of the structure, function, and principle of divine things. Nondual contemplation, however, is a more or less permanent state in which the desires of the world are diminished, and the life of prayer becomes central. These passive states of consciousness are vocations, and the monk may move between levels or experience aspects of each. They are, however, spiritual and interior, and thus ultimately are divine gifts not accessible through desire or will. We cannot "do" or "make" mysticism happen. It is an intimate, obscure, and silent communion between the soul and the hidden divinity. It is the height of love, the journey of lover and beloved, the alleviation of distinction, and the attainment of enlightenment, peace.

The contemplative journey of the new monk is radical, if for no other reason than it requires that we get to the root of the meanings that constitute daily life. It is radical as well because contemplation demands a certain kind of honesty and a certain pure intention that clears away the debris of the mind and the sloth of the heart. It subverts our understandings of reality, our time-honored structures of meaning, our economic and social constructions, and leads us to the doorway of freedom and authenticity. But, far from being a denial of the world, contemplation leads to a refinement and distillation of our whole being until we are able to realize the beauty and simplicity of everyday life. It is not a reality ever fully achieved; it cannot be captured by the intellect. This is enlightenment; if not an ultimate or final one, then the sweet process of being awake, of knowing and experiencing a liberatory state of consciousness.

As an adoration of the soul at rest, contemplation is being carried away into God's own life that dissolves the soul's separate identity and lays the heart bare. Thomas Merton writes:

> Contemplation is also the response to a call: a call from Him Who has no voice, and yet Who speaks in everything that is, and Who, most of all, speaks in the depths of our own being: for we ourselves are words of His. But we are words that are meant to respond to Him, to answer to Him, to echo Him, and even in some way to contain Him and signify Him. Contemplation is this echo. It is a deep resonance in the inmost center of our spirit in which our very life loses its separate voice and re-sounds with the majesty and mercy of the Hidden and Living One.[11]

Emptied of "self," the Divine permeates the entire personality. Seized by an intensity nowhere abated, it is as if an invisible thread or force is drawing the soul into the mysterious center of reality. It is the call of beauty leading us to Beauty; it is the call of silence absorbing the person into Silence; it is the call of humility beckoning the heart to let go; it is the call of surrender, light, and love.

The fruit of prayer and the natural consciousness of those who venture into the deep self, contemplation is a river of intimacy that flows between the soul and the Divine. The two are so intertwined, so precious to each other, that prayer is nothing more than a continual desire to pour our depths into God, who is no longer outside us, but within. In silence—emptied and freed of separateness—we discover that nothing can divide us. In this mystical dimension, there is not a merely mental common denominator, or a false sense of communion, but a more holistic awareness that perceives the unitive energies that give rise to multiplicity.

Far from being unfocused, ephemeral or rare, contemplation and mysticism unveil the precision of reality as it truly is and seed a person's consciousness with the ordinary and tangible presence of mystery in every facet of existence. They affect the whole of one's life by opening the heart to the luminous presence within all realities. These profound qualities of being are both the culmination of the religious life and the place where we *begin*, recognizing that the divine process or power is already present within us.

Through consistent practice, contemplation reveals the spiritual structures of consciousness that inhabit the divine and human worlds. In this realm, we are in contact with the founders and metaphysics of religion: Jesus and Trinity, Lao Tzu and *Dao*, Abraham and *Sefirot*, Mohammed and the ninety-nine names of Allah. But contemplation has an even higher, more supernatural range. Able to pierce these metaphysical veils, contemplation is like an arrow that aims for the root of being. As a divine energy in us, contemplation is purely creative; it is a nondual, highly subjective consciousness that is transformative and catalytic, generating creative interactions that heal wounds, reconcile differences, and produce new illuminations.

Darkness and Light

CONTEMPLATION is not detachment from the world, although we have to practice self-discipline in order to override distractions and habits. Rather, it is detachment from the self, from the ego's demands, will, and resistance. It is detachment from the selfishness at the center of the person, in order to give our life to the divine will. It is an act of faith, given freely, for that which is wholly other.

Everything we know will be transformed and lifted by the intense light of the Divine. We will not be able to cling to any form, even a mystical one. Every identity used to stave away the inevitable slide into nothingness will be taken away. We have to pull up the root of craving, ignorance, and false attachment. Emptying the self is not easy. But confrontation with our thirst for transcendence guides us to an inexpressible openness. Weary of our own inventions, we learn to trust again our passion, and to embrace our need. We learn to bathe ourselves in forgiveness for our frailties and recognize them as strengths. As the bottom falls out of our pretenses, we abandon the fear of being naïve or unsophisticated. We give ourselves over to the impulse for love that is deeper than our own identity. Then—when we have become nothing more than a drop in the flowing waters of divine generosity—we arrive at an authenticity that no one can take away. We discover the heart's secret yearning and the true meaning of existence. We are what we have only dimly hoped for and sought.

We are called to a relationship that leads us beyond our own self, and even beyond divine names, to participate in the cosmic self-emptying. Our soul becomes the emptying, and the liberating pouring forth of divinity. God is birthed in us.

But, like all profound and worthy experiences, contemplation is not without its anguish. No one can hope to escape from conflict, ambiguity, and doubt. All our concepts about divinity, our holy endeavors, our worn-out words, and our feeble attempts to control our lives are turned to ash by the interior flame. Merton called this "a terrible breaking and burning of idols, a purification of the sanctuary, so that no graven thing may occupy the place that God has commanded to be left empty: the center, the existential altar which simply 'is.'"[12]

All forms of contemplation, but particularly the more advanced stages, usher in a deep revolution of the spirit. The interior life becomes disordered. The usual forms of consolation are taken away. The direction the soul has followed diligently and with fervor no longer makes sense. The intoxication the soul experienced has departed. Prayer is shallow and spent or fractured and erratic. The certainty felt in other spiritual stages is left behind, and the path ahead is obscure or hidden. There is nothing a person can trust, no direction that he or she can follow. God is guiding now in darkness, and only surrender moves the person forward. The purity of divine love overwhelms some souls and shocks and repels others because the intensity of the light reveals the seeker's hidden temptations and flaws.

This radical questioning and annihilation of our identity even strips away the claim to a final and absolute faith. In the dark luminosity of being, we are torn from the god of culture and tradition to behold and ultimately savor the namelessness that is freedom. The sign that the soul's interior revolution comes from the Divine is this: even in our darkness we have an obscure feeling of "rightness." Despite our trials and pain, the soul clings to its unknowing and aridity because it knows that some high spiritual achievement is at stake. Through painful experience, we learn that the tangle of worldly desires that we have been encouraged to seek will never make us happy or lead us to freedom. At times, we have despaired of finding happiness and have been lost in a wilderness of our own wants. But we should not lose hope, for contemplation honors our true yearnings, drawing the silent, often obscure movement of the soul toward its Beloved Home.

Re-Visioning the Contemplative Heart

ONE OF THE SEMINAL insights of the new monastic movement is that contemplation is accessible to all humanity. Emerging from its historical confinement to cloister, tradition, one gender, or an exclusive hierarchy, today contemplation is cultivated in daily life and decision-making. Since contemplation refers to the inner presence of divinity in one's life, it occupies a unique role in the formation of monastic consciousness. Our understanding of the intimate relationship between our emotions, brain, psyche, and spirit increasingly enriches us.

Another revision in the understanding of monasticism is its embeddedness in everyday situations. Rather than placing revelation or the advent of new spiritual paradigms outside of history in a transcendent deity, the mystical heart of new monasticism seeks to recover the sacred function of humanity through our being-in-the-world. This renewed understanding of contemplation emphasizes the participatory nature and mutuality of spirit and mind, and the integral necessity of divine-human cooperation in the building of a new Earth. It recognizes humanity's essential ontological function: we are beings who co-create the world. Our capacity to co-create may, in fact, be our fundamental anthropological imperative. This view of divine-human symbiosis is not alien to the world's religions; it is captured in numerous scriptures and sacred texts, such as the Hebrew phrase, *tikkun olam*, which indicates human responsibility in healing the world.

This contemplative approach to monastic life is embodied; that is, it honors the body as a force of holiness. Spiritual practices increasingly recognize the body as a site and presencing of the sacred. As an extension or becoming of spirit into physicality, our whole bodily organism—cells, organs, nerves, mind, spirit, sexuality—is the vehicle through which love and truth, as well as our personal distortions and pains, are manifested. Constantly communicating its spiritual-physical wisdom, the body is a vessel for the co-incarnation and marriage of spirit and matter. What happens to our body affects our spirit, just as the strength and resiliency of the spirit nurtures our body. Learning to listen to our body, and experiencing it as a site and sign of wisdom, is central to our path.

Healing the many types of injustice that exist on our planet is another essential dimension of an embodied, monastic spirituality. Of necessity, today we must integrate and understand how violations of race, gender, sexual difference, religious belief, and charity wound the soul. Further, our concern extends to the suffering of the planet, injury to life forms, and violence caused by religious superiority, national self-interest, poverty, homelessness, starvation, and war. Any authentic spirituality takes into account how the rejection of difference—as the despised "other"—has distorted the heart of the world. Today we know that it is spiritually unhealthy and soul-damaging for a person to deny his or her unique embodiment—female or male, black or white, gay or lesbian—because the variety of life on Earth is not only evidence of the interdependence of spirit and matter, but also of the Divine Presence in creation.

This unifying vision sees the entire cosmos as intersubjective—all beings are alive in webs of relationship that are interdependent, and constantly being co-created and reinvented. Our journey of spirit honors the divine imprint in creation and the crucial contribution every living element makes toward the building of the sacred reality we call "Earth." Without rocks and trees, water and air, coyote and deer, lilies and daffodils, whales and cuttlefish, quarks and protons, our bodies and our souls would not survive.

In our re-discovery of mystical wisdom, we touch on a way of knowing that has been with humanity since our early beginnings. I imagine that early human communities lived in a mystical state of consciousness and used the metaphorical mind for tracking animals, studying the cycles of nature, and reading the stars and planets. In my view, it is through mystical awareness that ancient societies established sacred rites, and called upon the intuitive intelligence that transcends thinking. In fact, the scriptural traditions of the world's religions—from the pre-written Vedas to the compilation of the teachings from Buddha and Jesus, and Mohammed's dictation of the Angel Gabriel—descended into conscious awareness through the portal of the illumined mind.

On the mystical path, the inner light of truth teaches us. It is not the ordinary knowledge of the intellect, but infused knowledge that comes from the divine. Transcendent knowledge is not a rarefied capacity of human consciousness; it is an essential way of knowing implicit in everyday life. It operates at all times in the human spirit, perhaps hidden or oppressed by dominant modes of rational thought. Mysticism is the medium through which we know the unknown, say the unsayable, and see what is unseen.

There is an illuminative capacity to knowing. At times, we are graced to receive knowledge whole. Across traditions, mysticism asserts that through love, the human mind is able to comprehend the unity of the material and transcendent worlds. Here, knowledge and love are wed as two complementary states of being. Exemplified in the world's love poetry, the heart as an organ of perception symbolizes the integral relationship of knowledge and love. We are able to know through love, through being intimate with life. When we love someone or something, we know differently than when we know that same presence filtered through our reason or rational mind.

Frequently dismissed in popular media, mystical knowledge is forced underground or trivialized. We are not educated to be students of the intuitive, metaphorical mind or to honor the holistic, unitive knowing that has preserved indigenous cultures from extinction. Only recently, a radio show host—interviewing a guest who was promoting a book about a medieval woman mystic—pondered what mysticism is, dismissing it as a strange condition no longer present in the modern world. However, beneath this collective refusal to acknowledge the deep self, and the fear that accompanies probing below the façade of everyday reality, exists a teeming universe of wisdom. The reclamation of mystical knowledge and its integration with other forms of knowing, including the intellectual, aesthetic, and psychological, are vital to a global monasticism and to the future of life on Earth. For—until the modern period—spirituality was integral to the development of every civilization, and our comprehension of the world is incomplete without its wisdom.

In the cave of our hearts, a life-affirming, purely open monasticism is being born. Through this pure openness we are capable of healing differences and holding multiple spiritual realities in a unified whole. It is, in fact, the contemplative mind and heart that have the capacity to suspend naming, and thus to evaluate and interpret the world with unblemished sight. Contemplation prepares our minds and souls to seek truth with courage and ardor until we are centered in *The Center*.

The contemplative depth of your soul—in solidarity with Earth and Heaven—is creating a new monastic way, now. You may not consciously know you are participating in the formation of a new sacred path, but the fact that you cannot abide the disintegration of the holy is evidence of your soul's action. The call to the monk within is a profound and mysterious process that is taking place in the hearts and souls of people around the world. It's coming from the ground up; it's coming from contemplative people who wish to follow the Sacred Path in every aspect of life.

FOUR

The Desert Spirituality of New Monasticism

THE NEW MONASTIC is called to a posture of radical openness before the Divine. For many monks throughout history, this mysterious process of openness took place in the desert. Certainly, the women and men—who left the cities of Asia Minor for the Egyptian and Palestinian deserts in the fourth century—eloquently describe the stark beauty of stripping away external trappings to receive in the outpouring of God in the soul.

Although many of us have never lived in a desert, we are the heirs of the monks who found peace in the solitude and silence of these wild places. In the same manner that we—as modern monks in the world—transpose the physical monastery into an inner sanctuary, we also relocate the geographical desert into an interior metaphorical place that is eternal, without beginning or end, and cannot be circumscribed by time or place. By this I mean that we live in and practice desert spirituality, one that enters into and moves from a place of emptiness before God.

These two inner dwellings—monastery and desert—mystically are present in the very essence and intimate part of the soul. Nothing but the Divine alone touches this ground, and nothing but the soul's emptiness has the capacity to receive and live in its mystery. What makes this possible is not only divine generosity, but "a power in the soul," Meister Eckhart claims, "which touches neither time nor flesh, flowing from the spirit, remaining in the spirit, altogether spiritual. In this power, God is ever verdant and flowering . . . [and the soul is] free of all names and void of all forms, entirely exempt and free, as God is exempt and free in Himself."[1]

Eckhart "recognizes, as the desert monastics did," writes theologian Douglas Christie, "that a willingness to let go of everything that is less than God must exist at the very foundation of the soul. It is the posture of openness that makes everything else possible. It is precisely this openness that can and often does trigger the sudden upwelling of God in the soul."[2] "God must enter into your being and powers," says Eckhart, "because you have bereft yourself of all possessions, and become as a desert, as it is written: 'The voice of the one crying in the wilderness' (Mt. 3: 3)."[3]

The Wayless Way

THE SPIRITUAL PATH of new monasticism can be identified as the "wayless way" of the desert, which is neither given, nor wholly contained, by culture or religion. This way leads you to welcome in the depth of being—wholly, completely, in vulnerability and surrender—the transformation of love in your soul. To follow the call and surrender to wisdom greater than your own—abandoning doubt and confusion, intellectual resistance, and emotional reasons for not hearing the call. To be grateful for the call, for the preciousness of this life, for travelling the path of the mystics and saints and yearning for the Divine, for the mystery that can never be contained: That's following the call.

That's saying: "Yes."

It suggests that this desert spirituality represents the primordial place, the quickening moment of radical openness that initiates the upwelling of God in our souls. Here—empty of images and detached from possessions—we return to the advent of religious consciousness, the nameless source of every word and name, and the free and unencumbered darkness where God gives birth in us. The person on this path is able to perceive and identify with multiple religious expressions, holding plural worlds in a unified whole. This feeling of being "at home" proceeds from the divine genesis in our souls, into the realm of word and symbol, and is a divine-human co-gestating and co-birthing of an original and creative monastic spirituality for our time.

In one form or another, the world's religions identify desert spirituality with negative theology. This is the route of passive contemplation, whereby in silence, receptivity, detachment, and unknowing the person experiences the Divine Presence. Yet, the detachment associated with negative theology is not asceticism per se, but a necessary step in the transformation of false desire, achieved for the sake of abundance, dynamism, and the flourishing of life.

To understand the significance of desert spirituality in the maturation of the monk, I find it helpful to review how Dionysius the Areopagite distinguishes and clarifies two types of contemplative consciousness—the positive and negative theologies (in Latin, *via positiva* and *via negativa*).[4] Dionysius claims that we strive toward God through praising the "affirmative theology," and the conceptual names, symbols, images, activities, and emotions of God. And yet, as we rise from the things of this world up to God itself, we leave behind language and names because everything we *know* about God pales in comparison to what God *is*. Only one dimension of the journey, affirmation will cede to the more inscrutable "negative theology," the pathless path of contemplating God in its mode of nothingness.[5] The result is a language of paradox and the denial of names.

In terms of spiritual development, the positive theology is associated with earlier stages of the journey, when we rely on religious tradition, accepted names for God, and historically transmitted prayer forms and contemplative techniques. But, the journey of faith moves away from known into unknown, from belief into doubt, and from intellect into mysticism. This shift from affirmation to negation involves the whole person and everything that one has—up until this point—accepted as true or real. While Dionysius describes the Christian context of these archetypal paths, this movement from affirmation to negation as a method of spiritual advancement is evident in the world's religions. Mystics from traditions as different in their orientations as Buddhism, Islam, and Judaism tell us that it is in the radical ambiguity—or nothingness—of being that we are open to Reality in itself. As the fuel of self-emptying, negation takes apart the constructed or false self. It functions as a disruptive element in the spiritual life, designed to break down its linguistic coherence and structural logic, and thereby to shock the person outside conventional notions of reality into another plane of existence.

In a deeper spiritual sense, negative theology reflects the transformation of a person's core identity, performing in language the task that the mystic performs in the dark night or great death experience, when a person's false identity is given away. The corollary to the negation of concepts is the unsaying, undoing, and unwilling of the "lower self'—that entity defined by the world of attraction, ego demand, and economy—in order to find one's true self. Described in the world's religions by terms that evoke images of bewilderment or loss, negative theology quenches our fundamental thirst to be self-willed and heals us of illusions that separate us from our Source.

Dionysius held that the positive and negative theologies are stamped into our natures and we follow their ancient methodology—often unknown to our conscious minds—to the divine nature itself. They are not merely conceptual categories, but represent complementary paths to, and expressions of, ultimate reality; as such, each refers to techniques of prayer and contemplation, images and structures of language, ways of knowing, and views of the inner life of God.[6] Incorporated into each person's journey, consciously or latently, they represent the method and structure, and way and goal of the spiritual life. Without maintaining the dialectic of naming and un-naming, illumination and darkness, revealed and hidden, our lives would cease to grow toward integration and wholeness. Yet, he also cautions us to "not conclude that the negations are simply the opposites of the affirmations, but rather that the cause of all is considerably prior to this, beyond privations, beyond every denial, beyond every assertion."[7]

It is this "cause of all" that is the aspiration of the monk's journey—to live in God. Having surrendered to emptiness, the seeker is flooded with the inner life of the cosmos, of the universal intelligence that animates the stars and planets, that waters the greatest oceans and the smallest blades of grass, and fashions our souls. But, even more than this, the monk participates in the sacred passion—the personal, intimate Divine who cares for our world, suffers over injustice, has compassion for our sins, and loves without end. Made in the divine image, we are constituted to share in the supreme mutual intimacy and interpenetration of our being and the divine being.

The movement into the desert darkness is necessary in order for the soul to be so "pregnant with Nothing like a woman with child,"—as Meister Eckhart says—"and in that Nothing God was born."[8] The monk's journey, however, does not end here. He or she also flows out from God, returning to the world of ordinary senses and everyday existence. But, there is a difference. Now, the door between earthly and divine life is always open, and the mystic soul is continually watered with drops of night dew. Empowered by awe, the monk bears the gifts of a mystical life, and is called to be a witness to the loving, flourishing, merciful, and gentle Divine Presence activated in one's depth.

Eckhart views this entire mystical process as a "wayless way" that leads the soul to rest.

> The soul has three ways into God. *One* is to seek God in all creatures with manifold activity and ardent longing…The *second* way is a wayless way, free and yet bound,…well-nigh past self and all things, without will and without images.…
>
> The *third* way is called a way, but is really being at home, that is: seeing God without means in His own being.… How marvelous, to be without and within, to embrace and be embraced, to see and been seen, to hold and be held—*that* is the goal, where the spirit is ever at rest, united in joyous eternity![9]

The Meister contends that we enter the divine as "virgins," empty of images and demands. But, when we flow out from God, we are "wives" bearing gifts. His desert spirituality points to the root of the meanings and the states of consciousness behind religious names and identities. It is the longing of the soul—which Eckhart famously described—to want to "get into its simple ground, into the silent desert into which no distinction ever peeped, of Father, Son, or Holy Ghost."[10] To achieve detachment from images, the person "must collect all his powers as if into a corner of his soul where, hiding away from all images and forms, he can get to work."[11] In order to know the divine in the wayless way, Eckhart continues, "your knowing must become a pure unknowing, and a forgetting of yourself and all creatures."[12]

Thus, contemplative practices—if not kept alive and meaningful— can be another form of attachment that impede the journey and obscure the reason we pursue them. Eckhart is insistent that desert mysticism needs to be alert to the subtle manner of the ego, and to ensure that "all your works should be wrought without Why."

> I say truly, as long as you do works for the sake of heaven or God or eternal bliss, from without, you are at fault. You may pass muster, but it is not the best. Indeed if a man thinks he will get more of God by meditation, by devotion, by ecstasies or by special infusion of grace than by the fireside or in the stable, that is nothing but taking God, wrapping a cloak around His head and shoving Him under a bench. For whoever seeks God in a special way gets the way and misses God, who lies hidden in it.[13]

Unknowing, moreover, is not merely a stripping away of concepts, but a complete stilling of the mind. For Eckhart, therefore, the truest kind of prayer is thus no prayer, "in which the soul knows nothing of knowing, wills nothing of loving, and from light it becomes dark."[14]

Drawn into another dimension of the inner life, the wayless way requires that you accept—in the depth of your being—wholly, completely, in vulnerability and surrender, the birth of the divine and the transformation of love in your soul. To follow the call and surrender to wisdom greater than your own—abandoning intellectual pride and emotional resistance—is the path of the new monastic. To be grateful for the call, for the preciousness of this life, for travelling the path of the mystics and saints, and yearning for the Divine: This is "really being at home, that is: seeing God without means."[15]

When a person reaches into his or her depth, the pathless path is revealed because it is already imprinted in consciousness. Core mystical structures and techniques are present in every person's depth, even as their expression is uniquely individual. When we have the courage to enter the dark regions, a new monastic spirituality finds its way into our hearts. At the same time, this personal revealing is connected to the mystical well of every religion and to universal spiritual values.

This is the essence of the desert spirituality: to forge a mature vocation in solitude with the Divine. The person who is able to enter the wilderness of the heart, who has the courage to *be* in the desert, waiting for the divine voice—discovers the wayless way. Here is perhaps the challenge and fear, but also the great benefit and freedom of the monastic way. The monk gives his or her life to seeking the Divine in all things; but is not tied to whether the quest has a name—Franciscan or Tibetan or Shamanic—or whether it adheres to certain agreed-upon philosophies. Rather, it is a journey—perhaps similar to the one taken by our forefathers and foremothers—to seek truth in the wild places, away from dominant cultural and religious identities.

Eckhart also describes the wayless way as "living without why," a change so complete, so elusive, so deep, that nothing in our conscious behavior can be understood at this distance outside of God. This is not merely an ideal. It is an experience. It is the experience of naughting the self, so that we become every self.

To live *without why* is to throw ourselves into the unknown, finding the courage to seek this eternal place, without knowing at the outset where we will end up. For those who are genuinely and fully aware of our longing for union, this means that everything we do, every breath we take, every act we perform, and every moment of life is sacred. It is that momentary expression of the beautiful that dwells in us, which we offer to each other.

This is the path of high solitude, in the sense that it is the person's alone—no other can replicate or determine it. No theology or religious worldview can be imposed. Only the person's surrender to love—revealed and perfected—can be the way. This is our foremost capacity—to be divine-like, to be holy, to experience the openness of heart that gives life.

Just as the person who knows musical notation can play any score, the soul attuned to the universal, intradivine structures discovers the blueprint of every religious archetype. Then every path and every religion is a place of home. You may choose the path of Tibetan or Benedictine monasticism. Or, you may choose to live solely the wayless way. But, whatever path is chosen, desert spirituality will eventually reveal the master design of every particular form.

I imagine that all mature monks recognize that monastic consciousness is deeper and more universal than its unique, religious expression. It is ontological—an intrinsic aspect or archetype of being. The new monastic—perhaps more explicitly than the Buddhist monk or Hindu *sannyasi*—must take this realization a step further by temporarily abandoning all named religious traditions in order that the seeds of revelation can take root in his or her soul.

The challenge of our era is to co-create with the Divine (and with each other) new monastic landscapes. We are bathing in the waters of spiritual renewal gushing from a spring. Our participation in these waters grants us agency to develop a new type of religious consciousness, inviting all to enter.

This is the meaning of the arduous path, of the glorious journey into the heart of the Divine: to *be* alone, discovering the tremendous gift within us.

Birthing the New

BIRTHING OF THE NEW involves spiritually dying to old habits and ways of being. Every authentic practice involves the un-formation, deconstructive process that dismantles the false self, societal distortions, and violent, authoritarian elements within human consciousness. It thus travels a unique mystical path. It includes within the purification of the soul— described variously as a "dark night," "great death," or "annihilation"—not only the release of personal illusions and errors, but also of oppressive elements within society, institutions, and religions. A seeker on this path undergoes a spiritual dismantling that exposes the hidden internal assumptions and contradictions that wound a person's cherished ideals.

New monastic spirituality affords us an opportunity to rectify these past omissions. It draws upon timeless practices of meditation, prayer, and other purifying disciplines to combat the many instances of spiritual oppression imbedded in our religions and mystical paths. It also offers insight into how damaging states of consciousness impact our soul health and healing. But more significantly, desert spirituality opens a new potential for transformation. By sinking into deep mystical structures, the practice of monastic spirituality uncovers a way into and through painful and wounding aspects of our individual and collective consciousness. It thus offers insight on the path of reconciliation and renewal.

Questioning of our religious belonging and attempts to discover a more benevolent view of God often bring the spiritual pilgrim to inner conflict. Standing between two or more worlds, many souls suffer an impasse between religious worldviews. Unable to go back to who and what we once were, but uncertain about how to enter the future, feelings of confusion, betrayal, disinterest, and anguish are not uncommon. In fact, many people confide the pain of their alienation from traditional religious norms. As an essential aspect of healing, this process of impasse and anguish is a mark of the substance and authenticity of the path. When the self is pushed against darkness and unknowing, the impasse itself becomes a catalyst for a more honest understanding of reality.

In the lives of unimaginable numbers of people today there is evidence of this unique birthing process. Here, mystical union is more than a personal experience. Rather, it entails an apprehension of the sacred in the grandeur of the cosmos, variety of living systems, and the spirits of Earth. Similarly, it embraces the scope of humanity's quest for the holy, offering one's soul as the *site and activity* of unification. Through uniting the apparent opposites of one's self—male and female, reason and intuition, judgment and mercy, heaven and Earth, my religion and your religion—we co-create the eternal oneness already present in the Divine. This attention to healing the internal dichotomy dispels the falseness of "us and them," actualizing within our inner lives the true contemplative heart of faith.

The unifying path is directed toward both an inner and outer reconciliation of what divides us from each other and from ourselves; by such practice we expand our heart's capacity to love. The monk seeks to achieve the internal unity that is in essence the foundation of all religions, and of a true global family of shared responsibilities and benefits. The point of this global passage is to become more pure of heart, to discover how to lift our world up to its loving potential. If this new spiritual path is to endure, it needs to guide us toward the highest religious ideals. It must be attentive to practices that advance peace on Earth; and provide ethical guidelines to instruct us in moments of conflict, adversity, and pain.

History illustrates that every religious path holds the promise of a fulfilled human person. It opens up our capacity to transcend baser human behaviors and to aspire to the realm of the holy. In the Asian traditions, a sense of identity is established in the injunctions: atman is Brahman or samsara is nirvana.[16] Here, our original identity with our Source is affirmed; beyond the illusion of separateness is our true belonging to the Holy. Similarly, an early Christian phrase—"God became human so humans could become God"—establishes the basis of the path of perfection. We have the capacity within us, already present, to grow in wisdom, to aspire toward sainthood—to be all that we are capable of being. Further, these paths of holiness do not imply a fixed or final enlightenment. Rather, they assert the ongoing, continual movement of humanity toward spirit, and the cooperative divine-human effort to build a more loving, more harmonious planetary society.

An Altered Worldview

MONASTICISM requires an altered worldview that looks at one's self and creation through divine eyes. In other words, it requires a consciousness of humility, of compassion and love, that seeks not the things of the world, but the transformation of whatever is diminished by the world into a higher, more spiritual mode of being. It is to submit to the palace of wisdom and to evaluate one's life and activities from the vantage point of the holy. The process of moving into a divine perspective takes time and grows incrementally, as the person learns to let go of ego attachments, practice humility and merciful conduct, spend time in prayer, and purify his or her heart.

It is an unlearning of the personality characteristics and social advancement valorized in culture, and the quest to achieve that marks the climate of contemporary life. It is an unlearning of the false self, the self that seeks its own pleasure or will at the expense of meaning or love. It is an unlearning of how we consider the divine and what we attribute to god consciousness. It is a deconstruction of dualism, from the most personal to the most esoteric levels of awareness; it is sinking into passive or receptive consciousness, where Spirit works in the soul, and activates the deep self and its quest for truth.

The receptive, passive action of contemplation in the soul is so counter to how we appropriate and live out our lives, that the altered perspective of true monasticism can be unsettling, challenging how and why we do things. But it is also the great motivator of faith, for it is only when the will of the person is taken away, when we can no longer "do" anything; when the normal activities of life seem hollow and cease to work, that our self-definitions unravel and we open to the inflow of an illuminating light.

It is not just listening to the Spirit within, but the radical inflow of divinity that shatters self-definition and prepares the person for the spiritual graces and consolations that lead to the establishment of a monastic center of consciousness in one's being.

But even more than this, the reverse vantage point of monasticism builds an inner hermitage, the intimacy of being in the "cave of the heart." The person now radiates from a center of silence, bringing a fragrance of the holy into daily life. In this emptiness of self, which is also, finally, everything, one participates in the inner life of divinity—as a particular expression of God's presence on Earth—that is the absence of specialness, identity, or grandeur.

Desert spirituality is at the center of monastic formation. It is being *monos* (alone, one) in the everyday, of offering one's soul as a home for the homeless and a birthplace for the divine experiment, and of devoting one's life to the pursuit of humility, love, and nonviolence, that is the call of the (new) monk. It is the passage that draws the seeker beyond identifiable religions and social constructions into a pure, undiluted encounter with reality.

Theology of the Mystical Feminine

FIVE

Via Feminina:
The Mystical Path of the Feminine

REQUENTLY, I am asked: What is the underlying theological or spiritual foundation of the new monastic movement? If a person is not living as a monk within a tradition, or not drawing on the spirituality of one of the world's religions, then what theology or philosophy grounds the seeker's path? I imagine that each monastic community or new monk responds to this concern differently.

Yet, there is a foundation that informs the theology and is the focus of worship in many religious communities, even if not explicitly stated: devotion to Mary (*Theotokos*, mother of God), Sophia (Wisdom), Virgin of Guadalupe, Guanyin, Queen of Heaven, Corn Woman, Durga, Lakshmi, and other female goddess figures and aspects of the mystical feminine. While the great women mystics and founders of female monastic communities developed sophisticated theologies *within* their religions, lacking is a monastic spirituality that is formed *primarily* from the vantage point of the mystical feminine, with its own comprehensive practices, theologies and spiritual paths.

In what follows, I briefly reference an historical approach, illustrating the personification of the Divine Feminine in religious life. Much of this I have covered in a previous work, *Radical Wisdom: A Feminist Mystical Theology;*[1] and many scholars and practitioners have written more eloquently and with greater comprehension than I about the history of women's wisdom.[2]

Rather, my interest lays in the deep theology of the mystical feminine, which I call *via feminina*. In Christian theology, *via* signifies the spiritual journey toward union with God; *feminina* conveys a quality of consciousness that includes but is not confined to biological females. Thus, while the feminine is an archetype in both women and men, perhaps embodied and expressed differently in females and in males, *via feminina* is also a spiritual practice and way of life. This chapter is the contemplation on my practice, theology, and path of the feminine. Although even now—after more than forty years—I cannot offer more than personal insight into the depth of this mystic way.

Via Feminina

A NUMBER OF YEARS AGO, I was leading a weekly seminar on the contemplative life. One of my final lectures was on images of the Divine Feminine in the world's religions, the day's topic goddess figures in Christianity. During a discussion of two Christian paths of union with God, *via negativa* (the negative way) and *via positiva* (the positive way), I spontaneously claimed there was a third way: *via feminina*, the way of the feminine, or the feminine way.

Having spoken the phrase, *via feminina*, a treasure trove of meaning suddenly sprung open. The conceptualization was electrifying because it was a linguistic affirmation of another mystical path, one that unlocked new horizons in religious consciousness. *Via feminina* required a way of expressing that was poetic and polyphonic, its perspective organic, holistic.

Via feminina offers a new vantage point from which to perceive reality, a perspective that is implied and intrinsic, much as an underground spring nourishes seedlings even when the rain does not fall. That is, in a similar way that the monastic archetype is within all of us so, too, is the mystical feminine. Embedded in every religion—in overt and subtle ways—and every facet of creation, the mystical feminine is relevant to females and males, the life of the spirit, social justice, ethics, the community of earthly inhabitants, and how we access and evaluate knowledge.

Via feminina is the emergence of a truth yet unplumbed that draws us to a radical mercy, traces of which our mystic seers know too well, challenging us to redefine what it means to be human, and what the pathways of devotion entail. It is a way of being that approaches reality through the lens of benevolence, compassion, and love. It is a nondualistic, nonhierarchical, holistic path of embodiment *and* transcendence, of humanity *and* divinity, of earth *and* spirit, without division. It is the place where we sink into a depth of being that echoes the rhythm of the monastic day, allowing the rhythm of silence to become the matrix for reflection and wisdom. This is really the experience of the dark light of contemplation where no names are given and the Divine Feminine transfigures our inner lives, ennobling our hearts.

As a distinct spirituality, *via feminina* is attentive to the multiple wisdoms of body, psyche, and soul, placing primary importance on healing those social factors—whether of gender, culture, race, sexual orientation, religious belief, etc.—that stigmatize persons, rob them of dignity, wound their souls, and betray the highest aspirations of religious life. It thus is an invitation to divest one's being of subtle forms of injustice imbedded in the categories that define the religious life—redemption, salvation, *nirvana*, *samadhi*, soul, god—as well as in the processes of mystical ascent—purification, great death, annihilation, union—and hinder the full integration and liberation of the self.

Via feminina weaves together the secular and the sacred, and loves the earthly realm with all of its life-affirming attributes. It is, thus, the source and content of a theology of embodied transcendence, that is, the capacity and responsibility to integrate spiritual wisdom into daily life, to strive to be divine-like. To be wedded to humanity-creation-cosmos and to God in one, integrated vow. To celebrate life events in their mystical potential, and to see with contemplative eyes, the true state of the world.

In my usage, *via feminina* refers to impersonal divine energies and spiritual pathways, which I describe in nongendered language as the mystical feminine or "it"; it also points to the highly personal communion of the Divine Feminine in various personifications: Sophia, Lakshmi, Guanyin, Mary, etc., signified by "She." In this book, I will refer to divine manifestations and figures alternately as the Divine Feminine or

Divine Sophia, and to energies and paths as the mystical feminine or *via feminina*.

Via feminina is a mighty tributary within the universal spiritual quest, intertwined with and flowing alongside the dominant paths described in the world's religious texts. This way, or *via*, emerges from the revelatory inflow of the feminine being—of which Divine Sophia is one archetype—into human consciousness. As the free self-disclosure of divinity directly illuminating the higher faculties of the soul, the Divine Feminine is *birthing herself* into the world. *Via feminina* is a deeper, more hidden path. It is a more silent and nondual path. It is a more intimate and nonviolent path. It is a path of radical love, radical mercy, and surrender. It is a path of the openhearted and guileless. It is a path that leads to the expansion of our full humanness.

As a constructed phrase, *via feminina* is related to the wisdom teachings inspired by or inscribed within patriarchal religions; but it also disturbs and transgresses them. Standing outside or beyond the logic that formed their language, spirituality, and theology, its liberating mysticism functions as a continual unsaying, a continual disruption of the previous thousands of years of "saying," by pulling up the roots of injustice and the seeds of oppression that were handed down from generation to generation and planted in our souls.

Perhaps *via feminina's* single most distinguishing feature is its *intimate wholeness*, a vision of reality that encompasses and combines feminine and masculine, including everything within its merciful, benevolent, and joyous fold. It is a specific path of reconciliation that begins from a different premise of trust and indissoluble intimacy that moves deeper into unitive states of being beyond opposites and paradoxes. Yet, it simultaneously is able to hold paradox and opposites in a higher, more creative state, leading the seeker to the mystery of divine-human co-creation.

From the perspective of the mystical feminine, the Divine Presence—and, therefore, the underlying reality that informs everything—is dynamically open and nondualistic. A holistic reality that is not susceptible to subject-object divisions, *via feminina* eludes dialectical thought and excessive rationality because it is beyond dichotomy and mind. It reveals nondual intimacy—a dimension of numerous mystical states—in its transcendent aspect. That is, it is not only a spiritual practice, or a way to apprehend the divine, but also the primordial paradigm of life. From communion and intimacy, life comes into being. *Via feminina* heralds the power and profundity of Divine Sophia, and the wisdom of the Mother whose mercy is entirely free, without a trace of anything "other."

In my experience, complete participation in and understanding of monastic spirituality involves integration of the Divine Feminine into our hearts and minds. It indicates that the fullness of human spirituality— enlightenment, salvation, self, soul, god, ethics, morals—will not be realized without the wisdom of the mystical feminine. History bears this out as the unveiling of new religious forms take place within the context of prior views of reality. The power of new revelation always affects the whole constellation in which a human community asserts self-definition. In this sense, *via feminina* is a breakthrough into new consciousness and thought. At the same time, it is mysteriously bound to the traditions that have come before.

In following *via feminina*'s monastic path, we suspend attachment to religious forms and spiritual identities. Yet, *via feminina* is not a rejection of religious traditions, but a mystical deepening and transformation from within. We put away named practices and orthodoxies because we have faith that we will not be abandoned. That there is not a judgmental or jealous god who will strike us down or accuse us of betrayal. We need not fear the loss of known religious and spiritual paths, because they will always be within us, even as Mystery constantly gives birth to new expressions of itself.

Monastic life is ideally suited to express the mystical feminine, with its emphasis on interiority, silence, and solitude. It is entrance into the mothering heart of reality—that origin that is not opposite or opposed to anything. It cannot be dissected or dismissed. It is non-possessable and non-dogmatic. This mothering energy is bound to incarnation and embodiment, as it is the essential offering of forgiveness and freedom. It guides us into the compassionate heart beyond cause and effect, and into a new revelatory landscape that is absent origin stories of disobedience and sin.

So diverse and all encompassing is the shift in perspective from patriarchal religions to that of the mystical feminine that—to understand the differences in any complete way—requires reflective analysis. These are some of my questions about the ways in which the Divine Feminine brings change: How would theology and the stages of spiritual growth differ? How does *via feminina* help us to be spiritual advocates for rectifying the world's poverty, violence, homelessness, and war? How does it help us to engage in a global spirituality that embraces diverse religions and cultures? How would this vantage point alter our relationship with religion?

Further, in what way does the mystical feminine help to remove or heal spiritual forms of oppression that are ingrained in the world's religions? What deep structures of religiosity, akin to neurological patterns in the brain, have become entangled and misfired, afflicting humanity with fear, faulty hearts, and impaired states of awareness. Examples include emphasis on fallen-ness and original sin, over-dependence on institutional authority, rejection or vilification of outsiders—race, gender, sexual orientation, etc.—control of personal faith experience, and fearful, judgmental speech.

I—and many other people drawn to the monk within—choose to follow and practice in the liminal space, between realities, receptive to the inflow of revelation from the Divine Feminine, without identifying exclusively with one religion. I suppose one could say that we seek, to the best of our ability, to embody the message of this vast Wisdom-Realm, this revelatory landscape, directly, and without limiting its fullness to what is already expressed in cultures and religions. The mystical path of the feminine is not a panacea, or universal cure, but a path of healing and remembrance, of mercy and love that liberates forgotten and abused aspects of the human spirit in order to bring into our lives a more true vision of our humanity.

Personifications of the Divine Feminine

There is in all things an invisible fecundity, a dimmed light, a meek namelessness, a hidden wholeness. This mysterious Unity and Integrity is Wisdom, the Mother of all. There is in all . . . a silence that is a font of action and joy. It rises up in wordless gentleness and flows out to me . . . speaking as Hagia Sophia, speaking as my sister, Wisdom.[3]

IN THE ABOVE-CITED prose poem, "Hagia Sophia" (Holy Wisdom), Thomas Merton describes Wisdom as both a "hidden wholeness," and an "invisible fecundity," that is in all things, animating them from within; and, as the personification of the Divine Feminine: speaking as "my sister and the Mother of all." Sophia is both the transcendent, idealized Feminine, and the embodied, spiritualized woman.

Sophia is a return to origins, a retrieval of the "forgotten mother tongue," bound up in the mystery of our anthropology, the life story of the spirit. "For Merton to invoke the name of Sophia," Christopher Pramuk writes, "is to remember both the Name of God and our own deepest identity; it is to be drawn intimately into the realm of . . . sanctified time. . . . Sophiology is a theological response to a name we already have, a name to which we will respond, when it is called out, when it is remembered."[4]

Descriptions of the Divine Feminine—as Sophia (Wisdom)—are found in the canonical texts of the Hebrew Scriptures—Proverbs, Job, Sirach—and in the books of Ecclesiastes, Baruch, and the Wisdom of Solomon. Included in the Greek and Latin Vulgate, these last three apocryphal texts were omitted from the sixteenth-century Protestant Bible.

In the Book of Wisdom, Sophia is Creator at the beginning—*When God set the heavens in place, I was present*—and also part of the ongoing creative process that gives birth to humans, creation, and God. At the same time, she is the active force who illuminates the earthly world and "it is only through her . . . that humans can find their way to God."[5] She is prophet and redeemer who—out of compassion for the human condition—dwells within the material realm.

The Divine Feminine appears in later Jewish mystical texts as *Shekhinah* (feminine "indwelling presence"). In the *Book Bahir*—an important twelfth-century work of Jewish mysticism—*Shekhinah* is eternal, not created. In other Kabbalistic texts, She is not just a personification or quality of God, but "is always God Himself."[6] Similarly, *Shekhinah* is the receptive vessel (*shidda*) in which all the divine powers are contained, and is symbolized by the ocean to which all the rivers of the world flow. She is the crown within which all creation is held. She is understanding (*binah*) itself. She is the innermost chamber of mystery, and "to this humankind . . . has no access."[7] "Only in this state," says the *Book Bahir*, "can human beings see her and speak with her; her actual place, however, the place of her origin, continues to be hidden from their view."[8] She is erased; we are her unveiling.

In her dwelling among us, *Shekhinah* willingly goes into exile from her divine origins and suffers isolation (*meyuhad*) and the tragedy of the human condition. When we sin, she mourns. When we follow truth, she rejoices. She is the embodiment of the highest form of love—mother-love—and we use the metaphors of daughter, sister, and mother to express the "exceptionality and intensification of this love."[9] Our love is the overflowing of her love, our earth the formation of her plenitude, our body her holy temple.

To Muslims she is the womb (*rahim*) of the All-merciful, established in a famous *hadith*: "My mercy precedes My wrath" (*rahmati sabaqat ghadabi*). Ibn al-'Arabi—the renowned thirteenth-century Islamic mystic—also situates the essence of the feminine in both the heavenly and earthly worlds, and as prior to and inclusive of male and female. As a reflection of higher divine unity, "woman," Ibn al-'Arabi writes, "is the most complete and perfect [contemplation of Reality]."[10]

As the source of life-giving mercy, her tears overflow into creation, healing our sins and woes. Through her, all things come to be, in her, life brought to its fruition. She is pristine awareness, undefiled mind, and sinless purity. She is the sacred heart of Mary and *mater dolorosa* (mother of suffering) to millions of Catholics. Source of the ten thousand things in Daoist philosophy, she holds creation in her womb. She is nondual consciousness, who encompasses emptiness and form; *yin* and *yang*; happiness and sorrow; heaven and earth; creation and destruction; birth and death. In Celtic spirituality, the Divine Feminine is held in deep reverence, and Brigid, the goddess of fire, symbolizes fertility and abundance.

In Nigerian creation stories, *Woyengi* (Great Mother) molds human beings in her image and breathes life into creation. In the *Lakshmi-tantra*, a popular Hindu text, Creator Goddess Lakshmi pervades all creation with vitality, will, and consciousness. Undertaking "the entire stupendous creation of the universe with only a one-billionth fraction of herself, [she is] so transcendent...so beyond the ability of the mind to circumscribe her, that only a miniscule fraction of her is manifest in the creation of the universe."[11]

> I alone send (the creation) forth and (again) destroy it. I absolve the sins of the good. As the (mother) earth towards all beings, I pardon them (all their sins). I mete everything out. I am the thinking process and I am contained in everything.[12]

In the Chinese Buddhist personification of Guanyin—Bodhisattva of Compassion—She is depicted as pure light, eliminating darkness and extinguishing the fire of pain. Buddhist teachings on *Prajñāpāramitā* (*The Perfection of Wisdom in Eight Thousand Lines*) also describe Her as "The Mother of All the Buddhas" and as the "storehouse of the Supreme Dharma." She is both the repository of the Universal Mind, of Oneness, and the active flowing, in and out, of myriad dharmas. In the most famous *Prajñāpāramitā* text, *The Heart Sutra*—which is chanted daily in Zen sanghas—"Form does not differ from emptiness; emptiness does not differ from form." These sutras emphasize *Prajñāpāramitā* as both a personification and a practice of nonduality.

The power of Woman, a divine figure, and the feminine is elevated in many Indigenous communities and rituals. Native American poet and scholar, Paula Gunn Allen writes, "In the beginning was thought, and her name was Woman."

> There is a spirit that pervades everything.... The colors of this spirit are multitudinous, a glowing, pulsing rainbow. Old Spider Woman is one name for this quintessential spirit, and Serpent Woman is another. Corn Woman is one aspect of her, and Earth Woman is another, and what they have together made is called Creation, Earth, creatures, plants, and light.[13]

At times, the Divine Feminine is the ultimate divinity in her own right, uncreated and eternal. In this aspect, she is identified in Christian texts with the Holy Spirit or with the uncreated aspect of the Trinity. She also is worshipped in the *Devī-bhagavāta-purāna* of medieval Hinduism as the supreme truth, who lays the foundation of the world and flows forth in the wisdom of nature's evolution. She is the soul of the world. In addition, She is the unmanifest Godhead before God, the empty silence preceding and birthing the world of forms.[14]

The richness of the world's traditions provides ample evidence for the vision of the feminine as both a way toward divinity and as divinity itself. This vision is not a plea made against any prior reality, a claim of what should be, or a retrieval of the past. An ultimate category of divinity, the Divine Feminine does not emerge from a prior, more holy male god, divine attribute, or messianic form. It addresses our future and what we are becoming, now.

Several Attributes of *Via Feminina*

Radical Gentleness

Via feminina is a gentle path, subtle in its ways. It comes silently, and in such a deep interiority that often you do not recognize its call. And this is no wonder, since the sound of Sophia's voice is so holy, and the form of Her words so profound, that even the purist soul struggles to hold and bear them in memory. It is as if our Beloved Mystery is calling you to give birth to Her truth, to cradle Her words in your heart, until you have the strength and the wisdom to let them be incarnated in and through you.

Our souls, numbed by the harshness of daily life, almost cannot bear the soothing gentleness that *via feminina* brings. So deeply loving, so fully open, so completely healing, our Beloved Mystery offers Herself, in holy vulnerability. It is in the gentleness of spirit that we find the deepest truth, and the rest that our whole being desires. It is in silence and solitude that Holy Mother Wisdom guides us deeper into love.

So gentle are Her ways! She calls us to Herself over and over again, helping us to discover that She loves us in every way. She wants us to experience her heart, which is so merciful and kind that no wounding is possible. She desires to fill our spiritual memory with *via feminina* until we finally come to rest, and our soul is swaddled in the cradle of pure peace.

Unifying Spirituality

Via feminina is a radically unifying spirituality, different than the dominant mode of historical religions. It calls us to reassess our notions of ultimate reality in a context that includes the whole of life, seeks salvation for all creation, and protests a spiritual worldview that excludes, segregates, divides, or belittles. It is a way to live in a new mode, when we have left behind our attachments to a punishing and retributive God, and to a God of exclusion and domination. It is a contemplative path that brings an experience of complete and unconditional love, without opposite.

It is related to historical spiritualities, but it is does not entirely fit into prior religious categories; similarly, it does both the Divine Feminine and you an injustice if you try to conscript it to old patterns. While you will find elements of *via feminina* in all the world's major religions—Christ's teachings, the wisdom of Buddha and Lao Tzu, Sufi mysticism, Indigenous spiritualities, the Hebrew Scriptures, etc.—we are the recipients of another divine disclosure that emerges on its own terms and is not subsumed under or absorbed into the world's named religions.

Most significant, is that the unifying ethos of the mystical feminine does not imply a single, pregiven essence, or perennial philosophy that underlies and is the apex of every religious expression. Rather, one-ing is the source of pluralism, with its distinctive and often incommensurate religious worldviews. That is, the dynamic mystery of being, the unknowable, openness of ultimate reality, reveals itself in the manyness of religions, and their unique practices, languages, and meanings. A humble and sacred injunction of this path is to hold—in a unifying embrace—the manifold ways in which the Divine is expressed on Earth.

The mystical feminine is the grounding foundation of spiritual pluralism. It includes within its purview nonviolence, global spiritual consciousness, mystical oneness, and interspiritual paths of liberation. It offers unique insight into the inner life of the Divine Feminine, which has not been fully revealed or articulated in history. It is an as-yet untapped depth of spiritual consciousness.

Suffering & Mercy

Women and men suffer adversity in each physical and spiritual birth, and in acts of violation to their bodies and to their souls. Through pain and fragmentation, they also experience the Divine's own suffering—the wounds of Suffering Sophia—who laments with our world.

Those of us who follow *via feminina*, like *Shekhinah* in exile, identify with and give ourselves to the defiled and the outcast—to all who hunger and thirst. We discover that compassion is more resilient than fear and that nonviolence is deeper than retaliation. We realize that in those instances in which the inherent oneness of life is violated, our souls mystically experience the wounding of creation, absorbing the anguish of the poor, the victimized, and the exploited. We feel how Mother Earth is also possessed, discarded, expendable, sacrificed, and consumed, and how our pain is reflected and absorbed in her body. Our souls suffer the Divine's suffering, and see with the eyes of the Divine. We see our very self through this suffering because "my eye and God's eye," writes Meister Eckhart, "are one eye and one seeing, one knowing, and one loving."[14]

The fourteenth century mystic, Julian of Norwich, writes with great insight about our capacity to suffer, and the unconditional love and forgiveness of the motherhood of God. When we sin, Julian says, Mother Jesus looks upon us with such mercy and tenderness, which Julian interprets through the closeness of the mother-child relationship. Liz McAvoy writes:

Julian presents the mother figure as the one who feels in her own body every hurt her child receives, both physical and psychological, and so this lord feels the suffering of his servant and is united with him in his anguish. The pain of the fall unites them both, just as the pain of childbirth and the suffering involved in the child's acquisition of experience unites mother and child in a continuous cycle of reciprocity.[15]

To reach a depth of spiritual maturity, the person travels the gospel of mercy, the path of profound forgiveness. Images found in mystical writings of the soul's absorption, annihilation, and melting into the Beloved illustrate that the great truth we seek is found in mutual intimacy. This high degree of surrender opens the soul to Sophia's tenderness and benevolence, and the pouring forth of Her mercy into the mighty river that flows between the soul and Divine Love.

Via feminina heals our hearts of the violent and punishing way in which we treat each other and creation. It calls us to assert the dignity and worth of every life form and that of our planet. The balm of forgiveness in which the soul is graced is restorative not only to oneself, but to divinity as well. Our healing is God's healing.

The force of Sophia's presence leads a person's soul away from temporal and spiritual desires to make a primary mystical claim: I am holy. In order to utter such a phrase, the self must be brought to zero. Only a no self, a not-I can speak the truth of its own divinity. Only the person who is no longer separate dares to claim the graced state of freedom. This is not a liberation that can be earned; it is only found through the process of spiritual dying and rebirth.

The most revolutionary aspect of this path is the immensity of divine benevolence. Punishment and violence are removed, negative views of the self cannot be sustained, and sins forgiven. There is nothing that is outside the realm of radical mercy. It is true in everyday life that we falter, believing that we are "only human." But the Divine Feminine imprints into the soul something more: the desire to hold sacred oneself and the world.

The Mother Seed

Divine Sophia is the mother seed from which sacred consciousness grows, and the starting point for a new monastic spirituality. This is because in the hiddenness of the Divine Feminine is the principle behind every principle, the root consciousness that incarnates in various forms.

When you experience intimacy beyond religious identity, everything is as it should be. Everything is the source of further illumination. You enter into the heart of truth, before it takes on a particular identity. You discover the path of emptiness and the dwelling place of the Divine Mother. When you find Her source, you understand all spiritual traditions and essences, and you sit at the lotus juncture, a recipient of new revelation.

It is here that we live the formless form, the wayless way that is capable of bearing ambiguity, uncertainty, paradox, and plural realities. Through this mother consciousness, which endures all things, we glimpse the divine that is always within and with us, is always on our side and supporting us, is always present to us. As well, it is never against us and it never withdraws.

The revelation of Divine Sophia is the underlying foundation of a monastic spirituality that is both "new" and immeasurably ancient. If the inflow of divine mystery into the heart and soul of the seeker is sufficiently comprehensive, it not only reveals previously inaccessible dimensions of reality and the next phase of divine-human self-disclosure, but it also changes the structure and equations of reality. New monastics that live by *via feminina* are tasked with bringing Sophia's voice into consciousness, living her wisdom traditions and transforming spiritual life on Earth. Like all true revelation, the manifestation of the Divine Feminine will develop over time, as we—in our own lives—and those who come after us, engage with and embody Her profound message.

Follow the simple beauty of Her path, and the quiet manner in which She enters your heart. She is calling you! Sink into the silky gentleness She brings—like the gray down of a morning dove—and you will be enwrapped in folds of love, your whole being at peace.

SIX

Four Dimensions of *Via Feminina*

A DISTINGUISHING FEATURE of many new monastic communities is that the Divine Feminine is not solely an aspect of monastic spirituality, the Divine Mother to whom monks pray, or the archetype of the soul's feminine aspect of personality. Rather, this is a monastic sensibility born within and through the Divine Feminine that is bringing into our world a way of being faithful to that Faith which is beyond religion, and a contemplative heart open to the majesty and tragedy of life. It is a reconfiguration of the human soul on a subtle level, which is so profound and elusive that the agent of that reconfiguration is glimpsed only by her traces, much like subatomic particles that cannot be observed without dislocating presence.

Emerging from the indwelling of Holy Sophia in our souls, new monastic spirituality is tasked with making deification—the capacity of the person to achieve holiness—real. That is, living in such a way that the integration and embodiment of the divine-human, especially the relationship of the physical and spiritual, is woven into the fabric of daily life. It means redefining personhood not as fallen or wandering, but as the self who carries the seeds of transformation and future renewal. It is to change the focus of humanity's progression in history from deficit to surplus, from deficiency to strength. This is the vital shift in consciousness needed to embrace the blessedness of creation, and to assist in the building of a more holy and peaceful Earth community.

Key to understanding the foundation of this contemporary monastic spirit are four interrelated themes: *Via feminina* as Revelatory and Prophetic, Theological Method, Spiritual Journey, and Contemplative.

THEME 1:

Via Feminina is Revelatory and Prophetic

VIA FEMININA is an event-time, that period when the Divine breaks into history and calls us to listen again to the prophetic voice and gaze again on Wisdom's suffering face. It is revelation because it is Sophia's gift of unveiling what many have longed for and dared not hope: the feminine heart of divinity and the full spiritual equality of women and men.

For the last five thousand years, divine self-disclosure in its most comprehensive and universal form has been the record and the experience of males. Women mystics, prophets, and saints are not unknown during this period. Yet there is no major world religion that traces its beginnings to a woman, and there are few spiritual lineages—Teresa of Avila's discalced Carmelites, for example—where the teachings and practices of women monks and masters are the source.

Reasons for the absence of women's spiritual voices are found worldwide: a disproportionately greater literacy of men, exclusion of women from practice and participation in religious institutions, domination and oppression of women's lives from birth to death, and social prohibition against women assuming positions of spiritual authority.

The presence of God as Blessed Be She is nothing short of revolutionary. Carrying new visions of the sacred into the noisy marketplace of the world, we are bearers of the Divine Feminine. In the small and private ways that mercy soothes the habits of our hearts, and as pioneers and prophets of dissent, our struggle to name and to be named are revelatory acts. In the variegated tapestry of our claim to spiritual authority, courageous outpouring of speech, and insistence on equality and dignity, it is the Divine Feminine who weaves.

There are certainly human interpretations and constructions of *via feminina*, but its wisdom springs from the revelatory mind, overflowing as divine communication in our hearts and souls. It is an inner experience that offers a contemporary unveiling of the sacred feminine. This is an exciting historical moment, the seedling ground for a fresh way of living and breathing.

Struggle Gives Birth to Revelation

The revelation of *via feminina* bursts forth out of the struggle to find our true selves. Doubt and darkness form its borders. It is in the hopelessness of living without a divine figure who speaks to our alienation that we recover the presence of the living light. In secret anguish, we are made receptive and sanctified. Our identity is annulled in darkness. We are left with nothing to hold onto. Words and theories splinter "in order to search for freedom in the darkness of the undisclosed."[1]

Revelation is difficult and demanding. It calls its recipients to leave behind the tried and the true, and requires another way of thinking and being. It is radical, as revelation always must be, and creates scandal, doubt, and dissent. It unleashes the temperamental fear of those who guard the past, and causes those called to be god-bearers anguish and despair. And why not? Are we not being asked to hold in body and soul the living presence of the Divine Feminine's unconditional offering? Revelation disturbs our most hollowed traditions, our sense of who and what we are. We cry out: "How do I know you are calling me? Are you sure, God, that the time is now?"

In the tension where we no longer know who and what we are, whether there is a god we dare call God, whether there is anything other than betrayal, comes a Presence, Light beyond Light. This unveiling of our own sacred feminine is nothing less than a reordering of knowing and being. We discover that our true self exceeds religious traditions. From this vantage point, something radical happens: the center of our subjectivity shifts. Touched by the Divine Feminine's liberating voice, we have been named as Her own.

The Prophetic Voice

Prophecy is revelation's speech. *Via feminina* is prophetic because it inspires change in the underlying conditions that generate violence and misery, offering spiritual insight into social, political, and religious struggles for equality.

Prophecy is a personal encounter that becomes—in the intensity and completeness of its message—universal and potentially applicable to everyone. An extraordinary process, the prophet enters into his or her temptations, weaknesses, sufferings, and strengths to be gradually transformed by grace, then to emerge and speak out into the world's denial. Prophecy involves interpretation, criticism, and theological argument. But it also requires spiritual depth, because the prophet's speech emerges from an unrelieved distress that springs from his or her "fellowship with the feelings of God," and from intimate involvement with the world.[2]

The prophet recognizes that the global dimensions of injustice, war, and poverty rob women and men of dignity and inflict on their consciousness a lasting sense of worthlessness and inferiority. These are the most political of acts, thinly veiled attempts to mute the prophetic voice, blind the eyes that look upon our concerns, and deny the compassion for human frailty that comes through and by the Divine Feminine.

Out of silence, the prophetic call today rises from an awareness about the violation of our souls and of the feminine in our world. It is the presence of Holy Sophia, who breaks through our denial, floods us with tears, and shouts out for justice.

Creating a New Language

An incompletely mapped territory, the mystery of *via feminina* is more hidden than the language of the Fathers, or the visible religions of male gods and patriarchs. It requires the silent forbearance that prophecy brings—as well as the pain of birthing—before being able to name this gift.

If we are called today to be bearers of the Divine Feminine, then our task is to give words to Her new offering. If religious languages continually diminish, reject, dominate, marginalize, or demonize, if the language of the spirit is spoken almost exclusively in male terms, if God is predominately He, if prophets are always "he," and if messiahs are singularly embodied in a male person, then language itself betrays what Divine Sophia *is*.

To bring into speech what we truly know and are, requires both break-through and breakdown. We must break into the collective storehouse of memory and retrieve our mother-tongue. Without language, feminine wisdom is lost and its contribution erased with each person's passage from this world. This ancient *lingua feminina* is brought to word through experience and re-inscribed in our minds and hearts each time we name what we truly know.

In recovering what has been lost, we dismantle those languages that deny Wisdom and that marginalize and dominate. We also commit to the difficult task of giving up partial truths, which name only a fragment of our nature.

Via Feminina as Theological Method

VIA FEMININA is alert to whatever marginalizes, injures, or violates the sacred in our world. The focus of this theological stance is that a person's spiritual oppression is the foundation of all his or her other oppressions. Acts of violence—overt or subtle—are often directed unconsciously at the core of one's nature. While all forms of injustice involve a spiritual intent, worldwide violence can be seen as nothing less than a desire to destroy our unique and particular embodiment of divinity.

Like other liberation theologies, *via feminina* is on the side of free-dom. Critically evaluating Scripture and male-dominated languages and church hierarchies, it exposes the religious roots of social and cultural cruelty. It concentrates on a more subtle but equally powerful form of oppression—the oppression of a person's soul. It investigates how the violation of the feminine afflicts us in heart and mind, harming the growth of our full humanity and betraying the vulnerable and fragile in us all. As a theological method, *via feminina* provides a starting point for naming and healing spiritual oppression.

As a quality of consciousness, *via feminina* is a reminder that the journey of truth is never over. Although we may fear that no spirituality authentically speaks to us, we are challenged to remove the veils of grief that blind, learning that the true satisfaction of our desire involves constantly moving forward with our quest and never suspending our intent.

If Divine Mystery is offering us today a new spiritual life and a new way of being human, we cannot understand it solely by probing past traditions. We cannot cultivate it by relying on the testimony of others or on the authority of experts. We are alone, in the enclosure where the Divine speaks directly into the soul. In the desert solitude, one to one, we listen to the voice of Holy Mother within.

A Theology of Gestation

The contemplative spirituality of *via feminina* begins with the practice of gestation. From darkness and uncertainty, it waits for the Divine to be born in its own time. The process doesn't try to contain new revelation in the dry, crusty soil of old forms, but germinates each seed in the moist openness of heart, fertile and hollow like the womb, receptive and waiting. It is the qualities of Wisdom, the Mother of all—merciful, gentle, humble, nondual, holistic, benevolent—that we tenderly bear. Verdant, womb-like theology welcomes new seeds to take root. Round and hollow in imitation of divine fecundity, gestation cannot be forced; new life cannot be prescribed. We cannot change the color of the eyes, or the shape of the nose. Similarly, we cannot fashion divine self-disclosure to our own liking. Impregnated with its seed, we simply support it, and watch it grow.

And once your pregnant soul comes to term, and the holy seeds are born, the secret door to *via feminina* will open, right inside your being. Divine Sophia has never been separate from you. She waits now. Incarnated in you—pressed into body, mind, and soul—you are an embodiment of the Divine Feminine.

A Theology of Nonduality

Nonduality—*advaita*—is the name of the ultimate state of consciousness in Hindu mysticism. When the person transcends the ego (the conception of self as separate), transcends the discursive mind and the intellect, then he or she enters the realm of pure unity or nonduality. Nonduality also has been described as the state of unity, and thus present in all spiritual paths.

There is a power in the soul—a power of unification—that draws the seeker into the reconciliation of divisions or opposites, which is accessed by direct experience. Here, the distinction between self and other breaks down, and reality is grasped in a new and expanded way. In many of the world's religions, this state of dissolving of boundaries is achieved at the apex of mystical events. Whereas, in the mystical path of the feminine, nonduality is a starting point, spiritual attitude, and basis of inquiry. It is the guiding beacon of the seeker's spiritual quest, probing ever deeper into the myriad realities discovered on the other side of the opposing forces of good and evil, god and human, and the dialectical mind. The radicalness of being established in *via feminina's* mysticism of nonduality should not be underestimated. It is an entirely original vision of life.

This breakthrough into nondual wisdom leads to action. Thus, contemplation on *via feminina* leads to the recovery of our innate unity and enables us to function in the world of pluralism while experiencing that world in terms of divine simplicity.

A Theology of Pathos

As a way of thinking and living, *via feminina* is a catalytic force in healing and transforming the human heart. It expresses a divine sympathy with the Earth's suffering, the human family, and all of creation. It is concerned not only with the inner life and its spiritual implications, but also with improving the conditions that breed violence, subjugation, and hatred.

Woven throughout history—especially among the women mystics—is a strong tradition of divine pathos. In this interpretation, God not only cares about human suffering, God suffers with our pain or suffering (Greek, pathos). Our suffering is Her suffering. Divine suffering is our suffering. Imbedded in the interplay of the divine-human, our hearts mystically identify with and ache over the violation of the sacred.

The injustices perpetuated on living things, which rob us of dignity, become the context within which to revision our notions of divinity. A theology unable to contextualize the vulnerability violated by the brokenness of the world, is a theology whose heart has become closed. Here the mystical feminine revises our notions of an omnipotent, unfeeling God around images which reflect more directly divine compassion and involvement in global trauma. *Via feminina* embraces metaphors of the Divine as mother, lover, sister, and friend, who cares for and stands by the outcast, the homeless, and the destitute. The Divine Feminine shares in our hardship and suffers with us, as we suffer whatever diminishes the Divine on Earth.

A theology of pathos reminds us that love entails suffering and human responsibility in the face of suffering. Love includes openness to the ones loved, a vulnerability to their experience, and reorders the human ideal toward compassionate solidarity. Such caring results from a friendship with the complexity and wonder of every being. Daily events call us to embrace the sanctity of creation, and to mourn the loss of innocence to which we are subjected to every day. There is no religion, authority, or person who can overcome the tender kisses and nurturing embrace of Holy Sophia.

THEME 3:

Via Feminina is a Spiritual Journey

THE TRANSFORMATION of the seeker's social and personal identity and the healing of his or her soul oppression are ultimately spiritual acts. Thus, every journey toward wholeness maps a spiritual method and mystical pathway toward liberation. As in all spiritual journeys, the path is marked by purifying experiences that take apart our beliefs, illuminations that provide the courage to continue, and profound transformative periods of spiritual dying that prepare us for intimacy with life itself.

Via feminina is a journey of the heart, when the Divine is most intimate and draws us ever closer to her hidden chambers of love. It is entrance into the well of mercy, a way of approaching the spiritual life that is mysteriously etched into our beings.

Transforming the Spiritual Journey

In seeking an authentic spiritual life today, the context and content of the seeker's experience and relationship to the feminine refine and transform the spiritual journey—its interpretations, techniques of enlightenment, and understanding of divinity. In embodying the possibility of divine-human, the person's specific soul suffering offers a unique way of appropriating God-questions, leading us to new ways of *being human*. We ask:

What spiritual path, soul wounds, and dark nights does a person experience in his or her journey toward the Divine Feminine?

Who is the One we see, unite with, and reveal if we travel the path of *via feminina*?

How does the mystical dimension of consciousness contribute to healing the soul oppressions of humanity?

The mystical path of the feminine explores how restrictive social norms and religious communities affect the person's inner life, spiritual health, and ability to reclaim his or her original nature. It investigates the structures of consciousness of mystical traditions as a resource in our struggle for liberation. *Via feminina* supports a person's discovery of this mystical core, the dynamics of its development, and his or her quest for meaning and love.

Via feminina recognizes that full liberation is not only social and cultural, but also ontological and mystical. A person's inner life, and her or his ability to grow spiritually, are integral to emancipation. It charts the subtle attainment of a person's reclaiming of his or her full humanity. An arduous spiritual process marked by the night of contemplation, *via feminina* is born from a person's experience to heal the ancient fracture in consciousness that distorts the feminine. It also fuels the desire to promote the spiritual transformation of society.

This integrative mystical path emerges from the deepest core of the person, not just the mind. It embraces the struggle of not-knowing, the uncertainty of shadow and void, the sting of betrayal and rejection. Likewise, it rewards with moments of illumination, wholeness, and awe. The pioneering efforts of new monastics most likely arise from the challenge to experience and bring to speech what has been deeply heard and fiercely felt.

The Impasse: Through Crisis and Suffering Come Healing

As women and men awaken to the great divide that gnaws at the bottom of their souls, many discover that they cannot go back to a hierarchical worldview—winners and losers, privileged and disadvantaged, superior and inferior religions—or to outdated beliefs. Neither, however, can they move forward. "Imprisoned in a night of broken symbols,"[3] we are caught in an impasse between inherited religious systems that subordinate and a future that we hope to become. The experience of crisis, restlessness, and hopelessness that marks such an impasse—that I have named the "dark night of the feminine"—is the crucible in which our images of God are transformed, to discover the radical freedom and loving compassion that Divine Sophia brings.

By sinking down into our specific soul wounds and lifting them up to the silence that heals, a deeper stratum of reality is discovered. In the pain and darkness of not-knowing, when our identity has been erased and there is nothing to hold onto, love teaches us in secret. Rising up from our most holy nature, *via feminina* nourishes us with the nectar of heaven and heals our wounds, leading us to wholeness and freedom.

THEME 4:

Via Feminina is Contemplative

WHEN HUMAN CONCEPTS and meanings fail, impasse challenges us to uncover a deeper faith that can guide us to a new horizon. Only a personal encounter with truth can heal the roots of the person's suffering and reveal his or her original holiness. Distinguished across centuries of religious practice as mystical or contemplative, this process of healing demands a certain resiliency, an honesty of spirit that no ordinary life can hold. It is not merely a spiritual way of living or a code of conduct; it is the Divine living in us, and uniting us to Her own life and unity. The fundamental liberation we seek comes through contemplation, which leads to a personal realization of the inseparable oneness of life.

Via feminina is contemplative in three senses: the true self is found in silence and solitude; mystical heights are obtained in darkness and unknowing; and it is a revolutionary act to approach the world from Divine Sophia's perspective.

True Self: Individuating Through Silence and Solitude

Truth recedes into positive, holy silence. In the practice of silence, we reconnect to what precedes all knowing and being, all theology and word, as well as the wounds of religious superiority or injustice. The enclosure of our being is the silence in which Divine Sophia transforms our nature and leads us to new life. In solitude, the Holy One speaks to us in secret and teaches us in love.

This mystical self—silent, intimate, and empty—is not a miserable imitation of the supposedly greater and more valorous constructed self. Rather it is a glimpse of the *true self* enkindled by love, perhaps realized unconsciously, or not sufficiently understood and articulated. But nonetheless, this realized self—the self that is open to life—once it has become confident in its capacity for good, finds that solitude is basic to every act of kindness, and is the source of pure compassion. "If it could," writes St. Teresa, "love would want to discover ways of consuming the soul within itself. And if it were necessary to be always annihilated for the greater honor of God, love would do so very eagerly."[4] It is the soul annihilated by love that is finally secure, finally receptive to everything, that is the true source of the seeker's dignity and empowerment.

Self-nature is not something that can be acquired or possessed. It belongs to none. In the cave of the heart where the Divine speaks directly into the soul, the true self comes to full maturity and strength. As contemplative receptivity overflows into a creative encounter with the world, it is the essence of pure action.

To See Her Light: Emerging from Darkness

Via feminina is a higher and more holy aspect of the spiritual life that emerges out of the darkness of inner transformation. If we ascend the ladder of awareness by way of affirmation, and we find divine intimacy through negation of self, then that self-negation is the doorway to the mystery of the Divine Feminine. It is in nothingness, when the self has been brought to zero, that *is* the advent of the mystical path of the feminine.

The tension of unknowing and obscurity involves not only the loss of one's concept of self, but also the loss of corporate spirituality identity. Those elements in religions and in the collective spiritual imagination which exclude and dominate, and which distinguish the sinners from the saved, are confronted and healed. Sophia's starting point is oneness, her root sight is intimacy, and her liberation unbounded mercy.

The person who discovers *via feminina's* unmarked passage confronts the roots of violence and the invasion of his or her soul by an outmoded spirituality. An intense and lonely aspect of the spiritual life, the path is all encompassing because no one escapes the fire that is love itself. It is love that teaches us now, healing all our pains, troubles, and woes. In the dark night of the feminine, Sophia's *revelatory consciousness* is birthed in the restless resiliency of a person's soul.

Contemplation is Revolutionary

The spiritual journey of *via feminina* is revolutionary because it asks that we see the world from Divine Sophia's contemplative perspective. It protests the fragmentation and distraction of our lives and the selfless renunciation that is women's routine circumstance in much of the world. And it challenges the rampant materialism that makes our bodies and the body of creation objects to be bought and sold. Contemplative sight pierces the veil of convention, seeing into those hearts of stone, those hearts capable of inflicting wounds, and it incites an ethic of compassion that desires peace, which alone leads to lasting change.

Whenever we turn away from our depth and wisdom, we diminish our spiritual potential. We become *less* than we *already are*. When we cease to deny the inner voice, and cease to believe that what is outside is superior, we find that *via feminina* has always been with us. When we shed our inadequacy and our fear, we touch the source of blessedness. We experience the emptiness from which all religions grow and the mother seed that is the progenitor of the universal call to contemplation. Through mother consciousness, bearer of all things, we are embraced by Mercy, which is always for us, never against us.

SEVEN

The Dark Night of the Feminine

EVERY SPIRITUAL PATH involves stages of faith development and crises of growth as the seeker moves deeper into self-knowledge. Monastic life, in particular, is geared toward simplifying whatever stands in the way of the person's maturation and providing the resources—community, shared beliefs, spiritual practices, etc.—that supports his or her search for love and human wholeness. As the monk's divine pursuit increases in significance, the transformative process becomes essentially contemplative—that is initiated by the Divine—and the effects more purgative. This more advanced and intense stage of soul purification is described variously as "dark night," "great death," "nothingness," or "annihilation." It is usually framed as an interior struggle—a tearing of the soul or being —that the person must undergo to breakthrough conventional, constructed, or "normal" ways of seeing the world, and to establish a free, integrated state of being.

The mystical process entails extended periods of inner suffering as the disjuncture between the world of human senses and the world of celestial light is confronted. The soul's anguish is a specific experience that arises from its inability to resolve its profound conflict, which is experienced as a roadblock or impasse. Carmelite monastic, Constance FitzGerald, defines impasse:

By impasse, I mean that there is no way out of, no way around, no rational escape from, what imprisons one, no possibilities in the situation. In a true impasse, every normal manner of acting is brought to a standstill, and ironically, impasse is experienced not only in the problem itself but also in any solution rationally attempted.[1]

I have found that the new monk is especially susceptible to the annihilatory stages of transformation in part because the fundamental thrust of the mystical path of the feminine—which is to integrate the highest spiritual states with embodied life—occurs not only in rarefied moments of illumination, but through every day and in every deed. Thus, the impasse he or she is negotiating belongs not only to the realm of self-discovery— loss of ego, repentance of sin, and desire to be pure of heart—but also to the nature of religious truth, and to the state of the world. While it could be said that every seeker eventually passes through the dismantling of his or her limited worldview, I believe that the new monk—who has a non-exclusive relationship with religions and is often interspiritual—confronts a more complex task. Raimon Panikkar—Catholic priest and scholar of interreligious dialogue—realized that the difficulty and the price of being cross-cultural and truly intra-religious

> is death, surrender, the ego, world, being itself. [It] is to descend into the abyss and to drink from the very source where the human experience draws the water and the thirst; one might say that it is not a crossing but a cross.[2]

Similarly, Benedictine monk and Hindu-Christian *sannyasi*, Abhishiktananda, anguished over how to reconcile his mystical realization of Hindu nondualism (*advaita*) with his Christian faith. He writes of being "torn to pieces" by "my advaitism [that] has prevented me from feeling settled in my Christianity and my Christianity from feeling settled in *advaita*."[3]

In a sense, the new monk—especially the interspiritual—is undergoing at the very least a three-fold impasse, or transformative tension: personal, societal, and religious. The first includes the general state of self-emptying, involving a breakdown of the ego's resistance, willful-ness, refusal to repent, arrogance, doubt, and despair. The second occurs through the striving for justice in the world, compassion for suffering, and healing the fracture in consciousness that defies the sacredness of life. The third impasse involves the person's religious identity, including descriptions of ultimate reality, divine figures, cosmology, theology, and revealed truth. The reality of impasse occurs simultaneously on two levels: the mystical—that is, initiated by God in the soul or deep self—and in the person's lived experience to unite and heal all that is fragmented, unjust, or oppressed.

In my spiritual direction practice, I began to see that classical descrip-tions of the soul's journey did not completely address the issues confront-ing the person or nascent monk striving to forge an integrative, contempla-tive life in the world. Most striking was my observation of women's unique soul struggles in the context of church politics, religious marginalization, feminist self-identity, and the grief and rage born of personal and genera-tional violence. I found that females tend to have a more porous sense of self than males, wounded in specific ways by misogyny, physical abuse, and other forms of oppression. These violations of the soul's integrity are internalized, leading to feelings of unworthiness, failure, and despair. Frequently, traditional spiritual remedies do not address the basis or cause of these sufferings.

In ministry and spiritual guidance, the feminine dimension of mystical development lacks adequate recognition and appropriate language. All too often the spiritual remedies traditionally applied—prayer and spiritual guidance, giving oneself over to God's will, being humble or contrite—offends people and distracts them from a problem with roots deeper and more primordial than the religious interpretation used to cure their ills. In addition, historical accounts of the soul's journey have either been written predominately by men or express a male understanding of the inner life. This observation does not render the history of patriarchal spirituality wrong or misguided; only that it is partial.

I also found that many men are caught in an impasse, unable to access the soul distress associated with a rejection of their own feminine archetypes. The social emphasis that leads to an excessive individualism or self-autonomy of the male personality; male-on-male aggression; relationships based on power over women, nature, and vulnerable groups; and fear or shame about weaknesses and intimacy—often culturally prohibited, repressed, or ridiculed when expressed by males—impact the soul's health. As one of my male colleagues remarked,

> There is a shadow side of the masculine that wounds my deepest longing. There is a suffering and shame I feel over the extent of my gender's violation of women through the centuries that makes me afraid to confront the feminine within, or to take responsibility for my complicity. I am truly afraid I will not be able to contain or heal the waves of grief inside me.

I eventually found a way to frame the unique soul challenges people were experiencing. I was drawn to the idea through research on the subject of the soul's "dark night," first introduced in the sixteenth century by St. John of the Cross, and by St. Teresa's autobiographical accounts of her soul oppression as a woman. In Christian spirituality, the soul's journey to God is said to follow a threefold passage of purification, illumination, and union. John's dark night is a refinement of this classical journey, inserted between illumination and union and described as a more intense and rarefied stage of soul development.

In Spanish, the noun, *noche* (night), is feminine. In keeping with the gender signified in John's dark night (*noche oscura*), I named this more interior passage the "dark night of the feminine," and contend that it is a distinct, mature phase of spiritual development that—to my knowledge—has not been described in the world's religious literature. I now understand the dark night of the feminine to be a radical stage of interior transfiguration that is critical to the fullness of an integrative human-spiritual life and the person's "becoming divine." It opens the soul to the primordial state of intimacy and compassion, and initiates the process of birthing, of being a co-creator with Sophia, who forgives all sins, opens our hearts to endless compassion, and liberates our souls.

Dark Night of the Feminine

WHEN I SAY it is a feminine night, I mean the soul experiences the afflictions of its most receptive and intimate nature, both in terms of the negative wounding sustained from the violence of the world, and the positive touching of Eternal Wisdom, which opens it to deeper reserves of communion and oneness. This is the gestational ground in which the soul prepares to offer over its separate identity into the fiery flame of divinity to be transformed into a life of intimacy, relatedness, and communion that is not a negative giving-over of autonomy, but a new and exalted quality of being.

The feminine night is the soul's movement into the higher theophany of the Divine Feminine. A theophany is a visual manifestation to humankind of the divine reality and, in the case of Sophia, leads to participation in becoming a person of Divine Compassion. The soul undergoes a gradual process of identifying with and embodying the rarefied states of compassion, mercy, and benevolence, mystically becoming a co-creator with the feminine being. In the dark night of the feminine, we discover unity and intimacy beyond opposites and paradoxes, and yet simultaneously are able to sustain opposites and paradoxes, giving birth to new consciousness and new visions of god in the soul.

Henri Corbin—Islamic scholar and mystic—writes, in the context of Sufi metaphysics that to become a Compassionate One is to become the likeness of the Compassionate God experiencing infinite sadness over undisclosed possibilities:

> it is to embrace, in a total religious *sympathy*, the theophanies of these divine Names in all faiths. But this sympathy, precisely, does not signify acceptance of their limits; it signifies rather that in opening ourselves to them we open them to the expansion that the primordial divine *sympathesis* demands of them; that we increase their divine light to the maximum; that we "emancipate" them—as the divine Compassion did in pre-eternity.[4]

In his study of the mystical thought of the Andalusian Sufi master, Ibn 'Arabi, Corbin writes that in "the figure whose Name encompasses the entire secret of divine Compassion we can thus discern the features of Creative Sophia."[5] Further, he emphasizes the high status that Ibn 'Arabi accords the Divine Feminine:

> A mystic obtains the highest theophanic vision in contemplating the Image of feminine being, because it is in the Image of the Creative Feminine that contemplation can apprehend the highest manifestation of God, namely, creative divinity....
>
> The spirituality of our Islamic mystics is led esoterically to the apparition of the Eternal Womanly as an Image of the Godhead, because in her it contemplates the secret of the compassionate God, whose creative act is a liberation of beings. [This] intuition [is] set forth with the utmost clarity in our authors, that the Feminine is not opposed to the Masculine as the passive to the active, but encompasses and combines the two aspects, receptive and active, whereas the Masculine possesses only one of the two.[6]

Ibn 'Arabi's mystical apprehension of the Divine Feminine brilliantly illuminates the contemplative process of the feminine night, whereby the soul becomes feminine (all-compassionate) and takes on an actual mode of being as creatrix. Drawn into the inner life of Sophia, the seeker mystically participates in the divine sympathy for all persons, religions, and creation. Worldly actions and events, however, continually subject the most sensitive and tender aspect of divine likeness in the person to ridicule, violence, suppression, and even death. Thus the soul that enters the dark night of the feminine will experience the embodied pain inflicted on the gentle ones, and be pierced by the light of mercy to *be* different and to act *differently*. In sympathy with all beings, the degree to which the person embodies divine compassion, to that degree his or her soul is "feminine."

Adding the dark night of the feminine to our understanding of the soul's journey situates the reclamation of the feminine at a deeper level of consciousness. Highlighting the intensity of our struggle for wholeness, it emphasizes that the violations we experience in social, personal, and spiritual relations have a direct impact on our ability to release the false self, heal, and discover our true life. During this time, we experience the systematic reviling of the feminine in our world. At the same time, the dark night of the feminine is our emergence into a hidden womb of love and mercy "in which," Constance FitzGerald writes, "[our] God images and languages [are] transformed and a feminine value system and social fabric generated."7

Yet, I am not describing a rigid movement from one linear spiritual category to another. Nor am I suggesting that every person will proceed to the dark night of the feminine, or that everyone experiences this passage similarly, or at all. Rather, I raise the category and contemplative process, the "dark night of the feminine," to alert us to other stages of spiritual growth and to inspire further insight and conversation in the practice of new monastics.

Dark Night of Injustice

IN THE DARK NIGHT of the feminine, the afflictions of the soul's receptive, intimate, and benevolent nature—in terms of the injury sustained from the world—is experienced. This night is that mystical passage when a person confronts the pain of the violation of the divine feminine in one's self and in society. Further, it is a feminine night because there is a specific, embodied, and socially constructed aspect to it that acknowledges the historical oppression of females, violation of the Earth, and suppression of the anima—Karl Jung's term for the feminine aspect of a man's personality—in males.

As the singularly vulnerable and emotionally tangible of the mystical life, the night of the feminine does not withdraw the soul from the world in an ascetic detachment nor is the soul shielded from the world's cruelty and disgrace. It must confront the desecration of the holy in one's self and in every aspect of life.

Throughout spiritual history, religions have emphasized the role of individual and communal sin or karma as critical areas of spiritual development. For example, John writes that the soul's sufferings are caused by a purging of its "weakness and imperfections" during the dark night. Paths of enlightenment focus on individual virtues and abstinence from unhealthy attachments and habits. While critical self-reflection is necessary for a person's spiritual growth, the world's spiritual traditions must be more urgently aware of the impact that religious and socially sanctioned and accepted oppression—such as sexism, racism, homophobia, and institutional violence, including inquisitions, genocide, bride-burning, incest, and rape—exerts on the soul of person or society. It is imperative that we understand how deeply imbedded these various forms of injustice are in our religions, and how we live out these oppressive states of consciousness without fully recognizing their impact on the health of our communities and our souls.

I imagine that our spiritual foremothers and forefathers were aware of the importance of a person's unique physical and cultural history. But rarely in religious literature were their insights about social injustice— racial segregation, sexual violation or rape, women's subordination, wars and inquisitions— recorded as vitally significant to the soul's growth or union with God. Instead, classical spiritualities more frequently ignore, deny, or denigrate the importance of emotions, physicality, sexual orientation, gender, and race. In the mystical passage of the feminine, healing of spiritual injury is critical to the soul's advancement.

The night of the feminine turns the soul away from the purely spiritual realm and back to earthly reality to bear the harm that both self and divine have sustained from the world. In turning back to the world, the person is not supposed to reject, suppress, or mystically transcend his or her feelings, but to bear them to the point of healing and integration, until they bring forth the birth of our full humanity. Spiritual feelings are intensely felt, as the soul suffers a person's rejection, alienation, or difference. The pain that we are taught and labor to universalize or overlook cannot be merely transcended. The detachment of the senses, considered to be a hallmark of spiritual maturity, is inoperable in the realm of the feminine night. If we don't confront and heal the causes that generated our suffering, then dispassionate awareness is simply a suppression of truth.

Because our bodies and spirits live *in* the world, our personal suffering is inseparable from soul suffering. The feminine night digs down into our abused humanity and the violation of our divinity. Its trials extend from the spiritual dimensions of consciousness into the deep memory stored in our cells. Thus, while traditionally we are led to believe that the soul's dark night results from its own sins, purifying personal weakness only partially addresses the power of the feminine night, which aims, as well, to heal the ways in which a person's divine worth has been trampled by society. When the tender and vulnerable is violated within a person, he or she internalizes the pain, turning against one's self and expanding the soul's wound.

If we find intimacy with God through emptying—suspending divine names in silence and solitude—then that self-emptying is the doorway to Sophia. The soul now feels the violation of divine mercy and compassion in thought, word, and deed. Divine Sophia's endless capacity for forgiveness and gentleness stands in stark contrast to all that a person does to violate or injure Her pure heart. A person's felt experience of his or her rejected humanity becomes a point of recognition of being brought to zero—of knowing a divine-human injustice interpreted through one's own life experience. These trials are uniquely his or her personal battleground, but they also represent the birth of divine compassion in the soul.

Having once glimpsed Sophia's splendorous ways, the soul cannot turn back on itself; it can never be free from having known the potential of the spirit and the great wonders that await it on the other side of everything partial and conditioned. The positive touching is caused by love's flaming arrow, which pierces and opens the windows and doors of the soul. The power of Sophia's way leads the soul to the unifying qualities of "one-ing" and the consciousness of nondualism—unknowing, unbeing, and undoing. Because the unifying faculties precede the division of subject-object consciousness, the positive touching leads the soul to contemplation, and to the Great Silence from which word is formed.

In this feminine passage of night, the soul enters the womb of nothingness, the void of the mother, to touch the feminine Divine Face. Awed by the sinlessness of the face before we were born—and before which the fathers brought forth gods and religions—the soul is innocence itself. In the feminine night of anguish, the soul bears the violence and ravaging of the self, Earth, and Divine Mystery. Healing the broken symbols of all that separates and divides, and of religious languages and traditions that lead us away from her holy love, Sophia pours fragrant oils upon the soul. Aware of the Divine feminine manifesting through each and every revelation, but rooted in the fecund silence, the soul remains in a state of awe.

The night of the feminine is an inflow of Divine Sophia into us, Her desire to incarnate and restore in us the oneness of spirit and matter. It is thus an embodied dark night that takes us back to the beginning—to a refiguring of the ground upon which we stand. It is a restructuring of being that takes place at a primary level—at the outflow of all our religions and spiritual traditions and definitions of the self. This process of the dark night of the feminine seldom occurs all at once; more usually it repeats in cycles over days, months, or even years.

Dark Night of Religion

THE MYSTICAL PATH of the feminine involves not only the loss of one's concept of self, but also the loss of corporate spirituality identity. Even the form and concept of language and the structures of consciousness that constitute the religious imagination are not adequate to hold Her offering. The soul is led to an intimate understanding that includes all of life, seeks salvation for all creation, and protests the spiritual worldview that excludes, segregates, or tries to possess. It is the mystery of creation in a new mode, when we have left behind our attachments to a punishing and retributive God, and to a God of supremacy and domination. It is a contemplative path that brings us to an experience of abundant freedom and love.

The dark night of the feminine is directed at reforming the emphasis that religions place on transcendence and universality over the fact of human diversity. The world's religions are fairly consistent in their belief that the true spiritual life transcends earthly differences. We are encouraged by religious texts and practices to raise above our particular embodiment—female, male, Black, Asian, Jewish, Muslim, married, single, lesbian, and gay—to experience a unifying realm beyond ordinary life. While oneness is the universal measure of mystical consciousness, all too often in history uniqueness has been ignored, ridiculed, violated, or shunned. This must be repaired in the spiritual life.

Other soul-damaging structural beliefs that are confronted and healed in the mystical night of the feminine include the higher value accorded the male god and the consequent diminishment of females and feminine consciousness; limitations on who is authorized, and in what manner, to achieve wisdom; control over the rights and access to religious office (such as priest, roshi, rabbi, minister, or lama); and the privileging of truth formalized by a religion over intuitive, personal faith. The refusal to acknowledge the implications of religiously sanctioned oppression on the inner sanctum of individuals and communities has led to abuses of personal dignity and group integrity.

In the feminine night, there is not a denial of transcendent consciousness, or the vision of oneness that compels the mystic quest. However, the process forces us to experience the injury sustained in our souls precisely because our earthly differences are trivialized, ignored, or actively harmed. Because universal claims unfortunately are used to justify an entire range of abuses, transcendence is only authentically possible when oppression is acknowledged and healed. As we are reminded on a daily basis, to truly achieve peace, we have to mend the fractures and wounds that prevent us, and our world, from being whole.

A common theme in the feminine dark night is that spiritual transcendence is not the highest form of development unless and until it is embodied in persons and in institutions, offering up to divine healing what is damaged. The spiritual journey thus inspires a sanctification of all aspects of life, in order to aspire to holiness on Earth. Birthing of the new involves spiritually dying to old habits and ways of being. Illumination leads to transfiguration. Every authentic practice involves the un-formation, deconstructive process that dismantles the false self, societal distortions, and violent, authoritarian elements within human religious consciousness in order to allow the Unconditional, and the Nonviolent to dwell in our midst.

Questioning of our religious identities and attempts to discover a more benevolent view of God, bring the spiritual pilgrim to an impasse between religious paradigms. Unable to go back to who and what they once were, but uncertain about how to enter the future, feelings of confusion, betrayal, disinterest, and doubt are not uncommon. In fact, many people I see in spiritual direction confide the intensity of their suffering over the depth and extent of their alienation from traditional religious forms. As an essential aspect of healing, this process of impasse and anguish is a mark of the substance and authenticity of the path. When the self is pushed against darkness and unknowing, impasse itself becomes a catalyst for a more profound and honest understanding of reality.

The way of the feminine night heals the sin of "otherness"—the exclusion, violence and rejection of difference—in our hearts. It is God's dark night in us. It purifies spiritual and religious egoism in which one's truth, path, or scripture is secretly or overtly proclaimed to be greater, more holy, or truer than any of its competitors. Contemplation, as the force of letting go, also frees us from disguised forms of religious selfishness or pride that believe there is a privileged place of salvation, enlightenment, or pre-destination. Compunction over our failure to truly love the divine manifestation in every religion takes on greater depth and complexity as a personal and institutional critique is applied to the foundational texts, beliefs, practices, and hierarchies of our religious heritage.

As the soul moves into deeper states of contemplation, the brilliance of Sophia's presence propels the person into progressively intense degrees of emptiness. This process moves the soul from the dark night of being, to the dark night of God—emptying divine names and attributes, and then beyond to the dark night of religion—in the bewilderment of the Undisclosed (that is, the great doubt of faith). Culminating in entrance to the darkest night of the God beyond God: the womb or generative power of the Divine Feminine.

The entire cycle of the dark night of the feminine heals the wounds generated by whatever is unjust, prideful, harmful, or violent in our religions. Shedding harsh images and painful memories of gods and religions is the necessary precursor that prepares the soul to leave behind what came before and travel with Holy Sophia to what lies ahead—another way of being and loving. Most important, the process of awareness, suffering, questioning, loss of faith, doubt, and awe that arise as we learn of and about other religions are signs of a spiritual pilgrimage taking place within the soul. For the person who has sympathy for all faiths, and whose heart is open to every religious form, the dark night of the feminine leads to another type of mystical union or ultimate liberation that is simultaneously interspiritual and sophianic—that is, divinely feminine.

Although I use feminine imagery and metaphors to express this passage, the night of the feminine is not solely metaphorical. It is a mystical inflow of the Divine Feminine into us—Her desire to incarnate and restore in us the oneness of spirit and matter. It is thus an embodied dark night that takes us back to the beginning, to the outflow of religions and spiritual traditions.

Before the soul was formed, and gods and religions were born, Her contemplative vow was uttered.

Realized Divinity

AS THE MOST ESOTERIC and embodied of the mystical life, the soul, having passed through the dark night of the feminine, now participates in the flourishing, creative joy of Holy Sophia. Everything has changed. The source of a person's being, self, psyche, and thought is rooted in benevolence and compassion, approaching reality from the vantage point of oneness, affirmation, embodiment, and love of the world.

Below are five unique indicators of the effects of the feminine dark night:

1. **Never Alone**. Holy Sophia never abandons the person suffering through these dark nights. The touching and wounding of her Presence intensifies the soul. But, never withdrawing, the Divine Feminine instills the soul with the courage to withstand the radical integration and healing radiating through its spiritual and physical bodies.

2. **Co-Creator**. The dark night of the feminine is not solely passive. That is, the idea of mystical union often is interpreted as a static or

final state of being that requires no further cooperation on the part of the person. Rather, mystical union is an ongoing, dynamic process of participating in divine life. As the soul is increasingly made vulnerable in the feminine night—becoming emptier and more humble—it is being prepared to be a co-creator with Divine Sophia. Now the soul, in addition to being a recipient of mystical unity, becomes the site and activity of unification or one-ing. The person who has undergone the radical process of the feminine nights can bring about positive change by uniting differences in the self and serving as a divine-human agent for transformative peace.

3. **Birth of New Visions**. The night of the feminine purifies and heals divisions both within and outside of us that prohibit the merciful, gentle, intimate, loving, and benevolent from being born and received in the world. Rooted in mystical consciousness, it gives birth to new forms of creativity and new aspects of our humanness. Engaged with the fate of creation and the dignity of all life, the soul enters Sophia's hidden revelation to bring forth the virtues of humility and radical compassion, and apply them to the protection, preservation, and development of spiritual wisdom for the entire community of earthly beings.

4. **Realized Divinity**. A certain naïve and intuitive connectedness with life is branded by the fire of our pain. We now come to a realized intimacy, which is not only the natural intimacy of feeling close to some one or some thing, but a realized awareness of the web of relations, and how profoundly interdependent all creation is. It is a heroic and brave night when our souls voluntarily turn toward the world to bear the marks of alienation, and to heal the ancient fracture in our hearts. The dark night of the feminine heightens our sensitivity to the utter holiness of creation, and instills the desire to realize the Divine Presence in our lives.

5. **Supreme Love.** As painful and subversive as the dark night of the feminine is, it is also the supreme experience of love. It is the night of

healing that leads to a new life of communion, joy, and compassion. It is celebration, and that joyous night when our souls are raised to their highest potential.

EIGHT

An Embodied Spirituality

A BASIC ORIENTATION of *via feminina* is the spirituality of benevolence, which focuses on love of creation and the flourishing of life. From this perspective, it affirms humanity's responsibility to critically evaluate religious history, express sorrow over excess and abuse, and co-create new wisdom traditions. This understanding of divine-human cooperation is found in all of the world's religions, depicted in numerous scriptures and sacred texts, such as the Hebrew phrase, *tikkun olam*, which indicates human responsibility in repairing the world. The new monk seeks the actualization of these promises, and a more embodied and comprehensive realization of humanity's role in building a world community of justice, equality, and peace.

It is this merciful, benevolent attitude that gives new monks the courage to break through destructive elements within religious consciousness, uncovering an original or primary vantage point—one that precedes our many stories of creation and human genesis. In this re-imagining, we leave behind stories of sin and vengeance, a punitive and harsh God, or a spirituality of fallen-ness. Metaphors of divine intimacy, flourishing of life, and love of the Earth are not only significant; they also are instrumental in transforming our self-definition and tangible actions.

A spirituality of benevolence avows to the unwavering constancy of the Great Spirit as ever-present, neither judging, rejecting, arbitrary, violent, capricious, indifferent, or unforgiving. We are made and composed of Divine Love; we know a loving God who does not withdraw. We know a suffering God who bears the arrogance and deafness of our small selves, and of our closed hearts and minds. We honor the female ground of divinity while working to actualize the holiness of the Divine Feminine in our world. If we let go of the survival strategies and damaged beliefs that conscript us to being less than we are, transformation is possible; harmony and wisdom are possible. Healing of soul wounds and of societal repression can begin to transform into reality.

There is no part of us—neither wound of soul, personal failings, or sins—that is not of great value in helping uncover our true selves. We learn to approach the veils and shields of the false self with detachment and love. We discover that all violation of truth is an aberration of the Great Mystery within us. We thus become excavators of our own truth, digging through the rubble of our anguish, confusion, and missed opportunities for the keys to where and how the spirit has been repressed or denied. Our life—in all of its wonder and pain—is our teacher. It is through the process of spiritual awareness, love, and humility that we discover holiness within.

All our natural gifts are precious because they are both the medium and the method of the path. We use our intellects to study wisdom and to discover patterns in spiritual consciousness. We employ the gift of reason to question and test our perceptions and to make connections to other people's experiences of God. Our emotions become pure notes connecting our soul to the universal soul. If we follow our emotions to the depth of spiritual feeling within us, we will find the strength to question the falsehoods that obscure the truth.

Our bodies help us to stay grounded on Earth. They teach us to focus and to listen to the wisdom of being physical beings, and to honor the body as a manifestation of spirit. Through our words, actions and non-actions, and our capacity to love and inspire, we glimpse our potential. Similarly, our psychic intuition attunes us to subtle energy fields that compose sentient life, while our mystical capacity to strive toward oneness points us toward the unseen dimension and to the immense energy of love that forms us. Access to these higher realms of knowing and insight are our birthright; their wisdom is vital not only to every spiritual path, but also to expressing our full humanity.

The body is also the place where revelation takes place. It is through the body and through culture that we are illumined. This fact of bodily assimilation accounts in part for why the same essential divine message is expressed differently wherever it is received. We also acquire knowledge through our bodies. It is not just the mind or the sixth chakra, but the energy systems of the whole body that constantly are attuned to, and absorb knowledge. Thus, the body is not a prison of the spirit to be transcended. It is essential to grounding the spiritual transformations that we undergo. Through its earth-focused, slower energy vibrations, the body is able to hold and absorb higher, spiritual states of consciousness.

In this way, when we approach the mystery of our nature with love we find the courage to seek the true self. We use the heart of the divine in us to have compassion for our failings; and the eyes of the divine within us to uncover the harmony always present beneath turmoil and pain. Having experienced divine benevolence, we no longer ascribe our afflictions to punishment or sin. Rather, we seek the nature of our affliction, to discover what it can teach us, and how better to live, drawing closer to God.

It is natural to wonder how much energy spiritual awareness costs. Or, to be concerned that our whole life will be consumed by the need to question every emotion we have. But this is an unfounded fear. The awareness of which I speak can be cultivated as a daily alertness, as a way of living in the world. It is, in fact, a way of life that arises from a sensitive, but fierce determination to know oneself, and to pierce layers of numbness. It is the wayless way of all spiritual paths, and the methodless method, by which we achieve our one true desire.

A spirituality of benevolence, moreover, consciously practices the alleviation of suffering, especially inner suffering. It directs the soul's journey toward a wider understanding of liberation that expands from the personal or collective to the whole family of creation in its multiple aspects and forms. Spiritually, it recognizes the profound healing that we as a human community must undergo at deep levels of consciousness. Most significant is the unpacking of distorted beliefs on the spiritual or soul level in order to free our inner lives and social institutions from subtle forms of violence against self and others, including the Earth and the cosmos that sustain us.

Embodied Spirituality

STUDIES IN NEUROBIOLOGY recognize the importance of physical contact between mother and infant, and its positive effect on brain development and social integration. The growth of the full person is dependent on the health of body, emotion, mind, and spirit. Developmentally, each level of physical growth affects every other level, such that dysfunction in the cell division of a fetus changes the operation of the brain, heart, and other organs. If a child is deprived of loving contact, and does not receive sufficient care and attention, his or her psychological and emotional development will be impaired.

Emotional and psychological deficiencies have an effect on our spirits, and our ability to live fully. Every aspect of sentient life is integral to every other aspect. The emerging insight of neurobiology clarifies how love or deprivation influences the developmental wellness of the whole person.

This knowledge is something that every good parent knows—treating infants and children's bodies as sacred, tender gifts has a positive lifelong effect on the stability of the personality and the generosity of the heart. It is even more incumbent on adults, and especially those who choose a monastic path, to honor the preciousness of human life, and the miraculous gift of the body.

Bio-spiritual studies affirm the importance of an embodied spiritual practice and worldview. I am indebted to my friend and colleague Jorge Ferrer—Professor of East-West Psychology at the California Institute of Integral Studies—for his use of the term "embodied spirituality," and for his clarification of the difference between the classical spiritual vision—which has been called "disembodied"—and embodied spirituality. He writes,

> Regarding prevalent Western and Eastern spiritual history, I suggest that "disembodied" does not denote that the body and its vital/primary energies were ignored in religious practice—they definitely were not—but rather that they were (most often) not considered

legitimate or reliable sources of spiritual insight in their own right....
and were actually a hindrance to spiritual flourishing [liberation,
realization].

Embodied spirituality, in contrast, views all human dimensions—
body, vital, heart, mind, and consciousness—as equal partners in
bringing self, community, and world into a fuller alignment with the
mystery out of which everything arises. Far from being an obstacle,
this approach sees the engagement of the body and its vital/primary
energies as crucial for not only a thorough spiritual transformation,
but also the creative exploration of expanded forms of spiritual
freedom. The consecration of the whole person leads naturally to
the cultivation of a "full-chakra" spirituality that seeks to make all
human attributes permeable to the presence of both immanent and
transcendent spiritual energies.[1]

New monastic spirituality draws strength from an embodied spiritual
ideal. In fact, much of its focus is on reversing and healing the energies
of judgment, sin, cruelty, and punishment that are imbedded in religious
practices and thought. Nowhere is this need more apparent than in the
often-negative attitude toward the body—especially female bodies—
enshrined in religious texts and traditions. Instead, a spirituality of
flourishing and love of the world seeks an integrated relationship with all
dimensions of the human person, and actively creates literature, sacred
texts, spiritual practices, and rituals that affirm the holiness of creation,
and the aspiration toward the divine good.

An embodied spirituality offers a path for the whole of creation, not
only for humans, taking into account the variety of life forms, the cosmic
circle, and our other-than-human kin. It thus promotes an ethic of what
German philosopher Hannah Arendt called *amor mundi*, love of the
world. Embedded in worldly events, the new monk works to protect the
dignity of all beings, including the social realities, politics, and religions
that serve humanity. The spiritual journey is neither gender-neutral nor
free from the social impediments of its historical development. The
true mystic is concerned for the whole of creation and works toward its
sanctification.

An embodied spirituality recognizes the importance of the physical body and its symbiotic relationship with spiritual growth. The contemporary monk is especially tasked with lifting each relationship to its spiritual potential. He or she is called to identify the ways in which the deep self or soul identifies with human, planetary, and divine suffering in everyday experience, and carries both the responsibility to protect the dignity of all beings and the challenge of being an agent of divine compassion.

Body as Hierophany

EACH BODY is a hierophany—a site and presencing of the sacred. The body as a whole organism—atoms, cells, organs, mind, spirit—is the medium through which love and truth, as well as personal distortion and pain, are brought into daily life. The body is constantly communicating the wisdom of physicality, as the spirit is the carrier of divine wisdom into our full humanity.

Acceptance of the body as essential to spiritual practice allows the body to awaken to its natural rhythm. As the agent of mindfulness, it is through our bodies that we become aware of other people's energies, of the difference between falsehood and truth, and of positive or negative spiritual affects.

All of us, at one time, probably have experienced the "voice" of our physical bodies. Perhaps we were in a situation where a lie was being perpetrated, and our body registered a visceral response: throat constricted, or stomach hurt. Or, an office mate congratulated us on a recent success, but was actually jealous, and we were left feeling confused or angry, but didn't consciously know why. How often have we physically felt, "Enough! I can't do this anymore," but we refused to listen, forcing ourselves against our bodily wisdom?

Monastic traditions in general have tended to ignore, reject, or shame bodily experience. Yet without a body, there would be no spiritual transformation. Harshness toward the body is enshrined in harmful spiritual practices, which are supposed to tame the flesh and quell its desires. Monks were expected to sublimate genuine somatic or sexual desire as a catalyst for spiritual breakthrough, employing practices of self-flagellation, excessive fasting, wearing of hair shirts, and other forms of bodily control. Today, we may believe we have given up these "medieval" practices, but the daily ways we push our bodies beyond their natural balance are indications that we do not honor the physical form.

It is important to ask: In what ways have I accepted the rupture between body and spirit? What authentic desires have I given up for the sake of an elusive or transcendent goal? How do I treat my body as holy? How can I become gentler with myself? How can I be more attuned to bodily needs? When you start bringing the body into your spiritual prayers, you will receive different answers.

Your body is the vessel for the extension of the spirit while you are alive. There is not an artificial separation between spirit and physicality. While the body lives, there is an intimate co-incarnation of bio-spiritual energies. Learning to listen to your body, and to experience your body as a site and sign of holiness, is distinctive to new expressions of monastic life.

Body as Place of Insight

REALIZATION OCCURS through the physical body. We do not experience enlightenment or mystical union in a disembodied form. The body is the vessel of spiritual realization and its vital energies the source and goal of spiritual practices. The sacred marriage or integration of body and spirit generates the mutual transformation of their essential energies.

Many examples of the marriage of body and spirit are found in the long history of humanity's religious quest: The forest dwellers of ancient India, whose mystical life gave voice to the *Rig Veda*, a collection of sacred Sanskrit hymns, and the wisdom texts of Upanishadic seers; Patanjali's yoga sutras, or words of wisdom, the guidebook of classical (*raja*) yoga; the art of Ayurvedic medicine; and the complicated and brilliant system of Chinese acupuncture. These traditions resulted from the spirit's transmission into the mind and heart of a particular person or persons, who received and co-created an entire system of spiritual and medical wisdom.

I hear people say, "I'm just an empty conduit for spirit," as if we were disembodied. But that is actually not true. The totality of the being, the totality of the soul, mind, emotion, and body, is a bio-spiritual miracle. Wisdom is differently expressed depending on the individual person and his or her cultural, religious, and sociological context. The physical incarnation of every human and every lifeform is precious.

The body is the place of spiritual insight. In what form do we find the meaning of life, if not through our bodies? It is in our bodies that we learn to love and to seek the Divine Presence. It is through the miracle of the human body that wisdom comes to us. The body is also a microcosm of the universe, and houses a unique configuration of the cosmos. The Jesuit mystic and paleontologist, Teilhard de Chardin, wrote: "My matter is not a part of the universe that I possess totally; it is the totality of the Universe possessed by me partially."[2] Our physical bodies are a microcosm of the totality of the universe in its innermost structure. The body-spiritual entity known as "the self" is interdependent with the cosmos: we literally are composed of seawater, stars, and clouds.

The body is also central for enduring transformation. Psychospiritual growth involved in the soul's journey is experienced in the body. Vibrating at a slower rate than spiritual energies, the physical body serves as a grounding force, integrating somatic changes into cellular, mental, and emotional memory. Intense mystical realization consumes bodily identity, creating an opening for the birth of insight and wisdom. Every incarnation has a cumulative effect on the emergence of spirit in matter. That's how important our bodies are to our spiritual Lives, and why life is a miracle.

The Body as Subject

THE BODY IS BOTH the subject and the vow of spirit. When we treat bodies—all bodies, human, animal, etc.—as subjects instead of objects, we honor the divine mystery that generates life. Bodily joys or sorrows, longings or repulsions, are the means by which the spirit-body relays to consciousness its quivering, finely tuned energetic and emotional fields.

Our body is the locus of freedom, the way we walk our spiritual path. It is not a defiled realm that needs to be transcended. It is not sinful or shameful, needing to be disowned or beaten down. We need to replace the often-expressed religious view that the body is a prison for the spirit, with the idea that the body is our planetary home. Where else are we conscious, if not in our bodies? Where else, if not in this time and place?

The mystery of being born is the spirit becoming flesh. It is not the entrance of the spirit into flesh, it is not the descent of the spirit into flesh, but the spirit *becomes* flesh. A mysterious interaction occurs between spirit and the gestation of life that never will be totally understood.

Another aspect of bodily awareness is the sacred function of sex. While historically monasticism has placed celibacy as central to the monk's vow, many new monastics view healthy sexual partnerships (in or outside of marriage) as integral to living an embodied spirituality. Unfortunately, religious attitudes toward the body have been historically ambivalent, often relegating sexuality, pleasure, human contact, and sensual experience to an inferior, and sometimes defiled, realm. In embodied spirituality, denigrating sex leads to unhealthy practices, because whether or not we engage in sexual acts, sexuality is part of the full body experience. It is a part of creativity and a way of expressing one's body-wholeness.

When sexual energies are diverted or sublimated against the will of the person, his or her full creative energies become congested or nonfunctional. When we harbor feelings of shame about our sexuality, the heart and psyche suffer. Sexuality is de-sacralized when it is used as a means of control, possession, or dominance. Then, instead of these intimate psychic and physical energies being raised to spiritual states, they are pulled down to lower vibrations. Our distorted beliefs around physicality, sexuality, sensuality, joyfulness, pleasure and so forth, are consciously re-evaluated and healed in the practice of many new monastics.

Sexuality is related to being comfortable with the intimacy of your own body, and body intimacy with others, where there is no violation of free communion. Any act—sexual, mental, emotional, spiritual, or physical—that involves possession, domination, or suppression is potentially destructive. Any act that involves true communion, intimacy, and coequality, is potentially liberating, and can lead us to truth.

Wedded to Earth

CENTRAL TO AN EMBODIED SPIRITUALITY is the importance of the natural world. Being born on Earth is not a secondary byproduct of spirit, a mistake, or irrelevant. It is profoundly central to who we are. Earth is home. Nature is the source of our nurturing, and the sustainer of our life on Earth. It is the first sacrament. All creations of the cosmos—plants and animals, insects and fish, mountains and waters, and stars and planets—have wisdom. They, too, emit divine energies into creation. They, too, are the home of the spirit in this world. Through the living universe we discover transformation, healing, and liberation. Nature welcomes our body-spirit to be at home on Earth. When we embrace nature, we return to and complete the circle of beings.

In religious traditions, there has been an unfortunate tendency to represent the spirit as an otherworldly state divorced from the body. In many cases, the body is denigrated and a dichotomous relationship is established between spirit and matter. But the mystery of embodiment is central to the theology, practice, and meditative life of the new monk. Affirming the spiritual significance of the body and of physical contact, he or she embraces the whole breadth, depth, and extent of creation in spiritual life and practice. Recognizing the inseparable mystery of body, emotions, mind, psyche, and soul, the divine journey maintains a loving respect for all genuine ways in which the human spirit seeks truth.

As we shift from ascetical and world-denying aspects that have damaged planetary integrity, to a celebration of our incarnation in the natural world and the flourishing of life, we experiment with a language of wholeness. We accept no story of separation, exile, or sin to mar the first moment, the genesis of life. Whatever divisions we harbor or wounds we have inflicted are not in the beginning. They are human interpretations, and therefore capable of being reinterpreted and transformed. Thus, the process of spiritual growth is different. Spirituality is not primarily the reconciliation of lost or fragmented parts of one's self. It is not focused on the expiation of sins, or the search for an unfeeling or distant God outside human contact. Rather, our work is directed toward an integration of the Divine on Earth, and to the experience of meaning and love.

We are not here for ourselves alone. It is incumbent upon us to realize how our actions or inactions profoundly affect our soul health, relationship with all beings, and the diverse and complex biosphere of the Earth. We need a voice and a vision from which to awaken the heart of the world and to rescue ourselves from endangering the spirit of life. Injustice and war strike more deeply into the sacred web of creation, generating a hopelessness and despair that wound all our souls. The integrity of our planet and the fate of ecosystems are dependent on an excavation of our hearts and minds—and our souls and spirits—to discover a more generous benevolence and a sturdier vow of humility.

A new revelation or universal story is necessary to guide our world today, one that respects the biodiversity of life, tapestry of human cultures, and wide expanse of the cosmos. We need to imagine our world in its sacred and prophetic dimensions, in the virtues of all religions and spiritual traditions that are part of our collective inheritance, and in the dignity of all species and life forms. We need to recover the ancient vision of wholeness and closeness to nature that sustained countless generations, and at the same time broaden and deepen this vision beyond local, tribal, or national boundaries to include the entire Earth community and the cosmos. What we need is a sacred attitude of heart, and a global spiritual perspective that is not a substitute for our present religions but is a fulfillment of the promise of faith.

At the core of our collective journey is a vow. When we place Divine Mystery at the center of our hearts, then we truly are living a religious consciousness, whether or not we belong to a named religion. When we place the earthly realm and its entire human and more-than-human inhabitants on an altar of devotion and consecrate our lives each day to their benefit, then we are living a monastic path—a personal, organic spiritual path. When our daily monastic life becomes a prayer, then we are a prayer of love and healing for the world.

NINE

A Theology of Intimacy

I N ORDER TO FRAME this chapter, I have adapted the notion of the "social imaginary"—advanced by philosophers and psychoanalysts—to the spiritual life. The social imaginary is the creative and symbolic dimension of the social world, and the collective representations a society gives itself, with respect to the diverse concepts and functions that organize it. These deep-seated modes of understanding provide the normally pre-reflexive parameters within which people imagine their social group and collective life. Each culture has its own social imaginary.

Based on the work of the British philosopher of religion Grace Jantzen, I call my adaptation the "spiritual imaginary," which I define as the space, literally and symbolically, from which religious thinking is done and which frames what we think in relation to spiritual attitudes and behaviors, moral virtues, and the divine nature itself.[1] I'm not referring to imagination as illusory or unreal, but to the collective representations by which we define ourselves as subjects.

The spiritual imaginary involves the norms, assumptions, prejudices, pre-judgments, as well as the divine figures, religious commandments, symbols, and mythic consciousness that give content to our disposition to act spiritually and determine what is actually spiritually thinkable.[2] This includes the way a person understands the self, and the religious life that he or she imagines is possible to live. The entirety of a religious worldview—symbols, texts, theologies, and scriptures—forms, informs, and controls what we can imagine and think. This symbolic universe is so deeply intertwined with cultural identities that it cannot be dismantled or transcended simply by virtue of retrieval or reconstruction.

Each of us inherits a certain type of spiritual imaginary from our parents, culture, and religion. It is, in a sense, imprinted in us or born into the world with us, and thus involves an unconscious level. The spiritual imaginary impacts how we construct self-definition and the thought processes we employ to identify the self without being conscious of doing so. We imbibe and carry with us a self-definition that mirrors both the virtuous and immoral aspects of human nature expressed within our religions.

The implications of the spiritual imaginary are most deeply felt within the soul, where spiritual practices and theological beliefs implicitly or explicitly repeat our personal and collective symbolic inheritance. The capacity of the soul to transcend the imposition of the spiritual imaginary in the world's religions is described as enlightenment or salvation: *samadhi, sunyata, nirvana,* or *unio mystica.* Nonetheless, even in these high spiritual states of consciousness an element of repetition occurs, the person reflecting aspects of his or her primary religious experience.

Of course, there are extraordinary instances when a person does break out of a cultural and religious paradigm. Although these events tend to be rare, usually involving some form of transcendent intervention or revelation, we each have the capacity to open the spiritual imaginary and to cross a threshold into an uncharted world. Today, we find many examples in which the boundaries of religions are stretched. Emerging wisdom traditions—among them the ecological, liberationist, feminist, developing world, and interreligious—offer critical insight into the ways in which marginalized communities are reforming the bastions of belief.

Opening the Spiritual Imaginary

ONE OF THE MORE entrenched beliefs I encounter in discussing the spiritual life with others is fear of a harsh, unsympathetic, and punishing god.

No doubt this fear can be traced to Scriptural images and stories, creation myths, and to the religious formation we receive as children. Conflicted by origin stories of disobedience, ignorance, and violence, our hearts falter. We suffer over our lack and for the divine figures that come to expiate our sin. The fear of a punishing God is evident, as well, in the atmosphere all around us, in societies that extol violence over compassion, and wage war as a tool of control. While our minds and religions inform us that God is love, too often this is simply an intellectual awareness—one that we do not and cannot feel with our whole being.

If we do not know love, there is no benefit in being told that God is Love. If we are imprisoned by fear of divine retribution, it is difficult to know God as a friend and companion. These collective stories infiltrate our hearts and minds, distorting our inner lives and corrupting the spiritual journey itself. How do we dispel these beliefs that are rooted in our deep memory and damage our soul's longing for truth? How can we travel a path that leads us to an integrated, embodied realization of divine love within us? One of the great mysteries of life is that we do not know and cannot remember who we already are. So great a shroud has been placed over our intuitive beginnings, that we must struggle to find our way back to our Source.

Much of what impedes the quest is the suppression of our instinctive passion, the natural yearning of our being toward the divine being. Like a plant turning toward the sun, we are constituted to turn toward the divine light. Yet, our memory is afflicted; our native wisdom silenced. And so we must learn to suspend our rationality to become intuitive and simple again, to release the cry of passion in us that has been suppressed for too long.

One way to assist in healing the source of our infirmity is to tell new stories of our origins. If anything is needed now, it is an awakening of our inner knowing, and of the inseparability of our lives from the generative womb that animates all of creation from within. Somewhere deep within us lies a distant light, a reflection as old as the universe itself, of our beginnings in the mother womb of spirit.

Beneath our fear of sin and before our Scriptural imperatives is a reality so radiant, original, and eternal that it appears to us as *new*. We are given the freedom to break through traditions of consciousness and to discover a palace of freedom where our souls are not bound to a repetition of religions, or even to the spiritual paths of sainted figures and enlightened beings. We have been granted the capacity to see through the transparency of historical fact and religious dogma and to be delivered from *all* names and *all* ways. In the moment of suspension, when no thing identifies us as *this* or *that*, a path, hidden from view—yet with us all along—is revealed and becomes our own.

We must know the truth of our beginnings to survive the tender kindness, and passionate benevolence that gives life. We suffer no absence of divinity or revoke of love; this force, this Mystery never withdraws. Our challenge is to acknowledge how much we feel and how much we know of suffering and love. Our only safe harbor is to admit the expanse of passion we have for life, while we cling in desperation—or is it faith?—to our raft of nothingness. If we keep steady, if we take up the courage to advance beyond historic conventions and religious names, we will glide toward the distant shore of an impossible hope.

This is my story of our beginnings.

In the Beginning

GROWING UP, I had a compelling desire to pour myself out, to experience a seamless intimacy with the stately oaks and white-tailed deer that graced the woods around our house. I could feel my "self"—if it can be called "self"—extending beyond my body, touching the "self" of ant, leaf, cloud—knowing each with a knowing beyond language, a pure experience of the other as oneself. There was no volition on my part; yearning for communion with the radiant life all around me was not intentional. It happened. In spring, as a riot of red and yellow, purple and pink poppies and irises burst open, I fell upon the round, warm earth, breathing in the silky, moist air coming off Long Island Sound, and allowed my tender heart to heal. Often I felt a sweet anguish in this flowing out of myself into the wild Earth energies, and a visceral yearning to dissolve in their vibrant embrace.

As I reflect on this period of my life, it occurs to me that the intimate belonging I felt was more than a heightened sensitivity to nature, or a child's unfettered apprehension of the unseen world of spirit. I have come to understand it as a living, organic theology, as an embodied theology speaking from within the cellular and spiritual energies that made me. Before the world could claim me, I was caressed in the cradle of a time before beginning, when no separation divided us. Through nature, I was coming to know the borderless regions and gleaming jewel of light that is divine. A gentle, intimate vision took root in my being, and despite all attempts to disown and dislodge its radiance—to suffocate me with doubt and to ridicule my hope—it grew. I know now that these experiences of intimacy were a precursor of a more fully formed theology of the Divine Feminine, which flowers, thrives, and tenderly tears down our resistance, falling in love over and over again with all of creation.

These early experiences were my catechism, teaching me wisdom my mind had forgotten. Somehow through the stir of leaf and stream of light casting shadows upon my unformed heart, I glimpsed creation's beginnings. This was not the origin story I had been taught in Sunday school but something *wholly other*. For in the beginning, even if we say there is time or beginning, was not word or sound, but Intimacy. *All life* is pregnant with intimacy. In the beginning, we belong to the innermost, exquisite tenderness. The harmony of the cosmos, organisms that make up life, cells of our bodies—and how our minds work, hearts feel, and spirits love— are sustained within a mysterious matrix of affinity.

Concealed from our deepest nature, we are united in a circle of compassion, we are held by an intensity of divine passion; we belong to each other and to the Holy. We are nothing but belonging to the innermost divinity. Our belonging can never be repealed, cancelled, or destroyed. No sin or error can revoke our origins. Everything that *is*, began in intimacy. We swim in the cosmic amniotic fluid; we are connected through an umbilicus to the Source, to the Nameless who is Intimacy itself.

This vision of our founding impetus necessitates a revision of the stories of exodus rooted in human consciousness. We are not in exile, struggling to return to innocence prior to separation or sin, but are breathing in and living out our primary closeness in each moment. Intimacy means that our inner lives are bound to the inner life of Mystery, we share the same life, one and yet distinct. We live on the other side of a transparent door, a veil of gossamer through which we seldom venture. Yet separated from us by the thinnest of veils, by the imperceptible film of identity—I-hood—is the immediacy of belonging to and being held within the generative womb. This inseparable beginning invades the stars and heavens, subatomic realms, cells, our bodies, and our feelings, minds, and souls. We are artists without paint, poets with no language, trying to find a way to express the inexpressible.

Our struggle toward meaning is our own prayer of empathy, of feeling the flow of life toward its Source. The divine compassion that gives rise to our first breath becomes everywhere visible in nature's luminous self-communication. The longing of divinity, of a god who is affected by human events and feelings, implies that passion is not solely an attribute of a transcendent being, but also is the divine relationship of closeness in us. This divine initiative, of Mystery turning toward human beings, is reciprocated by the conversion of our hearts toward the Divine.

The hidden name of divinity is not infinite and all-powerful, but intimate and all- benevolent. It is not final and only, exclusive or demanding, but the relationship of longing, the love that binds us together as one, making of each moment a prayer. It springs from the capacity to be faithful to love, which bends our beings toward the divine being. Thus we touch the inscrutable Mystery that longs to be known in us and through our lives. By opening our hearts to nature's silent communion, we learn that divinity—by whatever name—is the source of benevolence and compassion, as our capacity to be loving and present with others gives birth to holiness in the world.

A theology of intimacy is already encoded in and present within the organic mystery of life. We can no more escape our spiritual belonging than change the color of the sky. Children of a cosmic desire, we are born with the sigh of compassion in us; we are beings who *feel* the world, connected to each other through a sympathetic state that unites creation in a bond of love.

In English, the word "intimacy" connotes positive meanings of closeness, friendship, and sexual affinity; as well as the potential to unleash its shadow side, domination and possession. But the dictionary definition is anemic in relation to the expansive, ecstatic expressions found in mystical literature, where intimacy is more than emotion, a state of relating, or the closeness of sexual contact. Rather, intimacy expresses the highest level of divine-human fire; it is a state of consciousness and being that compels realization of the inherent interdependence of all realms through surrender or annihilation of self. The language of expression is evocative: *atman* dissolves in the ocean of *Brahman*; the soul, kissed under an arbor of delight; the Sufi's surrender of the ego to *fana* (annihilation); *devekut*, a cleaving and closeness to God in Kabbalah.

Our spiritual forefathers and foremothers no doubt were groping for words, often using a language of negation—poverty of spirit, emptiness of self, nothingness—as ciphers to express the letting go of all that stands in the way of opening our hearts to the inflow of Divine Passion. Having experienced self-surrender, they knew that renunciation of separateness is the method of the spirit, for only that which is undivided can withstand Mystery. Only that which is undivided is wholly itself.

Silence and self-emptiness are means by which the oneness of life is tangibly experienced on Earth. Silence opens a state of inseparability within our souls. It teaches us to abstain from whatever stands in the way of our original belonging and flourishing. We practice renunciation not from fear of failure or sin, but to be close to our Source, to rejoin the circle of holiness. We disown self-interest; in this warm, inviting embrace, there is no "otherness," no "I" and "mine."

I believe this is what Mahatma Gandhi called perfect nonviolence. By bringing himself to "zero," by an abstention of self-interest, he harnessed the potential of our flourishing, abundant beginnings. For Gandhi, the manifestation of divine love was perfect nonviolence, a spiritual attitude of non-harm that recognizes that we humans are not qualified to punish. While it's an ideal that may never be fully achievable on Earth, Gandhi devoted his life to striving toward its perfection.

Like Gandhi, our beginning cannot be accessed merely by an intellectual pursuit, but is discovered through a surrender of the heart, which releases the already-present unification in us. We must feel with all our senses the inseparability that made us, allowing benevolence to reform from within our bodies and souls the harsh words and violent actions of cultures and religions.

It is not our mind or heart alone, ascetic practices, or meditation and prayer that entice passion from its radiant dwelling place. "It is the burning of the heart I want;" Rumi writes, "it is this burning that is everything, more precious than the empire of the world, because it calls God secretly in the night."[3] The Sufi mystic poet recognizes that passion, not language, is the secret path back to our original natures. Is this not why, in the presence of those who do not speak human words—oak, manatee, saguaro, zebra, ocean, wind, sky—we *feel* awe?

An ontology of intimacy underscores that we have never been separated from the cosmic mystery, from the divine. Even when we have been injured or forgotten or lost, beneath and more prior to our feeling of divine rupture or abandonment is communion, closeness. We are not exiled humans, unconnected from the web of relations, suffering a theology of separation. Rather, our subjectivity is founded on intimacy, on the birth of the maternal bond between soul and divinity.

The entire universe exists in harmonious cohabitation. The notion of a distant, unfeeling god is an antiquated metaphor. We groan with the world; we feel the pangs of the other. We share in each other's joys and triumphs; and we suffer in each other's and our own suffering. The interdependence of the world is shattering to the individualistic self. We are called again and again to being-in-the-world in unconditional love. Bodies, birth and death, family and relationship, marriage and sexuality, prayer and devotion are highly personal, relational endeavors. Biologically, the air we breathe and the ecological homeostasis that sustains our planet reflect metabolic, physiologic intimacies. Stones and rocks and water, trees and air and wind, deer and eagle and coyote, sun and moon and stars, silently intone the All. We are each part of the matrix of being. We are meant to nourish each other, and to be part of the reciprocal recycling of life's unbounded generosity.[4]

In true intimacy, subject and object disappear. Two become one, an experience the Vietnamese Buddhist monk Thich Nhat Hanh calls "interbeing"—a nondual state of reality. Intrinsic to our deepest nature, we experience interbeing through our longings for relation and understanding. It is mirrored in a woman's body when she offers herself as the birthplace of each human life, and in a man's commitment to justice. It calls us to recognize and uphold the friendship and deep affection of the whole human family for each other and with all species and creative life forms.

A theology of intimacy evaluates our religions and our lives through a different lens. Subverting the tendency to claim absolute and final truths, it recognizes that truth is tested in daily existence, when the self melts away and both God and the world are undone. It brings us into deep association with creation, tears down the walls of segregation and exclusion, opens our hearts to the mysterious patterning of life's wholeness, and teaches us not to turn away from suffering and pain. There is no salvation for one without salvation for all.

Three Divine Passions:
Benevolence, Mercy, and Love

EVERY RELIGION MAINTAINS a cosmological story to describe its sacred origins. Christians believe, "In the beginning was the Word, and the Word was with God, and the Word was God" (John 1:1). Jewish mystics hold that the manifest worlds—the *sefirot*, or ten supernal lights—are the off-spring of the *Ein Sof* (the nameless); while Hindu tradition attributes the creation of the world to the sacred sound, OM.

In my re-imagining, Intimacy is the first breath and creative act of the cosmos, and the Divine's first series of manifestations are what I call "Divine Passions," which bring spiritual and material life into form. When I use the word "passion" in this context, I am referring to the spirit of fire, the creative impulse that sparks the unmanifest into being, and not to emotion. How does emphasis on Intimacy as the primordial force of life change the story of our origins? I explore three ways.

Perfect Benevolence

In the beginning, we are swaddled in perfect benevolence. Our minds and hearts, our spirits and souls vibrate on its frequency. Every element of creation, from the smallest subatomic particle to the vast expanse of space, is infused with its radiance. Consecrated to a sacred purpose, irrevocably devoted to the Holy, the whole luminous orb of existence is attuned to the prayer of benevolence imprinted it its depth.

Perfect benevolence is the passion of divine care for creation. Creation didn't come into being in an apathetic, unfeeling way. We experience its perfection in the velvety petals of the rose, the grandeur of the elephant, or the wonder of the eye. To know our origins is to care for our selves and all creation with reverence.

Perfect Mercy

In the beginning, creation is swaddled in perfect mercy. Mercy implies compassion that foregoes punishment even when justice demands it. Compassion, from *compati*—to "suffer with" in Latin—indicates that we are beings who have the capacity of empathetic concern for the misfortunes of others. We are also constituted by our capacity to experience Divine suffering, our souls attuned to the harmonious vibration of each other and the universe. This ability to participate in and feel suffering leads to selfless action and is the power in us that is able to unite and heal. Thomas Merton writes:

> Sophia is the mercy of God in us. She is the tenderness with which the infinitely mysterious power of pardon turns the darkness of our sins into the light of grace. She is the inexhaustible fountain of kindness, and would almost seem to be, in herself, all mercy. So she does in us a greater work than that of Creation: the work of new being in grace, the work of pardon, the work of transformation from brightness to brightness.[5]

Perfect Love

In the beginning, we are infused with perfect love. Whenever we experience unqualified love for another, we swim in the ocean of divinity; we draw from the root of being. We are bathed in warmth; endearingly embraced. Imprinted in us is a higher understanding of spiritual love, a love without self-interest that is concerned for the good of others. By the steadfast desire breathed into us from our origins in the Divine, we are instilled with a capacity to know and feel unconditional love, and to suffer its absence.

Love is a real force or energy. It can be transmitted; it is cumulative. Because we are composed of perfect love, we can harness its energies to motivate action and change. We should always remember that its source is already present within us.

• ◆ •

FROM DIVINE INTIMACY, these three Passions, and more I presently do not name, the sacred sounds and words of our religions are born. Before the beginning present in each moment, when nothing is named, reality is in communion, concealed. Our beings vibrate with and are attuned to the heavenly realms. Here, the search for our origins is freeing; we may suffer, rejoice, or doubt, but we are never expelled from the state of oneness. This is the journey of the mystical heart, which heals all that stands in the way of a holy life.

As the force of newness and renewal, our founding Intimacy is catalytic. It is the starting place of transformation. In every beginning, new things happen. The person who experiences the Source realizes its potency. For here, what is oppressed, freed; sinned, forgiven; and wounded, healed. What afflicts the heart and soul is not accommodated, but broken open, erased, or liberated by grace, by the intensity of love.

One of the most breathtaking aspects of opening our hearts to Intimacy is this. By renouncing everything false and inauthentic, a vast goodness blankets our beings like a New Mexico sky. Whether felled by sin or shame, or torn by tragedy and pain, holy intimacy paints our souls with hues of awe that are never withdrawn. We are never separated from the cradle of exquisite tenderness in which we are held. Divine Mercy bends down to embrace our broken, swollen hearts, leading us toward a palace of forgiveness and healing. Holy Benevolence quickens us from within, beckoning us to shed ancient stories of retribution, and our own internal fears and sins. We are led to the sanctuary of peace where each of us, and all of creation, is Loved with intense delight.

Love as a
Spiritual Force

TEN

Love and Emptiness

IN THE FOURTH and fifth centuries of the Common Era, women and men left the cities of Asia Minor for the Egyptian and Palestinian deserts. Known today as the Desert Fathers and Mothers (*abbas* and *ammas* in Greek), these spiritual pioneers became the forbearers of the enduring contemplative traditions of Christian monasticism. Faithful to the qualities needed for surviving in the stark wilderness, they set off alone to map the trackless mystery of their hearts. I imagine them to be much like many of us today: having found modern culture wanting, we have given up the daily buying and selling in order to seek the truth that lays the soul bare.

The desert offered the *abbas* and *ammas* the freedom of a way of being that was purity itself, that knew that only love brings us to Love, that only the devoted find Devotion, that only the humble enter the gates of Heaven. They tell us that most essential to the journey is the soul's spiritual emptiness, and its willingness to traverse all obstacles that stand in the way of its Beloved. Contemplation requires an intention, say the Desert elders, that is similar to "the one who has seen the hare [and] follows it till he catches it, not letting himself be turned from his course by those who go back, not caring about the ravines, rocks, and undergrowth."[1] So it is with those who seek truth. Ever mindful of the desire for God, we care for none of the obstacles that stand in our way until we reach the divine abode.

Having left the marketplace of contemporary society and begun the quest for the authenticity of the contemplative life, like the Desert Fathers and Mothers we wonder what is essential to this life. In this chapter, I describe two of the most important aspects of monasticism: love of the Divine Mystery, and emptiness of self. Without these two qualities of being, the contemplative life is without substance. Through attentive love and loss of selfishness, contemplation transforms our quality of life and the way in which we live. It opens us to loving the world with all our hearts. It gives us the courage to let go of the false self and shows us the pathless path that liberates our souls.

Love of God Alone

THE PASSION of the spiritual quest is more ardent and more intense than most earthly romances. The soul that is seeking truth is consumed by an emotional necessity to be one with its Beloved. It is a love of the most profound sort that is not often found in this life. It is a love that dissolves the boundaries of the self, opening us to the infinite dimension of being. A yearning of our whole being for the Divine, it is love of truth that we seek. Desires squandered on lesser things are but unrealized attempts for a more noble future: to *be* a new person, to *be* holy. And it is this yearning to experience the holy and then to be holy that is love of God alone, the first and foremost principle.

Sufi mystic-poet Jalal al-Din Rumi tells us that all love is in fact love for God, since all existence is the Divine reflection or shadow: "All the hopes, desires, loves, and affections that people have for different things—fathers, mothers, friends, heavens, the earth, gardens, palaces, sciences, works, food, drink—the saint knows that these are desires for God and all those things are veils."[2] When we love God alone we see in the ordinary events of life something of the miracle and majesty of Mystery itself. When we see the world without veils, we finally realize that there is only one object of our desires: to see the divine face to face in all things.

Loving God alone is never exclusive, because all life is the Divine imprint. It is always inclusive, an embracement. Living in a state of "awakeness," it is the practice of profound and compassionate awareness. It is a commitment to open our hearts to love, and to hold the world and each other in divine embrace. Compassionate awareness is the sight of God's own eye, looking upon our hurts, worries, and despairs. When we include all creation in our hearts, we unlock the chamber of holy awareness. What would the Divine see or how would the Divine act toward our suffering or the suffering of others? What makes the cosmos dance with joy; what brings to others holy grace? This is what loving God alone means.

We love the Divine for its own sake. We do not love God because we seek forgiveness or receive gifts. We do not love God on our own terms and in our own time. We love because love makes us whole, it is all we are; it is all we wish to be. In love we find Love; we discover the source of Love: God alone. We stretch our love like a sail against the wind and allow the current of our passion to guide us straight into the divine heart.

God is not the object of our affections, or the answer to our prayers, but the length and breadth of our adoration. All desire is but this one desire: to see past the veils and coverings to the reality of that One Thing. When we love the Divine intently and with passion, the fragrant perfume of our desire intoxicates our spiritual senses. In this blind stirring of love, our whole personality is a reflection of beauty.

Loving the Divine means that although we recognize the broken spirits and wounded hopes of our collective body, we long to experience the manifest wholeness of creation. In fleeting moments we are granted a glimpse of the mysterious oneness that weaves all our relations into holy cloth. As the illusion of our separate existence is dispelled, we are awakened to the interdependence of life. Our very existence depends on the interlocking web of being, on the sanctified essence brought into form.

As we love purely and completely, we see past our lives straight into divine life to lift everything up to its true image and likeness. Overwhelmed with compassion, we see that the flaws and failings of human existence are a veil over our unborn and undefiled natures. We begin to have compassion for our sins, fragmentations, broken bodies, broken spirits, willfulness, angers, and apathies. We are able to hold in our hearts what Buddha called the two truths of existence. Side by side in the great unfolding drama of humanity's evolutionary quest, we see the illusions, doubts, and actions born of ignorance. But we do not stop there. In the midst of the suffering we see also the possibility of the divine presence in every situation. We learn to bear the truth of both states of consciousness and to recognize the difference. Of course we are selfish at times. Of course we fall and fail. But we are also and always in movement toward divinity. Awareness of these two aspects of our nature does not convey perfect awakeness. But it calls us again and again to remember the two truths.

This loving is a commitment to see with a spiritual eye and hear with a spiritual ear every day. When we remember the Divine in all things, our minds and hearts are baptized into an enlightened *quality* of being. An awareness of the divine in all one does and all one is sanctifies creation. This is our salvation here and now in each moment of our lives. We find our true selves and our true purpose for living in awakening to the holiness of life. As we become more and more awake, as the conventions of our minds and hearts are poured out, awareness is its own form of liberation. This is what seeing God in everything is: loving the Divine alone.

Many of us may fear our own divinity because we think we have to abandon everyone and everything, and give up our material life. But while loving God alone leads us through the narrow path and into the dark nights and the radical reordering of being, it is not a rejection of ordinary existence. Rather, love lifts everything up to its spiritual potential. It reinforces our ability to be parents and spouses, and to champion friends and colleagues. As the beginning of seeing reality from the view of the whole, love of the divine includes everything, uplifts everything, and offers everything over to fullness and fruition. Not an abandonment or betrayal of materiality, loving God alone brings us to ecstatic devotion for creation itself.

Emptying the Self

WE EMPTY OURSELVES to let the divine flood us with love. We are empty so we may be full. We give away our small self for the great benefit of being one with *that*, which exceeds every self. For this is the way of all real love.

The lover will give everything away, even her self, for the one she wholly loves. And this love does not pass away, for she will always choose self-forgetting as the surest intimacy with her Beloved.

As the sign of authentic spirituality, this desire of love to be free of self is so common across cultures that it may be considered a primordial dimension of human consciousness. Defined as the releasing of selfishness and ego attachments, loss of self is a central characteristic of spiritual life. Let us for now refer to emptying of the self in a twofold sense: as a breaking down of our cherished self-identities, wants, demands, and ego struggles; and as an openness of being, where all the doors and windows of the soul are thrown back to allow in the splendor of life. Since in a body we will always have elements of personality traits, self-emptying is not an absolute state but the *practice of letting go*. And this practice of detachment, in which we experience the fluidity of presence that is deeper than identity, becomes the medium for the great transformation of being that demarcates a contemplative life.

Of course we harbor many ill-informed notions of self-emptiness. Afraid that it implies an unhealthy rejection of legitimate ego needs, or a self-abasing type of privation, many people fear the relinquishing that is central to contemplative life. St. John of the Cross, one of Christianity's great mystic voices, depicts the pathway of self-emptiness as climbing to the summit of Mt. Carmel. He draws the pathway as a progression of negations in which the soul rejects the possession of desires, and becomes detached from both suffering and glory. Following the narrow path of successive *nada* (nothingness), the soul finds perfection.

Many people, when they first read St. John, are repelled by his repeated emphasis on *nada* and consider it to be an unhealthy form of asceticism and world negation. Yet John of the Cross is not speaking about rejection, but of a higher affirmation that occurs when we leave behind conventional attitudes, personality traits, and social constructions for what is more fundamental to our lives. The way is deconstructive: we take apart our thoughts, ideas, and motives. The roots of craving, ignorance, and false passions have to be pulled up. Emptiness requires a total self-honesty that is willing to pass through the fear that no "true self" exists. But instead of self-abasement, we find a freedom from the grasping of our minds. We find a flexibility of heart that liberates us from concerns and attachments. Emptiness of self is the great gift of being, for through its practice we become dissolved in the living stream of divinity.

For this reason, emptying the self is essential to all contemplative forms. For there are no absolutes in the spiritual life in the sense that we imagine: of having arrived, finally "captured" truth, and achieved the ultimate. We discover instead that there are degrees and progressions of letting go. There are states where we come to the end of the long, dark tunnel of self-centeredness and we are filled with the fragrant mystery. Yet even in these states there is always more. Awareness of our inability to arrive at final knowledge is both our anguish and emancipation as we are drawn ever deeper into the divine nature.

Emptiness of self entails hardship. To be contemplative one must not be afraid of adversity, or be afraid of the woundedness that life will bring. Suffering inflicted by others—when friends and family do not understand our motives or willfully ignore our intent—can be painful. Every day we are bombarded by the insensitivity of others and the blatant disregard for the codes of ethics, civility, and compassion intrinsic to any healthy life. Life's mistakes, unrequited desires, ego struggles, doubts and betrayals— these test the mettle of the soul, the strength of one's character, and the capacity to give of oneself in the midst of all that wounds and takes away. But there is another form of suffering, more difficult and stark, and this is the internal suffering of our existence. "Every man has plenty of cause for sorrow," says the anonymous author of *The Cloud of Unknowing*, "but he alone understands the deep universal reason for sorrow who experiences *that he is*."[3]

Self-emptying brings divine rest. "The charism of the monastic life," wrote Thomas Merton, "is the freedom and peace of a wilderness existence, a return to the desert that is also a recovery of (inner) paradise.... a kind of permanent 'vacation' in the original sense of 'emptying.'"[4] It is a reversal of the self's demands and aggressiveness, and we are challenged by its serene comfort to learn of our goodness and to practice a new kindness for ourselves. How difficult it is to wean ourselves away from the command to do something or to be somebody! We are so accustomed to subtle forms of self-wounding, willing ourselves to do things out of self-inflicted demands, that we literally do not know how to rest. Unable to see our cherished illusions, we repetitively re-inscribe the code: push, exert, demand, achieve.

Reversing this foundational orientation of want and scarcity is one of the most difficult aspects of emptying the self. Turning inward and accepting that we are spiritually guided, that our wills can rest, is contrary to everything we learn. Habituated to production, accumulation, and progress, we are startled by the ancient injunction to rest. More than bodily respite, this is the soul falling into the arms of the Divine. Cradled in a faith greater and more profound than our very life, all of the soul's inordinate fears are healed. In the "permanent vacation" of paradise, the soul does not work: she is sustained by the deepest goodness of being, a goodness that lifts from her the weight of sins and karmas.

True emptiness is also an openness of being. It is an ongoing receptivity to the wonder of life. Having an ability to flow with what life offers, we are able to pass back and forth from the interior chambers where our soul and the Beloved meet into the world. Intimacy with the Divine offers a new quality of heart. The contemplative life teaches us how to sustain this openness that is natural to our natures, and how to employ spiritual disciplines to preserve and protect our vulnerability. Contemplative experience moves us from the intellectual idea of openness that we glimpse in fragments and in starts, to the meditative exercise of openness, and then to the orientation of our whole being toward surrender and receptivity.

This hidden divine-human intimacy is always present, even though in certain aspects of the journey we may feel the holy is absent, and we are lost and in the dark. Yet it is our nature always to be one with our Beloved in the primordial garden of rest. We have the freedom, of course, to turn away. We have the freedom to reject and deny our own natures. But even when we have closed our hearts to intimacy, the eternal bond between God and ourselves is present. As we let go of the resistance and fear of being holy, our communion becomes progressively more open and free, and the contemplative life is deepened. For everything we are and everything we know in contemplation comes from the divine.

One Thing Necessary

THE MONASTIC LIFE is arduous because it takes us to truth, to the brilliant light of Divine Mystery. It will shine on the hidden flaws where the soul suffers shame, guilt, apathy, anger, or doubt—any place where we are attached to false and destructive self-identities. All forms of contemplation, especially the more advanced passive and nondual states, will usher in a profound revolution of the spirit. We will go through periods where the interior life is disordered.

We may become lost in dark nights, and bewildering, confused journeys. Yet, the silence gained in contemplation provides the fortitude needed to withstand and realize the productivity of interior darkness. We enter darkness because the purity of Divine Love overwhelms and shocks us. We are sometimes repelled when the intensity of love reveals our flaws, attachments, and possessiveness. We may be fearful or push away friends, family, and loved ones. Our choice of monastic life may shock or scandalize them.

Visual forms of consolation are taken away. The direction the soul has followed diligently, and oftentimes for many years with great fervor, no longer makes sense. The intoxication of the soul for its source has departed. The life of prayer becomes shallow, fractured, or erratic. Suddenly, the direction and confidence felt in other times of our lives is lost. The way is obscure. We feel we can trust nothing and follow no direction.

Especially during these times, faith guides us. The Divine is more present; the light is stronger. We are being taken on a path completely unknown to us, because the mind, will, memory, or understanding cannot grasp it. Only the heart knows. Before, we felt confident because we had sight and illumination. We knew where we were going and this knowledge gave us courage and strength. Now there comes a point in the contemplative life where the Divine brightness obscures our direction and our faith. Our inner voice and will cannot be trusted. We must go against the tendency of the self. The Divine is saying, "Let go and let me carry you." Our whole being rebels against this, because the roots of the ego are attached to the independence of the will. As we are being carried and held, resistance and doubt consume us. Quite often this rebellion takes place so deep inside that it defies language and we find ourselves lost and alone.

Remember, however, the monastic life is joyful and happy. Remember this particularly when in darkness and negativity. The pain is endured for the affirmation of something more splendorous and holier. As divine wisdom exuberantly or quietly infuses the soul, we realize not only why we exist, but also why we struggle, and why we are willing to give of ourselves. Having once embarked on the path, we will never turn back, even though at times we ask, "Why did I do this?" Even the darkest nights we would not give up, because we know we would lose the quest for truth, without which we cannot live. Observing the self, we realize that our apparent weakness and lack of discipline is only part of the story. Some fierce place inside of us has never given up, and would not give up, even when offered the opportunity.

If this is a true path, even though there is pain and darkness, we do not want to let the hidden suffering go and succumb to the lure of ordinary events. We know obscurely, obstinately, that if we prematurely apply an antidote to the soul's illness, we will be letting go of the great achievement or ability of our souls. On some level, we desire darkness and aridity, even while we yearn to be released.

When we devote our hearts to love of the Divine, and offer daily prayers to be made empty of "self," a mysterious expansiveness begins to flourish. Something opens within our being and the divine being, and we finally understand we have found the one thing necessary.

ELEVEN

Divine Love

LOVE OF TRUTH is at the center of spiritual life. Love seeks truth and adores the unnameable. The illuminated heart loves passionately in this way, not because we know what we are going to find or have proof of God, but because love creates us. Love sustains us. Love is the beginning. We do not love God because we want something. We love God because love is the first prayer, the first passion; love poetry gave birth to us.

When we love purely, without motive, with our whole being, and without desire for love in return, we co-create and participate in the flowing out of love. We don't ask for a demonstration, we don't demand to be healed of errors or wounds. We can make a commitment now, we can vow to love and learn to love the way Divine Mystery loves us.

Loving the Holy in all things is the beginning, middle, and end of devotion. The capacity to love without condition puts our hearts in touch with the original spark that animates creation. The miracle of love is that even if we have never received unconditional love from another person, we have the capacity to be the home of love. We have within ourselves the ability to be the source of love. Love can be our daily practice.

The prayer of the heart seeks to love how the divine loves—to love without condition—in order to heal the inhibitions that prevent love from being welcomed into the world. In this way, you become a conduit for the Living Spirit. When you love without condition, it doesn't matter if love is reciprocated, because you have touched on the Source itself.

Loving inside the monastic cloister or in the still night when there are no disturbances is much easier than loving God and others on a daily basis. Loving others requires wisdom. We must be wise in order to recognize how those who do not yet know how to love, trample love. It requires wisdom to be mindful of the forces of ignorance that fracture and divide, while at the same time keeping love alive in the heart. True love is capable of holding in unity both our capacity of love, as well as our capacity of unlove. Wisdom does not require that we love to our detriment, love against ourselves, or sacrifice ourselves for unholy love. This is a misunderstanding of love.

How, then, does the Divine love? What is divine love?

Divine Love is Freeing

The universal force of love moves in the direction of freedom, of all that is good. Divine love, loves us in freedom, and is our greatest liberation. Divine love, loves without possession or demand. Therefore, Divine love never asks us to sacrifice the true self to be loved, or for the sake of love. Love can never be possessed.

Over the course of our lives, how often have we given away our true selves in order to be loved? How much of our freedom have we given away in order to be loved? God's love is not that kind of love. Like divine love, our love also has to be free, without sacrificing our spiritual need to be part of the crowd. It never opposes or diminishes the practical realities of life—getting a job, finding a place to live, taking care of children, or sustaining one's self physically. Practical reality is a sign of love, as the Divine permeates the specific context of each life history.

Seekers often are idealistic. They imitate a saintly historical figure, but ignore how that person's history affected his or her quest to love. A person's lived experience is the medium and the modeling of love. If, for example, you have a history of deprivation, it may not be in your best interests to embark on a path of extreme asceticism. Rather, spirit may be calling you to heal the wound of deprivation. Similarly, if your life story includes excessive materialism or envy, your call may be toward simplicity as a means to balance love. The will of the divine is always imbedded in the practical events of a person's life.

Spiritual freedom is a difficult concept to grasp: it does not refer to individuality or to unbridled self-interest. Instead, it is the freedom to be fully one's self, to be fulfilled in one's own being, and to strive toward the innate capacity of love itself.

True love opens the soul to its greatest possibility, the richness of our humanity. At times, God's love may seem to be against our wishes or will because, in truth, we don't know what is good for us. What is good for us is freedom, and true freedom is not what we usually want because we do not know what it is; we have no measure of its gift.

Seeds of Love

Divine love wants nothing. When we love spiritually we do not demand to be loved, valued, or powerful. When we want nothing, then we know a love without self-interest. In wanting nothing in return for our love, we are present: open to experience whatever is before us right now. How many times have we been told that love is conditioned on how we behave or what we do? Divine love is not like that. It is open and receptive; it is gentle and tender; it comes in quietly, leading us to compassion.

Divine love is non-violent, non-dogmatic, and non-absolute because love is uniquely expressed in each situation. There is no *rule of love*. Love has no demand. When someone says, "You must be this way!" then that is not love. The reason the soul's journey can be difficult is because we cannot conceive of a universal force that loves us in freedom—that wants the best for us. When there is true love, when someone loves you as the divine loves, then he or she wants the best for you.

Love heals all things. It mends wounded souls and soothes the broken-hearted. It simultaneously recognizes both the mystery of altruistic love and the limits of conditional love. At the deepest level, love knows the capacity of the heart, as it exists right now. Love is wise. Just as the fullness of divine love isn't poured into the soul all at once (because we wouldn't be able to hold it), so does the sage measure love according to the person's need. Wisdom may say, "I am not able to give now." The body may say, "I cannot do more now." The perceptive person knows that certain limitations of love are gifts of mercy and compassion.

Our hearts grieve over the absence of love. The belief that we do not deserve love harms the soul; these pains perpetuate self-rejection and shame. God never withdraws. Divine love is never absent, even when we fear its distance. In darkness, dryness, and turmoil, even when prayer is not possible, seeds of love are planted in the soul, waiting to be watered by the power of love within you.

Love is Universal and Personal

In the book, *The Little Prince* by Antoine de Saint-Exupéry, the Prince loves a delicate rose. He takes care of this precious rose, waters it gently, and puts a fence around it, in a gesture of devotion. Like the little Prince, our personal love for another is a form of fidelity to the good. We do not love in the abstract. Anyone who has a relationship with a child, spouse, or friend has a particular relationship, because each one of us is unique. We need personal love. If we felt we were loved only in general, it would not be the same.

There is tendency to think that spiritual love is only universal, that it must entail loving all beings equally and nothing less than that. Yet, while true love loves all beings in equal measure, personal love is a special kind of commitment born out of universal love. It involves a channeling of universal love into the vow of loving someone in particular. The mystery of love is magnified in personal instances of loving someone or something with one's whole heart. Through the lens of personal love, when we open our hearts completely without self-denial or deceit, we discover love's mysterious work in creation.

A student of mine once pondered the paradox of universal and personal love. She wanted to know if it is true to say: "I love you universally, but not in the particular." I felt this type of statement could mask a subtle form of rejection. Every love in some way is personal; even universal love can never be practiced wholly in this life. When a relationship has been formed and woven by love, then it is incumbent upon us to be faithful to personal love.

Children, especially, need to feel they are uniquely loved by their parents, and not in the abstract. A child and parent separated by divorce may lose contact, to a point where the parent feels, *I have an obligation to you, but I do not have a special love for you as my child.* This harms the child's soul, because the spiritual bond that claims the child as the parent's own is not developed. Of course, a true bio-spiritual bond is not possessive. The love we have for our child, for example, should enable us to embrace all children with love, just as the uniqueness of our marriage or partnership should help us understand the significance of relationship and, therefore, want to preserve that for all people.

Monastic orders have tended to deny, diminish, or control personal relationships. The intention to suppress genuine feeling is a violation of the way that love is. We shouldn't deny that love grows and develops over time through experiences that people share together. When asceticism becomes a rejection of personal bonds, love is wounded. The mystery of embodiment, the mystery of interpersonal union, cannot simply be torn apart and discarded.

Love is universal and personal and needs to be honored in both dimensions.

Love Reveals Your Call

Only love can reveal your true nature. If you are called to a monastic or contemplative vocation, then you cannot live in the old way and hope to be healthy and whole. If you are called to community service, working with the poor or leading a corporate career, then contemplation can assist in centering an active life. To know your capacity to live in conventional society, to realize what you can handle on a daily basis, this is an expression of love. The insightful person discerns the subtle call of love. You may be good at many things, but are these the roles to which you are called? Love knows the difference. Love calls you to the mystery of self, the practical truth of your nature.

The Heart is a Spiritual Organ

Many spiritual traditions refer to the mystical heart as a high organ of perception, thought, and reason. When we think and perceive with the heart, we see the world through love's eyes. Our culture is directed toward cognition and rationality. We are trained to privilege thinking with the mind over the thinking with the heart. Individuals and societies who are heart-centered are often shamed and ridiculed by cultures that give preference to the mind. The heart is not the center of modern culture. Accolades and awards are given to the rational, to people who demarcate the limits of mind and reason. We need a heart consciousness; we need a consciousness that allows us to affirm the power of love to transform reality. The heart is the source of volition and decision: spiritual intention. What does the heart desire? Too often we wait to find out, asking: what can God give us or what is God telling us to do? But, we also are co-creators with the Divine. We can use our heart's intention to change the world.

The heart is also the center of feelings, of the spirit's deep passion for life. We are taught to suppress love and privilege the intellect. To keep the heart small, something that can be controlled or understood. But the heart is not to be contained; when we allow violence or anger to close the heart, we harm ourselves. This is a difficult lesson. It is natural to react and want to shut down or ward off further affront. When you succumb to the constriction of love, you are controllable; you are possessable. Your limit is something other people understand; it is not threatening to the status quo. Yet, you don't need to be someone other people understand. You need to be your true self.

The contemplative person, therefore, is inexorably drawn toward an open heart, a tender heart that feels the state of the world.

Homelessness of the Heart

St. Augustine wrote, "My heart is restless until it rests in You." This is the positive side of the homelessness of the heart: the heart longs to rest in God. The monastic is one who longs to live in the divine heart.

There is another side to homelessness: the world in contradistinction to the divine heart. The world can be the rival or debasement of the pure heart. Many have experienced a spiritual homelessness in society: "I can't find a place to rest my head. I can't find a place to be at home in the world."

Feeling that you can't find a place to rest in this world is only half of the journey. The work of the monastic is to replace the homelessness of the heart with the heart that is a home. Here the estrangement from life that many people feel, the sense of not belonging or alienation, and anger at the way the world is, is a kind of passivity and acceptance of the world's violation of the sacred.

If we experience estrangement, we should never let it define us. We experience rejection, but we should never accept rejection as final. We should never let it break us or destroy our path to love. We can transpose estrangement from life into inner protest, a refusal to accept alienation as the final word. We must refuse despair and restore our souls. We are co-creators with the cosmos and all beings. If we become estranged from life, use this painful sense of separation as a positive dying or letting go, where our soul and psyche pass into a deeper level of reality. Death is not the final outcome, but the transition into a new birth, a new life.

We become home. Our hearts become a home for the homeless: the outcasts, downtrodden, fearful, and poor. Then you will recognize co-communion with God in bearing all whom are spurned and debased.

When the heart becomes a home for the homeless, we participate in the continual rejuvenation of life. Feeling the wound, feeling sorrow, feeling love, but never succumbing to the belief in ultimate estrangement. Never succumbing to rejecting the world as unholy or impure. This world was created in the image of the Divine. We were created in the image of the Divine. Our work is to restore the holy sparks, to continually be a home for the homelessness of the heart.

Divine Love is an abandonment of all that keeps us separate, small, and divided. It dwells within our deep center, expanding our souls and illuminating our minds with the gift of compassion. Love is freedom itself, the overwhelming gift of cosmic rebirth and renewal.

TWELVE

The Illuminated Heart

WHEN I LIVED IN THE MONASTERY, the sisters often spoke about someone having "a monastic heart." I love that term, "monastic heart." It is evocative of the essence of monasticism, which is a heart centered on love of creation. The monastic heart is an ember burning brightly that illuminates the seeker, focusing him or her on the sacred.

We all have a monastic heart, an illuminated heart centered on love of the divine in all things. We are born with it, and are also constituted by it. This is not an achievement of our being. It is that by which we are made: a heart illuminated, longing for its source.

The heart illuminated by the light of spirit sees through our desire for attainment, prestige, possession, and achievement. It sees through the veil of these distractions to truth alone, recognizing holiness within and beneath everything.

The monastic heart overflows with gratitude for the gift of life and for the opportunity to spend our lives in search of the holy. The vows, rules, and observances that are central to monastic consciousness are the means by which we express our love of truth. Vows arise from gratitude, and through gratitude we find wisdom. Without gratitude and humility, we cannot pass through the door of the holy. Truth is so pure and so comprehensive that an attitude less than adoration inhibits our ability to experience fully.

Sufi masters say that the heart is the greatest spiritual organ—it is the seat of divine memory and of self-awareness. It is also the vehicle of our inwardness. How do we draw into our center? We go through the heart. How do we transcend the phenomenal world? We go through the mystical heart. In this way, the heart represents the human person as a spiritual subject within the divine. The heart sees the entire world, and all things in the universe, as subjects, not as objects. Therefore, all creation is bound together by the reciprocity of the beloved relationship, the communion of all beings.

But the monastic heart is more than this. It is an interpretation of life, and the symbol of wholeness and undivided unity in us. The heart is the invisible, illuminated spiritual organ of perception by which we encounter the world. In mystical texts, the heart not only signifies emotions and psychological feelings, but also the point of integration of divinity and humanity. It refers to both a physical reality and a psychic and spiritual center. In some way, our hearts are broken spiritually because we want to be with the Divine, in peace and love. Interestingly, cardiologists and other integrative physicians have discovered this wisdom. They now recognize that a broken heart can actually lead to heart attacks. If you succumb to a deep emotional wound—someone you love has died or you have been betrayed or rejected—your heart may be broken, which can translate into a disease state. Here we have physiological affirmation of ancient mystical wisdom: that the heart is the locus of the physical reality but also the psychic and spiritual center.

The heart also is the moral compass of the person and the center of passion—an intention of the heart toward our Creator. It is this movement from the center of our beings toward the center of the divine being that activates the mystical longing. Right now (as you are reading this) a river of feeling is coursing through your spirit, drawing you to the divine. Through the monastic heart we grow closer to truth and transparent to the spirit, experiencing ourselves as belonging to the realm of the holy.

The Heart Suffers

THE MONASTIC HEART symbolizes our fellowship and communion with each other and the entire universe. It is the organ of empathy, mercy, and compassion that participates in and identifies with what either elevates or violates the sacred presence. A result of the mutual longing between the divine-human, the mystical heart within us cannot exploit for its own purpose, because it experiences that all things are beloved in the divine.

The mystic heart is in tune with what is going on in the world, and feels at a profound level. Unfortunately, much of our time is spent suppressing our spiritual unity with others. When you realize—"I'm never going to be free of feeling the state of the world"—and are stabilized in solitude, your heart becomes capable of holding tragedy and sorrow against the horizon of joy and beauty. When the spiritual life matures, individualism melts away, which can bring experiences of universal—and divine—suffering. For the deeper you enter into solitude, the more your heart intimately senses the subtle vibrations of creation.

In these encounters with alienation and aloneness, the mystic in us seeks the sweet tenderness of the divine and suffers over its absence or loss. Yet, there is no permanent transcendence of this world: the idea that once we become enlightened, we live ever after in bliss is a fallacy. Anyone who pursues monkhood knows that our hearts never will be perpetually beyond the travesties and simple joys of life. Instead, the monastic heart sinks down into the world to engage in the daily moments that make up "now," honoring all we have received.

The deepening of solitude brings into stark relief what is not resolved or is imbalanced in the person. This can be shattering, especially if his or her spiritual life lacks a foundation or suffers from delusion. As the heart opens and the person is drawn deeper into solitude, the monastic heart— often without self-knowing—assumes and bears the tragedies of the world. More than ever, such a person needs to be grounded in prayer and meditation to sustain an interior sensitivity to injustice and pain, beauty and awe.

For solitude is not a denouncement of the world, but the mystic presence *in* the world, whether you are in a monastery or the middle of a bustling city. This way of living is actually the embodiment of divine reality in everyday life. To repeat: the monastic heart is not taking you away from the world. Rather, the monk belongs to the world more than ever—his or her heart integrates, embodies, and incarnates, creating a place for the divine that is conscious and tangible. And therefore the monastic person approaches daily events with renewed awareness.

This sense of the unity of being—of our capacity to feel another—is expressed in our yearning for a moment of selflessness, for a spiritual love without self-interest. Having experienced the loneliness that besets many people, we temporarily are left without a home. For compassion has nowhere to rest its head, except in the arms of every other who has been abandoned by the side of the road.

One of the problems inherent to the mystically sensitive person is that it is easy to overdo. An important spiritual lesson is to learn how to balance compassion with worldly concern. This is different for everyone. But if you do not find balance, you will be torn by what you experience. That's where the wisdom of the body is helpful. It says: "Wake up! You're pushing me. You're overdoing it. Stop!" The body also speaks out of solitude, out of divinity. It has wisdom and requires attention.

Heart of Solitude

THE MONASTIC HEART astonishes us. It is the fountain of silence that relinquishes our attachments. It is the inner hermitage of solitude that rests on three spiritual vows: dedication to the divine within; commitment to inner transformation; and prayer, the life of adoration. An intense desire for union with divine life seizes the monk's will and becomes the compass of his or her entire being. This essential first step is the fuel that ignites the fire of the soul and provides the inner strength to pursue the arduous path.

Solitude also benefits from a commitment to inner transformation, which in some cases will be difficult, anguishing, or painful. It's not always full of light. This is the paradox of the solitary life: we do not have control over the journey. We will experience stark places. We will feel stranded between heaven and earth. We will question, because the commitment to transformation does not tell us when or how we will encounter the holy. This is the gripping, wrenching sorrow of the spiritual nights when the whole structure of the clinging self is brought down and there is no stable point of reference.

The anguish of these great doubts is that there is no tangible reality ahead of the self that can dictate what or who will be known, seen, or experienced. The proof you want that there is a god is taken away, because the intensity of divine light is so pervasive that you no longer see or know what is calling you. Here is where you surrender. If the divine is *calling* you, all you can do is follow the call. All you can know is that you long to love and you will love. You will put your whole being on this longing to know the unnamable mystery. But how it happens and what you will experience, you will never know beforehand, because you are being taken to a place that is beyond your capacity to understand.

The greatest pain is not understanding what you are going through in this process of letting go. We move into a subject-less place; the self is gone and the "I" is gone. We just "are." The identity is gone. This is the place within us that is no longer in debt. No longer conscripted to payment in return, we discover a divine reality that is the flowing in of grace that can never be repaid. We are not punished, or inadequate, or tempted, or in sin. We are simply given with an abundance that overwhelms and humbles every self. This inflow of superior benevolence cancels our debts, wiping away our tears, and all the old retributions, karmas, and sins. This is the place of solitude. This is "The Beginning," that stands before, or outside of, the veil of tears, the anguish we suffer, and our fears.

If the first part of the journey is a dedication to the divine within, and the second is self-awareness and transformation, the third is prayer, the life of adoration. Prayer is healing. The heart that prays has no demands: there is no right way to pray. Prayer engages the whole self and the entire world. Life itself is prayer. It frees those who feel they are inadequate or don't belong, because prayer is communion. Communing with life is always occurring. The power of prayer restores and reconnects the heart to its Creator.

The heart knows and feels differently than the mind. It approaches life through the vantage point of the divine. Thus, every spark of illumination that ignites the soul renews the original vow: giving one's self over to be transformed and transfigured by grace. An excavation of old ways and a rebirthing of new ways occur as the person interprets life from the heart.

The Order of the Heart

SELF-DISCIPLINE is the royal road of the heart. Discipline harnesses all of one's desires, fragmented goals, and digressive motions, and directs them toward love of the holy. Without discipline we cannot achieve our goals. Discipline, however, does not refer to following a set of rules, reciting prescribed prayers, or punishment. True discipline is the ordering of your heart. It is spiritual training in the art of living from a divine perspective.

To remain faithful to a spiritual path requires self-discipline. Only you can find what is important in your life and take steps to reform whatever distracts you from your deep desire. The more profound the spiritual life becomes, the more subtle the distractions. The ego becomes more clever, the sense of self-reliance more hidden and elusive. Self-discipline is vital at this point.

Discipline also is necessary to sustain the creative monotony of monastic life. Much of spiritual life is extremely ordinary. The more you surrender to the divine presence, the more ordinary life becomes. At the beginning of a spiritual life, it is not uncommon to experience visions and extraordinary events. Yet, as life matures and one's soul grows in wisdom, many of these spiritual events disappear. The experience of God's presence is more embedded in the everyday things and "ordinariness" overcomes previous heights of spiritual awareness.

But do not be fooled. Spirit is still working in you. In fact, in these seemingly ordinary moments, spirit often accomplishes the most work. Even when you do not feel the divine—or fear you may be off your path—

the heart is being illuminated by an intensity of Presence. This hidden love is touching the soul on a different vibration than the one normally used to think, feel, or know. Self-discipline helps us to remain steady during times of absence or upheaval. It helps us to sustain prayer and meditation practices, and to be faithful to our vows even when we are not aware of inner progress.

The illuminated heart practices renunciation from destructive habits for the sake of freedom. Monastic renunciation gives up the conventions that keep us from living the rule of our lives. Mindlessness, distractions, diversions, and grasping for possessions are certain kinds of habits. Other norms include the need to be over-active or involved in many things to the detriment of inner peace, the need to be noticed, recognized, successful, or prestigious. There is also the attachment to intellectual or spiritual pride, as well as to over-giving, not taking care of our bodies, and self-debasement.

Frequently, the habits that we cannot control or release resurface because they are in the soul, disturbing the pure heart. The great monks and mystics are consistent: the end or goal of the spiritual life is purity of heart. It is a quality of being and state of consciousness that honors oneself and others in their flaws and beauty, and in their fractures and wholeness, like a clear mirror reflecting life to life, spirit to spirit.

The pure heart and the pure of heart are cleansed of their errors and sins. This cleansing of the heart does not come from any power that the human being possesses. We can work to dismantle the offences we commit, but true cleansing comes from the Divine. It is God who transforms our hearts into pure hearts, who reflects the undefiled refuge that is already present in us, and gives us permission to claim it as our own. When the Divine touches your soul, hidden indiscretions and pains are purified. Even though the memory of your past may not be erased, the soul is freed from the effects of failure and sin.

The Tibetan mystic Milarepa—who was a criminal and a murderer before he became a saint—and St. Augustine, who was torn by passions and confusions, trace how intense prayer and meditation cleansed their profound failure. You, too, can pray, "Please purify me of all that stands in the way. Please heal me of my sins and errors. I long to be pure of heart."

One can commit outer sins and have a pure heart and one can have outer purity but have a sinful heart. One can perform external offense—out of ignorance, immaturity, or pain—and still have a pure heart. And one can have outer purity and all the marks of maturity—unbroken relationships, attendance at church, financial security—and have an impure heart. It is thus imprudent and rash to judge others or yourself because only the Divine knows your inner life and true self. Only mercy frees your heart from its burden.

The task of seeking purity of heart begins by reversing the seeker's habits. Our sins and errors loom large in consciousness. We see them in "living color." The good things we do naturally from the heart, we rarely remember. But we often remember the painful acts we have committed. For this reason, it is imperative that you surrender your heart and soul to mercy, which can take away your sorrow. And thus to rest in the Holy One, praying for your burden to be lifted.

Testing the Heart

THERE ARE TWO unspoken tests of the spiritual life. One is the strength of your heart. In other words, how strong is your spiritual heart? How strong is your love? It is resiliency of the heart that guides the seeker through life's trials. Strength and abundance of heart are vital to every spiritual path. Even if your heart is closed, this does not indicate what your heart is capable of giving. This is where one must draw on inner wisdom for guidance. We all have experienced restrictions placed on love, which diminishes the heart's capacity. Some people have experienced a trauma so extensive that the spiritual heart is weakened. Until the heart can be given spiritual medicine to make it strong and fight for what it needs, such a person must learn to work slowly and not too arduously, or the effort can bring further harm. But if the spiritual heart is strong, there is nothing that cannot be accomplished.

The second test of the spiritual life is this: what are you still able to give when you are in pain, feel diminished, or suffering? Our capacity to give is an important test of the heart. We often harbor a false belief that there is a limited supply of love and compassion. Our hearts have been trained to be selfish, to hold onto material and spiritual possessions. Of course, an open heart does not over-give, give against oneself, or is self-deprecating. I want to be very clear about that. The giving heart requires a subtle level of understanding, with the idea that giving is not oppressive, demanding, or self-abusive. I am referring to a spiritual state when—even in pain or fear—the heart is willing to remain open. The natural reaction or habit is to withdraw or withhold.

The monastic heart beats with excessive love. Even if we have never received love, pure love composes us; it is within the reach of our own hearts. We are not deprived. No one can take the divine heart away. It is possible to be giving and to offer love when you think you have nothing. And the practice of giving, when you believe you have nothing to give, or when your habits prevent you from giving, transforms and transcends your self-imposed limitation.

The antidote of feeling unloved is to love. The antidote for feeling that you do not have enough is to give. The antidote for being attached to self—selfishness—is to practice generosity. These practices will allow you to scale the illusory wall of deprivation that has developed in your soul. The love you have not received in your life can be given to others as a test and a testimony of the heart.

Few have experienced the wonder of pure love. Yet many have witnessed your ability to love and to overcome the detriments in having been unloved. This is testimony that the Divine is working in you. You have stood in protest to the world's injustice and what the world says you should be. You have worked to bring the spirit into your personal life, relationships, or community. This is the illuminated heart that lives and breathes in you.

While you may judge yourself as a sinner or in error, you are embraced in the heart of mercy. This divine act of benevolence allows us to see ourselves in tenderness and in sorrow, to recognize that we have pushed ahead against odds, often without spiritual guidance, not knowing where we are going, certainly without the grounding that would have helped along the way.

In humility, we all feel that we have not accomplished enough in this life. We always will feel there is more to do, because there is no end to our capacity for love or compassion. But in those moments when the Divine touches us, we are given a glimpse of what life *is*, in the immensity of Spirit.

The daily work of the monk is to continually welcome the Divine into the hermitage of our hearts. Through offering hospitality to those we meet—by giving food, water, clothes, attention, a home—we replicate God's abundance bestowed upon us. The vows, rules, and observances that are central to monastic consciousness—which the monk performs and proclaims—can be synthesized into a simple phrase: they are the means by which we live out our love of the Divine, and offer hospitality to others.

The great gift of the monastic heart is that within each being resides the hidden mystery. Love is a force of the universe.

May the flame on the Altar of the Divine illuminate every heart!

THIRTEEN

Purity of Heart

THE PHRASE "PURITY OF HEART" expresses a central theme in the spirituality of the Abrahamic religions—Judaism, Christianity, and Islam. Seen as the crossroads between divine and human, the heart is the intersection of love for the Divine and love for the world. It is, in fact, the foundational axis around which the contemplative life revolves, in the sense that the clarification of intentions and the purification of desires are the necessary means by which a person gazes upon the holy. The comprehensiveness of the phrase indicates its importance in meditation or contemplation, especially by concentrating the seeker's practice on the virtue of inner authenticity—true love.

The Pure Heart in Jewish Scripture
"Create in me a pure heart, O God, and renew a
steadfast spirit within me." (Ps 51:10)

THE TERM "HEART"—*lev*—is used in the Hebrew Bible not only to describe the physical heart, but also refers to four spiritual sources of heart in the individual: thought and reason; volition and decision; emotion; and human wisdom. Within this understanding of the term "heart," purity of heart emphasizes the completeness or perfection of one's thoughts, decisions, emotions, and wisdom. Further, it points to a sense of freedom and emptiness, to openness of heart on all four of its levels. It refers, most basically, to an integrity and honesty of each of the heart's levels, which also could be called moral purity.

One of the characteristics of a pure heart in the Hebrew Bible is wholeness. The pure heart has singleness of purpose; it is not divided but is focused on the one thing necessary. Wholeness also refers to virtue and obedience to God's commandments. Judaism's essential core is the covenant between God and humans. Wholeness of heart, in this context, refers to the commitment and fullness of heart with which one obeys God's commandments.

Another characteristic of the pure heart is that it is empty and open, free of deceit and wrongdoing. It is upright and honest, a sincere heart, and a friend of the Divine. The heart that is near to God knows goodness and is morally blameless. Yet, the heart may have to be sacrificed. It may have to be broken. It may have to be humbled. In Biblical stories, God inflicts anguish, unveiling the fracture in our hearts. This cleansing requires surrender, because the deepest pain cannot be healed by human effort. In order to unveil the sinless heart, the Divine Physician draws out our hidden motives, expunging the heart's afflictions, sins, negativities, and impurities.

God is drawn toward the pure of heart. One may have committed outer sins, but have inner purity and an unblemished heart. God is drawn to the empty heart, the heart that has given up scheming and bargaining, deception, fear, and division. It is not that God will decide to enter or might consider entering, but that as you empty yourself out, God will enter. This does not mean God will decide that you are worthy. It can be thought of as a divine law: as you pour yourself out, God will pour God's self into you.

"Yet you know me, O Lord; you see me and test my heart about you." (Jer 12:3) "God knows the secrets of the heart." (Ps 44:21); God declares: "I the Lord search the heart and examine the mind, to reward each person according to their conduct, according to what their deeds deserve." (Jer 17:10)

Another wonderful passage, from Psalm 73: 23–26, speaks to the consequences of a pure heart. "Yet I am always with you; you hold me by my right hand. You guide me with your counsel, and afterward you will take me into glory. Whom have I in heaven but you? And earth has nothing I desire besides you. My flesh and my heart may fail, but God is the strength of my heart and my portion forever."

As the heart empties and expands, it experiences God's direct presence. When we don't feel God is with us, God says, "Open the door of your heart. I am here." We might have an intense experience of the divine that quickly dissipates. Our bodily cells cannot sustain the pure light of the divine if there is impurity or brokenness in us. This is not to say that you must be perfect to experience God, not at all. But purity of heart is a reciprocal love for the divine. It is the heart, speaking to the divine: "I will purify myself in order to be closer to you. I offer myself to you. I want to give away my imperfection because of what you have given me." Thus, cleansing one's heart is not punitive, but the activity of loving mutuality.

The Hebrew Bible also describes the heart as the vital center of wisdom, and the affective seat of human emotion. As the vital center, the heart is the driving force behind conceiving and planning, and involves memory and understanding. Affectively, it concerns self-will, the things we long for, and the emotions we have. Do we long for things that draw us closer to our true natures, or further away? Are our emotions loving, gentle, kind or are they conflicted, hateful, or selfish? Do our choices lead to wisdom? God speaks to us in our pure hearts.

The Pure Heart in Christian Spirituality

PURITY OF HEART is the abode of divinity within us, and is, therefore, central to Christian monastic spirituality. In fact, extensive writings on the pure of heart and purity of heart are extant in every era of Christian spirituality, requiring that this section be no more than a general overview.

The most concise and powerful expression of purity of heart in Christian spirituality is the Beatitudes, from the Sermon on the Mount (Matthew 5).

Blessed are the poor in spirit, for theirs is the kingdom
 of heaven.
Blessed are those who mourn, for they will be comforted.
Blessed are the meek, for they will inherit the earth.
Blessed are those who hunger and thirst for righteousness,
 for they will be filled.
Blessed are the merciful, for they will be shown mercy.
Blessed are the pure in heart, for they will see God.
Blessed are the peacemakers, for they will be called children
 of God.
Blessed are those who are persecuted because of righteousness,
 for theirs is the kingdom of heaven.
Blessed are you when people insult you, persecute you, and falsely
 accuse you because of me.

This passage is followed by Jesus' sermon on turning the other cheek in Matthew 5:39: "But I tell you, do not resist an evil person. If anyone slaps you on the right cheek, turn to them the other cheek also."

We are shown that God's love is for all; none are privileged above others. Purity of heart is not to be applied selectively, but to everyone—those who have harmed us, those who are considered our enemy, those who have sinned. To live this way is to practice nonviolence and to experience divine intimacy: "Blessed are the pure in heart, for they shall see God." This is the greatest prayer. It is the divine within us.

The fourth century monk, John Cassian, is commonly held to be the monastic theologian most closely associated with the theme of purity of heart. In *The Conferences*, Cassian's treatise on prayer, purity of heart is singled out as a central theme in religious life. He reflects on purity of heart from God's point of view, especially the readiness to please the divine by acts of mercy and kindness toward others, and by having a heart free from anger and ready to forgive. Considered by Cassian to be more important than any specific ascetical or religious practice, purity of heart is itself the goal of Christian life, an arduous stripping away of anything less than love. So comprehensive is its meaning, this one phrase can encompass the entire monastic experience.[1]

Other monastic theologians, writing in Syriac (a Semitic language related to Arabic), drew on the word for heart, *lebba*, to emphasize its role as the vital center, seat of human emotions, and driving force of a person's conceiving and planning. One of these theologians, Martyrius, a seventh-century Syriac monk, exemplifies the Christian concept of purity of heart in this passage from *The Book of Perfection.*

> Happy is that person of love who has caused God, who is love, to dwell in his heart. Happy are you, O heart, so small and confined, yet you have caused him whom heaven and earth cannot contain to dwell spiritually in your womb as in a restful abode. Happy that luminous eye of the heart which, in its purity, clearly beholds him before whose sight, the seraphs veil their face.... *Blessed indeed are the pure in heart, for they shall see God....* Blessed are you, O heart that is luminous, the abode of the Divinity; Blessed are you, heart that is pure, which beholds the hidden Being.[2]

In our hearts we hold divine light. The heart that is pure is a vessel for the Holy Spirit. We must recognize that it is in our thoughts, cultivated in our divided hearts that negativity and sin reside. So if remembrance of God is important for a pure heart, then we must discover where remembrance has been blocked.

Another seventh century Syriac monk, St. Isaac of Nineveh (also called St. Isaac the Syrian) makes reference to "purity of heart" in his discourses on prayer. Exhorting the "disciple of truth" to reflect on virtue during the time of prayer, St. Isaac clarifies that virtue "is not a matter of someone being totally without thought or reflection or stirring, but rather it consists in the heart being purified of all evil, and in gazing favourably on everything, and considering it from God's point of view..."[3]

If you can live in the material world maintaining a single-minded purpose of heart, then you are on your path; you are in your "monastic space." Abba Moses said, "The end of life is God alone, and the goal is purity of heart." When we are consumed by a desire for material things, in effect we make them gods and ends in themselves. Ask yourself, which ephemeral things have I made more important than my heart's longing? It is a process of discernment to recognize the difference between temporary happiness and the profound and lasting kind.

The desert isolation of the early Christians was for this precise reason: to remember God, and to be attentive to distractions that led them away from God. To become aware in a way that they weren't aware in the bustle of daily life, and through prayer to practice driving out that which disturbed the heart's pure longing. Thus, awareness was brought to every deed, and the heart became an altar, a term described in various ways in Syriac liturgies. Here is one, from the *Book of Steps*, a fourth century anonymous set of homilies:

> There is a hidden fasting of the heart, fasting from evil thoughts. . . . The body is become a hidden temple and the heart a hidden altar for ministry in the spirit.[4]

It's a beautiful image, that our heart is an altar in the temple of our bodies and in the altar of our heart, we offer ourselves to the Beloved. And what do we offer? Everything: suffering and pain and joy and pleasure. We often think we can only be with God when we are in a good mood, when we have something good to say, when we come with everything polished, our bow tie on or ribbons in our hair. No, it is your afflictions that God wants. When you cry out: *God where are you? Why have you betrayed me, why have you left me to suffer? I anguish over my imperfections. I don't know you. I don't know how to pray to you. I am angry with you*, these are offerings too, because it is a moment of truth. The Divine can take it.

It is the tumultuous emotions that finally force us to surrender and allow the Beloved into our hearts. When we try to be perfect and polished, we are still in control. But when we offer ourselves in weakness, we pour ourselves out. That is when God pours in.

But you see, we don't believe that. We believe that we could be abandoned. We could be rejected. We could possibly be banished. We could possibly lose our last and only chance. This mentality is the result of punitive views of the Divine. It is not possible to be abandoned or rejected. As you realize and probe feelings of fear, anger, and abandonment, you are purifying your heart. Don't push those feeling away; don't try to control them. Let them come out. God calls us to communion. God in the Hebrew and Christian Scriptures is described in emotional terms: God mourns, angers, punishes, weeps, loves, soothes. God is not a distant, non-caring being, but feels what we feel, a God to whom we can offer our true selves at any and every moment.

Ascetic practices or virtues were considered necessary to the development of a pure heart, among them: not eating much, wakefulness, sleeping on the ground, manual labor, and poverty. In addition, reciting the divine liturgy, reading scripture, mourning, tears, and weeping were associated with the heart's cleansing freedom. Christian monastics contend that the sources of sin are the negative thoughts cultivated in the heart and not primarily the result of outside forces.

Basil of Caesarea (330-79), founder of a community of ascetic Christians and bishop of Caesarea in Cappadocia (modern day Turkey), taught that one should do everything as if God were watching every move, trusting that such awareness would promote correct behavior.

> Prayer is to be commended for it engenders in the soul a distinct concept of God. And the indwelling of God is this: to hold God forever in our memories. We thus become temples of God whenever earthly cares cease to interrupt the continuity of our memory of Him, whenever unforeseen passions cease to disturb our minds. And the lover of God, escaping all them retires to God, driving out the passions which tempt him to incontinence, and abides in the practices which conduce to virtue.[5]

The Heart in Islamic Spirituality

IN SUFISM—the mystical, esoteric dimension of Islam—the heart (*qalb*) is the organ of perception, and one of the centers of mystic physiology. It operates with a subtle body composed of psycho-spiritual organs, which are distinguished from bodily ones. The person's mystical heart is the organ or eye by which God knows and reveals God's Self in divine epiphanies. Although love is related to the heart, the specific center of love in Sufism is the *ruh* or spirit.[6]

The power of the heart is a secret force or energy, which signifies the act of meditating, imagining, projecting, and ardently desiring. This is the vital force or intention that powerfully realizes its creative function to unveil the unconditioned into manifestation.

In Islamic mysticism, the physical Ka'ba in Mecca represents the spiritual heart and the place within the human being where Allah dwells. The spiritual heart is the original source of prayer, and the journey to its perfection is the intention and goal of every seeker.

The organ of prayer is the heart. Prayer is the highest form, the supreme intention of the heart's creative imagination. This intimate dialogue between the heart of the seeker and God opens out into contemplation, and is a secret psalm recited in the mystic's depth.

Ibn 'Arabi, the esteemed fourteenth century Sufi mystic and theologian, understands that it is the science of the heart that releases the mystic interpretation and makes it possible to read and to practice the Koran: "When He shows Himself to me, my whole being is vision; when he speaks to me in secret, my whole being is hearing. . . . The entire Koran is a symbolic, allusive (*ramz*) story, between the Lover and the Beloved, and no one except the two of them understands the truth or reality of its intention."[7]

Prayer or *dzikr* evokes a constant reminder of God in thought, emotion, will, memory, and so forth. Sin is the act of forgetting to remember God in all your actions. When we turn toward material things at the expense of the divine, we cause affliction in the heart, for the heart becomes divided, turning away from its purpose.

For Ibn 'Arabi, the heart is not primarily the place of emotions or feelings, but the house of knowledge, where God is known; it's also the temple in which God already dwells. Our heart is God's heart, not our own. What intervenes between the heart and God as the owner of the heart are ignorance and an absence of knowledge of the divine, living heart within us. "The greatest sin is that which kills the heart, and it is not killed by anything except lack of knowledge of God, which is called ignorance (*jahl*). Because it [the heart] is the 'house' (or temple, *bayt*) which God has chosen from this human formation for Himself."[8]

This mystical heart is central to Sufi spirituality as the meeting place of soul and mind and as the focal point where the mind, which is all-knowledge and light, is reflected in the mirror of the soul. Ibn 'Arabi understands the heart of the perfected human to symbolize the synthesis and whole experience of the Oneness of Being. God is the unseen manifestation in the heart and also the sensible manifestation in the world. "It is from the former type that the predisposition of the Heart is bestowed, being the essential Self-manifestation, the very nature of which is to be unseen."[9] It is this capacity of the mystical heart to synthesize and unite that underlies Arabi's unity at the heart of reality, and the oneness of multiplicity. He writes, "That is because he who has attained to realization sees multiplicity in the One, just as he knows that essential oneness is implicit in the divine Names, even though their [individual] realities are various and multiple.[10]

The heart-center is also the place of Divine Light and occupies all the degrees of existence. The heart possesses the capacity to turn from state to state and is free flowing, unable to be shackled, as is the unenlightened mind. But when the mind is married to and in service of the heart, it is capable of infinite change and can act to transmute spiritual knowledge. Ibn 'Arabi reflects on how the marriage of heart and mind generates infinite receptivity to revelation, illuminating the mystical capacity of each heart:

> When God created your body, He placed within it a Ka'ba, which is your heart. He made this temple of the heart the noblest of house in the person of faith. He informed us that the heavens, in which there is the Frequented House, and the earth, in which there is the [physical] Ka'ba, do not encompass Him and are too confined for Him, but He *is* encompassed by this heart in the constitution of the believing human. What is meant here by "encompassing" is knowledge of God.[11]

Symptoms of an Impure Heart

MONASTIC TRADITIONS emphasize asceticism and detachment as a way of getting beneath thought and action, and recognizing what thwarts an open heart. The pure of heart have a singleness of purpose, a heart not divided in its affections. Søren Kierkegaard wrote, "Purity of heart is to will one thing." What does it mean to will (or love) one thing?

If we were to say, "Truth is at the center of my life," or "Non-violence is at the center of my life," how does that play out in a life? Let's say you tell your spouse or partner, "I love you," but you're always looking out for yourself. Or, "I want the best for you," but you don't trust your partner, so you hold something back. Do you see how the heart is divided in this instance, how it cannot be in truth?

The heart focused on God struggles to be undivided. Of course, we are human, life is complex, and we have our wounds. We are not always completely honest and open. But we can strive to move toward the purification of our daily lives, to be truthful. Sometimes inner conflict takes us away from our spiritual goal. Sometimes divisions in relationships are subtle: we harbor feelings of despair, are afraid to talk about them, or believe we do not have permission to be pure in heart. But remember that any relationship that is called by the spirit will flourish as we risk opening our hearts and being honest with each other. If the spirit has called a relationship into being, it will be able to weather stormy days.

In some ways, it is easier to maintain singleness of purpose alone than in community or relationship. But, even when we are unclear and indecisive, the deep self yearns for oneness. Remember St. Basil's words: "The body is become a hidden temple and the heart a hidden altar." It is not a metaphor; it is true. When we are divided in heart and mind, we are not truly happy. The disjuncture between our conflicted wills causes anguish. Augustine writes in *Confessions*, Book 8, "My will for the world and my will for God are in mortal combat and they are laying waste to my soul." He cannot escape the conflict. His divided wills afflict his soul and illustrate that there is a state of unity beneath and greater than our dividedness. The quicker we move toward unity, the less painful it is.

What are the conditions that cause duplicity of heart? The desert monks listed greed and gluttony. Remember, the Hebrew Bible mentions four levels in which these causes can take place: thought and reason; volition and decision; emotions; and wisdom. Greed or gluttony is not only about material objects. There is also intellectual greed, emotional greed, or spiritual gluttony, which can manifest as an inability to settle into one spiritual practice, or follow one precept instead of chasing every spiritual tidbit. If I resist simplicity, is that causing division in my soul?

Pride and ambition are another cause of a divided heart, which extends into pride of thought, pride of possessions. Ambition is different than passion. Ambition implies a competitive advantage over others: envy, love of money. Cassian also cites injustice, avarice, and pride, as well as the subtler types of duplicity: reluctance to do one's duty; desire to receive praise; and excessive love of temporal things. Other examples of an impure heart are a contentious or quarrelsome attitude, and arguing and taking positions (not for the sake of truth but simply for the love of differing). He also cites the fault of questioning others for the purpose of acquiring information in order to accuse them.

An important caution is not to allow good intentions to be mixed with impure motives. We may have good intentions but our motive may be divided. Meister Eckhart offers scathing commentary on priests who buy and sell God like a cow, and on religious people who perform the letter of the law, or try to look spiritually perfect, but are not pure of heart. Augustine says something very close to this: "Therefore, no one has a single heart—and this is the same as a clear heart—unless he rises above human praise...that is to say, unless his thoughts and his efforts to please are directed solely toward Him who alone is the discerner of conscience."[12] Note that in this, Augustine is asking us to walk the narrow path, to discern what is good and true, and not to worry about what the world says about our actions.

Augustine also recognizes how the desire for others to think well of us while doing a good deed allows pure motives to be mixed with impure ones. "It is not that being praised by others for a good deed is an evil in itself; but an object does not have to be evil to debase a higher object."[13] An example is given of two metals: gold and silver. Gold is the more inert metal, and is considered to be more pure than silver. It does not mean that silver is less important than gold, but when they are mixed gold is debased by silver. These wise thoughts clarify that we cannot depend upon the praise of the world to do what is right. We have to depend upon our inner voice.

Qualities of a Pure Heart

ONE OF THE MOST IMPORTANT qualities in the monastic tradition is humility. Humility is the virtue that celebrates being less rather than more. Cassian says that the antidote to greed, gluttony, and other sins is humility. When we think of all that divides us from the Beloved and from others, we see it is an attempt by the ego to make more of ourselves. To be humble is to celebrate being less.

Humility is the simultaneous experience of participating in the majesty of the cosmos, and the recognition of how small we are in its midst. The concept of poverty of spirit—being distilled, becoming less—is central to every spiritual path. If you discover the sweet experience of knowing you are but a drop in the ocean of divinity, you will be surrendered into the divine flow. What makes the practice of humility (and perhaps all ascetical practices) so difficult is social and cultural norms. To be less, to give your self away, can be incredibly painful. If a society does not recognize the dignity of persons, and denies them a true sense of self, the virtue of humility may be misinterpreted as another debasement.

The journey toward faith and wholeness of self involves tests and travails. Cleansing of the heart involves wisdom, which cannot be achieved by the intellect or empirical mind alone. Only through a movement of the heart—through love—can truth be found. In the beginning of this chapter, I equated purity of heart with love. Love is a way of knowing. The knowledge discovered through love and faith is unique and not reproducible. Those who insist on seeing before believing "are like blind men," says

Augustine, "desiring to see the physical light of the sun in order to be cured of blindness, whereas they cannot possibly see the sun unless they are first cured."[14] Augustine describes the demand that we make on reality. We don't want to surrender; we don't want to have faith without proof: Prove to me that there is a God who loves me. Show me that if I go down this path, I am going to be holy!

But the heart cannot be cleansed without faith. To know if God loves us, we have to ask if we have ever really loved God. Have you ever in one moment of pure, unconditional offering, just loved life or God without proof? You start where you are, and that is in the heart. Love springs from the heart. Augustine writes in his *Confessions* that he was arrogant because he had become a brilliant rhetorician. He could argue himself out of anything. He could find fault with anything. He realizes that it is only faith that reveals a new reality. It can be described as opening a door into a territory that cannot be seen until one passes over the threshold. This is cleansing of the heart. These are the vital keys to the door. To quote Augustine:

> It is not God who must change and become visible for those who are unbelievers, but it is they who must realize that their very salvation depends on a change of outlook and heart. They must be willing to prepare themselves to see before they see—to step out in trust and accept as true what is not apparent.[15]

This is true, profound transformation. This is how the heart is cleansed. It is how we recognize our sins. Faith seeking understanding helps us to accept everything that happens without resentment or resistance to the divine will. Resisting, or contrariness, distorts the heart. And we don't want crooked hearts! Further, discontent agitates the heart and clouds the mind, which prevents divine light from penetrating. Faith frees us from needing reasons for why things happen. At times there is no reason for why things happen, which is a profound spiritual lesson. It frees us from hubris, from believing that we know how the world should be, thinking we can present a rationale for suffering or joy. We can't know. We must trust that the world is mystery and sometimes all we can do is be present, hold each other, cry, or laugh. Sometimes faith leads to suffering, just as fire will separate gold from its impurities. So too the soul is purified of its attachments.

Purity of heart is the loving means of living for and with the Divine. Yet, many people are afraid to follow the humble path because they believe it will take them away from some material or spiritual good. The Divine never denies our longing. God's will is never against us; it is always for our freedom. It is never opposed to our deepest nature. Acceptance of the divine will—which also is our true will—can feel dangerous because layers of distrust may obscure the true self. It's as if we have been imbibing small doses of poison and, over time, we no longer taste the poison and it doesn't make us sick.

A similar process happens in the spiritual life. We take little doses of the things that are not good for us, and eventually we develop fear that if we give them up, we're going to suffer a fatal illness of the spirit. This fear is contrary to the true freedom the Divine wants for us. Because we cannot see beyond our self-loathing to realize and accept that we are called to be holy. Our hearts are beautiful. God loves us and calls us to equality. The radical transformation of consciousness occurs when you are being led to true freedom, the thing you most deeply want: to experience holiness and to be completely loved, one and undivided. The mind cannot conceive of such a place.

And so as the divine is drawing our heart into truth, we are suffering the pain of letting go of all that's not true, of all that has prevented liberation. Thus, the darkness of being is not an ascetic renunciation of one's flaws. Rather, it is the practice of remembrance, and the mental and spiritual discipline to remember the divine in everything we do. Then the heart desires peace and silence, a happiness that material things can never provide.

Unless the Beloved is loved by faith, the heart cannot be cleansed. For love is the unspoken hidden element. It is love alone that changes the heart. Prophecy and spiritual gifts will not in themselves change the heart unless there is love.

Thus, we are reminded of how comprehensive purity of heart is. I have only introduced it here, but this is a meditation for one's lifetime. It is all this: We seek the one pure abode that is the altar on the temple of our being. There, God finds us; God touches us.

Living the
Monastic Heart

FOURTEEN

Treasures of the Monk's Journey

A MONK'S LIFE of study and solitude, prayer and work is imbued with sweet fragrance and hidden treasure. It is only by entering into that life—as a vowed member, oblate, or temporary guest—that the person glimpses the richness and wonder of living in and for God. Spending an extended period of time in a monastery or retreat center, embraced by silence and solitude, elicits a singular deepening of the self.

During my residence in monastic settings, I have been enriched by the quality of presence mirrored in the daily life of the monks and in the atmosphere of their communities. In what follows, I describe eleven jewels of monastic spirituality that are practiced and held in esteem by diverse religious orders. Especially relevant to the new monk seeking to establish a day-to-day contemplative orientation, these virtues highlight the transformation of self that the monastic vocation ushers in. They also indicate the direction of the monk's life, as well as the expansion of holiness and peace.

Solitude

One of the foundational attributes of monasticism is solitude of self. Solitude is not aloneness for the sake of separateness, but an interior sanctuary reserved for divine communion. It is a state of preserving holiness in your own being, to be with God's being, the divine being, allowing no other to intrude. "Solitude may perhaps be more helpfully considered from a psychospiritual point of view," writes Bernadette Flanagan, "that place within each person that is the center of spiritual consciousness . . . and a quality of heart."[1] The monastic or contemplative person seeks singularity of purpose as a response to the divine call and as regular withdrawal into the inner room of one's being.

As spiritual practice, solitude has both mystical and practical implications. In the deep well of contemplation every person is one with the divine. Here, nothing else may penetrate the mystical intimacy between the soul and its Beloved, felt through inner consolations and spiritual touches. On a practical level, solitude of self implies detachment—where we extract ourselves from daily concerns, professional conflicts, and social situations in order to foster and preserve the right to be alone. Solitude makes freedom possible. There is no necessity to maintain superficial relations.

The energy and wisdom of a person who lives in solitude is tangible. When you meet someone who has achieved spiritual solitude, you experience a different kind of presence: one that is open, free. He or she emits a centeredness that is self-contained, that does not violate or transgress other peoples' space and, by such a gift, acknowledges their freedom. The natural solitariness exudes an aura of gentleness and love.

It is in solitude that we discover our true selves—our relationship to God, the meaning of our existence, our place in the universe, and the challenges of the interior quest. Alone, we finally seek self-illumination: "Who is this person that I call myself? In what ways do I fail myself? What elevates my being and what things instigate my false self? What kind of life do I want to live?"

As a quality of being, solitude is essential to monasticism. Ideally, everything in monastic life is ordered around this primary vow. *The Cloud of Unknowing*, an anonymous fourteenth-century text, urges us to center our lives in solitude, placing all daily strife under the "cloud of forgetting." We have to let go of all our worries and concerns, surrender to being alone with the Source of all happiness, and rise up into the welcoming arms of Wisdom.

Solitude is risky because it compels you to the depth of your own personhood—to conflicts, attractions, and demands—to discover the soul's burning fire that is not quenched by worldly things. It is to claim the right to stand alone, to be unafraid of others' opinions and desires; to be exempt from having to be special or accepted, known or important.

A helpful practice is this: Imagine a flame at the center of your being. Every time you tend the flame, you devote yourself to God. Whenever the world intrudes on your devotion, or whenever you feel obligated to neglect your sacred task, ask: Is this action of benefit in my life? Is it taking me closer or farther away from my true desire?

Respect

The utter respect that each monk accords to every brother or sister is evident in healthy monastic communities. There is a sense that each of us is a living example of divine possibility and, therefore, is worthy of gentle regard. Our journeys are mysterious. We will never fully know another person's soul and can never presume to have crossed over the boundary of his or her heart. Whatever glimpses we are granted into each other's lives are glimpses of grace. The true monk honors others' search for God and, by his or her presence, shares in their trials and frailties, their joys and strengths. Therefore, we offer each other mutual respect, which always tries to see through the eyes of the heart, and tries not to judge, ridicule, or in any way offend the divine mystery in each person.

In my visit to monasteries—Carmelite, Benedictine, Zen, Orthodox, etc.—the respect the monks showed toward each other and each guest was palpable in their actions and in their desire to be of service. It filled the monastery with a presence of holiness. Whatever impurities we carry in ourselves—and these monks did not hold themselves up as enlightened beings—are kept in check by the command for mutual respect, this command of the heart.

Reverence

Another quality I have experienced in monasteries is reverence for life's gifts—the small and grand creatures, workers in the fields, food, and people who support the vocation. And in the case of Catholic and Buddhist communities, for example, monks express reverence for the mystery of their faith—the Eucharist, Christ's life and death, and the books of Scripture; Buddha, *dharma, sangha*—and the teachings of love that inspire these seekers. At one Benedictine monastery I visited, there were sisters who had been living their vows together for fifty or sixty years. Invariably, I found myself sitting next to one of the older sisters in the oratory. Now and then a sister, with tears in her eyes, would comment: "I am so grateful. I just cannot believe that I have had the privilege to live here for so many years seeking God, with so many good and kind women."

Members of this community pray seven times a day. Seven times a day for fifty or sixty years they have listened to the Rule of Benedict, read passages from Scripture, and chanted the Psalms. Still, there is reverence. The monks in the oratory are attentive. No one is slouching or distracted. This was a moving experience for me to witness.

Everything about the monastery was held in high regard—the flowers, vegetable gardens, forest paths, and outdoor sculptures—as were the religious sisters who came from Europe to found the monastery in the 1800s, and the lineage of Prioresses who guided its growth. There was simply a palpable love and devotion for God, each other, their heritage, sisters who had died, and visitors, all sustained by a motherly embrace of reverent gratitude.

All who enter are embraced in their welcoming hearts. Unconditional love sees you and holds you and celebrates you for who and what you truly are. It is so rare to be *known*. This monastic quality of consciousness is something we all can learn and model in our lives.

The Cell

The monk's cell is historically a place of enclosure; but also it is a metaphor for inner transformation. Thus, a vital aspect of a monk's life is self-transformation in order to aspire toward or achieve mystical depth. It is daily confrontation with a person's façade of personality—the illusions, desires, and attachments of the false self—to discover the divine within. The monk stakes his or her life on the capacity to be transformed, to be divine-like, enlightened, or free.

Monks throughout history advocate the value of retreating into one's cell as the practical means of self-purification. The main obstacle to union with the Divine is in a soul disturbed by desires, wounds, and fears. The cell, then, represents the triumph of love over the false self, and the resilience to enter into the night beyond faith, intellect, or hope.

Monastic elders understand that the cell is the locus of transformation, initiating a potentially life-altering catalytic process. Numerous monastic stories recount some version of this advice: You don't know what to do? *Sit in your cell.* You have inordinate passions? *Sit in your cell until you break through.*

Why is the cell efficacious? Because alone in one's cell, the Divine concentrates the monk's being, revealing what has been concealed, and purifying the soul guides it to freedom. The cell, however, is not a prison of asceticism. For the monk enclosure is celebration, found by passing through the narrow gate into intimacy with life itself.

Renunciation

Monastic commitment is difficult and sometimes obscure or dangerous. Renunciation of worldly desires is prescribed as the means of harnessing one's inner life toward the highest good, and all traditional monastic forms involve some type of asceticism: poverty, chastity, obedience, detachment, nonviolence, and so forth. Restraint in food, deed, coupled with discipline over mind and body are foundational. Often the first stage of the monk's spiritual development is directed toward overcoming his or her vices. Self-mastery is an essential element of monasticism, which is attained through the order of the monk's life— training in the community's rules, regulations, and liturgies. The aim of monastic formation is purification of heart so that the monk's outer behavior is reflective of his or her interior quest. For this reason, monks recognize the benefit of an experienced elder in wisdom to support their efforts and show obstacles to be avoided.

Prayer

The rhythm of a monastery is predicated on a daily schedule of prayer or meditation, the monk's primary work. As the first language of the soul, prayer is the fulcrum of monastic life, from which all-else flows. Some monastics live in cloistered places, where their entire day is ordered around meditation, work, reading, and rest. However, many monastics are not cloistered, and are actively engaged with their wider community. For example, in one Benedictine community where I lived, the sisters had commitments as professors, nurses, schoolteachers, etc. But they thought long and hard about any activity that could interfere with prayer, and always asked before embarking on a choice: "Can I maintain the prayer schedule of my monastic commitment?"

At scheduled times of the day from all over the monastery, the sisters would converge in the oratory, chanting the liturgy of the hours. This rhythm gave their day order and meaning, and kept their lives rooted in what was most essential. In addition, many of the sisters prayed in their own rooms, or prayed together in smaller groups. Sisters who lived in a hermitage and did not attend regular liturgies also maintained the monastery's regular call to prayer.

Prayer or meditation is the most important element in monastic spirituality. The space, geographic location, and natural surroundings of the monastery buildings are chosen to be beneficial for these devotional activities. Likewise, the internal atmosphere, respect for each monk's solitude, and non-hurried movement in hallways are important to the conversion of life that monasticism requires. Awareness of one's manners, including the correction of specific daily habits—slurping soup, discarding towels on the floor, talking loudly, banging dishes—are aspects of mindfulness. In this way, the monk creates a sanctuary in his or her heart where the Divine Presence dwells.

Thomas Merton describes the monastic atmosphere of prayer:

Everything in the monastery, then, is ordered to produce the atmosphere propitious for a life of prayer. The isolation of the monastery itself, the work by which the monks strive to be self-supporting and independent of secular contacts, the reading and study which are done in the cloister or in the cell, and the office chanted in choir all have for their function to keep the monastery what it is meant to be: a sanctuary where God is found and known, adored and in a certain way "seen" in the darkness of contemplation.[1]

For those of us living outside of a monastic community, our days can be chaotic and fractured. The patterns of our lives do not seem to match the self's inner order. Thus, essential to a monastic commitment is discovering how to foster a sacred rhythm in your life. To do this, you have to learn your rhythm. You have to feel how your practices—prayer, meditation, walking, reading, and contemplation—seep into the cells of your body, instilling another manner of being.

Hospitality

Monastic life is designed to mirror the highest possibility of religion, and one manifestation of that is hospitality. The cenobitic communities place special emphasis on hospitality, welcoming others into the house of God, of making a home for the homeless. Here I refer primarily to the homeless soul, not only the homeless person. Hospitality welcomes the homeless *soul* into the house of spirit, showing the pilgrim charity, blessedness, joy, and love. Christians strive to be like Jesus, filled with divine, sacrificial love; Buddhists to be like Buddha, with a pure mind and compassionate heart; Hindus to be the indistinguishable, infinite *Brahman*. Monastic hospitality rests on this question: "What does the Divine want of me? What is the greatest good that I can achieve in this life?" Hospitality calls us to celebrate the bond that is much more powerful than our differences of culture and religion, and to invite visitors and pilgrims to share in the bounty of love.

Discipline

One of the more misunderstood aspects of monastic life is discipline. In my visits with the Benedictines, their respect for following the Rule of Benedict—a book of precepts written for monks by Benedict of Nursia (c. 480–550)—is realized as a living spiritual practice. The Abbot or Prioress of the monastery always seeks new ways of understanding monasticism in the context of contemporary life. The Rule holds the community together, gives the monks something to measure themselves against, and reminds them daily of the importance of solitude and reverence. Because the Rule fosters obedience to God and respect for fellow monks, each day serves as a model of contemplative love, each moment an opportunity to be grateful for the monastic way of life.

A person's life need not be predicated on society's materialistic concerns. It does not have to be based on the competition, ruthlessness, and lack of kindness we witness every day. There is another way of being. Yet, to live another way, requires discipline. We need daily reminders because we are human and we forget or become distracted. Monastic rules are designed to remind us that we can forgive, we can trust. We can look for the best instead of the worst in others; we can strive to be less rather than more; we can put our egos in abeyance, especially when they thwart our deepest desire.

The discipline maintained by elder monks is held naturally and easily. It is simply a living expression of the order of their lives. It is no different than what orders trees to bloom, or rivers to flow. For these monastics, the Rule is not externally imposed, but is an internally flowering expression of their vows, and thus brings luminosity to their daily existence. The internalization of the monastic rule at a cellular and soul level is vital, particularly in our contemporary culture, which can be disordered and distracted, with so many people desiring the kind of freedom that is not freedom at all.

Work as Service

Monastic communities recognize work as a means of spiritual development, especially the work of one's own hands. Work is help for prayer. During the long hours of solitary meditation, the desert monks did simple work like plaiting baskets or making ropes to avoid distraction and to anchor their thoughts. Many cenobitic monks do some form of manual labor like tilling in the fields, building fences, or making cheese. The monk gives up worldly commerce and in exchange is supported by the community, but shares in solidarity with other men and women outside the monastery by working in order to earn his or her living. Some of the world's monasteries are quite wealthy. Others are poor and self-supporting.

Monks perform individual acts of kindness and merciful service daily, while many monastic orders also function as charities in an organized way. The first Christian monasteries supported almshouses and hospitals for the poor, and much of Western civilization has benefitted from the charitable work of monks building schools and hospitals, and caring for the dying, homeless, displaced, and the poor. Throughout his teaching, Buddha was clear that we should do whatever we can to alleviate suffering, and to care for the sick and those struggling through disasters. Although charity was most often conceived as an individual act, more recently monks have applied Buddhist teaching to social and economic issues, such as the "Engaged Buddhism," proposed by Thich Nhat Hahn.

Freedom

Monasticism leads us away from bondage and toward the freedom of the true self. At times it can be difficult to uncover all that binds us. But monasticism is designed to liberate us from false desires and toward the soul's freedom of choice, a reality that the ego-self and the material world are simply unaware of. Being driven by self-will, we experience this unbinding as loss.

We must, at times, follow the obscure and uncomfortable path to uncover hidden layers of being. Thus, the monastic enclosure not only physically preserves a sanctuary for the holy, but also protects the monks from the intrusion of the world. As previously mentioned, the main obstacles to freedom are in the mind and soul, disturbed by its desires and passions. The process includes an analysis of the human heart, for peace is the fruit of striving to combat inner defects and to purify one's intentions.

Monks are not necessarily enlightened; they, too, sin, gossip, and create and suffer injury. However, it is within the difficulties and benefits of community that they learn what love really is. Love is not total dependency and identification. Rather, love is the integrity to stand in one's light and to also celebrate the light of others. Thus, detachment and its attendant ascetic practices are designed to foster freedom, to strengthen the monk's ability to ward off distractions and focus his or her heart on longing for the Ultimate.

"The whole purpose of the monastic life," writes Thomas Merton, "is to purify man's freedom from this 'stain' of servility which it has contracted by its enslavement to things that are beneath it. Hence the true monk is one who is perfectly free. Free for what? Free to love God."[2]

What is beneath us? We are in bondage to material things that we believe are important, necessary, and give life meaning. We are in bondage to an idea of what we have to do, be, and perform, and what the spiritual life is supposed to consist of. The desert monastics called these worldly illusions "demons," the shadow side of personality, where we are trapped by subservience and subjugation to temporal desires. These cultural demands are inferior to the luminosity of being that is already within us. Every day we trade the glorious for the mundane.

To achieve freedom requires a continual reaffirmation of our sacred existence in the midst of all that denies its validity. And certainly there are many things that refute the dignity of life—domestic violence, terrorism, war, starvation, and the misery of those who've been forced to flee as a result. Yet, if we succumb to this kind of thinking—the demons of despair—then we have given up on life. Abraham Joshua Heschel, who barely escaped the Holocaust (in Hebrew, *Shoah*, "catastrophe"), said his greatest fear was that humanity would succumb to despair and believe in the death of God. But despair is also the collapse of the self, and the destruction of hope. This is how we lose freedom. The freedom of being cannot be achieved in one lifetime because it is infinite. Thus monks work to eradicate the little demons of despair that constantly tug at faith. That is the goal of their effort: to be free to love God.

Rest

Monastic life can be arduous. It is not by any means an easy life, for the majority of monastic communities support themselves through making products to sell or tilling the land or working in schools and missions. Despite the fact that many monks lead active lives, there is a palpable presence of rest in monasteries. I believe this comes from the monks' hearts, which are resting in the divine. The monastic gives up the notion that a meaningful life has to follow the norms of civil society and have credibility on the world's terms. This can be a challenge or a significant struggle for someone who has lived with the opposite belief—The Puritan Work Ethic, for example—that doesn't allow for much rest.

In the spiritual traditions we talk about active and passive contemplation. Active contemplation refers to everything we do to bring ourselves closer to God—meditative practices, study, prayer. Passive contemplation is not the absence of a positive motion. Rather, it is the action of the divine in your being. It is God's work in you. It is here that we surrender to the divine within, sinking into the state of restful awareness. We listen to the Voice: *Come this way. Rest in me.* Agitation ceases, emotions steady.

We do not understand how un-restful we are until we experience divine rest. Much of the way we live does violence to the spirit, because it demands things that our true self has no intention of doing. We labor to fulfill obligations. But by being "useless" on the world's terms, we can live honorably and uphold our deepest commitments

If you desire to be monastic, you will find peace of heart when you realize that the Divine is already working in you, calling you to solitude. This is passive contemplation and divine rest, and the essence of the call to monkhood.

FIFTEEN

The Monastic Personality

IF THE MONK is a universal archetype, as Raimon Panikkar eloquently stated, then we all contain, to a greater or lesser degree, a monastic personality. We share a common mystical anthropology, by which I mean the study of humanity from the perspective of the spirit. Here, the deepest core of the person is situated in silence, in aloneness with the Divine source. The monastic personality reflects a particular type of temperament and personality trait especially evident in people whose contemplative nature has been awakened. I am not referring to a specific monastic expression—Zen or Tibetan, Benedictine or Carmelite monks, for example—each with its unique flavor, but to the universal, contemplative heart instilled in us and of which we are made.

Modern psychology has identified a variety of temperaments and personality maps; among the more popular are the Jungian and Enneagram types. While these valuable categories are widely used today, I set them aside in this chapter and focus instead on the spiritual characteristics of the person drawn to the monastic archetype. Found along every spectrum of personality—extroverted, introverted, intuitive, etc.—and in every profession and cultural context, the contemplative soul is uniquely attuned to spirit.

Qualities of the Monastic Personality

Need for Emptiness

While I believe that all humans have a monastic dimension, and would discover a deeper self-understanding if they sank into contemplation, it is also true that there are people who are especially called to silence and solitude. Like someone born with a unique musical or artistic talent, there are people who come into this world with a more open connection between the outer personality and the inner self. This particular type of personality needs space for emptiness, free from the world's demands, in order to develop his or her full potential.

Thomas Merton writes that there is a point of nothingness—*le pointe vierge*—at the center of our being. It is

> a point of pure truth, a point or spark which belongs entirely to God, which is never at our disposal, from which God disposes of our lies, which is inaccessible to the fantasies of our own mind or the brutalities of our own will. This little point of nothingness and of absolute poverty is the pure glory of God in us.... It is like a pure diamond, blazing with the invisible light of heaven. It is in everybody, and if we could see it, we would see these billions of points of light coming together in the face and blaze of a sun that would make all the darkness and cruelty of life vanish completely.[1]

Whereas others may thrive on the stimulation of daily activity and social networks, the contemplative person needs an environment of interiority, and one that is not excessively other-directed. When the nourishment that aloneness, solitude, and silence provide is not present, when a person is too active in the world, his or her soul suffers.

You may have wondered this about yourself: Why don't I fit in? Why are the activities and concerns that others find important not of interest to me? It's because you are awakening to the fact that you have tried to live in a mode of consciousness contrary to your deepest nature! It is important to realize that your desire to have time alone is not for selfish reasons; it is not to be distant from the world. It is food, nourishment for your soul. It is essential for your spiritual survival, and to function well in society.

Married to Silence

Each day, each person embarks on a journey from silence to speech, bringing unspoken and unseen worlds into form. Silence perfumes reality with its essence. Language, in a sense, is formed by the silent spaces between letters and words. We seek respite from external forms of noise in order to experience the silent place, where art, music, revelation, and other creative activities form.

The monastic personality ultimately discovers that regardless of personal attachments—whether one is married or unmarried, separated, has a partner or children, and so forth—a person's ultimate spiritual commitment is to the divine within. Once we accept that we are wedded to silence, it is easier to enter relations with an open heart, centered in *the center* without fracturing our bond to spirit, self, others. But if you have a contemplative soul and you neglect the need for silence, you will never make it in the world of relationships; you will always be fractured, pulled in contrary directions. Part of the problem is that you don't fully realize the extent and power of this interior desire. Thus, you are always trying to negotiate your relationships, but are never content.

Silence composes us; we simply have to uncover its hidden presence. By embracing silence, everything in life is included, and nothing is excluded. Every relationship has the potential to mirror and reflect the holy place within. In fact, when you finally accept your primary commitment, you will love and honor your relations more. You will feel more, and your connection to others will be strengthened. But to get to that place you must tell the world: Don't invade my silence. Don't possess my solitude. You must learn to be a fierce protector of, and advocate for, your inner monastery. None of us does this perfectly. We forget or get confused. But we have to remember what sustains us.

It is valuable to recognize the social constructions and familial impositions we learn in childhood about acceptable behavior. For example, I was taught that if you love someone, you are supposed to merge and be in each other's mind and reality constantly. This never felt right. I always sought solitude in nature. My parents could not understand my behavior and claimed I was detached and unsympathetic—a loner. But that wasn't the issue. I was ashamed to admit how happy I felt to be alone.

A person of contemplative temperament truly loves to be alone, without noise and distraction, in order to just *be*.

Thus, once you admit how important silence and solitude are in your life, relationships will change. Some will grow deeper, while others may wither. You'll be amazed how everything looks different, in a good way, when you accept this. When you make a vow to silence, you will be shown how to change your life. If you stop resisting and accept your need, it's easier and faster in the long run. Your resistance doesn't help at all, because resistance is a reaction. So you have to trust that spirit is working in you. Your search for truth is working in you, and it will show you the way.

Being in the absence of noise allows us to connect to the silence that created us. It allows us to concentrate, to bring our energies into focus and deeply listen. Prayer and meditation retrain body, mind, and spirit, uncovering our original, pure nature. When we consent to sink into the silent well at the center of being, Presence is there. Here spiritual activity arises from non-action, action that is a spontaneous movement of the heart. It is not self-willed, but a purely motiveless movement of the Divine in you.

Permeable Soul

A person with a contemplative temperament often has a pliable or permeable soul, naturally receptive to the Divine. Of course, every person ultimately has a mystical soul. But in a person born with an affinity toward contemplation, the veils between divinity and humanity are thinned. At times, such a person finds it difficult—and often doesn't know how—to distinguish between worlds, or establish boundaries with others. In the Divine, however, boundaries are not necessary. Nothing is rejected; communion between spirit and the soul is a natural flow, like a river moving without obstructions. There is no need for boundaries because nothing is false, nothing is harmful, nothing is unloving. You can *be* fully yourself.

There is a tendency of the contemplative soul to misread the world, to see others in light of a higher reality, and not to see the limits of a person's current understanding or love. One of the monastic personality's great lessons is to discern the practical aspects of life, without idealizing spirituality or viewing others through a mystical lens. Similarly, the permeable soul will be absorptive of energies in its environment and must learn to guard its divine enclosure. This is where spiritual practices are invaluable because they train us to recognize our energy and to distinguish it from energies that are not our own.

Sensitivity to Suffering

The person of mystical temperament usually displays an unusual depth of sensitivity to others, even from a young age, and often is in touch with the mystical dimension of life. As children, most of us probably didn't understand or were afraid of our sensitivity. Perhaps our attunement to the fragile web of life was suppressed or injured. Or the denial of an intimate resonance with the living universe led to harmful ramifications, affecting one's health, relationships, and search for meaning and love.

Due to a natural openness and intuitive grasp of reality, the monastic personality has a natural ability to identify with, draw out, and bear another's pain and suffering. Striving to heal injustices and imbalances—actions often accomplished intuitively—such a person often is not aware he or she is doing anything. The monastic personality also is susceptible to the absorption or accumulation of other people's emotions, thoughts, and psychic scars. This ability is particularly strong in childhood when the ego identity is not established and energetic imprints can take hold. Often a lifetime is spent struggling through these unearned and unwanted obligations.

Since the soul feels more profoundly than the body, acts of violence that injure sentient beings, damage Earth, and destroy communities open a wound in the consciousness. This capacity to experience mystical solidarity with others' suffering is inherent in people who have a compassionate heart. At the same time, the heightened sensitivity to and compassion for others can be confusing, because a person may not be able to separate the pain of the world from his or her own.

An anonymous medieval author, in a chapter titled, "How the Friend of God Suffers," describes four ways that a true friend of God suffers: in one's actions, will, soul, and in God. Here he writes about soul suffering:

> The third suffering of a friend of God occurs in his soul when the spirit is seized by the divine spirit. God's garment of love is so wrapped around her [the soul] that she relies on it and this bond becomes so pleasant that she finds everything else unpleasant. If the friend of God then meets anything which does not spring from the Holy Spirit, it causes him pain. And all that he sees and hears, all that is not divine, pains him and causes him suffering.[2]

The above quote conveys an important theme for the monastic-type person: the wise author knew that those who love share in whatever wounds the Holy. They feel God's suffering in their souls; they experience the desecration of the sacred in their bones; they lament the death of innocence in their hearts. Like prophets they cry out, demanding that people awaken.

If you are born as a sensitive soul, you will biospiritually react to things that are harsh or that violate your integrity. Our bodies respond, communicating through illness, anxiety, fear, and other physical disturbances. Yet it is this same sensitivity that fosters intuitive awareness, and receptivity to change. When the soul is aligned and connected, openness to the sensate and somatic energies of life can become a source of wisdom and inner strength.

The monastic personality, attuned to the subtle vibrations of sentient life, tends to be a healer, absorbing the anguish and affliction of the world around him or her without conscious intention or volition. Such a person cannot help being united, one, with the entire web of creation. But it is therefore vital that the monastic grow in spirit by harnessing meditative and prayer practices, which stabilize the heart and expand the person's inner light.

Thrives on Reflective Work

The monastic personality thrives on reflective work, on seeking truth, and is empowered when truth is experienced, acknowledged, or heard. For example, think of times when you may have been distraught or upset. If someone is able to explain the spiritual truth about your situation, there is the experience, "Oh, I feel better." Whereas other personalities may not be interested in these spiritual depths, or get upset when confronted with deeper insight, finding it to be uncomfortable and necessitating a reaction. But the person who has a contemplative personality needs the acknowledgement of spiritual wisdom. He or she thrives on it, and when truth is obscure, there is pain.

Many people have experienced difficult childhoods because of unacknowledged feelings and untruths within our household environments. There was no permission or safe environment by which to address these unspoken realities. This need for a deeper, reflective engagement—to have emotional truth affirmed—may have set you apart from your family and made you believe you didn't belong. But really, where you belong is in the family found in the depth of spirit.

Thus, a person of this type can feel alienated in conventional situations where platitudes are the norm, as well as in relationships where people refuse to be emotionally truthful. For example, the monastic personality often has a difficult time with empty chatter, or cocktail party small talk. It can actually be wearing and wearying. It's not that you're antisocial; it's actually that your true self can't take it.

Like a redwood tree, which grows only in a specialized region of Earth, the monastic person thrives in an environment that is spiritually open to wisdom. The most honest thing you can do for yourself is to be truthful about your spiritual life. Whatever else you may or may not be able to give—material gifts, intellectual goods, and so forth—be a fierce advocate for the pure center that seeks truth.

Need for Freedom

When I say that the monastic personality has an intense need for freedom, I refer to the self-integrity that cannot be co-opted by anyone or anything. For such a person, the freedom to find one's own way and to make one's own mistakes is essential.

The need for freedom often runs counter to the wishes of family, friends, colleagues, and even monastic companions who either don't understand you or who ridicule you (or both). But happiness comes from following—often blindly and in the dark—where you are being called. So the monastic person has to become a very strong and determined person who is paradoxically very open. As St. Teresa of Avila advised her monastic sisters, we must practice *"una grande y muy determinada determinación"*—a great and very determined determination. If you get pushed down, get back up. Someone tells you "No," tell yourself "Yes." This determination is pursued not by following your own will, but by the grace of the Divine will, guiding you to your inherent freedom of being.

Again, the personality who seeks inner freedom often finds it difficult to understand how relationships work. But once we accept why our need is so intense, we will find others who also value freedom and solitude. In 1904, the poet Rainer Maria Rilke, in *Letters to a Young Poet*, encapsulates how the freedom of solitude sustains and empowers relationship:

> This advance (at first very much against the will of the outdistanced men) will transform the love experience, which is now filled with error, will change it from the ground up, and reshape it into a relationship that is meant to be between one human being and another, no longer one that flows from man to woman. And this more human love (which will fulfill itself with infinite consideration and gentleness, and kindness and clarity in binding and releasing) will resemble what we are now preparing painfully and with great struggle: the love that consists in this: that two solitudes protect and border and greet each other.[3]

The person of monastic temperament feels this liberating call very intensely: to be free from all definitions; oppressive cultural, religious, and gender roles; and social constructions that are harmful to the interior life.

A Place Apart

The spiritual person needs to create designated times to be apart from society in order to be with alone with Mystery. He or she will seek natural places of solitude—forests, oceans, deserts, or mountains—as well as established spiritual environments, such as a retreat center, monastery, or church. This ability to be alone, and to stand away from the crowd is a positive attribute that prepares one's heart to listen for the divine voice. The posture of being alone is necessary, especially in deep spiritual states, to preserve inner wisdom, and to distance the ego from the temptation of distractions such as popularity, intelligence, and fame.

We all find ways to preserve the right to be alone. My use of the word "right" is intentional, because I consider solitude of self to be a spiritual right, on the same level as other universal rights. Perhaps as a child you learned to distance yourself from anything that was violating body or spirit. You found ways to stabilize your emotions by separating from family dynamics. Or, you escaped false silence, the silence that is deafening by what it is not saying, by what it refuses to say.

The Indigenous Peoples who revere the Earth and honor the spirit of place interconnect with the sacred bonds of silence. They understood that wilderness is necessary for the human soul, and if wild places are not preserved, our humanity is impaired and Earth's sovereignty overrun. They wisely intuited that all living beings require spaces of pure emptiness, untainted by human activity or development. Similarly, the American naturalists—John Muir, Aldo Leopold, and others—who advocated for the preservation of vast tracts of pristine land bestowed upon us the priceless gift of solitude.

As monks living in the modern world, we can replicate a tiny portion of their vision by honoring all holy sites, creating solitary prayer or meditation spaces in our homes, and by dedicating our hearts as "wild places"— where we enter to rest in our inner monastery, alone with Mystery.

Communicating the Deep Self

People who have a contemplative consciousness often have difficulty communicating the deep self. Because the deep self is unnamed—a mystery that belongs to spirit alone, it is seldom given space in popular culture. We may suffer for many years with the notion that we cannot communicate who we are to others. Perhaps we think this inability is a particular malady of modern, Western societies. Perhaps it is. But Black Elk, the Oglala Lakota medicine man, describes in *Black Elk Speaks* his difficulty as a child telling his family about his vision of the six Grandfathers. Although visionary experience and spiritual ritual were a regular part of the Lakota culture, Black Elk feared he would not be understood.

> When I got back to my father and mother and was sitting up there in our tepee, my face was still all puffed and my legs and arms were badly swollen; but I felt good all over and wanted to get right up and run around. My parents would not let me. They told me I had been sick twelve days, lying like dead all the while, and that Whirlwind Chaser, who was Standing Bear's uncle and a medicine man, had brought me back to life. I knew it was the Grandfathers in the Flaming Rainbow Tepee who had cured me; but I felt afraid to say so. . . .
>
> Everybody was glad that I was living; but as I lay there thinking about the wonderful place where I had been and all that I had seen, I was very sad; for it seemed to me that everybody ought to know about it, but I was afraid to tell, because I knew that nobody would believe me, little as I was, for I was only nine years old. Also, as I lay there thinking of my vision, I could see it all again and feel the meaning with a part of me like a strange power glowing in my body; but when the part of me that talks would try to make words for the meaning, it would be like fog and get away from me.[4]

There seems to be a kind of universal difficulty in expressing not only internal truths, but also the visionary worlds that many contemplative personalities experience. We may find few people with whom we feel safe to communicate. And so when we discover people or communities with whom we can share, we should treasure them.

One of the maturing aspects of the monastic life is that we overcome the fear of speaking. Since the natural tendency of this personality is to prefer silence, it often requires a conscious intention to overcome the sense of feeling unsafe, and instead takes on the mantle of making changes. *I am going to speak.* The monastic personality can tend to feel misunderstood, or alienated by the lack of genuine friendships, but by sharing his or her inner world, that person can become a voice of healing and transformation.

Dying to Self

The mystical personality is often capable of moving back and forth between the permeable membranes of divine and human realities, or visionary and intellectual worlds. There is a fluidity of the self that knows how to spiritually let go without actually physically dying. What is defined as "self" is not a discrete entity or static identity, but "nothingness"—the dynamic motion of flowing in and through a spectrum of consciousness.

If this natural ability to move seamlessly through realities is stifled, rejected, denied, or hidden, it can be detrimental to one's spiritual, mental, and physical health. For example, your religion or relations may impose restrictions on what is actually possible to believe, feel, and see. You may have been told, as Teresa of Avila was by her male confessors, that your spiritual visions and way of prayer are bad, from the devil. And, like her, you may have tormented yourself, wondering what is wrong, why are you so sinful? After years of pain, Teresa eventually realizes that these accusations were not designed to help her root out selfishness or error, or even initiate a process of dying to self, but were aimed at suppressing her true nature.

The monastic personality balks against the constriction of its natural rhythm—it is like a dying, a real dying—because such a person finds meaning in the ability to move between realities, to flow unimpeded with the spirit. In such cases, patterns in the brain can become configured in ways that are antithetical to our true nature, which can lead to fractures or wounds in the personality and to much confusion. Then the rhythm of our being is distorted, unable to access the divine within or shed the ego's hold.

The ability to spiritually die to self without physically dying is one of the miraculous gifts of being alive. We should practice dying to self, and celebrate our capacity to participate in the process of death and rebirth that earthly and spiritual realms actualize every moment.

Contradiction and Paradox

Contradiction and paradox are intrinsic to this life. It is possible to receive spiritual illuminations, and even be touched by mystical union, and still be a flawed and struggling personality. We live in contradiction because the human person is not fully formed. We are born to participate in and co-create divinity on Earth. Our flaws, karmas, and sins are part of what we are working to resolve in the world, striving to transform our hearts. We should not be surprised that we still seek to be whole. Our imperfections and sins are not evidence that the Divine is not present with us, that we cannot change things. They are the fuel that motivate prophetic action and teach us about redemption.

Perhaps this is the original human story of tragedy: that we are granted divine life and we are still flawed. But this is what being human entails—we are beings who stand at the juncture of Heaven and Earth, wisdom and ignorance, love and despair. We have to honor both, by having compassion for our foibles and by our willingness to be transformed.

More than anything, the monastic personality needs to experience mercy and compassion for one's self. Because of a native sensitivity, this type of personality can be excessively self-critical, viewing one's sins with a magnifying glass. It is thus necessary that we experience humor and gentleness, and grant to ourselves the love that the divine has for us.

Called to Contemplation

A monk seeks a meditative and prayerful existence. But there are signs that a person is called deeper into contemplation. These include a desire for more solitude; the move from active to passive contemplation, with attendant confrontation with sins or spiritual impasse; and disaffection with prior ways of living and being, even those that previously gave solace or pleasure.

Additional signs might include a heightened awareness of your life and relationships, and an inability to balance the pull of the inner life with the demands of job, family, career, and so forth. You may feel tension between the Divine, which is drawing you into deeper communion, and daily obligations, which pull you into social engagements and a go-go-go lifestyle. Or, you may feel an habitual attraction to going out, to denying your deepest need, and to attending activities that are against your wishes, perpetuating and re-creating demands that keep you busy and fractured, without a chance to catch your breath let alone practice meditation or prayer in a genuine, non-hurried manner.

Associated with the movement into deep contemplation are feelings of doubt, dryness, despair, and general dissatisfaction with one's life that are occurring at a subterranean level. Where you once found consolation in prayer, or had a community that supported you, or experienced love, now you are in darkness and can't rely on anything that worked before. These experiences can throw you into a kind of desolation. Oftentimes, these feeling states are not even in your conscious mind. You just don't feel the same, but you don't know why.

These are some of the uplifting and challenging signs of being drawn deeper into the mystical life proper. There are positive signs: seeking silence, thriving alone, experiencing God's work in your soul. And then there are the painful signs: wounding, desolation, isolation, tension, impasse, and darkness. In all these ways, you are being led by the action of the spirit into the mystery of divine life.

There is a nuanced difference between the contemplative call to solitude and isolation. Acknowledging the monk within is a way of transcending isolation and seeing the blessing it offers in the form of solitude.

Living in Sacral Time

The monastic personality is made to live in God's time. The person drawn into intimate communion with the Divine cedes his or her worldly concept of time to flow in the waters of the sanctification of time. Here every hour is precious and unique; every moment imbued with Presence.

To enter and experience the holiness of each day, we must go away from the clamor and labor of the world and from, writes Abraham Joshua Heschel, the "betrayal in embezzling" our lives.

> Six days a week we wrestle with the world, wringing profit from the earth; on the Sabbath we especially care for the seed of eternity planted in the soul. . . . . Labor is a craft, but perfect rest is an art. . . . . the seventh day is a *palace in time* which we build. [This is] the love of the Sabbath.[5]

An astonishing benefit accrues from giving up the incessant demand for activity and allowing our souls to bask in divine light. By sinking into the holiness of time, the contemplative person makes progress through inaction. Our time is not God's time. When we follow the rhythm of what is eternal and immaterial, we have entered an enchanted universe—a freedom of being and a sanctuary of rest. Taking a long-term perspective, the monastic personality recognizes the role of patience in following the way of Sabbath, and the blossoming of love in one's heart.

· ◆ ·

THE PERSON OF MONASTIC TEMPERAMENT exists—consciously or intuitively—in mystical discourse with the expanse of creation. He or she is constituted to participate in the spiritual realms and to share in the fate of the world. While daily busyness surrounds us, the contemplative personality makes progress through holy inaction. This is not a refusal of engagement, but a more authentic commitment to develop a mature humanity, giving of one's self to others and honoring the monastic call.

SIXTEEN

The Monastic Ideal

THE NEW MONK, seeking a deeper orientation to the Divine, often struggles to convert his or her worldly existence into a more spiritually attuned life. This occurs in part because we tend to think of monasticism the way we think about everything else: something we have to do, make happen, accomplish, or achieve. But the contemplative or monastic life is a reversal of this attitude that we are in charge, that our will alone can motivate change, that we can get by in the normal frame of reference. What is shattering about monastic spirituality is that it aspires toward a state of receptivity, in which nothing impedes the inflow of mystery. It is a life of humility and non-violence, of peace and love, but mostly it is a life that has surrendered the self in an act of unknowing. This means to let go of the mental gymnastics disturbing the mind and instead simply experience a moment of openness.

Initially, we approach contemplation from the intellect and the rational mind. But contemplation is a state of non-doing, a consciousness without division—a consciousness of one-ing. Non-doing defies the structures of language in which we normally think, because we are not educated to understand unitive awareness, the wholeness of things. It also defies religious realms because it is beyond identified spiritual states: verbal prayer, metaphysical systems, theological orthodoxy, all of which are the fruit of active consciousness. Contemplation is more mysterious.

We are drawn away from the known into the unknown, from active into passive consciousness. This is because contemplation is entrance into the divine life itself, which only can be grasped through direct experience.

The mystery of contemplation is often associated with a quality of being that is surrendered, receptive, vulnerable, compassionate, and merciful. True contemplation is so tender, so devoid of violence, punishment, or judgment that our minds cannot grasp its essence. It is the divine's secret speaking in our souls. Secret, because it is an intimacy so total, that it cannot be fully expressed.

We resist intimacy. We are more concerned with wanting to be appreciated and successful. We want to be respected, recognized, or rewarded. We want to be perfect. These aspirations can be categorized as a form of self-violence. Contemplation is peace, a solitude of self that gives up the incessant quest to be somebody, to do some thing, to be acknowledged, to have all the answers, to insist that reality measures up to one's demand.

A Reverse Perspective

Monasticism is an unlearning of the personality characteristics and social advancement valorized in culture and the quest to achieve that marks the climate of contemporary life. This incessant demand to be recognized infects the purity of the soul every day. Impregnated into the personality, it controls what constitutes success and how a person is situated within society. Motivated by our own desires and our own will, rather than by the will of the Divine, we do what we want and then offer it to the Divine for approval. We do not think first and foremost: What does Spirit want of me?

The mature person undergoes trials and pain, seeking to be transformed into the numinous light. Thus, you can see that monasticism is the reverse perspective of how the world operates. The "worldly" is not seeking the highest spiritual aspiration of the human being, ethics, or the planet. It pursues expediency and self-motivation.

The monk aspires each day to humanity's spiritual potential, which affects everything: what one does, how one lives, and one's relationship to money, possessions, and so forth. This aspiration is highly personal, as a person works to transform whatever is diminished by the world into a more spiritually integrated mode of consciousness. The heart feels what is lacking, and reaches out to transform and heal, because interior to the self is love. Although we may never have experienced love, we know what it is. And because we know love, we suffer. If we didn't know love, we wouldn't suffer. We suffer because we know the path of radical love, and our heart reaches for it.

The reverse perspective of monasticism means that we submit; we say "yes" to the wisdom that elevates our lives and activities. We consent. We have the freedom to refuse, to say "no." But the monk is distinguished by his or her consent. This is the vow. I may move very slowly, I may be a turtle, or a snail, but I say "yes!" *Show me the path. Open my heart. Live in me.*

The process of establishing a divine perspective in the monk's heart takes time and grows incrementally as he or she learns to let go of ego attachments. We suffer because we resist movement into the sacred. We don't intend to rebel or struggle. But we have been trained to fear change and to deny the transcendent. As we divest the ego of falsehood, denial and fear can flood the mind, and obscure the heart. In these moments, it is important to remember that letting go is for our great benefit. It is cause for celebration, to experience inner paradise now!

Monasticism is not essentially about cloister, robe, or ceaseless meditation. While these are central aspects of many monastic lifestyles, the heart turns away from worldly attractions that inhibit our receptivity to God within. It is an unlearning of the theologies, divine names, metaphysical systems, and spiritual demands that identify and conscript our direct contact with reality. It is also an unlearning of dualism, from personal to esoteric levels of awareness: self and other, mine and yours, God and soul, male and female, rationality and intuition. The monk, in her or his small way, protests the buying and selling of the soul.

The most astounding thing about the interior life is accepting that you are beloved and cared for by the Divine. There is a force of consciousness working in you for the good. This is the shock of the monastic life—not asceticism, not nonattachment—that we are the recipients of divine love, continually.

Because contemplation is often counter to how we live out our lives, the reverse perspective of monasticism can be unsettling, challenging how and why we do things. Even the degree to which we have learned to surrender and to give up our will, there is more. There is always that mysterious capacity for intimacy, which will never be exhausted.

At times, contemplation is associated with passivity. What is the difference between passivity and passive consciousness? Passivity is what we do when we don't do anything. In other words, we accept the status quo. Many of us are passive in this sense. We get stuck in the banality of social consensus, and don't believe it is possible to change. Even our lament, blame, anger, and protest can be forms of passivity. This is not passive consciousness. Rather, passive contemplation involves inner receptivity and humility; a state of being that is vulnerable to the action of the Divine in one's core.

In order to be effective, the monk uses meditation and prayer to uproot the incessant mind chatter, which clouds the soul and obscures direct experience. Instead, the monk takes the stance of nonviolent protest: "I refuse these thoughts!" Most of us don't take that step. We wallow in our weakness, in defeat.

The monk within us seeks self-wisdom. It is the practice of understanding our unique energies, how we respond to the world, and why certain actions and not others affect us. It requires a refined and conscious awareness of the self, at the same time being divested of "self." It requires dispassionate awareness of the ego in order to clearly distinguish wisdom from other forms of consciousness. It is a way of being vigilant and attentive to the influx of ideas, sentiments, and emotions that intrude on a person's inner peace. It requires that we learn, train, and practice the art of being the guardian of our own divinity. It is a life activity, this process of considering that everything in one's life—family, children, partners, work, food, play—provides an opportunity to restore and ignite the divine spark in the world.

Prayer, meditation, and awareness spiritualize our energy. It is difficult to raise one's energy when we harbor negative beliefs about the self and fear we never will achieve spiritual wisdom. The transformation of consciousness also has to be a transformation of the attachment to self. We think we are honest when we say, "I can't do it," but this is simply another naming. While it is easy to see arrogance and pride as self-attachment, one of the more insidious identifications is unworthiness or inadequacy.

The Divine reveals no ultimate dichotomies, opposites, or negativity. It is purity itself, which eludes naming, but includes all wisdom—love, compassion, mercy, grace, benevolence. When we diminish ourselves and deny our sacred origins, we create division in our hearts. We create an opposite that doesn't exist! Then the fullness of divine life can only break into us when we are not paying attention, when we have a moment of "weakness." This is why so often conversion and mystery come through suffering, tragedy, and illness.

Many of the world's mystics have been imprisoned, martyred, or exiled. The prison serves as a metaphor, illustrating how violent the world is and how far away it is from God. Why would love, non-violence, and intimacy be threatening? Why would peace incite violence?

Buddha asks: who is the one who dies, who is the one who hurts? *Anatta*—no self. He clarifies the illusory nature of a fixed identity. We have to transform our attachment to memories, especially bad memories. The repetition of memory solidifies consciousness and leads to stagnation of being. This inner or spiritual stagnation manifests in the cells and energy of the body, and may be expressed as immovability or rigidity.

The monk also abandons attachment to negative or obsessive thoughts and emotions. How painful it is to let go of remorse and anger at one's self! How often do we hold onto thoughts expressed as "I could have done better, been better?" Liberation becomes a reality when we experience the truth of a benevolent and compassionate universal force. It's staggering and can be frightening that everything is forgiven in the Merciful Heart.

Ultimately, the transformation of consciousness that monasticism ushers in divests us of religious images handed down through the generations. This state of consciousness beyond divine names is both luminous and obscure. Luminous because it is infused by divine light, a blazing light of brilliance, obscure because it cannot be ascertained. For this reason, enclosure is beneficial. Here, again, we turn to the passive consciousness of contemplation, for it is God alone who takes us beyond God. The inner transformation that occurs in monastic reversal is always in dynamic movement toward letting go, toward liberation. This capacity is built into our nature. It is simple—we are constantly in search of God. While this quest may be impeded by pain and confusion, our job is to cast off these impediments so we are always moving in the direction of the "not-yet." If we think we can remain static, have finally arrived, and can cease to be self-aware, then we don't understand the inner life. Deep within there is a willingness to never let anything impede our access to peace and to love.

Sometimes we get stuck. We think we are our sins and our karmas. We think we are someone else's words, someone else's heart, or someone else's mind. But only as we search for the undefiled state do we find the liberating force at the core of being, the divine desert that frees our souls, where Mystery speaks to us anew and we co-create a sacred world here and now. The path is active and passive, intentional and unintentional, full and empty, conventional and radical, but always a movement of the heart toward truth. We can only pray to be guided to this awareness each day and to find the courage to attend to the path of radical openness. If we do this, we will walk the way of liberation and we will be happy.

May we have the courage and strength of heart to practice the liberation of self for each other, for our relations, and for all living and non-living beings. May we participate in the great journey of spirit. May we discover peace, may the divine be in our hearts forever.

SEVENTEEN

The Deep Self

F ROM A MYSTICAL POINT OF VIEW, the deep or true self is not an individual identity or personality, but rather the openness or nothingness of being that belongs to the entire cosmos. "Nothingness" in this context means communion, surrender, and intimacy, where your being and the divine being are without distinguishing attributes; they are undivided, nondual. This is the moment of utter spontaneity, just openness itself. It is a state of vulnerability at the center of being that belongs entirely to the Divine.

To know the deep self is to recognize that you will always be on the way, basking in the paradox of fullness and emptiness, knowing and unknowing, living and dying. It is these paradoxes and contradictions that draw us into contemplation. The deep self has the capacity to travel back and forth between living and dying now. It is not a fixed or stable state, but the flow of universal consciousness pouring through and in all forms.

The deep self is groundless. Groundlessness is before every beginning, the place of the infinitely deep, the Deep that is also you. The true self is always before the beginning, emerging from the point of emergence. Whereas the personality or identified self is restricted by names and emotions—an entity called "self" or "myself"—the true self is limitless, formless, unfettered by images and attributes.

The true self is revealed through a continual un-formation process, or letting go of everything divisive in us. This is the universal consciousness—Great Spirit, Mystery—the place of zero. When you consent to being zero—nothing—then your whole being radiates the eternal light. Thus, a person's search for the Divine, the search for one's true self, is never a selfish, individual act. It becomes universalized in the process.

A deconstruction of the false or ego self often is initiated by sorrow or suffering over one's self-absorption and self-limitation. This turning away from self-interest is spurred by recognition of the abundance we have been given and how little we give in return. Our world is sustained by the labor of all beings: microorganisms, ants, spiders, trees, flowers, fish, animals, mountains, air, water, and people. What do we give back?

Perhaps we believe that we can give to God in the esoteric sense, but we can't give to our fellow humans who are here now. Contrariwise, we can give things to other people, but we are not going to give anything to God, because we don't know who or what God is. Both of these errors of reciprocity are related to the construction of the personality: the self that is co-opted for worldly purposes, the self as consumer, who achieves at the expense of others. The false self is cultivated for gain and achievement; it seeks recognition and satisfaction. Its untempered need becomes a subterranean, insistent drone that justifies possessiveness, and is the cause of so much sorrow.

The deep self, the point of nothingness, can never be possessed; it cannot be owned or developed, it cannot be perfected. It already *is* what it is; it is Mystery in Mystery.

Our true subjectivity is seeking to accomplish nothing, not even contemplation. It's not trying to pray, it is not trying to be holy. It is not trying to get ahead. It is not trying to do anything; it is moving in the waters of divinity, in the waters of sacred time. But since we all have to achieve a certain degree of material well-being in order to survive, it is difficult to live according to God's time. We are always on someone else's time. If you cannot at this point transform your life in order to live in spiritual time, then at least recognize the conflict that you feel. Because the more you are pulled toward the deep self, the more you are called to sacred time. "Be with me," the Holy says. "Come with me. Let us communicate. Let us share the deepest kind of love."

There is a natural rhythm to the divine flow within you. It is a different rhythm of being, and it can easily be diverted and distracted by the noise and busyness of the world. Monastic communities ritualize sacred time through liturgy and established patterns of behavior, prayer, and meditation. Yet even in monasteries there is the pull to live outside the holy bonds of ritual, and even monks struggle to hear the spirit speaking in their souls.

Being Nothing

In seeking the true self, the trauma that you have to face is that perhaps you will be deemed worthless or a failure in the world's eyes. You have to be prepared to achieve no result at all, or a result in opposition to your expectation. To commit to the true self is difficult, especially in our media-driven culture, where we are bombarded with images of the best-selling book or movie; television pundits discussing the world's issues; multi-millionaire preachers hawking prosperity and self-actualization. These cultural images impress on a person's being that—without a certain level of achievement—you are nothing. The relentless media onslaught reinforces feelings of despair, loneliness, or alienation, and can raise questions of how a person fits in society, how his or her life can be of worth.

The true self does not stop achieving or making an effort to contribute to society. But all acts are made under a paradox or contradiction, between one's inner quest to be "nothing" and an outer desire to achieve. It is an act of faith to just *be*, without knowing whether your efforts will, in fact, achieve anything, without building a new, false identity.

This tension, or contradiction, is a shared experience of suffering. But, from a monastic perspective, when you acknowledge the tension, then you are going in the right direction. It is accepting that the world may never understand what you do or where you must go. This acceptance becomes the fertile ground in which to grow a different, more meaningful, life. It also shifts the focus from thinking that you are in charge and that your needs and wants are at the center, to the divine being at the center of your life. It is not so much about what you feel or what you think, as it is what the spirit wants and what the spirit is calling you toward. It is about the depth that is drawn out of you. At the same time, it is going to be the Divine working through you to transform and universalize you, so that you become more hollowed out, and more uniquely yourself. It's not about your psychological states: why you feel bad, why you are not fulfilled, why you are not on your path, why you are failing, why you are worthless. It's about the Divine longing in you.

The desert *ammas* and *abbas* had a number of sayings that illustrate this point. A pilgrim would arrive at the door of a monk's hut with a whole litany of problems: I'm spiritually bored. I'm not getting anywhere. I don't feel anything. The *amma* or *abba* would say (paraphrasing), "So what. Big deal. The spiritual life is taking place in you, whether you know where you are going, whether or not you have felt God." Teresa of Avila struggled for more than twenty years, not sure where she was going or if she was on the right path. I once had a former student write that she experienced twenty-seven years of continual dryness, where she didn't feel like there was any contact with God. And then all of a sudden, out of the blue—illumination!

Yes, we do want to help each other. Yes, we do want to guide each other along the way. But, in the monastic cell—literal or figurative—everything is being resolved. You have to find that proper balance between when you need help, when you need a spiritual guide or teacher, and when you need to just sit in your cell and say: "Get over it. It's all being taken care of. There is nothing that I can identify." Where is the moment of faith, when will I accept that I live in paradox, accept that I live in groundlessness, accept that my life is never going to totally "add up"? Because life is inscrutable, it never totally "adds up."

This is the true, mystical self: Living and accepting paradox. Living, and accepting, that one's focus is always self-centered. I don't say this in any pejorative sense. It just is. Every person stands where he or she stands. But a self-centered focus is not operable in the mystical life. It isn't that you are egocentric or that you are doing something wrong. It is simply that it doesn't work. You can berate yourself; you can lay yourself on the ground. Nothing is going to change that in sacred time, you will be taken where you need to go. Yes, you prepare the ground. Yes, you continue your devotions. Yes, you are loyal to dryness and emptiness. These psychological and emotional states are real and have value. But at a certain point, they need to be let go. You need to be able to tell yourself, "So what. Get over it!"

Therefore, as you develop inner solitude, a shift happens in which your consciousness is not as self-motivated as it once was; is not as self-focused or self-analyzing as it was. Things become simpler and more ordinary. There is a certain part of your spiritual life where you may have had visions and spiritual consolation. Then, as the spiritual life matures and grows deeper, these mystical states may diminish and sometimes disappear. Your experiences become less extravagant because you are consenting to a reality so *Other* that it can only be just what it is.

This path of the nothingness of self brings up questions: Are you willing and ready to walk the path? How many spiritual commitments can you make? How many books can you read, how many teachers can you study with, before you make the decision? How long will it take you to admit, "I don't know if this path is going to take me to spiritual union. I don't know if I'm even worthy of going there. But my whole being wants to go there. My whole being is finally saying, *now*." The paradox of nothingness removes the fundamental ego-thirst to be someone, to be something; to make the world sit up and take notice of one's self. And the reason that detachment or emptiness thwarts those efforts is that it is more spontaneous, more natural, and more organic. It is not contrived; it is not something you set out to do.

We can't understand how radical this relinquishing of identity is until we experience it, until the Divine takes action in our souls. Until something finally shakes us up. Because, until we get to this place—even when we practice emptiness—we are not empty. Even when we pray for humility, we are not humble. Even when we desire to be nothing, we are something. And this is the radical path of the monk: to pray to be empty, to meditate on nothing. To find where God dwells, you must go by way of what you are not. We will never understand this until it is experienced.

The action of the Divine in the ground of love takes us to a deeper, more solitary transformation. This singular contemplation heightens the aloneness we suffer in the world of humanity, commerce, and materialism. It is by being a marginal figure that the monk is able to pierce the veils of reality, to *see* divine love flowing through the veins of history. Rabbi Abraham Joshua Heschel says that the prophet is the one who feels in his or her being the compassion and suffering of the world, and cries out in anguish. The intensity of divine pathos inhabits the voice of the prophet, who speaks about injustice. The prophetic voice is not a voice of achievement; it's not a voice of accomplishment. It's simply the voice of divine intensity in us.

The challenge for the contemplative person resides in his or her ability to be groundless, to be poor of "self." Much of monastic practice is about protecting one's right to be free from another's identity or persuasion. It is the right to be "one's own person." But, to achieve the freedom of the true self, you have to continually be alert to becoming "something." This requires continual sacrifice, emptiness. Otherwise, you become "teacher," or "guru," or "great author." In the openness of divine love, there are no names. Of course, every such journey is always imperfect—and so it should be.

Living each moment aware of our own nothingness moves us into a new order of being. True activism is living an alternative life. It's not about whether you are a social activist; it's about finding what is an alternative life for you. This requires relinquishing of—among other things—intellectual pride.

Apatheia

In the *Confessions of St. Augustine,* Augustine recounts his struggle with intellectual sophistication. Educated to be a rhetorician, he leaves behind the life of the academy and the philosophy of Manichaeism in order to find faith. Similarly, Merton abandons a scholarly life and the career of a popular writer to become a monk. When asked by reporters or other curious individuals to define his work, Gandhi said he was a weaver and a gardener. My monastic friends—many of whom have advanced degrees or are renowned in their field—similarly seek the least identity, one that is almost nameless: "I am a monk." Each discovered how his or her worldly identity could become a burden, an excuse to not probe more deeply, or generate hubris and exceptionality.

The practice of letting go of the attributes of personality requires the cultivation of disinterest in one's self, what the early Christian monastics call *apatheia*. While related to the word "apathy," apatheia has a specific nuance: It is not disinterest in others or in the world, but in the self's needs and will. It refers to an interior struggle against inordinate attachments. It is a kind of mature mindfulness that seeks to transform the emotions— anger, fear, anxiety, doubt—that dominate or control inner peace.

Disinterest or *apatheia* teaches us to intentionally let go of all that keeps us from a single-minded pursuit of truth: feelings and thoughts that bind us, cravings and addictions that diminish our sense of worth, and attachments to self-imposed perfectionism. It is nourished by simplicity of soul. It's not a selfish action. It's not a move into exclusion for your own needs and desires. It's an awareness and recognition that you have been called. When you realize how often you are distracted, you suddenly understand how little you have given in return for all that the Creator has given you. It is easy to ignore these realizations, because we tell ourselves, "God could not be calling me." But, this is a convenient excuse that prevents us from facing the fact that we are called. It is not our ego or false self that seeks to be a devotee.

What distracts are all the "shoulds" and "oughts" that you have accumulated in your social and religious formation. The denial or refusal of the divine call manifests in everyone's life. You're sick or exhausted. You can't find a moment of quiet. You hate your job. These are signs that you are not listening to the deep self. You are still averting your face. What is going to break through the façade of the false self? Why are you not listening? Why are you not hearing that you are called to freedom from the round of events that supposedly construct a life?

To combat these social demands, you have to find a fierce, heart determination that practices active, nonviolent resistance: "I'm not going that way."

I'm not trying to diminish the struggle. It's not an easy thing to do. It takes everything; it takes full intentionality to uncover one's fabricated identity. The monastic path pulls in another direction. It's very difficult to turn your whole life around, to follow what makes you most happy. We think following what makes us happy is an indulgence. But it is not. What makes us happy is meaning and love. That's *God* within. I'm talking about the deep inner happiness where your whole being is free to say, "I don't need to be anything."

The formation of self-identity is strong. Everyone has some version of alienation and pain. These feelings accumulate and we take them with us through life. Thus, once you've made a conscious choice to divest your self of an identity, you suffer the consequence of leaving behind the definition of "self."

At the same time, something good happens: your self is hollowed out even further. Your inner space is bigger. Your ability to handle solitude and suffering, your own and that of others, is greater. You develop resiliency, the inner capacity that is at home everywhere, but resides nowhere. You begin to really live with those who have nothing, because you yourself have given up everything. Then, you accept solitude, and thrive.

It is in this divesting of the self that you can appreciate the spiritual wisdom that has been passed down through the centuries. You have to experience the wound of no-identity to let go of naming and claiming. You will struggle until you let go and give up. And even when you let go and give up, you will still struggle because other sentient beings are suffering. The journey never ends.

The inward journey to the deep self elicits compassion for others. It helps dissolve the distancing and specialness that the ego exerts in order to survive in the world. As we cultivate humility, we develop a tender, vulnerable, and expansive heart that embraces the humanity of all people and sees the world with the eyes of wisdom. As we move into solitude, we learn a new language—the language of the spirit, the language of heaven. For the desert solitary, prayer is not the speaking of words. Prayer is one's heart reaching out with openness to be touched by the divine heart. It is the cosmos praying in and through us so that all of creation dwells within our being. The true prayer and longing for God is really God praying in us. As we pray with passion and longing, we are praying out into the whole world, and drawing the whole world into us. Our solitude and aloneness, the simple path of poverty becomes, instead, openness to all.

The desert monks had a word of caution on the road to nothingness: *acedia*. Disciples of prayer, they recognized how easy it was to succumb to *acedia*, boredom or dejection that comes without cause, and is a temptation to give up the spiritual life. They called *acedia* the "noonday demon" that tried to lure monks away from their monastic commitment by faintly whispering, "Aren't you getting bored with all this prayer? Isn't this a monotonous life? Go do something; go create something; go be someone."

They called it "demon" because it subverts and discourages the inner journey toward freedom. The remedy required monks to be tenacious in prayer, determined on their path, and to trust their original desire for God in the midst of all that distracted them. Thus, boredom would pass.

The self—made in the divine image—will wander in shadowy alleys, and become lost on dusty roads, before it discovers its true orientation in this life. But no matter how long it takes, or what travails are encountered along the way, the deep self eventually will be unveiled in the heart and soul of every seeker.

Wisdom of the Elders

EIGHTEEN

St. Teresa on Prayer

CENTRAL TO THE MONK'S VOCATION is the deepening of contemplation. To maintain the interior focus necessary to become spiritually receptive to the divine voice, the monk is committed to the practice of prayer and meditation, and to the stilling of the intellect, silencing of the memory, and suspending of excessive attractions.

Yet, no amount of study, self-discipline, or practice on its own prepares a person to deepen her or his interior life. Rather, it is the cultivation of silence and the motivation of a pure heart that foster contemplation. When these intentions are fully present, then any healthy spiritual practice naturally draws the person into the more profound aspects of the life of prayer, and into spiritual attunement with history's wise and humble guides.

One master of the inner journey was the sixteenth-century Spanish mystic, St. Teresa of Avila. Drawing on her experiences—from entrance into the Monastery of the Incarnation as a novice sister to her role as prioress and founder of the reformed (Discalced, "shoeless") Carmelites—she composed a compendium of wisdom on the soul's development, and the stages and power of prayer. The spiritual journey recounted in her numerous written works attests to the significance of contemplative prayer in the maturation of the monk's vocation, and also as the essential means by which he or she is drawn into union with God.

A Vision of the Soul

IN THE WANING YEARS of her life, Teresa had been struggling with a weight on her heart and with fear that she would not live to see the fruit of her labors. Her physical suffering had intensified to the point that she wearily reported: "I have been experiencing now for three months such great noise and weakness in my head that I found it a hardship even to write concerning necessary business matters."[1] In addition to miserable health, everything she had worked for was in danger of being suppressed by the new Church authorities. The monasteries she had founded were constantly under scrutiny, and her personal integrity was subjected to criticism and ridicule as she labored to withstand the latest Inquisitional attack.

In the midst of these disturbing and painful events, Teresa of Avila—under obedience to her confessor—begins writing her sublime book on prayer, *The Interior Castle*, synthesizing her entire mystical corpus under "the magnificent beauty of a soul and its marvelous capacity."[2] On the eve of Trinity Sunday, June 2, 1577, God showed her in a flash of light the whole book she would write and the glorious sensitivity of the soul made in the divine image. She comments:

> Today while beseeching our Lord to speak for me because I wasn't able to think of anything to say nor did I know how to begin to carry out this obedience, there came to my mind what I shall now speak about, that which will provide us with a basis to begin with. It is that we consider our soul to be like a castle made entirely out of a diamond or of very clear crystal, in which there are many rooms, just as in heaven there are many dwelling places. For in reflecting upon it carefully, Sisters, we realize that the soul of a just person is nothing else but a paradise where the Lord says He finds His delight.[3]

Teresa describes a vision of the soul as a crystalline castle with many rooms or dwellings (*moradas* in Spanish) that lead to Christ in its center.

She identifies seven of these rooms, distinguishing the three outer from the four interior *moradas*, which represent successive degrees of prayer and intimacy with the Divine. The three outer dwellings turn toward the world, and are susceptible to its pains, doubts, limits, sins, and sufferings. They represent what the soul understands through human effort, active contemplation, and ordinary grace.

The four interior rooms, however, are supernatural and mystical, and as such remain pure and untouched by earthly events. Of these, the fourth and fifth dwellings are achieved through passive—sometimes called "infused"—contemplation, while the last two *moradas* specifically address mystical union, or what Teresa terms "betrothal" and "marriage." Taken together, the entire soul—outer and inner—is singular and simple, facets of the same divine life. Progress from one dwelling to another is not linear, but occurs according to the maturity of the soul, in a spiral fashion, or alternately ascending and descending, or interior and exterior.

In writing of these seven dwelling places, Teresa points out that we must be aware that "in each of these are many others [*moradas*], below and above and to the sides, with lovely gardens and fountains and labyrinths, such delightful things that you would want to be dissolved in praises of the great God who created the soul in His own image and likeness."[4]

The Interior Castle is a record of Teresa's journey of self-knowledge and self-discovery, with each room of the castle signifying a state of awareness and a quality of prayer that eventually leads to centering one's whole life in God. Teresa understands that, due to human ignorance and sin, each person must undergo a journey from the outer *moradas* to the inner, from exile to home, in order to focus his or her attention on "another heaven . . . where His Majesty must have a room where He dwells alone" in the soul.[5]

Entrance into the castle is through prayer, writes Teresa, and the first dwelling place chronicles how the soul "is so involved in worldly things and so absorbed with its possessions, honor, or business affairs," that it is prevented from taking time for prayer and searching for the true light.[6] The second dwelling place is for those who have taken the first steps in the practice of prayer, and who are receptive to external means of communion with God, especially through books, sermons, good friendships, and trials. In moving from distraction to formal prayer practice, the third dwelling place is reserved for those who long not to offend "His Majesty," and who guard against sin and "are fond of both ascetical practices and periods of recollection."[7] However, due to the attachment to worldly affairs, "any threat to wealth or honor will quickly uncover" the extent of a person's true desire for perfection and for achieving the "delectable peace and quiet of contemplation."[8]

The challenge of how to explain contemplative prayer—called by Teresa the "prayer of quiet"—marks the fourth dwelling place. It represents the joining together of the active or natural and the passive or supernatural states of consciousness. At this stage, the person is more firmly established in prayer, which is motivating his or her life. Teresa reminds us that active contemplation begins in human nature and ends in God; while passive contemplation is more interior and is initiated by God, igniting the spark of intimate love and knowledge directly into the soul. "The important thing," Teresa writes, "is not to think much but to love much, and so do that which best stirs you to love."[9]

The soul progresses from the prayer of quiet to the "prayer of union": Teresa's description of the fifth dwelling place. Here the faculties of the soul are completely silent, which leaves a certitude that the soul "was in God and God was in it."[10] The stilling of the faculties occupies an important place in Teresa's understanding of mystical life. Just like we have five sense faculties—sight, hearing, taste, smell, touch—the soul has spiritual faculties. In Christian mysticism, the spiritual faculties are memory, understanding, and will (love). They assist in our memory of divine reality, our apprehension of hope and faith, and our willing intention to love. Yet, their operations are dependent on a degree of separation between the soul and the Divine. In the prayer of union, Teresa tells us that the spiritual faculties become silent, and it is this very stillness that allows the soul to receive the upwelling of God.

The sixth and seventh *moradas* deal with mystical or passive prayer, and how the soul is drawn into a deeper experience of divine intimacy through further purifications and raptures. Teresa uses the images of "spiritual betrothal" in the sixth dwelling, and then later—in the seventh dwelling—"spiritual marriage" to describe the nondual contemplation that joins God and soul in an inseparable oneness, instilling in the person the courage to be co-equal in love with his or her divine spouse.

For Teresa, the love and goodness in which the soul is enclosed subvert our notions of sin, and remove punishment and pain. Negative views of the self cannot be sustained and no sin is outside forgiveness, for there is nothing that divine mercy cannot heal. Progression from outer to inner soul, and from "wretchedness" to self-dignity is depicted in bridal imagery as the person is first betrothed, and then wedded to God. The spousal encounter conveys a mysticism of intimacy in which the person moves from occasional touches of divine union, to a more sustained union found in spiritual betrothal in the sixth *morada*. However, even in betrothal "union with the Lord passes quickly" Teresa writes [and] "in the end the two can be separated and each remains in itself."[11]

It is only at the center of the castle that the soul and God are joined in an inseparable unity "that is like what we have when rain falls from the sky into a river or fount; all is water, for the rain that fell from heaven cannot be divided or separated from the water of the river.... The soul always remains with its God in that center."[12] The intimacy achieved in mystic contemplation impresses on Teresa how the soul in its essence is always one with God, despite errors, omissions, and sins. So powerful was her understanding of the undefiled love between God and the soul, that it is not excessive to state that this equality of intimacy was the founding impetus of her life's mission.

As the soul advances toward the center of its castle, consciousness moves from the experience of oppression to freedom, from human love to divine love, and from doubt to certainty. The most difficult aspect of this spiritual process, according to Teresa, is not the trials a person endures, but the immensity of divine benevolence: God wants the soul's freedom; God draws the soul toward healing and integration, toward its true nature and source. Despite the noise, disruption, and wasted time that occur "on the outskirts of the castle," the soul is completely joined with God in the dwelling places very close to the center. "Terrible trials are suffered," Teresa laments, "because we don't understand ourselves, and that which isn't bad at all but good we think is a serious fault. This lack of knowledge causes afflictions of many people ... [who] don't reflect that there is an interior world here within us."[13]

In practical terms, Teresa conceives of the spiritual life as one in which the person must learn to detach from the temporary attractions of the world in order to experience a higher order of freedom and happiness. Beginners in the spiritual life are aware of two things: the struggle to mend an inherent divide within one's self, and the wish to achieve moments of illumination and love. Those more advanced in the spiritual life feel the pain of longing to be reunited with their beloved, of no longer living a divided life. They recognize that the more arduous and ultimately fruitful path is one in which conflicting attractions give way to centering one's life in God. Teresa recognized that a person's capacity to grow spirituality and to be harmonious and joyful is dependent upon healing the division between inner and outer soul. What afflicts our hope, faith, and love in this world has a corresponding impact on the soul, affecting its ability to be in touch with and experience the great goodness in which it is held.

Yet these sublime contemplative states often involve inner torment, as the person is called to give up his or her will, and to be espoused to God. As prayer deepens, and the soul moves from betrothal to the seventh and final dwelling place of marriage, it dies now to live in the Divine. To achieve perfect union with its Beloved, the soul experiences divine-human intimacy, captured in the Sanskrit word *advaita* (literally, "not-two"). In this nondual state, a mystical integration of body, mind, and spirit takes place. No longer a state we achieve occasionally or reach only during heights of ecstasy, this mystical marriage is the continual sharing in God's inner life, Teresa tells us.

In nondual contemplation, the person's being radiates the nirvanic, liberating state we think of as enlightenment. The soul becomes a source and fount of healing, wisdom, and transformation. Why? Our being and the divine being are consummated in such a way that the entire soul becomes a window into the holy. Contemplation is not something we do. It is a free gift of the spirit; all we can do is surrender and "let go." Every excursion into openness is a flooding in of the true self, remembering that the Divine is already within, waiting.

The Four Waters of Prayer

TERESA OF AVILA also uses the metaphor of watering a garden to help her sisters understand the unique value of contemplative prayer. In *The Book of Her Life*—written about ten years before *The Interior Castle*—Teresa employs another image to describe the soul's progress in prayer: four ways of planting a garden and drawing water from a well.

> Now, then, these four ways of drawing water in order to maintain this garden—because without water it will die—are what are important to me and have seemed applicable in explaining the four degrees of prayer in which the Lord in His goodness has sometimes placed my soul.[14]

Beginners on the path she likens to someone cultivating a garden in a stark, yet weedy landscape. "Beginners must realize," she writes, "that in order to give delight to the Lord they are starting to cultivate a garden on very barren soil, full of abominable weeds. His Majesty pulls up the weeds and plants good seed."[15] While God assists beginners, these seeds have to be watered by the seeker.

For the beginner, prayer requires effort. The tedious work of lowering the pail into the well, pulling it back up, and pouring water on the soil corresponds to the rational work of the intellect. We are strained by the work, and often must wait for the well to fill again before we can once more draw water. This first stage requires personal sacrifice and determination in seeking divine favor.

The second method of watering a garden is by means of a waterwheel to which dippers are attached. As the wheel is turned, the water pours into aqueducts and flows to the garden. Teresa calls this the "prayer of quiet," and explains that in this stage "the soul begins to be recollected and comes upon something supernatural because in no way can it acquire this prayer through any efforts it may make."[16] Much less labor is required, although the construction of numerous aqueducts demands human skill and effort.

Drawing closer to its divine source, the garden of the soul is now irrigated with water flowing from a river or spring. This third degree of prayer requires very little effort, as God so desires to "help the gardener here that He Himself becomes practically the gardener and the one who does everything."[17] The source of water is right there and the trough fills up without noise. The spring of contemplation comes from its own source in God, and it leads to great peace and sweetness in the very interior part of our souls. The soul longs for an intense freedom, and its virtues and good deeds are stronger than in the prayer of quiet. The flowers of the garden are in full bloom, offering sweet fragrances.

Yet, this degree of prayer does not culminate in further stillness or inactivity, but joins "both the active and contemplative life together."[18] Teresa claims that the person is able to conduct works of charity and business affairs while at the same time the best part of the soul is elsewhere. "For the truth of the matter is that the faculties are almost totally united with God but not so absorbed as not to function."[19]

The Prayer of Union, or fourth degree of prayer, is compared to water falling from heaven. Nothing can be done to bring the life-giving waters of rain; its blessing is simply received. The gardener is now joined with heavenly love and experiences intimate communion with God and the greatest tenderness in the soul. This prayer indicates a complete dissolution of that separate function of self-remembrance and self-communication. "In the previous degrees," Teresa writes, "the senses are given freedom to show some signs of the great joy they feel. Here in this fourth water the soul rejoices incomparably more; but it can show much less since no power remains in the body, nor does the soul have any power to communicate its joy."[20]

The shift in imagery is noticeable. In the early stages of spiritual growth, we must dig into the soil of our souls, and labor to water the divine seeds wishing to take root. But, as we mature in our spiritual lives, our souls move deeper into the divine nature, ultimately to experience a union or marriage with God. Here, the water of life rains down upon us, effortlessly, in excessive grace.

Teresa's four degrees of prayer provide evocative guidance on the journey. We ask: Am I laboring to dig in the soil, using my will? Or am I open to quieting my mind, surrendering my will, and letting rain fall from heaven to water my parched soul?

· ◆ ·

THE DEGREES OF PRAYER described by Teresa in *The Book of Her Life* do not correspond exactly to the seven divisions of prayer she described in *The Interior Castle*. Nonetheless, in both instances the soul's progression into deep states of contemplation is initiated by divine action in the soul, and by the person's relinquishing effort. The seeker has to quiet the mind, free the memory, and surrender his or her will.

Thus the deepening of prayer involves the divesting of identity and, along with it, the dismantling of prior modes of thinking and being. Of course, a lifetime of practice may be necessary to move from active into passive prayer, from the God of name to the God of no-name, from intellect and superiority to unknowing and humility. Contemplative prayer is not the recitation of words, but an invitation to live in the divine life. This process of deconstructing the self is often painful, generating suffering in the soul.

Because passive contemplation is the force of divine consciousness, it has transformative power to dissolve whatever stands between the person and his or her ultimate desire. Words are inadequate to explain or describe this experience. Teresa tells us that when we experience the touch of God, we will realize that the mystery of the universe is so profound that there is no need to labor—for faith or meaning or love—because all of this comes of its own accord.

Contemplative Vocations

WHILE THESE VARIOUS LEVELS of prayer represent categories of experience, Teresa's descriptions also correspond to spiritual vocations. A number of the world's spiritual masters—and many in our own time— were active contemplatives, living out their ministries united with the divine: Dorothy Day, American Catholic activist and co-founder of the Catholic Worker; Reverend Martin Luther King Jr., leader of the American civil rights campaign and a spiritual master; Rabbi Abraham Joshua Heschel, a scholar and Jewish prophet who spoke for justice; Mahatma Gandhi, an adherent of nonviolence and leader of the campaign for Indian independence from the British empire; and others too numerous to name.

Although all souls are called to some dimension of silence and solitude, isolation does not fit the active personality; eventually, their spirituality suffers. People called to active contemplation find closeness to God in relationship with others. As with anything, we can take the active contemplative life to an extreme, become stressed by its demands, and need to return to solitude. Similarly, someone in a monastic community may go too far in the opposite direction, lose contact with others, and need to be drawn out. Again, an interior discernment is helpful: In what way is the Divine calling?

Unfortunately, our pragmatic, individualistic society often devalues a life of withdrawal and prayer as useless, even selfish. If we try to force ourselves into one mode of contemplation, thinking that is the only way, we can bring our spiritual life to a standstill. If we are drawn to active contemplation but try to commit to an eremitic life, it is not going to work because that is not where we are called. Similarly, if we are drawn to passive or nondual contemplation and we try to emulate people in active contemplative life—we think we should be social workers or we berate ourselves for not feeling drawn to some spiritual service—we also do violence to our spirits.

Teresa, too, suffered from spiritual directors and confessors who did not understand the depth of her spiritual call. They tried to force her to conform to accepted modes of prayer that were contrary to God's desire for her. It cost Teresa much effort and anguish to trust the Divine Presence in her soul, and to follow the deepening call of contemplation.

In her community, Teresa suffered not only from monastic demands and restrictions, but also even more profoundly from the advice of male confessors who tried to corral her spiritual experiences into accepted modes of vocal prayer. Finding her all-absorbing surrender into the Divine to be in conflict with the active use of mind and imagination that were common to discursive (vocal) prayer, Teresa continually was torn between the passive contemplation to which she was called and the counsel of her spiritual companions and theologians. It was only when she accepted the validity of the contemplative prayer to which God was drawing her that she was able to affirm her genuine call: "This [discursive, vocal] prayer is the kind that those whom God has brought supernatural things and to perfect contemplation are right in saying they cannot practice."[21]

Teresa's life is an embodiment of all three contemplative streams of consciousness—active, passive, and nondual. Grounded in mystical marriage to Christ, Teresa found the strength to forge relations that reformed her spiritual order, and to generate contemplative wisdom that endures today. Active in the spiritual growth of her sisters and the larger community of family, neighbors, and spiritual friends, Teresa also founded seventeen monasteries while sustaining an intense mystical life.

Like Teresa, we pass through many phases in life. We may have spiritual guides who have not experienced the contemplative path to which we are drawn. We may be called to one type of spiritual expression or experience at a certain developmental stage and to another at a different time, or perhaps to a combination of these states. Further, many in spiritual guidance, whether counselors, spiritual directors, or clergy, may have never experienced passive forms of contemplative consciousness. But unless we understand the power of these multiple contemplative paths, we may be guided incorrectly, and falsely commit ourselves to an active path because it is all we know. This is why we must remember to open ourselves to the inner voice where the Divine whispers silently in our souls, calling us to a life specially chosen for our spiritual need.

NINETEEN

St. Augustine's Spiritual Journey

ACROSS THE WORLD'S RELIGIONS, the spiritual journey describes the person's progressive transformation into the divine nature. Despite lofty language and rarefied goals, the path to enlightenment does not progress smoothly and without hardship. It is the road upon which the self learns abandonment, conversion into divine likeness, and, ultimately, mystical union. The self undergoes a change of heart and a change of being that involves psycho-spiritual growth and deepening of consciousness. Such radical, life-changing transformation has its own spiritual method that, despite the diversity of the human spiritual quest, shares common characteristics across many traditions.

In her seminal work, *Mysticism: A Study in the Nature and Development of Man's Spiritual Consciousness*, the British writer, Evelyn Underhill (1875-1941), presents five stages of the mystic way: self-awakening, purgation, illumination, dark night, and union. "Taken all together," she writes, "they constitute phases in a single process of growth; involving the movement of consciousness from lower to higher levels of reality."[1] These stages are organic processes of soul development and are not linear or sequential, but progressive movements that "must be looked upon throughout as diagrammatic, and only as answering loosely and generally to experiences which seldom present themselves in so rigid and unmixed a form."[2] Keeping in mind that the spiritual path is deeply personal and contextualized by time and place, these stages are found implicitly—wholly or in part—in many mystical texts of East and West.

The Mystic Way

ONE OF THE MORE EVOCATIVE expressions of mystical growth is found in the *Confessions* of St. Augustine. Its pages chronicle one man's struggle to find truth in the midst of everyday weaknesses, lack of clarity, and pride. It is the very normalcy of the issues with which he grapples—childhood errors, adolescent losses, worldly loves, and career questions—that make Augustine's search both compelling and contemporary. Documenting the arduous climb toward the divine light, Augustine gives eloquent voice to the spiritual process that leads to a transformation of the heart.

Born in 354 on the eastern boundary of present-day Algeria, Augustine began life in the tension of differing spiritual views. His mother, Monica, was a devout Christian, while his father, Patricius, followed the pagan traditions until his conversion to Christianity near the time of his death. As a child, Augustine showed marked intelligence and received education in local schools, later traveling to Carthage to study rhetoric, grammar, literature, and Roman and Greek philosophy. It was at Carthage that Augustine became a member of the Manicheans,[3] a quasi-Christian sect, and fathered a son, Adeodatus, with an unnamed woman in 371 or 372. The metaphysical and moral dualism of Manichaeism, the ethical struggle (especially over his having a child out of wedlock) ever-present in his personal life, and the intellectual challenges posed by Christianity and Greek philosophy set the stage for Augustine's spiritual crises.

Augustine's spiritual journey begins with a self-awakening preceded by a series of intense, but short-lived, conscious experiences of a different order of reality that take place over many years. Two episodes echo his inner conflict and become the locus around which his eventual union with God occurs. The first in intensity, if not in historical sequence, is the self-awakening in which he sought release from his confusion around love, lust, and human sexuality. Unable to find a balance between the sexual exploits of his youthful friends and the tension between his mother's piety and his father's permissiveness, Augustine recalls his sixteenth year as a crucial point in his journey:

> Where was I in that sixteenth year of my body's age, and how long was I exiled from the joys of your house? Then it was that the madness of lust, licensed by human shamelessness but forbidden by your laws, took me completely under its scepter, and I clutched it with both hands. My parents took no care to save me by marriage from plunging into ruin. Their only care was that I should learn to make the finest orations and become a persuasive speaker (2.2.4).[4]

He records a second incident immediately thereafter in Book 2, Chapter 4—the theft with a group of friends of pears from a neighboring orchard. This episode in the *Confessions* stands out for its symbolic power, highlighting the purification of heart Augustine confronts as his soul searches for truth. In clarifying his motives, he recognizes that the stealing of pears was not for pleasure or need or even want, but for the will of doing what is self-willed, even if unlawful. Finding that his actions were motivated by a desire for his friends' recognition, Augustine reflects on his life as a tension between personal willfulness and spiritual awakening: "I fell away from you, my God, and I went astray, too far astray from you, the support of my youth, and I became to myself a land of want."[5]

As in every authentic spiritual path, Augustine's journey progresses through human afflictions and pains, in a psychological oscillation designed to goad the soul out of its self-absorption and into a movement of consciousness from lower to higher levels. The momentary glimpses of love and the intensity of Augustine's search trace another way of being, and underscore the distinction between divine love and human suffering. His soul is called to recognize the higher Self to which the lower self belongs in order to awaken from the slumber of perpetual habits. While these years find Augustine with a deepening understanding of God, he is unable to extricate himself from the snares of an undisciplined spiritual life:

Anxiously reflecting on these matters, I wondered most of all how long was that time from my nineteenth year, when I had first been fired with a zeal for wisdom. For then I had determined, if wisdom were found, to abandon all the empty hopes and all the lying follies of my vain desires. But see, I was now in my thirtieth year, still caught fast in the same mire by a greed for enjoying present things that both fled me and debased me. (6.11.18)

Yet his struggle is not without merit. The tension and bewilderment Augustine encounters in the disjuncture between what his mind and heart desire—and what his senses and body demand—bring him to a critical point of spiritual growth where the ego, or false self, is sufficiently effaced to "let go." What was originally an inchoate groping toward awareness now becomes a courageous, and conscious, effort of purification. The power of these gradual encounters with divinity magnifies for Augustine the distance that still separates him from God. Having glimpsed the beauty of divine life, Augustine is impassioned to purge himself of the fears, pains, and imperfections that impede knowing and experiencing God. It is purgation because the road to God involves a struggle with one's fears, and with the doubt and resistance that oppose every act of liberation from self-centeredness.

"From day to day," Augustine writes, "I deferred to live in you, but on no day did I defer to die in myself." (6.11.20) Aware of God's call, he laments how his weakened will still separates him from love of wisdom. "You beat back my feeble sight, sending down your beams most powerfully upon me, and I trembled with love and awe. I found myself to be far from you in a region of unlikeness..." (7.10.16)

Augustine's trials are worked out in the uncertainty and confusion of daily life; his struggles are the struggles that beset all humans; his fears those of every mortal heart. For Augustine, the divine will is sought in personal conflicts: his career and philosophical orientation toward rhetoric and the Platonists, his religious conviction concerning Manichaeism, and his torment over his unmarried life and parenthood.

Awakening grants Augustine temporary glimpses of divine truth; purgation chips away at whatever obstructs God's presence in his life. But

Augustine still has yet to experience the illuminative grace, which is able to lift him above the turmoil of his soul. Only as he detaches from emotional and intellectual acquisitions is he able to hone deeper spiritual virtues and gaze in mystic contemplation on reality. But, it is his philosophical conflicts between Manichaeism and Platonism on the one hand, and the Christian scriptures on the other, that set the stage for his breakthrough to the divine light.

Having questioned the Manichean denial of the divinity of Christ and the incorruptibility of the Word, Augustine now seeks answers to the question of sin and evil, truth and resurrection: "Whence is evil? What torments there were in my heart in its time of labor, O my God, what groans! When I sought an answer, bravely but in silence, the unspoken sufferings of my soul were mighty cries for mercy." (7.7.11) Affected by the difference between two modes of being and two views of life, Augustine says that God guides him to the breaking point: "Being thus admonished to return to myself, under your leadership I entered into my inmost being. This I could do, for you [God] became my helper." (7.10.16) The tension to be aware and awake, and to hear God's voice reaches a pitch that overcomes his whole being with illumination. "I entered there, and by my soul's eye, such as it was, I saw above that same eye of my soul, above my mind, an unchangeable light." This light is not a common light, he tells us, nor is it a physical light but a supernatural light.

Identifying this light with the truth, eternity, and love of God, Augustine finally recognizes the essence of the illuminative experience: the light is not above him because of natural law, but because of an ontological difference.

> Not such was that light, but different, far different from other lights. Nor was it above my mind, as oil is above water, or sky above earth. It was above my mind, because it made me, and I was beneath it, because I was made by it. He who knows the truth, knows that light, and he who knows it knows eternity. Love knows it, O eternal truth, and true love, and beloved eternity! You are my God, and I sigh for you day and night! (7.10.16)

Unable to keep the light present in his mind, Augustine unhappily returns to his old habits. At once aware that God is calling him and afraid of the depth of this call, Augustine cries out, "Not yet, God, not yet!" He writes, "I marveled that now I loved you. . . . Yet I was not steadfast in enjoyment of my God: I was borne up to you by your beauty, but soon I was borne down from you by my own weight, and with groaning, I plunged into the midst of those lower things." (7.17.23)

Augustine's early illuminative experiences permanently alter his perception of reality, but he still is unable to harness his passions and the moral order of his being. Overcome by emotional excess as well as the need for intellectual recognition and spiritual superiority, Augustine alternately resists and embraces the need to convert his whole life to devotion to God, as recorded in Book 8, Chapter 5:

> A new will, which had begun within me, to wish freely to worship you and find joy in you, O God, the sole sure delight, was not yet able to overcome that prior will, grown strong with age. Thus did my two wills, the one old, the other new, the first carnal, and the second spiritual, contend with one another, and by their conflict they laid waste my soul. (8.5.10)

A deep state of communion, illumination is an elevated, but not final stage of the mystic ascent, usually followed by some type of purgative contemplation.[8] His increasingly frequent illuminations prepare the way for Augustine to confront the roots of his self-thirst and to be stripped of false spiritual ambition. Not only does he undergo a conversion of intellect and memory, but also his self-will is made empty in order that he may enter into intimate union with God. Freed of intellectual doubts about his religious convictions and confident in the path he has chosen, Augustine still struggles to gain a moral and spiritual transformation of mind, body, and spirit.

One of the most poignant descriptions in religious literature, Augustine's battle with his "two wills"—the one mortal, the other divine— brings him to the brink of despair. One moment saying, "Let it be done now," and in another, "Not now, God," Augustine depicts the extent of the soul's struggle toward moral conversion and likeness with God.

I still hesitated to die to death and to live to life, for the ingrown worse had more power over me than the untried better. The nearer came that moment in time when I was to become something different, the greater terror did it strike into me. Yet it did not strike me back, nor did it turn me away, but it held me in suspense. (8.11.25)

This reflection "dredged out of the secret recesses" of his soul brings anguish and tears. Agitated and overcome with emotion, Augustine flings himself on the ground and cries out: "How long, O Lord, will you be angry forever?… How long, how long? Tomorrow and tomorrow? Why not now? Why not in this very hour an end to my uncleanness?" Contrition causes him to weep from the depths of his being, and is countered by a voice Augustine hears "like that of a boy or a girl" chanting over and over: "Take up and read. Take up and read." (8.12.29) Hurrying back to the place where he had left his Bible, Augustine silently reads the passage upon which his eyes first fell: "Not in rioting and drunkenness, not in chambering and impurities, not in strife and envying; but put you on the Lord Jesus Christ, and make not provision for the flesh in its concupiscence." (Rom. 13: 13, 14)

According to Augustine's account, all the "dark shadows of doubt" that plagued him instantly fled as if he were filled with a peaceful light streaming into his heart. (8.12.29) Beyond the world of senses, knowledge, and sacred text, Augustine is lifted above the mind to gaze upon God directly.

Transforming Union

AUGUSTINE'S CONVERSION reaches culmination about a year later, at age 32, in an experience of divine union with his mother, Monica, shortly before her death in 386. Resting in the garden of a house at Ostia on the Tiber, Augustine and Monica talk about the nature of God and the soul's journey. Reaching the height of discussion in spiritual matters, Augustine writes:

then, raising ourselves up with a more ardent love to the Selfsame, we proceeded step by step through all bodily things up to that heaven whence shine the sun and the moon and the stars down upon the earth. We ascended higher yet by means of inward thought and discourse and admiration of your works, and we came up to our own minds. We transcended them, so that we attained to the region of abundance that never fails, in which you feed Israel forever upon the food of truth, and where life is that Wisdom by which all these things are made, both which have been and which are to be. And this Wisdom itself is not made, but it is such as it was, and so it will be forever. (9.10.24)

Together Augustine and Monica experience mystical union and an intimate sharing in the inner life of God. Augustine's life is transformed; having come face to face with the glory of God's presence, he recognizes the power and certainty in the direct experience of faith: "God speaks alone...through himself, so that we hear his Word, not uttered by a tongue of flesh, nor by an angel's voice, 'nor by the sound of thunder,' nor by the riddle of similitude, but by himself whom we love in these things..." (9.10.25)

However, union does not bring changeless rest or the absence of conflict, pain, or despair. Rather it draws the soul to the wellspring of love in which the paradoxes and ambiguities of life are not finalized, but can be borne. Augustine raptly reflects how the gift of divine grace provides forbearance in the face of human suffering and tragedy. Scarcely five days after he and his mother share together their experience of mystical union, Monica becomes seriously ill and dies nine days later. As he lays his mother to rest, Augustine expresses the eloquence of his grief and the grandeur of his heart.

What was it, therefore, that grieved me so heavily, if not the fresh wound wrought by the sudden rupture of our most sweet and dear way of life together? I took joy indeed from her testimony, when in that last illness she mingled her endearments with my dutiful deeds and called me a good son. With great love and affection she recalled that she had never heard me speak a harsh or disrespectful word to her.

Yet, O my God who made us! What comparison was there between the honor she had from me and the services that she rendered to me? When I was bereft of such great consolation, my heart was wounded through and my life was as if ripped asunder. For out of her life and mine one life had been made. (9.12.30)

· ◆ ·

AUGUSTINE'S MYSTICAL JOURNEY reveals the elements of spiritual growth in the context of a distinctive personal pilgrimage. His experience of divine union is a culminating moment, yet even the term "union" is but one stage of successive penetrations into the divine life. Not only does the journey involve further degrees of purification and illumination, there also are states beyond mystical union—beyond the subject-object structure of language—described in nondualistic terms: annihilation, absorption, and intimacy. What we glean from Augustine's *Confessions* is how the stages of spiritual growth—self-awakening, purgation, illumination, dark night, and union—are both uniquely individual and yet universally relevant.

TWENTY

Gandhi's Threefold Path

T O COME IN CONTACT with Mohandas K. Gandhi through his works or writings is to be left with a sense of gratitude for his dedication to truth. Gandhi practiced a contemporary form of monasticism, in which activism was sustained by contemplation, and which contributed to the liberation of India from foreign oppression and changed the consciousness of the world. By virtue of his accomplishment, he continues to exert an enduring impact on the spirituality of our planet. His vision was comprehensive. He modeled a life devoted to silence and prayer; a life of mystical insight conveyed in the most accessible terms. Yet its depth was bottomless.

Gandhi's followers called him "mahatma"—great soul—and a karma yogi who selflessly devoted his life to the benefit of others. As active as his life was, he learned to carve out those spiritual necessities that allowed him to live in the world but not be co-opted by it. One such necessity was a weekly day of silence that he devoted to reading, writing, and prayer. As was the case for many mystics before him, for Gandhi every breath was a prayer. Arrested numerous times for civil disobedience, he did much of his writing in jail, finding prison a place of solitude and freedom that was rarely available in regular life.

Monastic consciousness was intrinsic to Gandhi's search for God realization. He claimed that his entire nonviolent campaign—to alleviate poverty and to change India's political fate—was conducted through his desire to see God face to face. This was his *dharma*, his divine duty. His central focus was to discover what God asked of him in each situation. And thus, to know the Divine directly was the guiding principle of his life, as it has been for seekers throughout history.

Gandhi desired to awaken truth within each individual. From the time he was a young adult, he realized that humans are caught in a struggle between two different ways of life. One is directed toward love of the Divine. One is directed toward love of the self. While these two ways can interact—love of the Divine does not negate love of the self—there must be a priority of intention. If attention is placed on love of God alone, a person will automatically come to love one's self in the way of truth, not from egocentric desire.

Gandhi recognized that in every activity, he was being called to discern between these two ways of life. He questioned: was he moving closer to truth, toward God, or was he seeking aggrandizement of the self? From his campaigns in South Africa for the rights of people of color, to his campaigns in India, he sought to ascertain the difference.

Satyagraha (soul force), *ahimsa* (non-harm), and self-sacrifice formed the heart of Gandhi's spirituality. If we draw on soul force, we may be asked to suffer in order to uphold nonviolence. Though he knew he would never perfect these practices—the mystery of the Divine was too vast and unknown—he also knew that by diligently practicing this eternal wisdom his soul would be woven deeper into the tapestry of love and devotion. What held these high principles together were his three-fold practice of ceaseless prayer, self-restraint, and obedience to seek truth.

Ceaseless Prayer

In the early morning I worship him
who is beyond the reach
of thought and speech,
and yet by whose grace all speech is possible.

I worship him whom the Vedas describe
as *neti, neti*—not this, not this.
Him they, the sages, have called
God of gods, the unborn,
the unfallen, the source of all.[1]

PRAYER WAS THE CENTER of Gandhi's life. "Without it, he wrote, "I should have been a lunatic long ago."[2] Rooted in the ancient and beloved Hindu scripture, the *Bhagavad Gita*, which he recited daily, Gandhi included Christian, Islamic, Jain, Sikh, and Buddhist prayers into his morning and evening services. As a devotee of nonviolence, he found companionship in Jesus' sermons, especially the Sermon on the Mount from the Gospel of Matthew. Gandhi's all-consuming passion to alleviate suffering was inextricably linked to prayer—his time of communion with the God of peace. It was a daily practice that strengthened his resolve to find in nonviolence the political equivalent of the *sannyasi's* quest for purity of heart.

Gandhi had a profound understanding of his fallibility, recognizing that the path of the human being is always one of struggle, conflict, and uncertainty. Through struggle, however, we find landmarks and recognize points of truth. Gandhi: "Man is a fallible being. He can never be sure of his steps. What he may regard as answer to prayer may be an echo of his pride. For infallible guidance, man has to have a perfectly innocent heart incapable of evil. I can lay no claim. Mine is a struggling, striving, erring, imperfect soul."[3]

Purification of self required hard work. Gandhi showed that if you lay your heart bare and strive for what you believe is true, you will discover divine principles. You will have touched the divine heart. One of Gandhi's central tenets was his insistence that prayer is necessary for enlightenment. He repeats often how as a child, his nurse taught him the word *Rama*, or *Ramayana*, which means God in Sanskrit. She taught him to say *Rama* in those moments when he was afraid, troubled, or conflicted. Prayer led him to austerities that purified his heart, and drew power from constant repetition of the divine name: "When a man has got to the stage of heart prayer, he prays always, whether in...secret or in the multitude."[4]

In each of the four yogic paths in Hinduism—(1) the path of knowledge or *jnâna*, the discrimination of the unreal amidst the unchanging; (2) the path of devotion or *bhakti*; (3) the path of *karma* or selfless work; and (4) the path of *raja* or mental concentration—we are called to prayer. Prayer frees us from self-will and is the vehicle through which we offer ourselves, connecting to the Eternal.

The Sanskrit word *yoga* means union, and the harnessing of one's senses. For the karma yogi, knowledge without prayer is just another accumulation. One must pray to understand the highest principle in one's actions. For Gandhi, it wasn't a question of Indians versus British, but a search together for truth, with equal respect. It required right action, selfless work to honor the British while striving for and suffering with the Indian people. It required intense prayer, which harkened truth. Gandhi held that no one was qualified to teach wisdom by mere charisma or self-appointment. Truth is born out of the work of prayer. It was the work of saying *Rama* for a lifetime that allowed him to question authority.

Ceaseless prayer harnesses the soul to God. It is recognition that we are not alone and that the world does not function on our individual efforts. It is recognition that we are connected to something greater than ourselves. Prayer lends fragrance to everything we do. There is a quality of consciousness that is tangible when a person's life is given over to prayer. Certain sweetness emerges from action that does not seek to attain, achieve, or demand. Action that arises from love, from no other intention than to love, is divine action. This is the power of ceaseless, loving prayer. This constant loving of the divine restructures our bodies, minds, and souls. It gives us the strength to bear all things.

Gandhi knew that prayer is the greatest strength, the most powerful protector, the answer to all our needs, the foundation and basis of wisdom, and the *mantra* that links our hearts to the Divine.

Self-Restraint and Receptivity

GANDHI LIVED AS A WITNESS to divine plenitude, and also with emptiness, in austerity and restraint. Rooted in the tradition of *Vedanta*, Gandhi recognized that restraint was vital to inner receptivity, to hear the voice of truth.

> Self-realization always comes through truth,
> austerity, true knowledge, and self-restraint.
> Seekers who have become free from sins realize
> the immaculate, refulgent spirit within themselves.
>
> Truth alone triumphs, never untruth.
> That way which the sages whose purpose is fulfilled
>   traverse,
> which is the way of the gods,
> and where is the great abode of truth,
> opens for us through truth."[5]

Self-realization comes through truth, and truth comes through self-restraint. We cannot know truth if we are partial, looking out only for ourselves. Truth sees the whole. It is apprehension of the oneness that underlies diversity. Truth goes to the core, the fundamental reality, the piercing wisdom of ultimate existence. For Gandhi, the ability to know truth comes from discipline and self-restraint. It is not something that we can achieve by charisma or self-appointment. It comes from a lifetime of being tested by the fires of desire, by the world's claim on the seeker. It comes from a lifetime of choices and decisions that draw one closer to or further away from truth.

Truth is beyond our senses, yet its laws can be discerned, experimented with, and relied upon. Blind obedience is not the way of truth. While Gandhi held that truth is unceasing and unchanging, it is not pursued or claimed without critical reflection. Each individual through personal experimentation must discover truth within. Since the totality of truth is beyond our human capacity to know, we can only approximate its vastness. It is an experiment of our hearts, and the challenge to practice the truth of our hearts. Only when we give our whole selves—body, mind, soul, and spirit—to the search for truth, will we begin to understand. If you seek truth partially, you will discover only a part of what you seek. If you seek truth fully, you will enter a new world of meaning and love.

Many of us are afraid of truth. We believe that it will turn against us, or that it is too arduous, too difficult. What will it mean, where will it lead? Will we become zealots, alienated from the mainstream of society? Are we being naïve, reaching for the unattainable? Are we elitist, believing that we alone can attain special status? Many questions arise when one decides, "I want to live a life of truth." What does that mean? In our post-modern world, truth is excoriated, antiquated, or up for grabs. Or truth is only for the naïve, unsophisticated, or extremist. Yet throughout history, people have searched for truth. Augustine suffers for truth. The seers of the Upanishads sing its praises. Moses is exiled for it. Buddha abandons a life comfort, and Jesus dies, for truth. The postmodern critique of truth is not new. Nonetheless, the angst and suffering is real. Because it is difficult to ask: "Who am I? What am I doing on Earth?"

Gandhi shows that the quest for truth will never become a caricature if we adhere to the principles of nonviolence and self-sacrifice. If we are demanding or controlling, punitive or retributive, we will not hear the inner voice of truth. To practice truth is to allow the quiet, inner voice to speak, a voice that always must be free. Gandhi tells us that every major decision in his life was made through ceaseless prayer, through listening to his inner voice.

What does it mean to listen to the inner voice? What does he ask us to strive for? When Gandhi was in South Africa with the Zulu rebellion, he made a decision that irrevocably set the course for the rest of his life:

> During the difficult marches that had then to be performed, the idea flashed upon me that if I wanted to devote myself to the service to the community in this manner, I must relinquish the desire for children

and wealth and live the life of a *vanaprastha*—of one retired from household cares.[5]

Once this idea flashed upon the mind of the soon-to-be Mahatma, it was translated into immediate action. He renounced possessions and sexual practice. He was thirty-seven, married, and had four sons. He would be as good a husband and father, as the immense demands on him would allow. But from that moment, he would live no more for self or immediate family. Three months from his decision, Gandhi's concept of *satyagraha* was born.

Gandhi's life illustrates the relationship between our desire to hear the inner voice, and the importance of following what we hear with a pure heart. This is one of his great lessons. For Gandhi, renunciation led immediately to lifetime opportunity. He heard and responded at once with all his heart. This is a spiritual law: acting on our inner voice leads to spiritual opportunity. When our inner voice calls and we do not act, we lose a precious chance. We might find we can come back to it at a later point, but that particular moment has passed forever.

Of course this raises questions: Is my inner voice authentic? Will I be led astray? Yes, surely, at times. Am I imperfect? Definitely. But there is a realm of reality that can only be known by faith. Yes, we are going to be imperfect in how we hear or follow our inner voice and yes, we are going to make mistakes. But we have to learn to recognize the signs of a true call from God. We have to learn to read the inner language.

He also teaches that in the midst of the call-response of hearing and action, we may not appear outwardly consistent. Gandhi was consistent with what he heard God calling him toward, but he remained open and responsive to the call, to a new message. He followed a principle: *ahimsa* (non-harm). Gandhi constantly discerned whether his actions were harmful or helpful to others. He would then know if he was drawing closer to God's intention.

Gandhi was not rigid or unchanging in his beliefs or practices. If at one point in his life, he understood truth to be one way, but as he became more purified he understood it another way, he would move in that new direction. In his autobiography, he cites an example. When he lived in his first ashram, everyone shared all the chores: cooking, cleaning of latrines, gardening, and so forth. Gandhi did all these chores. His wife, however, coming from the *Brahmin* caste, was not prepared for manual labor and resisted. He then tried to expel her from the ashram, telling her to go away, to leave the marriage. She responded by saying, "Have you no shame? I am your wife." He later claimed that it was his wife who taught him more than anyone else about nonviolence because she led him to realize that he was trying to impose his beliefs on her. He was telling her that since he wanted to be a votary of peace, that he would clean latrines—and therefore she must as well. But she taught him that she had to come to a decision in her own way, through God's presence within.

Gandhi's vision concerning the power of peace—the power of a world filled with people who are no longer looking out for themselves—and of India being a nation of peace, was always tempered by the principles of ultimate respect, ultimate reverence, and ultimate nonviolence for all life. Here is a model for the contemplative life. In fact, I think it is the only model that makes sense, which teaches how to simultaneously dwell in ultimacy, and yet not become dogmatic, aggressive, or punishing. Of course, we are all going to make mistakes; we are all going to fall back on what we've known and experienced. But we must keep calling ourselves, again and again, to non-harm.

Obedience: Acting on Truth

GANDHI READ the *Bhagavad Gita* every day. In this ancient sacred text, he found the path of nonviolence and the way of truth.

Spiritual principles govern the soul, its present and future manifestations, just as physical laws govern the material world. When we follow these principles of truth we move closer to happiness; when we violate them we move away from happiness. Gandhi held that the highest principle is nonviolence born of God's total goodness. Goodness is the foundation of reality; it is the motivating principle of life. *Satyagraha* and *ahimsa* are manifestations of ultimate benevolence.

Since the soul is divine, Gandhi held that humans were good in their core. Self-sacrifice was the method of unlocking goodness in each person. By offering himself as a person of peace and openness—which could entail physical or psychological pain, imprisonment, or even death—he believed the goodness in others would be activated, overriding the power of violence and evil. He held this belief unconditionally, as the philosophical core of his life.

This same principle is at the center of a monastic spirituality: deeper than our errors or sins is unconditional goodness. The belief that we are broken or incomplete is not the ultimate truth. Precisely where we believe ourselves to be unholy or unhealed is the place where the Divine bathes us in love. *Jnâna Yoga*, or the yoga of knowledge, is about uncovering false beliefs to see reality as it truly is. Similarly, one of Buddha's precepts, "right awareness," is necessary to break through our limited beliefs to reach compassion or wisdom. Through compassion, we learn to adhere to truth. We understand how violent we are to ourselves, to the tender, vulnerable goodness within.

Goodness, nonviolence of self is fundamental to every decision and every action. For example, if Gandhi planned a fast, he would examine his conscience: was his fast motivated by self-desire and control, or motivated by love and surrender.

God is One without a second: nothing is comparable; nothing is less. In Sanskrit this is expressed as *advaita*, which means "not two." It is the Hindu principle of non-dualism; reality is non-dualistic. While God is One, supremely good and infinitely merciful, God also has many names. Gandhi held that no truth or religion is privileged. While Gandhi was a devout Hindu, and it was the center of his spiritual life, he was also open to all traditions because truth is many. It is simultaneously one and many.

He understood the concept of obedience as "acting on the truth." Normally, we think of obedience as submitting to an authority, or giving in against our will. But obedience is not in relationship to an external actor or force. Rather, obedience is to truth, to acting on the divine truth within. And obedience to the inner voice entails risk. When Gandhi heard the inner voice, he had an immense opportunity.

If God is one, the world is one. Therefore, truth applies on every level.

There is no place empty of truth. This is one of the more difficult concepts to understand and apply to a person's life. Often I hear people express how hard they are trying to find God. They reveal that even though they have meditated and prayed for years, they are no closer to their goal. When I really listen, I often learn that for these people, prayer and meditation are given a life of their own, as privileged activities. Yet the rest of their life goes on relatively unexamined. Daily life proceeds in one sphere, and prayer life in another, unconnected. And of course there needs to be a change of consciousness, a waking to the fact that we are wholly made of truth.

We are composed of truth—spiritually and physically. Just as water is made of two parts hydrogen and one part oxygen, we are composed of divine principles: mercy, bliss, goodness, compassion, and humility. Our nature is divinely constituted. These attributes are not extrinsic to us; they are not something outside the self. They make us who we are. When someone asks, "Who are you?" we might say, "I'm a teacher," or "I'm a banker." But on a spiritual level the question is a *koan*, an inscrutable puzzle that breaks up thought patterns. Because you are made of divine attributes, they are part of who you are. Spiritual vehicles, such as prayer, meditation, fasting, and so forth, are designed to activate one's deep nature and to establish in one's consciousness the truth of being.

Obedience is faithfulness to truth, in the service of discovering our true nature. As I mentioned earlier, many people are afraid of truth, afraid that deep down they are terrible or despicable. Yet, fear of truth is lack of faith in reality. Why should our natures be less than or different from the divine principles that compose consciousness and the whole body of creation?

It is these great doubts and pains and violations of consciousness that prevent us from knowing. We live a deception. We do not remember. Yet because we are made of truth, when we go by way of truth, we draw closer to God. We can only do this in personal ways. There is no prescription that is viable in every situation of life. Your way is intrinsic to your particular life. Yet, if we were to look at all the ways we learn and live truth, we would find similar patterns, even though each one is unique.

This is why knowing self is so important. No one else can teach you how to know yourself. Only spirit knows your failings and strengths. Each day, with every breath, action, and thought, we sow the seeds of our lives. We dig and plant and weed the ground of our being; obedience is the method that helps us proceed on the path of truth.

In the monastic traditions, obedience is designed to help the monk avoid deceptions based on subtle aspects of personality and habituated thought. Obedience therefore helps us understand our motives. If we are afraid of truth, we will live both in illusion and in pain. Our choices will be the wrong choices. We may create a path of relative ease, but it will lack meaning. You can construct a life built upon a false foundation that hides what is painful or disturbing. You can tell yourself, "Beneath this façade of personality, I do not venture." Despite prayer and practice, if you refuse to be obedient to truth within, you will not know the secret of your being and your life will spiritually stagnate. But at some point, life's passion for truth will break the barrier. What seemed perfect will crumble, what seemed easy will be impossible to maintain. One day, you wake up and say, "My life has no meaning, Why am I on Earth?" Then, what seemed so radical before—a life lived for truth—is the only way to proceed. You may worry that you have waited too long; too much time has passed. But it is never too late. In your last hour, you still have the capacity to know truth.

Gandhi's life is a model for the contemporary monk. His was a life not bound by walls, but rather by the quest for and obedience to truth. Gandhi recited this ashram prayer about *satyagraha*:

> Soul-force is superior even to science,
> for one man having soul-force
> will shake one hundred learned men.
> When one has that force he is ready to go to a teacher,
> he serves him, then he becomes fit to sit near him,
> he ponders over what he has heard; he becomes wise,
> he does his duty, he has experience.
> The earth keeps its place through that force,
> the heavens retain their place through it,
> the mountains, the gods, mankind, the brute creation,
> birds, grass, plants, game, insects, moths, ants,

all life are sustained by that force.
Therefore cultivate that force.[6]

When you have soul force, you are ready to listen attentively or to be obedient. When you have *satyagraha*, you may serve a teacher, because soul force grounds your identity in that which is deeper than ego. You can thus sit at the feet of a teacher. Because you are not inferior to the teacher; you are not without wisdom; you are neither lacking nor deficient. You can serve because you have been served.

Soul force helps you to be ready to serve, to be fit and devoted. The integrity of the person who practices *satyagraha* generates the capacity to ponder, reflect, think about, and decide, which leads to wisdom. Here you discover your *dharma*, the path, or duty of your life. As a tree is made to be a tree, you were made to be something, to have a vocation. Not in the world's sense, but in spiritual terms. So when you follow receptivity and obedience, it will lead you to your true duty. When the teacher speaks, words fire your search. These are no longer just words to be imitated, but rather part of your nature.

· ◆ ·

IN DESCRIBING Gandhi's threefold practice, we have looked at ceaseless prayer, receptivity, or listening to the inner voice, and obedience, or acting on truth. Most of us are good at one or two of these, but seldom do we practice all three. Some people are good with prayer and receptivity, but not very good with obedience. Some are good with obedience, but are not attentive to the inner voice, and obedience thus is rote, or rigid. They follow the law, but are not listening to the divine voice. Some may be receptive and obedient, but do not pray.

When this threefold path operates, it leads to an interpenetrating way of being and a holistic insight into monasticism. For the contemporary person, the practice of prayer, interior listening, and obedience to truth stabilizes the monastic call, turning it into a living reality, without walls, without barriers, born from the primordial well of the soul. It is the call of the monk that bubbles up from a place inside us—where we live differently, where consciousness has been transformed. No one can impart it to you in words. Words can help, but it can only be the spirit of the words, the essence, that can offer the potential for the breakthrough into a new monastic way of life.

TWENTY-ONE

The Monk as Social Mystic

O VER THE COURSE OF HISTORY, saints and prophets have spoken out against injustice and have given their lives to help sufferers. We need look no further than the Hebrew prophets, sages from the world's religions, or Francis of Assisi who identified with and felt the pain of the impoverished and disenfranchised. But in the twentieth and twenty-first centuries, a critically different and stronger emphasis on spiritual engagement with the world—termed "social mysticism" or "engaged contemplation"—has become prominent. An important and overlooked resource in most cultural indicators is that exerted by monks and religious leaders, who have been a driving force behind some of the world's most important political and social achievements.

Social mysticism applies the deep experiences of faith to the struggle for dignity and human rights. The monk as social mystic approaches the world's injustices through the lens of the Divine. He or she is involved in a kind of messianic longing to see society transformed, whereby the personal spiritual journey is transposed into the national and international realm. By this I mean that the social mystic employs a contemplative ethic to address all forms of injustice, which emerges from the life of prayer, virtue, and silence. His or her intention, therefore, does not refer simply to action for social change, but to awareness that this action is the fulfillment of a divine desire. Alton B. Pollard III writes:

"Mystic-activism, therefore, is a praxis-orientation to the world which relies but in part—albeit a considerable part—on the political and intellectual arguments and dictates of society; the more demanding motive is located in the obligation engendered by religious experience."[1]

We see this commitment to mystic-activism operable in humanity's heroes, those men and women who challenged the powers and principalities, igniting the moral fiber of oppressed peoples. This was the path of Mahatma Gandhi, Martin Luther King, Jr., and Abraham Heschel, of Thich Nhat Hahn, Dorothy Day, and Thomas Merton. From silence came speech; from solitude came commitment; from prayer came resolve; from mystical experience came excessive love. They had faith—as Teilhard de Chardin once remarked—"That the day will come when, . . . we shall harness for God the energies of love. And, on that day, for the second time in the history of the world, man will have discovered fire."[2]

As lived by these mystic activists, the classical distinction between action and contemplation, transcendence and immanence, and the interior and exterior life is overturned. Moving away from the connotations associated with spirituality as a pessimistically, anti-material orientation, they retrieved spirituality as a relationship with God imbedded in a whole cultural, social, and religious orientation inseparable from the life of the community. Raising this notion up into a global context, the community becomes not a single, homogenous, group or religious tradition, but all human and non-human life. "I am absolutely convinced," Dr. King professed, "that God is not interested merely in the freedom of black men and brown men and yellow men. But God is interested in the freedom of the whole human race."[3]

To be effective and to live up to the message of the Hebrew prophets, of Jesus, Mohammed, and Buddha, etc., religion could be neither solely concerned with transcendence—waiting for liberation in a heavenly realm—nor with temporal justice without addressing the implications of inequality for a person's spiritual life. Thus, at the same time that large cultural forces were freeing millions of people from the clutches of war, colonialism, and displacement, the social mystics recognized a parallel process was taking place in the inner life of the person, in the depth of souls. They realized how poverty, segregation, and hunger violated the dignity of persons, destroyed hope, and inflicted on humanity a relentless series of soul wounds. Campaigns for social change—for example, non-violent civil disobedience directed at dismantling unjust laws—were the social and political equivalent of healing the spiritual depth of humanity. Civil oppression had its roots in soul oppression.

It was this ardent concern for the spiritual health of individuals and society that was built upon the prayer lives of these monks and mystics. More than a social issue, their passion was forged by the mystical imperative to remove all that prevents God from coming to fullness in the life of the individual, a belief strongly held by Howard Thurman:

> The mystic's concern with the imperative for social action is not merely to improve the condition of society. It is not merely to feed the hungry, not merely to relieve human suffering and human misery. If this were all, in and of itself, it would be important surely. But this is not all. The basic consideration has to do with the removal of all that prevents God from coming to . . . [fullness] in the life of the individual. Whatever there is that blocks this, calls for action."[4]

Monastics today—especially new monks living in society—are called to attend to the universality of suffering on our planet and to the power of an integrative, social mysticism. They recognize their responsibility as citizens of Earth to foster a spirituality of compassion, bringing the voice of nonviolence to social issues, and championing the rights of underrepresented or ignored peoples and groups, including our other-than-human planetary citizens. In these last one hundred and fifty years, efforts to integrate our wisdom traditions with social responsibility are practiced by so many religious traditions and spiritual leaders that, in the remainder of this chapter, I present only a brief sketch of this vast movement of hearts.

Four Practices of the Social Mystics

FROM HIS MONASTIC HERMITAGE, Thomas Merton spoke *against* the Cold War, Vietnam, and materialism, and spoke *for* nonviolence, peace, and love. Similarly, Rabbi Abraham Joshua Heschel not only felt it was his sacred duty to restore the soul of the Jewish people suffering from the atrocities of the Nazi Holocaust, but also to stand in solidarity with oppression wherever it is found. Marching alongside Martin Luther King, Jr., this contemporary prophet resonated with everything life-giving and flourishing in the human spirit.

Like Merton, Heschel, and King, African-American theologian and preacher, Howard Thurman was a champion of inter-cultural and inter-religious dialogue, and a tireless advocate for the spiritual unity of the sacred and the secular. Despite the havoc of political realities, the tragedies of our private lives, or the "dead weight of guilt,... in all those things," Thurman knew, "there is a secret door which leads into the central place, where the Creator of life and the God of the human heart are one and the same."[5]

Dr. King is known throughout the world as the leader of the American civil rights movement, and a political hero. While aware of the deep religious foundation of his ministry, articles tend to neglect or ignore the mystical intention that guided his life's mission. King's experiences of God, beginning as a child and present through his life, were the motivating factors in and the foundation of his commitment to civil rights. The extent of humanity's deviation from love—that condoned and permitted slavery and segregation, poverty and war—awakened King to the realization that religious experience, and not philosophical thinking, was the basis of societal transformation.[6]

His was a mystical heart that felt the spiritual fractures tearing apart the soul of humanity and—as all "friends of God"[7]—suffered for it. It was King's capacity for altruistic love that lent such power and credibility to his mission, and that demonstrated to a spiritually impoverished citizenry the miracle of God's presence in history. He wanted more for African-Americans than civil rights; he wanted more for the poor than a job; he wanted more for the victims of war than the cessation of violence. What he wanted was a spiritual revolution in which the forces that generated racism, militarism, poverty, and violence would be immobilized—weakened—and ultimately defeated by a world-world uprising of peace and love. He wanted redemption, even perhaps the erasure of the original sins we humans inflict on each other.

Drawing from their respective faith traditions, the contemplative orientation of the social mystics is founded on similar theological orientations. From days of solitude and silence, and practices of prayer and compassion, four universal principles guided their actions: Oneness of life, Experiments with Truth, Spiritual Nonviolence, and Self-Sacrifice.

Oneness of Life

It is not possible to enumerate all of the gifts that silently support our lives: air we breathe and sun that warms the Earth, food we eat and the clothes we wear, plants and animals that sustain our bodies. Connected to an invisible matrix of being, a web of relations so intimate and sensitive, we cannot help to acknowledge our depth of gratitude.

Oneness of life is the key to the mystery of our existence and the source of compassion, generosity, and hope. It is the mystic glance that tells us who we are, where we belong, and from whence we come. In a fleeting moment, we know and understand how profoundly loved we are, how profoundly connected we are, how profoundly desired we are.

Howard Thurman's soul was especially attuned to the interdependence of creation. His spiritual contributions—from his formation of the first intercultural, inter-religious, non-denominational church in California, to his inspired preaching, and lectures at universities and parishes around the Untied States—affirmed the mystical heart of reality:

My testimony is that life is against all dualism. Life is One. Therefore, a way of life that is worth living must be a way worthy of life itself. Nothing less than that can abide. Always, against all that fragments and shatters and against all things that separate and divide, life labors to meld together into a single harmony.[8]

Thurman's testament stems from his self-confession that the sacred and the secular—heart and head—are inseparable, "lost in wonder in the One." The Divine loves the world as one family: animal, plant, mineral, human. As a family we must attend to the well-being of the whole. His perception of the interdependence of reality was based on mystical realization: the greater the effacement of the ego self, the more gripping is the person's attunement to the indivisible harmony of life. Thomas Merton similarly recognized the relationship between nonattachment and mystical unity.

On March 18, 1958, Merton left Gethsemane Abbey to run an errand in Louisville, Kentucky. As he stood on a street corner, he later wrote in *Conjectures of a Guilty Bystander:*

> I was suddenly overwhelmed with the realization that I loved all those people, that they were mine and I theirs, that we could not be alien to one another even though we were total strangers. It was like waking from a dream of separateness, of spurious self-isolation in a special world, the world of renunciation and supposed holiness. ... This sense of liberation from an illusory difference was such a relief and such a joy to me that I almost laughed out loud.[9]

Awakening from a false ideal of the monk as a special type of human, Merton recognized that it was not possible to leave the world in any real sense. He experienced the truth of humanity's spiritual interdependence, challenging his concept of monastic existence as a holy endeavor separated from "the human race." Seeking to unify in himself all that is divided, he became ever more aware of institutional and religious exclusion and superiority, and of the callousness and entitlement that prevents vulnerability to the world's suffering. He also studied the wisdom and practices of the world's great traditions in earnest. From this point forward, his commitment was to a social form of mysticism. He began to write about Civil Rights, Vietnam, and non-violence.

In his first published journal, *The Sign of Jonas* (1953), "he quarreled with himself about the compatibility of monastic life and a writer's work. Here there was also something else astir in the book: the reluctant prophet who came to discover (and to proclaim) the unimaginable and universal mercy of God [that was] . . . not to exclude anyone."[10]

From 1953 until his death in 1968, Merton's interests continued to be ever wider. He began a correspondence with Boris Pasternak and with the Zen scholar and master Daisetz Suzuki. He exchanged letters with Abraham Joshua Heschel, a correspondence that developed into a deep friendship, and that formed a common bond in the struggles of Christian-Jewish reconciliation, and opposition to the Vietnam War. He resonated with Heschel's description of faith: "Well-adjusted people think that faith is an answer to all human problems. In truth, however, . . . [t]o have faith is to be in labor."[11]

The extent of Merton's study and writings deepened, as his concern for social and religious arrogance, and planetary strife took root in his soul. His reading of Gandhi and King inspired him to become the conscience of the peace movement and a tireless advocate for civil rights. Merton's immersion in Buddhism, Daoism, Sufism and other religions grew deeper and more interior during this period, as his meetings with Thich Nhat Hahn and the Dalai Lama instilled in him a tremendous respect for the contemplative activism of his monastic brothers. It was also the period in which his study of the Divine Feminine took on added urgency, and his critique of monasticism and the corporate Catholic identity came under closer scrutiny.

Centuries earlier, the Italian mystic and saint, Catherine of Siena (1347-1380) also would write about how spiritual cruelties violate the unifying ethics of the spirit. At sixteen she renounced marriage, choosing instead to be isolated at home with her family, undergoing many fasts, and practicing humility. However, when she was twenty-one, she experienced "mystical marriage to Christ," and in her vision was told to return to the world to help the poor and sick. She visited hospitals and homes, traveled widely, became involved with Church politics, and established a women's monastery. She composed over four hundred letters and the definitive work, *The Dialogue*, in which she dictates God's words to her confessor:

For you see that everywhere, on every level of society, all are giving birth to sin on their neighbors' heads. For there is no sin that does not touch others, whether secretly by refusing them what is due them, or openly by giving birth to the vices of which I have told you. It is indeed true, then, that every sin committed against me [God] is done by means of your neighbors.[12]

Committed to ethical involvement in the state of society, Catherine felt responsible not only for the world's sin, but also for its transformation. On fire with love and passion for truth, she served victims of the plague, preparing them for death and burying them. She sought to convert sinners, including rulers who caused wars, and Church leaders who neglected the poor and lived luxuriously. Pained by institutional complicity in the creation of social poverty, avarice, and injustice, she wrote to popes and kings with admonition and advice.

Catherine's life of prayer was the central fuel and source behind her ministry. "It was precisely what she experienced in contemplation," writes Dominican sister Suzanne Noffke, "that impelled her into action.... She was indeed a social mystic—but even more properly a mystic activist.... This integration is the characteristic that marks Catherine among the mystics more than any striking quality of her mystical experience as such, and makes her writings so very pertinent today."[13]

Similarly, a radical commitment to the unity of life inspired the activism of Mohandas Gandhi. In the depth of his soul, Gandhi felt the suffering of India's people. The starving masses were the face of God stricken with hopelessness, the belly of God empty of love, and the heart of God pleading for compassion. In this encounter, he sought the face of God in every person and life situation.

So powerful was Gandhi's mystical insight of oneness that he identified with the dignity of all beings and refused to privilege even his own physical survival over the survival of the least creature. As a sacred vow, Gandhi held all life to be one, a state of being that was acquired through persistent struggle:

I do not want to live at the cost of a life, even of a snake. I should let him bite me to death rather than kill him. But it is likely that if God puts me to that cruel test ... I may not have the courage to die but the beast in me may assert itself and I may seek to kill the snake defending this perishable body. I admit that my belief has not become so incarnate in me as to warrant my stating emphatically that I have shed all fears of snakes so as to befriend them as I would like to be able to do.[14]

Like Gandhi, Dorothy Day—the American nonviolent social activist and co-founder of the Catholic Worker—felt in her soul the world's pain and injustice. Her identification with the plight of others' suffering was intensified when she participated in a women's picket of the White House over the brutal treatment of jailed suffragists. Arrested and sentenced to thirty days in prison, the direction of her life was changed by "this ugly knowledge I had gained of what men were capable in their treatment of each other." Day later wrote about her days and nights in darkness, cold and hunger:

I lost all feeling of my own identity. I reflected on the desolation of poverty, of destitution, of sickness and sin. That I would be free after thirty days meant nothing to me. I would never be free again, never free when I knew that behind bars all over the world there are women and men, young girls and boys, suffering constraint, punishment, isolation and hardship for crimes of which all of us were guilty. ... I was that mother whose child had been raped and slain. I was the mother who had borne the monster who had done it. I was even that monster, feeling in my own breast every abomination.[15]

In a juxtaposition of images, Thich Nhat Hanh, the Vietnamese monk and Zen master, expresses a comparable sentiment of mystical oneness in this excerpt from his poem "Please Call Me By My True Names":

I am the child in Uganda, all skin and bones,
    my legs as thin as bamboo sticks,
and I am the arms merchant, selling deadly
    weapons to Uganda.

I am the twelve-year-old girl, refugee
　　on a small boat,
who throws herself into the ocean after
　　being raped by a sea pirate,
and I am the pirate, my heart not yet capable
　　of seeing and loving. [16]

These experiences of mystical unity echo Martin Luther King's call for a worldwide fellowship that lifts neighborly concern beyond one's tribe, race, class, and nation. It is in reality a call for an all-embracing and unconditional love of creation. In King's identification with God's compassionate love, he sought not a merely mental common denominator, or a false sense of oneness, but a more holistic awareness that perceived, along with the differences, the unitive energies on which differences rest. In his days of silence, and his intimate experience of God's Presence, King was freed of separateness, discovering in the Spirit that nothing can divide us. In this way, King was granted insight into the mysterious *oneness* that sustains and celebrates the dignity of all beings. The cosmos was interdependent, and human beings were essentially relational beings. In "The Letter from Birmingham Jail," King wrote: "We are caught in an inescapable network of mutuality, tied in a single garment of destiny. Whatever affects one directly, affects all indirectly."[17]

Experiments With Truth

We discover in the mystics' experience of oneness that ultimate truth is not capable of being fully expressed. In matters of truth, humility is prior to certitude, contrition more foundational than claim. Here again is paradox. Propelled by a vision of such certainty, the social mystics are able to convert mass numbers of people to their cause. But at the same time, every person's access to ultimacy is tempered by his or her awareness that any vision of truth is itself only partial.

"Nobody in this world," writes Gandhi, "possesses absolute truth. This is God's attribute alone. Relative truth is all we know. Therefore, we can only follow the truth as we see it. Such pursuit of truth cannot lead anyone astray."[18] The seeker grows closer to truth by conducting experiments in the political and spiritual arenas, and testing his or her choices. In *Autobiography: The Story of My Experiments with Truth,* Gandhi explains:

> Far be it from me to claim any degree of perfection from these experiments. I claim for them nothing more than does a scientist who, though he conducts his experiments with the utmost accuracy, forethought and minuteness, never claims any finality about his conclusions, but keep an open mind regarding them.... The various practical applications of these principles ... include experiments with non-violence, celibacy and other principles of conduct ... But for me, truth is the sovereign principle.... as long as I have not realized this Absolute Truth, so long must I hold by the relative trust as I have conceived it.[19]

Gandhi practiced the relativity of truth as his sacred duty. While aspiring toward a vision of absolute truth, Gandhi knew that the limits of humans' ability to know would impinge on the knowledge of truth in any final or absolute way. Truth is open to testing. It must be pursued with an open mind, to test its efficacy in real situations. Only those who know truth intimately know that it cannot exclude or segregate. We are not to wound others who believe differently, or demand they follow our way. Gandhi recognized that if his experiments with truth refuted the possibility of error, they were not to be followed:

> I hope and pray that no one will regard the advice interspersed in the following chapters as authoritative. The experiments narrated should be regarded as illustrations, in the light of which every one may carry on his own experiments according to his own inclinations and capacity.[20]

"The instruments for the quest of truth," Gandhi held, "are as simple as they are difficult. The may appear quite impossible to an arrogant person, and quite possible to an innocent child. The seeker after truth should be humbler than dust."[21] In states of high mystical consciousness, the foundation of everything is open to experimentation, testing, and—in this sense—non-absolute. In fact, these qualities are evidence of divinity. The liberating, experimental quality of "relative truth" does not signal an inferior reality, but the process by which the practice of truth honors divine ineffability. It compassionately holds what Gandhi termed the "manyness" of reality, and even what appears to be inconsistent or contradictory.

Aware of the frailty of human systems and theories, Dr. King also understood that "the strong man holds a living blend strongly marked by opposites. Not ordinarily do men achieve this balance of opposites.... Seldom are the humble self-assertive, or the self-assertive humble. But life at its best is a creative synthesis of opposites in fruitful harmony."[22] Truth-seekers do not arrive at a final reality where all ambiguity is resolved, but are, instead, on an endless pilgrimage. They are always beings *on the way.*

Spiritual Nonviolence

If truth is a constant experiment and one cannot know absolute truth directly, how do we proceed? In the parables of Christ, the method of Gandhi, and the life and writings of Day, King and others, nonviolence is the answer. Nonviolence is the active manifestation of divine oneness and expresses its highest light. It is the actualization of peace and the essence of contemplation. Nonviolence is the pursuit of the endless sea of mercy that God is.

As a social action, nonviolence is the outer manifestation of a mystical consciousness that is itself the outer garment of an even deeper truth—reality moves in harmony with love. It is not merely a cultural necessity or form of protest, but the whole configuration in which life can be seen as it truly is, in its deepest dimensions. The closer one gets to achieving nonharm, the closer one approaches the divine nature. Thus the practice of peace, the practice of nonviolence is its own spiritual path.

The modern world's first spiritually motivated political campaign was Gandhi's nonviolent movement of civil disobedience, which spanned the first fifty years of the twentieth century. Drawing on centuries of Hindu,

Jain, and Buddhism wisdom, Gandhi forged a stunning exemplar of contemplative activism. From his ashrams, he ran a pervasive political campaign that was instrumental in routing the British from Indian soil. Using what he considered to be the greatest weapon of all—the moral superiority of nonviolence—Gandhi's fierce spiritual commitment branded into global awareness the potency of contemplation engaged in the service of social change. Behind every tactic and victory in the Mahatma's arsenal, lay spiritual imperatives of silence, fasting, prayer, and sacrifice. Intertwined with Indian independence, was a monastic commitment to refuse the trappings of social comfort or political expediency for the sake of suffering souls everywhere.

Martin Luther King Jr.'s ministry of justice and reconciliation was tied to the adaptation of Mahatma Gandhi's comprehensive praxis of non-violence. Like Gandhi, King's involvement in civil rights emerged from personal experience of discrimination within his ministering community, which led to the moral audacity to confront and rectify abuses of a person's God-given dignity. He drew inspiration not only from Christianity, but also from the phenomenal spiritual experiment unfolding across the great continent of India. During the Montgomery Boycott, for example, King later wrote: "Nonviolent resistance had emerged as the technique of the movement, while love stood as the regulating ideal. In other words, Christ furnished the spirit and motivation, while Gandhi furnished the method."[23]

King also understood nonviolent activism to derive power and efficacy from its theological foundation in divine love. It was never for social trans-formation without soul transformation. While "principled nonviolence" was based on moral values and "pragmatic nonviolence" rested on practi-cal solutions, in almost all nonviolent campaigns these were interrelated paths.[24] However, King, like Gandhi and other social mystics, was especially concerned for the spiritual implications of nonviolence on the inner life of the person and her or his growth. For this reason, I modify the word "non-violence," with "spiritual" to underscore the self-awareness and personal repentance that King recognized was critical in liberation movements.

Thus, spiritual nonviolence was not solely concerned with the nega-tive impact of violence, but with what Gandhi called *satyagraha*—the "soul-force" that empowers the life affirming strength and moral resilience necessary for the conversion of the human heart and the transformation of culture. It was this spiritual core of the person that provided the strength of character to resist dehumanizing violence in Gandhi and King's campaigns.

As the common element in all human cultures and traditions, King recognized that the spiritual dimension of life was intertwined with all other rights. For him, nonviolence provided a path and an interpretative framework to analyze our failure to prevent the severing and wounding of God's presence on Earth. It demanded an accounting of how human acts of violence tear at our hearts, lay waste to our souls, and lead us to the brink of despair. It asked how these travesties against the spirit of life contribute to our collective grief, and afflict us in ways that even now the global community has yet to feel, name, or understand.

King realized that every advance in human dignity also involved the awareness and transformation of hidden states of consciousness that perpetuated acceptance or silence in the face of the inferior status of "the other." A vow of nonviolence led to growth in consciousness, which in turn obligated the oppressed to combat the inferiority, self-hatred, or lack of self-worth that demoralized personal integrity and crushed one's ability to resist. Similarly, on the side of oppressors and those obligated to effect remedy, there must exist inner repentance, or coming to terms with the shame and sorrow one felt and the suffering and pain one had caused. This reconciliation also involved engagement with the spiritual depth of nonviolence.

He had a keen sense of the fragileness and resilience of human communities, and the importance of a narrative able to unite divergent factions of the populace. He tapped into the river of wisdom that has guided religious leaders throughout history, and was especially committed to interfaith dialogue and to cooperation and reconciliation with members of the world's religions. King's fellowship with all men and women around the globe was based on "that force [of love]," he wrote, "which all of the great religions have seen as the supreme unifying principle of life. Love is the key that unlocks the door which leads to ultimate reality. This Hindu-Moslem-Christian-Jewish-Buddhist belief about ultimate reality is beautifully summed up in the First Epistle of Saint John: Let us love one another: for love is of God."[25]

King developed a critical awareness of the integral unity that sustained life, and by which he abandoned any narrow sense of superiority of religion or person. Not only was God revealed in all religions, God also brought new or unexplored wisdom through other religions, King held: "There is a need for individual religions to realize that God has revealed Himself to all religions and there is some truth in all. And no religion can permit itself to be so arrogant that it fails to see that God has not left Himself without a witness, even though it may be in another religion."[26]

Ahimsa means that we may not offend other religions or harbor a superiority of revelation. Often, we don't recognize how our religions promote or defend violent speech. We fail to admit the ways in which our sacred texts and religious practices employ a language of exclusion, rejection, or superiority. True nonviolence protests the assertion that there is a limited amount of compassion to go around, that salvation is somehow proscribed only for the few, the elect, and those belonging to a "superior" culture, race, gender, or religion. The world's violence is the outer garment of humanity's interior, spiritual violence.

The principle of nonviolence is quite subtle. It covers all aspects of behavior. Truth is harmed by evil thoughts, by undue hate (or haste), by lying, by hatred, by wishing ill. It includes inner states of being, and theological or spiritual nonviolence. Nonviolence seeks reconciliation and fosters an atmosphere of peace. We all yearn to be cared for. We all yearn to be embraced by holiness. We do not want others to violate us or demand that we change. We want to be reconciled in a loving and nonviolent manner. Non-violence opens the door of the heart so that truth can be shared, and heal.

Voluntary Self-Sacrifice

Gandhi held that, "Sacrifice is the law of life. It runs through and governs every walk of life. We can do nothing or get nothing without paying a price for it. . . . If we would secure the salvation of the community to which we belong, we must pay for it, that is, sacrifice self."[27]

The Mahatma practiced spiritual renunciation—self-sacrifice—that identifies with the displaced and marginalized, and which implies a moral persuasion based on the inherent goodness of creation. This giving of self occurs in daily family and community situations, in mystical solidarity with injustice, and in political and social action for change. Parents sacrifice for their children and police and fire responders for their community. Monks sacrifice a certain kind of freedom to identify with and heal the wounds of others. Others, like Gandhi and King, give their lives.

Considered the highest spiritual path and the catalyst of all true transformation, sacrifice erases the self in order that the person may become a divine conduit: "If you would swim in the bosom of the ocean of Truth," Gandhi wrote, "you must reduce yourself to zero."[28] In the depth of our humanity, we refuse to violate the code of humility and mercy; we refuse to cause suffering to others. The salvation we seek, the joy of *moksha* (liberation), is not an end in itself. It arises, Gandhi wrote, "through the agony of the Cross and in no other way. Joy comes not out of the infliction of pain on others but out of pain voluntarily borne by oneself."[29]

Thus, self-sacrifice is authentic and spiritually inspired when it is performed without revenge, coercion, or hate. Gandhi was strict to inquire whether his austerities, such as fasting and inviting imprisonment, where inspired by God's call or were egoistic. Self-suffering is not the act of a false martyr, but is voluntarily and consciously undertaken as redemptive. In "A Christmas Sermon On Peace," Dr. King clarified:

> I've seen too much hate to want to hate, myself, . . . and every time I see it, I say to myself, hate is too great a burden to bear. Somehow we must be able to stand up before our most bitter opponents and say: "We shall match your capacity to inflict suffering by our capacity to endure suffering. We will meet your physical force with soul force. Do to us what you will and we will still love you.... But be assured that we'll wear you down by our capacity to suffer, and one day we will win our freedom. We will not only win freedom for ourselves; we will so appeal to your heart and conscience that we will win you in the process, and our victory will be a double victory."[30]

During the Vietnam War, a number of Buddhist monks underwent the sacrifice of self-burning. This act was aimed at the heart of the oppressors, and called the world's attention to the anguish endured by the Vietnamese. These monks performed an act of determination to confront violence and hate, and to suffer and die for their people. Thich Nhat Hanh tried to explain self-burning to a Western audience, which was spoken of as suicide, but, "in the essence, he wrote, "it is not. It is not even a protest."

> The Vietnamese monk, by burning himself, says with all his strength and determination that he can endure the greatest of sufferings to protect his people. . . . What he really aims at is the expression of his will and determination, not death. . . . To express will by burning oneself, therefore, is not to commit an act of destruction but to perform an act of construction, i.e., to suffer and to die for the sake of one's people.[31]

From his cloister, Thomas Merton also discovered that social and political injustice was not separate from the state of his soul. Through his struggles and dark nights, he was confronting more than a reckoning of personal sins, lack of virtue, and inner egoism; he also was bearing the collective, global sins that wound our hearts, and the heart of God, in order to *be* a soul force of unity and peace.

It is increasingly clear that Thomas Merton understood his vowed monastic life to be a form of protest and sacrifice, and the necessary leaven required to raise awareness of the human condition. He was deeply concerned that technology and bourgeois commercialism would taint the souls of people and lead to a sloppy and immature development of personality. Most of all he wanted people to be concerned about the present and future of the planet and to feel the violation of holiness marred by armies, nuclear arms, civil rights violations, the Vietnam war, and "a kind of 'religious vaudeville' that trivialized religion."[32] He was calling for a mature reflection on life, a thoughtful, balanced observation of the forces that skew American politics and by extension the world atmosphere.

"Merton had reached the point in his life at which he was prepared to forego all other activities for the sake of a global unity in God."[33] As a monk he lived and immersed himself in lessons important to changing the world: disinterest in money for its own sake; integrity and the ability to stand alone in the face of opposition and ridicule; concern for the soul of humanity over against technology and commercialization; recognition of the deep goodness of each person; and thus contemplative action directed toward planetary peace.

He did not avert his heart from the tragic consequences of the greed, power, and insanity exploding the serenity of the planet. Rather, his solidarity with the mystical body of Christ made his soul ever more vulnerable to what global salvation means: "What impresses me most," he wrote, "... is ... the idea of solitude as part of the clarification which includes living for others: dissolution of the self in 'belonging to everyone' and regarding everyone's suffering as one's own."[34]

Advocating what he called the "third position of integrity," Merton was disinterested in the grab for power and control, even under the guise of liberal social agendas.[35] Instead, he placed his faith in love of the common good, and in the innocent victims of all sorts of institutional and governmental violence. Even though he branded himself complicit—as a citizen of the planet—in human tragedy, he continuously fought the complacency and dishonesty that tends to shield the deep self from the plight of others. In his astute study of world events, Merton was a prophetic cry in the desert of modern culture, exposing his soul to the actual fate of victims.

> I am on the side of the people who are being burned, cut to pieces, tortured, held as hostages, gassed, ruined, destroyed. They are the victims of both sides. To take sides with massive power is to take sides against the innocent. The side I take is then the side of the people who are sick of war and want peace in order to rebuild their country.[36]

The primacy of love over everything in the spiritual life transformed his understanding of the monastic commitment. "Love takes one's neighbour as one's other self," Merton writes, "and loves him with all the immense humility and discretion and reserve and reverence without which no one can presume to enter into the sanctuary of another's subjectivity. From such love all authoritarian brutality, all exploitation, domineering and condescension must necessarily be absent.... The saints of the desert... renounced everything that savoured of punishment and revenge, however hidden it might be."[37]

The monks and mystics who give their lives for the betterment of the world have much to teach us. Without the experience of voluntary self-sacrifice, we cannot understand divine suffering, or how suffering fully experienced becomes grace. Our capacity for sacrifice is the means by which the world is transformed. We learn from these masters of wisdom that our self-gift is the method whereby we can redeem society from strife and pain. Suffering voluntarily endured becomes a redemptive force in history.

· ◆ ·

THE SPIRITUAL PHILOSOPHY of the social mystics—which approaches the world from a holistic, sacred perspective—transforms the content and context of public discourse. While devout representatives of their respective religions each, in another sense, lives *beyond* tradition. To the social mystics, the pursuit of ultimate reality is not solely a personal quest, but is truly attainable only by engaging with the struggle for social and political justice. God-realization is held up as a mandate not only for the individual, but also for entire societies and the global community.

In closing this chapter, it is evident that monastics—new and old—are challenged more than ever to work together toward building Martin Luther King's "beloved community." Through mutual cooperation and sharing, we can find the means to mend the rift between rich and poor, body and spirit, and indifference and compassion. By attaining inner peace, we discover new answers to perpetual human problems—poverty, racism, ecological degradation, gender violence, war, starvation, and moral temerity. Through the witness and lives of modern saints, we can learn to direct mystical consciousness in the service of societal reform. Like the women and men of faith presented in this chapter, devotion to a contemplative ethic can be our guide to the soul's liberation from oppression. True concern for humanity and the Earth challenges us to probe our inner lives, and to uncover points of spiritual exclusion, violence, superiority, or rejection that wound our souls and diminish love. When we have the courage to face ourselves, we will realize that the true spiritual task begins in searching our own hearts for that one, holy source of unity.

Revisioning Monastic Principles

TWENTY-TWO

The Wisdom of Vows

ALL OF OUR LIVES involve some type of commitment, whether performed consciously or not. We each are vowed to someone or something: This could be the marriage vow, or faithfulness to a community or practice. It could be the daily obligations we enact to support our families or care for loved ones. Perhaps it is vowed to live in relationship to the ecology of the Earth, or to the practice of nonviolence. These represent a set of values that compel us to act—or refrain from action—according to a more humane and heightened sense of responsibility and harmony.

The monk's profession of vows maintains a similar ethos, with the distinction that it almost always has a juridical element, seen as a legally binding obligation to church, *sangha*, or congregation. He or she recognizes that these are consecrated commitments made to God, the Holy One, and are designed to be lifelong. In Christian orders—Catholic, Anglican, and Eastern Orthodox—these have been depicted as the three vows of poverty, chastity, and obedience, or the Benedictine equivalent.[1] Monks in diverse traditions distinguish between the primary vow to live a God-centered life, and a secondary one made to the community.

For example, Sandra M. Schneiders—Immaculate Heart of Mary sister—describes "the commitment to Religious Life" in Catholic monasticism as having a twofold significance: an "absolute, total, and unconditional commitment to Jesus Christ" in lifelong celibacy, and a commitment to one's monastic congregation that is "necessarily relative, partial, and conditional."[2] Schneiders also emphasizes that the language of vows is metaphoric, poetic, and "hyperbolic," that is, literary extravagance is used to "capture the totality of the commitment being expressed . . . the use of extreme language to evoke what is beyond expression."[3] Words like "poverty" and "obedience" are not literal descriptions of legal obligation, but rather represent the commitment of the monk's *whole self* to the love that has claimed him or her.

As new monastics, we are especially called to delve into the meaning behind vows, and to forge new traditions of commitment. These religious lifeforms can be practiced by anyone, with or without belonging to a formal monastic community, especially when the deep structures that underlie monastic vows are pursued. It is not uncommon for a person on a spiritual path to discover that beneath one's material wants and human desires, true happiness is found in the deep self, where we are connected to God within. When worldly distractions subside and we are left alone to ponder death or the transience of life and possessions, what remains is the permanence of silence, love, and truth. These core principles are the foundation of every monk's vow.

The Tree of Vows

IMAGINE THE LIFE of a monk as a beautiful fruit tree. The root of the tree draws in the spirit's life-giving sustenance, distributing it to the trunk, branches, leaves, and fruit.

The root is the monastic heart, anchoring the tree in stability, and without which it cannot exist. Reaching down and out into the soil, the root represents the intention for the Creator beating in every one of the tree's fibers. The trunk is the circulation system of a tree, forming a network of tubes that carries love up from the roots to the leaves, and carries wisdom from the leaves down to the branches, trunk, and roots. This is love for love's sake, because we were created in love, and through love we discover the secret teachings of love. When our hearts in their passion reach out toward the Divine in adoration, we are drawn into intimacy. Thus, the monastic heart absorbs and distributes the spirit's blood, like a trunk that circulates the tree's nutrients.

The branches of the tree are the vows we take, devoting one's whole self to the Divine through a faithful commitment. Vows are an expression of love arising from the primordial prayer of the heart, the first language of the spirit. When words are spoken from the depth of our hearts about what we long to be and how we long to serve, and the ways in which we want to devote our lives to the furtherance of divine life on earth, those are the vows.

The leaves on the tree represent the type of monastic commitment. These are the rules of life the monk follows to stay on the path. They are devised to harness and prepare our hearts through daily practice to strengthen our resolve and help us to be humble, being faithful to God's action in us. Surrendering our will to the Divine is the major turning point in the monk's life: to not be self-willed in a harmful way. A monastic rule also assists in deconstructing those habits that prevent the monk's quest for meaning and love.

The fruit on the tree is evidence of the love and wisdom that fills our souls with fragrances, and which we share with others. From the center of the monastic heart are born these tangible fruits, which nourish us, and those we meet. Gentleness of speech is nourishing. Gratitude is nourishing. Silence is nourishing. Love of God is nourishing. These qualities of the monastic heart feed us in ways that other things cannot.

In the term, "monastic heart," each word is significant. "Monastic" is related to the Greek word, *monachos,* meaning "single" or "solitary." Combined with "heart," the phrase points to a singular quest for the divine in a movement of love. The axis around which a seeker forges personal vows and a new way of life, the monastic heart is centered on love of truth in all things.

The monastic heart is the flame that ignites your love; the ember burning brightly that keeps you focused on truth; and the knowledge that all loves are in essence love of the divine. When life is assessed from the perspective of history, desire, progress, possession, achievement, great honor, and wealth, the monastic heart realizes that in all this, there is one underlying fact: God alone. Everything in life can be distilled into this single realization.

However, it is easy to become distracted by conflicting interests, and to forget that underneath everything there is a pulse from the Divine Heart calling you home. If only you remember that whenever you have a problem or feel alone, you can return to union with God in the center of your being. Part of the human journey is to forget and lose our way. All of us can review our lives and see where and how we have gone astray. We may have pursued honor, wealth, and accomplishment as a path to a meaningful life. But the road to fulfilling our deepest desire comes from directing our love toward the Divine Heart, where no attainment is required.

Society often is in conflict with the simplicity and direction that is essential to a monastic commitment. If you desire to be a monk in the world, then you must learn to distinguish between conflicting desires. This is because the mystical heart requires a unity of your whole being and life choices. The totality of the heart's effect on your inner life is so comprehensive that it is not possible to maintain a distance from its pulsing life force. No. The spiritual life, the monastic life requires that you give away protectionism and the desire to ward off what is too palpable, too emotional. Unconsciously, like the autonomic nervous system, you surrender to the torrent of love pouring into your whole being with each breath. In giving yourself away, you receive wisdom that cannot be known any other way.

Religious life is a movement of love. It is love of the divine lived out in the world. It is the desire to live life as the Spirit created us to live that draws us to the wisdom of monasticism. Monasticism approaches reality from a divine perspective, seeing with contemplative eyes, in search of silence, the source of awe.

In addition to the personal adherence to vows, monks—as members of an intentional community—dedicate themselves to the work of spiritual growth and to the preservation of solitude. Benedictine monk William Skudlarek describes this essential dimension of a vowed community:

...a monastic community is not simply a gathering of like-minded individuals who enjoy one's another's company and work together on a common project. It is, rather, an intentional community whose members are dedicated to the work of spiritual growth and who together fashion an environment in which each can engage in that inner work with a minimum of distractions.

In addition to being a *schola caritatis* [a school of love], a laboratory for testing and strengthening the day-to-day practice of unselfish fraternal love, a monastic community exists to create an environment in which solitude is cherished and protected.[4]

Vows are the pledge each monk makes to devote his or her life to the solitary quest for truth. Vows are a guiding set of principles that strengthens the monk's resolve—alone or in community—to be a source of peace, and to walk the humble path of service.

Gratitude

An abundant sense of gratitude for choosing the monastic vocation permeates the monasteries I've visited. Monastic men and women have confided how blessed and lucky they feel to spend their lives with others who also long to know God and develop a spiritual life. The silence that seeps from the walls—and the simple placement of candle or statue—glows with appreciation for life's gifts. Daily chanting praise and devotion, the monks' voices blend into one, unified affirmation.

The commitment to live a vowed life rises up spontaneously out of gratitude. Vows express an outpouring of appreciation for the precious gift of being born, for the gift of being able to seek truth. How miraculous that is! How incredible it is that all of us—and all of life—are connected to the Divine, which transcends our daily concerns!

Gratitude and appreciation overflow into the whole environment of the monastery and enter into the hearts and souls of those who enter its cloistered walls. It's a tangible feeling, a sweetness that fills your soul, reminding you of what is truly important. Gratitude and the monastic injunction to practice simplicity, emptiness, or poverty are interrelated.

These spiritual qualities peel away whatever is extraneous in a person's life to reveal the monastic heart, the core.

Gratitude overflows from the simplification of life, the honing of life into what is actually necessary and what really matters. We think, *Well, we can be grateful when we have many things.* But we discover that gratitude is not dependent on externals. It is dependent on our commitment and our desire to love life. Therefore it is within our capacity to achieve gratefulness. It's not dependent on what the world gives us, but rather what we give of ourselves to the world. I believe this is the fundamental principle behind monastic vows.

The ideal power of gratitude is expressed in a story from one of Christianity's early desert fathers. A seeker of truth says, "Abba, I want to know the truth." He is sent away because his attitude is demanding: "You owe me the truth." Without gratitude, we cannot enter into the heart of reality. Without humility, the soul will be prevented from achieving its great longing. Without giving ourselves away with devotion and love, we cannot enter the tabernacle of the Holy. Vows prepare us to receive God into our hearts. It's not something we demand, but something we give.

Vows are the manifestations of a grateful heart. It is a literal process. When the Buddhist monk is taught to be mindful of his or her actions and to treasure each breath, each washing of the dish, each step, this is gratitude in practice. Right action, right speech, right livelihood are the physical expression of a person's sacred vow. When Teresa of Avila says, "God lives among the pots and pans," and Benedictine monks read the Psalms, participate in Eucharist, and perform *lectio divina* ("divine reading")—the slow reading and pondering of Scripture—they express gratitude. These actions result from a desire to embody and integrate the Divine into every aspect of our lives.

As St. Augustine says, we can truly know only what we truly love. This is the point of the vowed life: to assist the soul in remembrance that there is a higher love seeking to be born in our hearts.

Obedience

In Latin, the word "obedience" means to listen, to really hear. We could say that obedience is listening with our hearts to hidden truths. We practice obedience out of gratitude and love; we want to live a holy life. We want to be obedient to the inner voice, to live in alignment with truth. Freedom comes from listening. The freedom God leads us to, however, is not a freedom that we can understand from our wills, from our personalities. It is so profound that we have to sink into a deeper listening in order to be guided to that which is beyond understanding.

Obedience does not always imply an external rule. But all spiritual lives are obedient, listening, to something. It is not a kind of unordered doing of whatever we want, acting solely according to our own will. Obedience is listening for God's will—a difficult concept for modern people. Our individualistic society has developed an extreme resistance to being told what to do. But the true monk, in following an interior order, realizes the need for spiritual guidance, because the farther a person moves along the path the subtler is his or her will and ego.

This inner order does not arise in a vacuum because it involves relationship, communication, and understanding others' desires. In a monastic community, obedience is designed to guide the monks, under the supervision of the abbot, abbess, roshi, lama, and so forth, to listen to the inner voice, which, due to secular habits, the monks may not understand or have forgotten. Mystically, obedience is an interior process of living according to the deepest and highest human possibility. Living not against ourselves, but giving to others what we have been given.

Are there abuses in monastic traditions? Yes. Are there times when obedience becomes pathological? Yes.

One of the most difficult aspects of the monastic journey is discerning when we are being called in one direction or another. If obedience means following the rule of God, and your resistance arises from your will seeking its desire—which may be contrary to the Divine Will and thus in conflict with your true happiness—then you understand how arduous discernment can be. Augustine's soul struggle, which he recounts in the *Confessions*, of the division within himself that is laying waste to his soul, is classic. He cannot reconcile what he knows God wants for him with what he wants to do. Even though Augustine wants to do what is right, his habituation to doing what doesn't make him happy creates internal conflict.

Obedience is also a form of renunciation. We try, in a celebratory way, to renounce those habits that we have been trained to enact—the habit of contemporary culture, habit of personality or family—and out of humility we work to re-order these habits in the service of liberating the self.

Being obedient to God within, listening to the stirrings of the Divine Will, is part of monastic training. It is the capacity to trust your inner voice and to follow the guidance of inner light that helps you through those times when your life is rough and the road is bumpy. Through this training of the soul, we remember, "Thy will, not my will."

Simplicity of Life

All over the world, monastics value frugality and simplicity. This commitment of solidarity with the struggles of earthly life is frequently translated into the vow of poverty, with monks giving away money and possessions before joining a religious order. The seeker gives away everything in order to be unencumbered before God.

Among the desert monastics, Buddhist monks, and Essence communities, poverty, in the form of divesting of everything but the barest necessities of life, was critical to mystical union or enlightenment. Others, such as St. Francis and his followers, espoused to "Lady Poverty" as an ontological principle and the most authentic imitation of Christ. Benedict's monastic spirituality associated poverty with interior humility, and the primary practice in the quest for God. Ascetic practices—which consisted of one vegetarian meal a day, sitting and sleeping on the floor, fasting, contemplation, and solitude—marked the radical poverty of the Hindu *sannyasi*.

In each of its expressions, poverty is not solely material, because the monk may be materially poor, but lack inner poverty. True poverty includes spiritual poverty; it is divesting one's self of superiority and willfulness, thereby purifying the heart's intentions. In daily life, our hearts are often divided, pulled in contrary directions. The monastic heart signifies a desire to be drawn closer to a unified heart, so that our inner and outer lives mirror each other. Purity of heart is poverty of spirit, a profound contemplation on detachment and emptiness, and is always relevant in the vowed life.

Celibacy

The spiritual aspiration of the monk is to work for the good of all living things. Renunciation of worldly goods and behaviors, including sexual behaviors, is considered a particularly powerful and exalted expression of this aspiration. Catholic monks choose to forgo marriage and to practice lifelong celibacy in order to love God with their whole heart and to love their neighbors as themselves. The goal is *caritatis*, fraternal and divine love, which is developed and enhanced in community.

Although celibacy has had a checkered history in religious communities, it is still considered to be the singularly distinguishing characteristic of the monk. As a sacrifice of the self for God in complete love, celibacy is understood to be on a different level than the vows of poverty and obedience. Sandra Schneiders writes: "The vow of consecrated celibacy stands by itself since no interpretation or particular law can alter its fundamental obligation to remain unmarried and to practice chastity in the form of total abstinence from genital sex and whatever leads to or flows from genital sex."[5]

For Buddhists, celibacy is the path to wisdom and liberation. "A Buddhist monk," William Skudlarek writes, "would not identify love as his motive for choosing to be celibate.... the goal for the Buddhist is liberation from *dukkha* ... [or] suffering ... To say that love is the goal of celibacy would not provide a sufficient rational for the Buddhist, for whom liberation is the ultimate goal of human existence." He continues:

The key insight of the Buddha in relation to sexuality and celibacy lies in identifying sexual pleasure as the most powerful sensual pleasure, the one to which we become most easily and strongly attached. To attain the highest way of life, it is necessary to relinquish the desire for

sexual pleasure because this form of gratification obstructs the concentration (*samadhi*), the one-pointed stillness that leads to insight
(wisdom).[6]

For Buddhists, the practice of celibacy is fundamental to the monk's
dedication to spiritual development and to harnessing the energy of
liberation.

Christian monks are celibate to learn to practice universal love, the
love that transcends the personal, and practice fraternal compassion, to
see all human beings without self-motivation. The celibate of Christian
monasticism bears witness to the radical existential solitude of every
human. Recognizing that God alone can satisfy the deepest longing to
love and be loved, the monk dedicates his or her life to the love of God
and all creation. "Celibacy then," writes Skudlarek, "is the practical means
to establish the monk in solitude, thereby making possible a more visible
witness to the fact that silence and solitude are at the very core of monastic
life, just as fruitful mutuality [children] is intrinsic to the married life."[7]

Chapters 24 and 25 further explore the relationship between celibacy
and sexuality for the new monk—single, married, in partnership,
abstinent, or sexually active.

Discipline

Training in discipline develops an inner core that keeps the monastic
heart focused. Violence, punishment, and oppression are spiritually
damaging; aggression robs the person of the gift of interior discipline. We
rebel against external demand: "You are going to do it this way and if you
don't do it, I'm going to beat you or deprive you." Something in the human
spirit resists violence. If we are continually subjected to punishment
and ridicule, resistance becomes a habit, an automatic response of self-
protection. While there may have been genuine survival reasons for our
resistance, at a certain point it becomes a serious detriment to spiritual
growth. Resistance to forced discipline will be in conflict with true inner
discipline. True discipline is a joy because it gives you direction and a path
to follow.

Our many resistances—suppressing love, anger with the divine, fear of the divine—are the inner, subtle blocks that monastic vows are designed to undo. Most monks will tell you that they, too, went through tremendous struggles in the beginning of their vowed life; they, too, experienced dark nights. Yet as they grow out of resistance and into inner discipline, sweetness and resiliency develop. If you toil and cultivate and plow the inner soil of your soul, someday you will reap the harvest.

The wonderful quote from the Book of Sirach reminds: "When you get hold of her, discipline, do not let her go because she is the rest you seek." Discipline refers to the order of one's heart. It's the spiritual training of living from God's perspective. Therefore it is reflected in certain shared monastic values, such as hospitality, loving kindness, and gratitude. Discipline is the harness by which you are joined to the Divine.

Contemporary Vows

MANY COMMUNITIES have developed vows in accord with their missions, including the vows of nonviolence, personal sacrifice, social justice, and gratitude. The selection of vows listed below are drawn from diverse sources—new monasticism, nonviolent campaigns, social justice, etc.—and serve to illustrate the interdependence of spiritual principles in transforming and transcending attitudes, centering the seeker in the divine heart.

Rutba House: Twelve Marks of New Monasticism[8]

Rutba House is a house of hospitality founded in 2003 by Jonathan and Leah Wilson-Hartgrove. Rooted in evangelical Christianity, Rutba House is a leader in the movement of new monasticism and welcomes the formerly homeless into a community that eats, prays, and shares life together.

1. Relocation to the abandoned places of Empire.
2. Sharing economic resources with fellow community members and the needy among us.
3. Hospitality to the stranger.
4. Lament for racial divisions within the church and our communities combined with the active pursuit of a just reconciliation.
5. Humble submission to Christ's body, the church.
6. Intentional formation in the way of Christ and the rule of the community along the lines of the old novitiate.
7. Nurturing common life among members of intentional community.
8. Support for celibate singles alongside monogamous married couples and their children.
9. Geographical proximity to community members who share a common rule of life.
10. Care for the plot of God's earth given to us along with support of our local economies.
11. Peacemaking in the midst of violence and conflict resolution within communities along the lines of Matthew 18.
12. Commitment to a disciplined contemplative life.

The Eleven Observances Taken by Members of Gandhi's Satyagraha Ashram[9]

Truth was the basis of Mahatma Gandhi's nonviolent campaigns, and inscribed in the form of life developed in his ashrams. His commitment to the alleviation of suffering of India's citizenry was stabilized and advanced through the following monastic vows.

- Truth is God, the one and only Reality. All other observances take their rise from the quest for, and the worship of, Truth.
- Non-violence is Love. Mere non-killing is not enough. The active part of non-violence is love. The law of Love requires equal consideration for all life from the tiniest insect to the highest man.

- Observance of chastity is impossible without the observance of celibacy. It is not enough that one should not look upon any woman or man with a lustful eye; animal passion must be so controlled as to be excluded even from the mind.
- Control of the palate is a principle by itself. Eating is necessary only for sustaining the body and keeping it a fit instrument for service, ... Food must, therefore, be taken, like medicine, under proper restraint.
- Non-stealing [not only means] not to take another's property without his permission. One becomes guilty of theft even by using differently anything which one has received in trust [or] if one receives anything which one does not really need.
- Non-possession [means] one must not possess anything which one does not really need ... to possess unnecessary food-stuffs, clothing or furniture.
- Physical labor is essential for the observance of non-stealing and non-possession. Able-bodied adults must do all their personal work themselves, and must not be served by others, except for proper reasons.
- Man ... serves the world best by serving his neighbor. Following this principle [swadeshi], one must as far as possible purchase one's requirements locally and not buy things imported from foreign lands, which can easily be manufactured in the country.
- One cannot follow Truth or Love so long as one is subject to fear. A seeker after Truth must give up the fear of parents, caste, government, robbers, etc., and he must not be frightened by poverty or death.
- Untouchability ... is altogether irreligious. ... The ashram does not believe in caste, which it considered has injured Hinduism, because its implications of superior and inferior status, and of pollution by contact, is contrary to the law of Love.
- The ashram believes that the principal faiths of the world constitute a revelation of Truth ... One must therefore entertain the same respect for the religious faiths of others as one accords to one's own, and [not] convert people to one's own faith. One can only pray that

the defects in the various faiths be overcome, and that they may advance, side by side, towards perfection.

Pledge of Nonviolence Taken by Marchers with Dr. Martin Luther King Jr., 1963[10]

A deep spirituality was the basis of Rev. Dr. King's Civil Rights campaigns and advocacy for the soul of humanity. His marches, built upon Christian principles of love and nonviolence, were a type of contemplative formation and vowed commitment.

- As you prepare to march meditate on the life and teachings of Jesus.
- Remember the nonviolent movement seeks justice and reconciliation—not victory.
- Walk and talk in the manner of love; for God is love.
- Pray daily to be used by God that all men and women might be free.
- Sacrifice personal wishes that all might be free.
- Observe with friend and foes the ordinary rules of courtesy.
- Perform regular service for others and the world.
- Refrain from violence of fist, tongue, and heart.
- Strive to be in good spiritual and bodily health.
- Follow the directions of the movement leaders and of the captains on demonstrations.

Nine Vows Developed by Interfaith Minister Rev. Diane Berke[11]

Rev. Berke is the founder and director of One Spirit Learning Alliance and One Spirit Interfaith Seminary in New York City. Ordained an interfaith minister in 1988, she is a widely respected pioneer of interreligious ministry education.

- I vow to actualize and live according to my full moral and ethical capacity.
- I vow to live in solidarity with the cosmos and all living beings.
- I vow to live in deep nonviolence.
- I vow to live in humility and to remember the many teachers and guides who assisted me in my spiritual path.
- I vow to embrace a daily spiritual practice.
- I vow to cultivate mature self-knowledge.
- I vow to live a life of simplicity.
- I vow to live a life of selfless service and compassionate action.
- I vow to be a prophetic voice as I work for justice, compassion, and world transformation.

· ◆ ·

MONASTIC VOWS emerge from our profound commitment to the Holy. As modern, multi-religious or interspiritual monks, we touch the center of solitude within us to draw out a method and a way. In many new monastic communities, vows are written by each aspirant, and represent his or her personal commitment to the Divine. Since Spirit calls each person to monastic life directly, I find that this method preserves the solitude between the seeker and God, while avoiding the corporate spiritual identity that too often has stifled the spirit of monasticism. For the person who longs to be a monk, God already speaks in his or her heart. Vows that arise from the person's deep listening take on the aura of authenticity and power.

At the same time, the new monk recognizes how mysteriously his or her path is connected to monastic wisdom practiced across centuries, cultures, and traditions, and in the hearts and minds of countless humans. Each aspires toward nonviolence in thought, word, and deed, and it is precisely the monk's vows that hone the personality and open the soul to love. Thus, study of monastic vows practiced by members of the world's religions is especially helpful to developing our personal vows and sacred commitments.

This revival of contemplative monasticism is a hopeful sign for the future of humanity. While a particular form of monasticism may become obsolete or extinct, the monastic archetype is intrinsic to the human heart and to the spiritual way of life. Vows are an expression of gratitude for everything we have been given. The formal profession of vows witnessed by the members of a spiritual community has a very powerful effect on a person's life.

TWENTY-THREE

Gandhi on Vows

MAHATMA GANDHI is a valuable guide for the contemporary person who is pioneering a new monastic expression. Gandhi did not live in the traditional ashram, where the scriptures, practices, and rituals were primarily Hindu and the lifestyle strictly contemplative, and often caste-bound. Rather, his ashram experiments were committed to the prayers and practices of many religions, and were inclusive of individuals from every caste. In addition, the ashram, far from being an escape from politics and societal turmoil, was a school of contemplative engagement, and a refuge in which Gandhi restored his spiritual strength in order to be of further service through nonviolent campaigns.

For Gandhi, vows were intrinsic to his entire way of life and the necessary counterpart to his faith in the unity of all beings and the oneness of creation. Perhaps his most profound accomplishment was his ability to know, speak, and act on truth in thought and deed. Arising organically from his experiments in nonviolence, Gandhi's practice of vows was a personal, sacred commitment that inspires us to ask: what is crucial to *our* paths? Gandhi would be the first to say that no one can perform his or her vows perfectly, but we can aspire toward perfection.

Two main principles underlie Gandhi's vows and are central to his spiritual practice. The first is, simply, human caring. Gandhi's development of vows was designed, above all, "to heal the hurting indifference which keeps one human being from another." His stance against untouchability, for example, rose out of this principle, for how can you love all creation, all humanity, and hold that one individual life is less valuable than another?

The second principle underlying his vows is the desire to achieve salvation, to see God face to face. Integrated with the first principle, salvation is achieved through upholding the family of creation and the oneness of life. Gandhi sought to heal the indifference within Indian society that segregated people. Instead of accepting that brokenness, suffering, and injustice would always inflict pain on India's people, Gandhi worked to create a world without injustice by adhering to his vow with unflinching determination.

An important component in professing a vow is that a vow is not something you undertake only as far as possible. Gandhi said that "as far as possible" implied that he had a way out, because then he could decide how far he wanted to go. He therefore would control what was possible, what was reasonable. What often appears to be reasonable or conventional wisdom is in fact an element of one's will. For Gandhi, it would be a fatal mistake to say "as far as possible" because you then would start with a compromise. It is an attempt to pursue one's own ends and not God's, refusing to give oneself totally to a higher truth.

He saw God as the epitome of a vow; he held that God would cease to be God if God swerved "even a hair's breadth from God's own law." The sun shines every day; it does not only shine as much as possible. Nature provides us with abundance and does not limit itself; it follows divine law. Gandhi understood this to be the law of God: that life is a continually renewing, overflowing possibility. Thus, every authentic vow must be founded on an unflinching determination to go where God takes us, not stopping at self-imposed limits. Gandhi was graced with an ability to push the boundaries of conventional reality; his life a testimony to how an unswerving love of truth can transform society.

Gandhi lived to fulfill God's desires. He seemed to feel with an extraordinary intensity the brokenness of the world. He could not tolerate the wall that separated him from the poor. And so he became poor in order to be one with them. Open to the physical and soul suffering of others, Gandhi offered himself as a sacrifice. He felt God's suffering for all of India in the depth of his heart; the starving masses were the face of God stricken with hopelessness; the belly of God empty of love; the heart of God pleading for compassion. In this direct connection with the suffering people of India, he came to realize that there was no truth in any vow that did not pursue action and change.

Gandhi embodied a new monastic model by uniting the monk's traditional life of prayer with that of the karma yogi—the person who practices the yoga of action through selfless acts of giving. The degree to which he wed solitude to action is unique in history, as was his ability to sustain the performance of his vows over a lifetime. His duty as a karma yogi was for one purpose: that his way of life would alleviate the divisions between people and contribute to the healing of the world's suffering.

His vows were all encompassing, covering every area of human endeavor—nothing was too small to attract his attention. He was interested in diet, illness, and health. He ministered to people in his ashrams, becoming proficient in applying bandages and Ayurvedic medicine, and practicing many types of healing modalities. He was deeply concerned with women's issues in India, with children, their education and health, with agriculture and, of course, politics. Each of these concerns stemmed from his belief that there is no division of the spirit in creation. With this one root principle, he focused his heart and mind on diverse areas of life.

The way Gandhi was guided to the development of vows, and how he transformed vows into political action, are sublime examples of practicing monasticism in the world. He once closed his ashram in protest of British colonial rule, explaining that the ashram would become a walking ashram, in exodus, but still an ashram because it was not dependent on structure. What made it a holy community was not the form or location, but the commitment to healing the divisions in India and to the performance of a unifying vision.

Vow of Brahmacharya

One of Gandhi's instructive vows is *brahmacharya*, the control of the senses or appetites, sexuality, and food. If we study this vow under the umbrella of Gandhi's larger principle of healing of divisions within humanity, we see that *brahmacharya* is conduct adapted toward the search for Brahma, or truth. In essence, this is the universal principle behind monastic vows: to seek God. *Brahmacharya* involved control of thought, word, and deed; control of sexual desire; control of ownership, possession, or demand; and control over food. His vow to control sexuality arose from his realization that he was demanding of his wife, that he lusted after her, that he saw her as an object of his affections and not as a person in her own right. He realized that until he could love his way into her heart and see reality from her perspective, he would not be able to heal the divisions between them.

Controlling his desires helped him identify with the suffering of his wife and the plight of women, and to work toward healing the inequities placed on women in India. He came to believe that there was no hope for India's emancipation while women remained enslaved. Gandhi writes in a pamphlet, *The Constructive Programme*, "Women have been suppressed under custom and law for which man was responsible and in the shaping of which she had no hand. Men have not realized this truth in its fullness in their behavior towards women. They have considered themselves to be lords and masters of women instead of considering them as their friends and coworkers."[1]

Those who knew him in his later life spoke of him as one who tried to understand what it was like to be a woman—the suppressed half of society—in the same way he tried to understand what it was like to be an untouchable. He came to believe that the only way he could understand the plight of women was to become sexless, to be someone women could trust, who did not want power over them. He writes, "Only by becoming a perfect *brahmacharyi* can one truly serve the woman."[2] He tried to become a person who didn't "want" something from women, but could relate—to his wife and all women—in a pure form. His stance is particularly striking for the cultural and historical period in which he lived. He once commented that it was his wife who taught him nonviolence—that her resistance to his advances became the foundation of his commitment to the power of love and nonviolent resistance.

The control over one's senses also includes control of the palate. This followed his central principle of healing divisions through physical and spiritual solidarity with the poor. He knew that control of the senses was a time-honored monastic practice, which he called "self-sacrifice." For Gandhi, controlling his sensual passions became a vehicle of transformation—you do not over-eat when millions of people are starving; you do not own excess possessions when millions have nothing. In your heart, you maintain unity and solidarity with those in need. Gandhi advised: Before you think about doing something, imagine the poorest person, and ask if that person will benefit from your action. Then you will know whether you are going in the right direction.

Vow of Self-Sacrifice

Self-sacrifice was the foundational vow behind every one of Gandhi's vows. He considered self-suffering to be the highest spiritual road, and the catalyst for transformation. Sacrifice erases the self, and thus contains the whole of creation. Gandhi knew experientially the suffering of India's people. The less he was, the more he mystically identified with their pain. "If you would swim on the bosom of the ocean of Truth, you must reduce yourself to zero."[3] Self-sacrifice is the force that transforms oppression and reverses the process of violence and hate.

This is a powerful concept: sacrifice heals humanity's divisions. And further, that the degree to which we are able to sacrifice is the degree to which society will be transformed. This makes vividly clear Gandhi's belief that a person cannot vow "as much as possible," because liberation is possible only when a vow exceeds the limit of belief.

On another level, Gandhi held that self-suffering was the expression of moral persuasion based on the inherent goodness of creation. This was the secret force behind vows.

Since creation is inherently good, he reasoned, when we perform acts of self-sacrifice, the goodness in anyone—whether enemy or friend—cannot avoid being touched by our sacrifice. Gandhi well understood that sacrifice is not an attempt to force people to do what you want them to do. That would be an act of ego. Genuine sacrifice is the result of a commitment to truth. For example, in the ashram, if someone broke a vow or rule, Gandhi would fast, not to coerce this person to obey, but because the system as a whole had contributed to the problem. Fasting was an act of healing for himself, the rule-breaker, and the entire community.

If the subtle principle of sacrifice is merely an external gesture, it is a form of control. Gandhi advocated, instead, the practice of nonviolence: you cannot punish; you can only offer penance. You cannot impose your will on others; you can only model transformation through your actions. Self-sacrifice is a catalytic force in caring for humanity because it tries to mend the divisions of the world by mending the divisions within the self. Instead of railing against the world, it is a path to self-transformation and, thus, to a renewed world. Gandhi often said that if he didn't believe in the power of nonviolence and the principle of love, he would not have been able to survive.

Vow of Non-Possession

Gandhi believed that inequity and poverty are caused by many of us taking more than we need. If we take more than our immediate need, we seize it from someone else. Thus possession is tantamount to stealing. "I venture to say, without exception," he writes, "that Nature produces enough for our wants from day to day, and if only everybody took enough for himself and nothing more, there would be no pauperism in this world, there would be no man dying of starvation in this world. But so long as we have this inequality, so long we are thieving."[4] Faith in the law of spiritual oneness was the basis of Gandhi's vow of non-possession, which he held was a fundamental law of nature.

The vow of non-possession, like his other vows, is mystically subtle. For Gandhi, stealing was the physical or mental desire to acquire anything that belongs to someone else—to covet. Non-possession was a deliberate reduction of his wants, and a vow of solidarity with those in need: "In India we have got three millions of people having to be satisfied with one meal a day...You and I have no right to anything that we really have until these three millions are clothed and fed better."[5] Non-possession was the way he loved the poor and cared about their suffering. He applied the vow of non-possession to all areas of his life, from the physical to subtle spiritual levels. For example—as previously stated—his commitment to chastity was a result of his vow of non-possession. He considered his desire for his wife to be a form of possession because he demanded sexual favors from her. Non-possession meant to not possess her soul, her thoughts, her body, or her relationship with God.

Gandhi's vows illuminate his understanding of God, who was total love, absolute freedom, and complete oneness. To live in God, we mirror these qualities in our lives. His vows, thus, extend from the physical to the mystical realms. He was concerned not only with external reality, but with all the interior, subtle movements of the spiritual life that can divert us from the goal of nonviolent love.

Vow of Ahimsa

We now come to the most well known of Gandhi's vows: the vow of *ahimsa*, or nonviolence. In Sanskrit, *ahimsa* means non-harm or non-killing. In Gandhi's usage, nonviolence is not passive, in the sense of the absence of something, but is an active term that means the performance of total love. Nonviolence applies to both the social and interior sphere, in which non-harm is practiced in thought, emotion, perception, and deed. He was especially sensitive to violence caused by religious hatred, superiority, or exclusiveness. For this reason, Gandhi personally and in his ashrams advocated openness to all genuine religious and spiritual paths, incorporating their wisdom into his practices and prayers.

Ahimsa means non-killing. But, for Gandhi it also carried the injunction to not offend anybody, and not harbor an uncharitable thought even in connection with our enemy. Nonviolence is the law of life; if we love those who consider us an enemy, we will have touched on God and will be of genuine service, because love is returned by love.

Ahimsa is the path to truth. Gandhi said that if you go by way of non-harm, you would find truth. *Ahimsa* and truth were intimately related. If truth is a constant experiment—and no one can know absolute truth directly, as Gandhi believed—then the only way to proceed is to unceasingly follow the direction of nonviolence. Violence of word, thought, and deed, and violence of religion is disallowed because no one has a privileged place on which to stand. None of us possess the total and absolute truth, and none of us is ever competent enough to judge or punish.

Ahimsa, as an expression of infinite love, requires that we look at the world with compassion. If we perceive the subtle nuances that take place within relations, we will see how, on a daily basis, we create suffering. Nonviolence was Gandhi's way of describing a life that upholds the virtues of kindness, mercy, and love. Suffering forms the basis of *ahimsa*, the principle behind the principle of all-encompassing humility. Because we understand suffering, we refuse to add to it.

Gandhi's stance on the theology of nonviolence asks: how does the world appear from the perspective of *ahimsa*? When we say there is an all-loving God, what are we saying? Is that metaphor or truth? For Gandhi, it is true: in God, punishment, retribution, condemnation, and judgment do not exist. This mystical vision of God as a loving, nonviolent, all-embracing divinity is the foundation for Gandhi's vows. If you are trying—as Gandhi was—to see God face to face—then how do you bring unending love into your life?

Gandhi embraced Jesus' injunction to "turn the other cheek" to those who call themselves "enemy," because he knew in the divine there is no such thing as an enemy. The vow of *ahimsa*, therefore, requires practice and discipline. We know how easy it is to respond in anger or in hurt to someone who scratches the surface of our wounds. He asks us, as he asked himself, to develop the resiliency and strength that can prevent us from reacting in anger or retaliation. Gandhi would be the first to admit his imperfection; he did not hide his foibles or fears. He shows us that no one can perform vows perfectly, but that we can continually aspire and work toward fulfilling them in our lives.

Vow of Truth

Gandhi held not only that "God is truth"—in that truth becomes an attribute of God—but also, "Truth is God." Truth is the way to God. Through practicing truth in every instance and circumstance, Gandhi had faith that he would be drawn deeper into the divine nature. This he did by following a relentless search for truth, realizing that he had not yet found it, and, further, that he must bear the paradox of this truth-seeking in the contradictions and disagreements of daily life.

What I want to achieve—what I have been striving and pining to achieve these thirty years—is self-realization, to see God face to face, to attain Moksha [Salvation—oneness with God and freedom from later incarnations]. I live and move and have my being in pursuit of this goal. All that I do by way of speaking and writing, and all my ventures in the political field are directed to this same end."[6]

The very method of seeking truth is one of impermanence and change, based on an understanding of the nonviolence at the core of reality. Every truth-seeking involves a sacrifice, Gandhi held, and each sacrifice requires a letting go of identity.

I am but a seeker after Truth. I claim to have found the way to it. I claim to be making ceaseless effort to find it. But I admit that I have not yet found it. To find Truth completely is to realize oneself and one's destiny, i.e., to become perfect. I am painfully conscious of my imperfections, and therein lies all the strength I possess because it is a rare thing for a man to know his own limitations.[7]

What did Gandhi mean by "Truth"? He didn't mean just external truth, although he did include that—a person does not lie or steal. He also meant the truth of your being, the truth inside, and the method of finding it. Who you are—the quality of your being—is your road to truth. Gandhi put the responsibility for truth on each person, in how a person lives his or her life. The more you adhere to *ahimsa*, the nonviolent path, the more you approach truth. He would remind others that non-harm should apply to one's self as well as to others. He gave an example of not wanting to hurt someone's feelings by telling a lie such as, "You're not disturbing me right now." But if you were being disturbed, then saying that you were not is a form of violence toward the self. The best response is to admit you were disturbed, but say it in a nonviolent way.

The vows Gandhi followed are living, eternal truths. They are perfections in themselves. We can never achieve such perfections, but the degree to which we perform them, even imperfectly, is the degree to which we walk on the path of truth. To discard them because we cannot perform them perfectly is to harm our desire to live in and with the divine.

In Gandhi's life, vows are not superimposed on events, but arise organically from the heart of one's quest for truth and understanding. He did not impose his beliefs on others, but followed the path to which he had been called. Thus, the taking of vows is always a personal, sacred commitment. His life challenges us to ask: "What do *we* have to do?" "What is crucial in *our* lives?"

TWENTY-FOUR

Mystical Celibacy: Divine-Human Intimacy

MYSTICAL CELIBACY, the soul's blissful union with the Divine, is our original state of consciousness. We are born enclosed in the tender embrace of the Spirit and as we leave this world, we are drawn back to our Source. While mystical celibacy underlies all types of intimate relationship, we are taught almost nothing of this holy state.

Mystical celibacy purifies the heart and reestablishes the integrity of being that is often lost in a world that does not recognize the sacredness of physical presence. It trains the body, mind, and spirit to preserve the enclosure where God and our souls are alone in love.

In contemplation, the divine garment of love wraps around the soul and holds her in a tender embrace. In the consummation of divine-human intimacy, celibacy is mystically born in the soul. Married to God, and single (*caelebs*) of men, the soul now gazes upon another reality. Whether joined to others in this life, married or unmarried, the soul is always intimate with her Beloved in the chamber of love.

Mystical Celibacy

UNDOUBTEDLY, sexuality and celibacy are two of the more mysterious aspects of contemplative life, reflecting deep roots in the human personality, and in the advanced stages of spiritual growth. In them, we experience the Holy Mystery in and through creation. Although celibacy is primarily associated with the unmarried state and physical abstinence from sexual relations, it also reflects a mystical state of being.

I call this state of being "mystical celibacy," and define it as the relationship of divine-human intimacy that is preserved from encroachment by outside energies. It is, then, a state of being that expresses the undefiled solitude of the self and its god. If this pure relation is present, we may speak of celibacy in two senses: as the *physical* absence of sexual relations, and as the maintenance of *spiritual* integrity, in or out of sexual relations. If this pure, interior solitude is not present, although a person may be technically celibate—unmarried and abstaining from sex—he or she is not practicing mystical celibacy.

In this expanded definition, celibacy and sexuality are two modes of expression of our primary relationship with the divine. The subtle interplay of these two phases of celibacy is often interwoven and even indistinguishable in the person. As such, each one, when understood in its depth, enriches, balances, and nourishes the other. Celibacy, as vow of abstinence and a state of consciousness, helps to redefine ourselves as sexual beings. Sexual relations, as the union of individuals in their mutual love for each other and love for the Spirit, instruct us in the balance of particular and universal love. Together, the evolutionary trajectory of celibate-sexual consciousness represents a range of possibility for expressing the mystery of embodiment.

Derived from the Greek noun *askesis*, the word *asceticism* means "exercise, practice, or training." Physical celibacy is one of the great ascetic practices found throughout all human cultures. In many religious traditions, celibacy has traditionally been seen as a lifelong abstinence from sexuality and/or from marriage for the sake of some religious obligation or commitment. In Christianity, the celibate abstains from sex to be available solely for the Divine, and by extension to all of humanity, without the constraints that incur in personal relationships. Luke's reference to celibate persons as "equal to angels" (Lk 20: 35–36) suggests their role as agents of God within our human sphere. In Buddhism, the monk abstains from sexual relations for the sake of the *dharma* and the *sangha*. The Hindu renunciate or *sannyasi* is *brahmacharya*, literally "walking with *Brahman*," and further reminds us that celibacy is associated with deep spiritual principles. It is mind-body-spirit training that heightens awareness; it preserves our inner being as a holy place, free from the emotional and biological demands of the body, and from the penetration of the mind.

Of course, people harbor fears about the celibate life. We may have heard the monastic vocation labeled "unnatural" and sexual abstinence dismissed as "sublimation." Negative perceptions about celibacy no doubt dwell in our consciousness. For example, many religious philosophies believe in a dichotomy between spirit and matter, and therefore associate sexuality with spiritual defilement. Woman, as representative of the darker forces of matter, becomes the archetypal temptress who draws males away from their higher life in the spirit. When practiced for these unhealthy reasons, celibacy denies the sanctity of the body and of human intimacy, and it distorts our perceptions of women and the feminine principle.

The "virgin" soul, a common theme in medieval Christian texts, depicts celibacy in a symbolic sense as the soul's purity. Empty and without image, the soul is as free as when she was uncreated. Naked of all things, and having nothing in common with anything, she receives into herself nothing less than the divine in all its splendor and vastness. Meister Eckhart employs this image to make a distinction between the soul as a married person, and as a virgin who is a wife. Some married people are "possessively attached to prayer, to fasting," he writes, "and to all kinds of exterior exercises and penances.... And I call these married people because they are pledged to possessiveness... and produce little fruit. A virgin who is a wife is free and unpledged, without attachment; she is always equally close to God and to herself." Her emptiness is fecund and she produces much fruit, "neither less nor more than God himself."[1]

Eckhart clarifies that a person may be sexually virginal, but mentally, spiritually, and emotionally consummated to the world. Sexual abstinence alone does not confer purity *of being*. One of my friends, a prioress at a Carmelite monastery, solemnly remarked: "We have women here who are seventy years old and virgins who do not know what celibacy is. They allow gossiping friends to intrude on silence. Or lack emotional maturity, susceptible to praise and blame, or suffer from excessive attachment to people, food, or possessions. They are, in their own ways, just as 'married' as their sexually active counterparts outside our monastery walls." What she meant was that some of her sisters did not understand the mystical dimension of the celibate life, far removed from physical abstinence alone. They had never learned that celibacy is not chiefly a physical renunciation, but is the interior preservation of one's solitude with God.

Eckhart's virgin soul conveys to us that mystical celibacy is the spiritual discipline of detachment that preserves the person's inner core from penetration. When we are attached to the outcome of our labors, when we are possessive and cling to people and things, we allow the world to step into the sanctuary where we are alone with the Alone. The practice of mystical celibacy allows us to bar entrance to our holy of holies, while being fruitful and passionate in love.

As we seek to understand the relationship of celibacy and sexuality, the monastic enclosure serves as a vibrant metaphor. As a symbolic guardian of purity of heart, the thick monastic walls preserve a way of life from intruders who might violate the vows of all those inside. Free to recover the simple health of one's inner life, our monastery is not the foreboding, asexual presence we might imagine, but the lively birthing place of the holiness of relations. Far from being opposed to sexuality, we practice mystical celibacy to discover the deepest possibility of human friendship and love. Understood in its spiritual implications, this freedom of spirit is available to all who preserve the sanctuary where the *monk within* rejoices in solitude. Celibacy shows us how to be both radically open to the whole of creation and deeply faithful to our primary relationship with the Divine.

Four Virtues of Mystical Celibacy

A PERIOD OF CELIBACY can be vital for restoring the monastic enclosure, and for reestablishing one's relations with the world on the basis of an inner freedom of being. But, as my Carmelite friend noted, celibacy is not conferred by physical status alone. It is a gift of the spirit to live in the pure solitude of being. We discover that beneath and more prior than our sexual exploits and the unholy way we treat our bodies, we are uncreated and free from attachments. We are free to enter and to leave the chamber of intimacies. We come and go as silently and as naturally as the wind on a warm day in May. Mystical celibacy teaches us to orient all our relations toward the spirit; it shows us how to maintain the monastic values of solitude and love as the central core of all our relations.

The new monk, who lives in society and does not intend to be a life-long physical celibate, benefits from a deeper understanding of mystical celibacy. Such a person also derives value from periods of sexual abstinence, in which he or she withdraws from consensual relations, and takes time to reflect on the cultural constraints or suppositions attached to gender roles and sexual performance.

The practice of mystical celibacy is a type of monastic precept for the person who lives singly, in partnership or community, or as a renunciate, whether or not he or she identifies as a monk, or chooses to engage in consensual sexual relations. It replaces the role that the vow of celibacy fulfills in historic monastic communities, in part because the vow of mystical celibacy refers to an ongoing and active spiritual practice that is pursued and forged in every relation as a means of fulfilling the commandment of love. The vow of mystical celibacy opens up the body, mind, and soul to four virtues: fidelity, passion, detachment, and intimacy.

Fidelity

Fidelity or faithfulness is central to the meaning of both physical and mystical celibacy. In Western spirituality, the union of the soul with the Divine is associated with the image of the soul, as the Lover, united in mystical marriage with its Beloved. Celibacy expresses the fidelity of the Lover transposed into the Beloved.

In Earthly marriage, we take a vow of exclusive commitment to our spouse: *in sickness and in health, in riches and in poor, till death do us part, I will love you.* The monastic vow of celibacy bodily assumes this commitment by offering the promises of the marriage vow to the Divine, and through divinity to all creation. We offer to the Divine the total trust and devotion that is ideally present in our most cherished relationships.

Mystical celibacy is faithfulness to inner solitude. It is a reconnection to the positive life energies found in children and in others who have remained free from spiritual and physical compromise. It is faithfulness not to a religious vow or social commitment, but to *one's integrity*. It is the reformation of one's whole being on a foundation of dignity that refuses to give one's mind, body, or spirit over unless the potential for respect and communion is there.

True fidelity is a spiritual liberation. Faithfulness opens a new panorama of spiritual growth and maturity. When we are faithful, we know what is central to our lives and what is simply a distraction. It gives us the freedom to practice purity of heart, to uncover the deepest desire of our lives.

Fidelity to inner solitude is not rigid or absolute. We cannot expect each other to be perfect models of communion. Untrusting and unholy relations test our faith. Possessive love shrinks our capacity for trust. But faithfulness can be practiced. When we offer to someone emotional and spiritual stability, we heal the scars of abandonment, betrayal, and absence in each other. We learn to recognize the importance of integrity in our lives. We can vow to ourselves to no longer be unfaithful, or to accept unequal or unfaithful relations. Mystical celibacy is the practice of remaining loyal to the monk within.

Sometimes, though, we may confuse fidelity with morality, and interpret it through the lens of moral judgment and outrage. Because fidelity is often portrayed in terms of an austere moral code, we may find it difficult to be faithful to god or to another person. But fidelity draws upon a core dimension of human spirituality: to be loyal to the inner voice of truth. Sometimes, fidelity means we are called to take actions that appear contrary to social or religious norms. Faithfulness requires mature and attentive discernment. It is not the unquestioned adherence of societal commandments or the comfort of belonging to the righteous and the elect.

As a result of various emotional or psychological injuries, we may associate faithfulness with an unhealthy or even dangerous kind of vulnerability. Our egos may fear that fidelity implies loss of freedom, or a stifling obligation to lovers, parents, or friends. We may not have experienced the faithfulness of love and are cautious about its value in our lives. We may have never given fidelity to, or received it from, another human being.

When we understand faithfulness as the source of liberation, we realize that until we give ourselves away, we will not touch the depth of our spiritual potential. One way to begin is to ask ourselves, *Have I ever been faithful to anyone or anything, and if not, why not?* We may discover that we have never been faithful to another human being. On the contrary, maybe our fidelity to the spiritual life has been greater than what we have given to our partner or our parents. Perhaps we have transferred from spouses or friends faithfulness to a cherished pet. It could be that we have been faithful to a certain commitment in life—our work, or our passion for nature. Facing the places where we have been faithful or have lacked fidelity is an important part of spiritual growth.

The vow of physical celibacy is not a true path for every person, and may be detrimental to one's journey. Nonetheless, periods of abstinence from interpersonal and sexual demands are fundamental to the healthy growth of the person, and can be life giving and extremely fruitful. Equally, the vow to practice *mystical* celibacy brings gifts of the spirit that can be found in no other way. It teaches us to channel our sexual energies toward a deeper understanding of interpersonal relationships. It is a path that invites us to discover the ways in which faithfulness is a part of our daily life and relations. Of course, mystical celibacy is challenging. It requires a high level of awareness to offer all aspects of our lives—the physical, emotional, sexual, spiritual—to the Divine. It requires a transformation of consciousness to heal the unfaithfulness that leads to social and spiritual disintegration.

Passion

Holy passion dwells in the soul. It is the wonder of a passion that is not reducible to the physical, but of which the physical is a seamless extension. It liberates us from the idea that sexuality is only related to the physicality of the body. It also frees us from the belief that passion is the exclusive domain of the sexual and cannot exceed the material boundaries of partner or spouse. It allows us to claim the holy passion that arises from the divine upwelling in the soul.

Temporary abstinence from the senses quiets the body and opens the soul to the Divine Presence. Elusive and obscure, the vow of mystical celibacy prepares the soul's holy chamber for divine union by dismissing all other suitors outside its doors. Filled with a sensual feeling of love that intoxicates the emotions, holy passion has physiological implications because in this life we are substantially one in body and spirit. But it exceeds both the consciousness and the physical limits of the body, because passion can neither be contained nor comprehended from our physical selves alone.

We find evidence of passionate celibacy in certain advanced spiritual practices, where there are accounts of orgasmic experience not triggered through physical stimulation, but through meditative techniques in the energy pathways of the body. These spiritual energies help us understand that even physical intercourse is not solely contained in the sexual organs of the body. In and of itself, the sexual act is simultaneously a psycho-mystical and bio-spiritual one.

Celibate passion makes us available to others in body and in soul. In some ways, it is more voluptuous and earthy than sexual passion because it is an expansion of heart and soul. Too many of us have been trained to believe that the highest expression of passion is only triggered or created in sexual intercourse. Dependent on others to fulfill our own deepest possibility (a possibility that is truly *sustained* only in the spirit), we may harbor feelings of inadequacy, especially when our sense of worth is related to sexual performance. But, in interior solitude, we experience life's passion for itself. We are led to a more true and holy understanding: our passion is *within* us. Our passion for the Divine is also our passion for physical relations, as the two desires are intertwined.

As a feeling that rises straight up from the heart, from the gut, from the whole person, passion is the exuberant awe for life. This feeling cannot be bought or claimed, it cannot be owned by another. Sexuality is only one star in its firmament; it is far more profound and majestic than that alone. In order to know our true selves, we have to know that physical passion is a reflection of this *other* passionate relationship between our embodied selves and the entire earthly-cosmic-divine realm.

We may need a period of sexual abstinence in our lifetimes in order to find the source of our passion. Separation from intimate relations, sexual and otherwise, begins the process of reintegration. We close the door on abuse, on inequity in love, on lack of commitment, and on physical or spiritual domination. We shut away, for a time, the attraction to physical touch and the desire to be held and to hold. We do this, not because we deny sensual pleasure, but out of a desire to find ourselves: *Who am I without the attraction or demand of sexual relations? Who am I when I am free to be in my enclosure with God?*

Celibacy does not kill passion. Rather, we learn that passion overflows from the well of holy energies in our souls. Even in the practice of celibacy, we still have a body through which we experience the spirit's indwelling. Our passionate relationship with divinity, in and through our bodies, continually enkindles the spark of love hidden in matter, teaching us about another type of fertility and birth. Spiritual passion glorifies the gift: *May the birth of the Divine take place again and again in our bodies and in our souls.*

Detachment

The practice of detachment is the positive ascension into what is most sacred in the human spirit. Far from suppressing passions, detachment instructs us in how to lift up the lower emotions—anger, greed, ignorance—that lead us away from the luminosity of relations, and to redirect them to what is more noble in human nature. Detachment opens up another kind of sensuality beyond mere pleasure.

Meister Eckhart says detachment leads us to be receptive to the Divine, because "detachment is so close to nothingness that there is nothing so subtle that it can be apprehended by detachment, except God alone."[2] Detachment draws us right next to God, and compels God toward us. We breathe God's breath and we see with God's eye, because there is *nothing* separating us. The Divine nothingness and our nothingness are one. We have discovered divinity in the material world.

Celibacy teaches us about detachment, and detachment teaches us about mystical celibacy. We learn about detachment through being sexually celibate, because we are confronted by the demands of emotions and of bodies. When we choose a celibate period of life, we realize the power these demands exert on our well-being, and how spiritually degraded our relations may be. We discover that dependence is not love, but often an unhealthy form of control that leads us away from our deepest wish.

Yet, physical celibacy alone does not confer the gift of wisdom. We must consciously apply the vow of mystical celibacy to our lives. The detachment of the monk within is conquered through the struggle to tame emotions, to the point where the whole being is shocked into a Zen-like awakening. We will suffer to give birth, in and through our relations, to the quality of intimate presence we experience with our Beloved. When we ascend toward greater unity and spiritual love, we sanctify relations; when we turn toward egoism, possessiveness, and materializing of pleasure, we debase our relations. Detachment is the search for what is most good and most holy in us. It is the choice we make every day to turn away from the direction of descent, and to release the bursting sparks of holiness from our hearts.

Detachment provides insight into the underground currents of ego that diminish love and thwart friendship. It guides us through the obscure alleys of human domination into the core of our beings, to uncover the root thirst of our personalities, and the hidden motive for existence. Released from the desire to attract, control, mate, and relate, we discover another, more authentic way of being.

In its way, detachment from the desires of the body is another night of the soul, only this time in relation to physicality. It plunges us down into the historical markers of human identity, the biological urge to procreate, and the painful chapters of humanity's capacity to possess, violate, or subjugate our cells and our souls. We discover the root of our need to be accepted, and to accept others, as sexual beings.

Abstaining from sexual relations can incite a withdrawal response similar in experience to the person who cannot confront her addiction to nicotine until she throws her cigarettes away. Likewise, when we abstain from sexual relations—for a temporary or permanent period—we uncover the ways in which the ego structure is controlled by want, possession, or ignorance. These cravings of mind, body, and spirit maintain deep roots in the human psyche that can be pulled up. Detachment from the lesser passions frees our bodies and our spirits from our own, or others' demands.

Whether as a temporary or permanent vow, detachment makes us aware of our thoughts, actions, and motives. It exposes the violence of a possessive heart, and the ways in which we are controlled by our passions. A heart liberated from attachment is alert to the primordial tension of love and possession, caring and domination. Perhaps, for the first time, we are alert to how much time and energy we expend on being sexually attractive—and how imprisoned we can be by society's messages that our personal value is related to our sexual worth.

In the unclarity of our attractions, in the confusion between love and possession, we trample each other's holy offering of body. Spiritual detachment teaches us about the integrity of personal space on the physical, emotional, and spiritual levels. We discover our sacred right to define and enclose our own universe of being. We find permission to close our monastic gates to the spiritual violation of a spouse, or the psychological invasion of a parent. Detachment fosters integrity because the return to our enclosure is not a negative reaction, but a positive affirmation of our right to be alone. We are reminded again and again that pure detachment polishes the mirror of our desires until they are reflections of God's desire, until we gain a glimpse of pure yearning of heart.

Intimacy

Described in mystical texts as an experience of absorption, annihilation, or intoxication, mystical union expresses the heights of intimacy. We are awakened to an experience of love so deep, so full of ardor, that the language of its expression ascends to the erotic heights of sensual pleasure. *O that you would kiss me with the kisses of your mouth!* sings praise in the *Song of Songs*. Ablaze with the savor of love, his soul intoxicated with passion for his Beloved, St. John of the Cross composes a lyric verse between his soul and Christ similar in sensual imagery: *There He gave me His breast; There He taught me a sweet and living knowledge; And I gave myself to Him, keeping nothing back; There I promised to be His bride.*

As expressions of the eternal, divine nature, each precious creation is a revelation in form. When we espouse to the inherent oneness of life, we participate in this living stream of love. We enclose ourselves in the bridal chamber with our Beloved to discover the joyful abandonment of being intimate with all of life. Never again alone, the divine union in us is reflected in the union we experience in the natural world, in community, and with lovers, spouses, partners, and friends.

The miracle of intimacy happens whether we are alone or in relationship. None of us are monads. We are always in relationship with life in some way. Whatever the nature of these relationships, something of the interdependence of the cosmos and all living things is revealed. To uncover deeper levels of this reciprocal revelation is part of the ongoing progression of the human spirit. Divine-human intimacy overflows in the direction of an ever-greater experience of mutuality within our selves, among each other, and with all creatures of the Earth.

The wisdom of celibacy frees us from the demands of a false kind of intimacy that masks selfishness, possession, or insecurity. It may be the first time in our lives when we can experience the integrity of body-mind-spirit for our own benefit and not under the control of another person—

positively or negatively. The vow of mystical celibacy prepares the ground in which the seeds of authentic intimacy are sown.

In fostering the integrity of body and spirit, we expand the range of human intimacies. Far from being the loss of presence or the unhealthy giving away of one's self, mystical celibacy has at its heart faithfulness to the monk within. When we do not abuse or give away inner solitude, we maintain spiritual integrity, and are capable of being more alive in all manner of relations: sexual or celibate, friend or family. When we expand the parameters of celibacy beyond its ascetic definitions, to include the principle of mystical solitude, a space is opened in our hearts. Into the mystical clearing comes the archetypal dance of life: the weaving and interpenetrating web of relations. *All life is holy.*

· ♦ ·

"PURITY IS OFTEN PICTURED to us as a fragile crystal which will tarnish or be shattered if it is not protected from rough handling and the light. In fact, it is more like the flame which assimilates everything and brings it up to the standards of its own incandescence. To the pure, all things are pure."[3] We are reminded by Teilhard de Chardin how mystical celibacy, as a state of consciousness, is a beacon guiding all our relations through the dark nights and deep intimacies of embodiment. It is a fiery flame of pure consciousness that challenges us to measure everything against its transcendent luminosity.

Mystical celibacy leads us to our true nature. It reminds us that here, in the woundedness of the human condition, we are radiant, untouched. We contain the seeds of pure consciousness; in our adherence to the vow of mystical celibacy, the divine works out the holiness of matter. It is more than a discipline of physical desires; it is a state of being that honors the sanctity of the living universe. Mystical celibacy teaches us to relinquish the bartering of our souls and the commodification of our bodies. We recognize, of course, that there will never be a time when we cannot be more holy.

TWENTY-FIVE

Sexuality and Mystical Openness

C ELIBACY AND SEXUALITY are complementary realities, both on a physiological and, more importantly, on an energetic level. When sexuality is approached through the lens of the solitude of self, physical and mystical intimacy intersect and mutually enhance each other. The soul in mystical union symbolizes what is the potential of sexual union between two people. This does not mean sexuality is otherworldly, falsely spiritualized, or abstract. Rather, it is an expression of divine possibility through the affirmation and love between physical selves. This chapter, then, explores the spiritual implications of human sexuality.

Sexual Intimacy as a Spiritual Journey

THE ATTRACTION between two people is also, in some way, an attraction between those individuals and the cosmos. The sexual act is the embodied experience of the convergence of human-human and divine-human inti- macy. This fits with our focus on the integration of sexual desire and tran- scendent consciousness, which "entails a mutual transformation," writes Jorge Ferrer, "or sacred marriage, of their essential energies. For example, the integration of consciousness and the vital [sexual] world makes the former more embodied, vitalized, and even eroticized, and grants the latter an intelligent evolutionary direction beyond its biologically driven instincts."[1]

While the world's religions have practices that affirm the sacred dimension of sexual intercourse—Tantra in Tibetan Buddhism and aspects of the Kabbalistic tradition in Judaism, for example—the relationship between mysticism and sexuality is, in many ways, uncharted territory. Both movements—the movement of love between two people and the movement of love between each partner and the spirit—happening simultaneously mirror or replicate the act of mystical union between the soul and the divine. Further, our capacity to unite sexual energy and divine desire enhances human love, drawing intense spiritual energies into our bodies, and furthering the evolution of an incarnational consciousness.

Perhaps at one point in our lives, we had a fleeting experience of transcendence in the sexual encounter, but lacked the ability to sustain its full bodily-cosmic expression. As a person ages and grows in spiritual maturity, he or she may become a more stable vessel for the integration of divine energies, and the sexual experience can become more meaningful and spiritually profound. This is due in part to the fact that youth is not a predictor of sexual satisfaction, and sexual intercourse does not happen only in the physical body. Rather, the symbiotic relationship between mind-body-spirit illustrates that sex involves the physical body, but also the soul and all aspects of the etheric body: the chakra systems, acupuncture meridians, kundalini, and so forth.

Healthy, intimate partner or marriage relationships are a spiritual journey in their own right. That is, two people travel a joint spiritual path—alongside and interwoven with the individual path of each partner—that involves inner growth, including release of old behaviors and illumined glimpses of the future; experiences of anguish and doubt; and surrender of ego or false identities. Similarly, partners travel together through phases of shared celebration, moments of intensity, and deepening commitment. Sexual love leads to the growth of intimacy and, in that, mirrors the soul's mystical union.

Openness to mystery creates an openness in the person's physical being, and vice versa. Because of an innate desire for union with our

Source, the energies exchanged during sexual intercourse imitate the capacity of consciousness to co-create with, and participate in, vital spiritual forces. Thus, knowing another's body, mind, and spirit is a type of divine intimacy. The intimacy the person has with God is reflected in the intimacy discovered in knowing another with his or her heart.

Since Mystery is infinite, all relationships are infinite. Relationships sometimes confuse us, because we think of ourselves as finite, even though we possess limitlessness. The danger in this lies in believing that we fully know and understand our partner. Many relationships break down because people are not willing to return to the point of mystery—captured in the ineffability of every face—and reinvestigate what is on the other side of their now-ossified views of each other. Both partners must be willing to challenge outdated conflicts and identities, but often one partner decides this is as far as he or she will go. A relationship can endure if there is an awareness of the mutual spiritual journey that both partners *are already* embarked upon.

Therefore, each person's inner growth contributes to and enhances the couple's affinity on all levels. If personal intimacy reflects divine intimacy, bodily interpenetration reflects the merging and flowing out of divine energies. Conceived in this way, the failure or end of love closes off one spiritual possibility in the world.

The passionate forces occurring in sexual relations reflect not only the passion we feel for life, but also the cosmic passion felt in and through our bodies. This passionate uniting of two spiritual forces is love to the exponential level. Passion is not only human love, as we understand it, but a divine, creative force we participate in and contain within our beings. Connected to the act of creation, sexuality includes the whole spectrum of creative energies and the power of fecundity —the generation of art, story, poetry, meaning, etc.—and the birth of sentient beings. It thus requires attention to the full range of the person's interior powers and longings, for in this expanded definition every act of creativity is connected to vital energies.

For this reason, we need to preserve our life force for whatever we deem most important. We tend to give away our sexuality. We tend to debase it because we debase our bodies. We truly do not believe in the spirituality of bodies. We give away our creativity, and do not conserve our energies. The value of celibacy may lie in this conservation of energies, rather than in any strictly ascetic or moral sense.

The sensitivity and vulnerability of the sexual act repeats the radical openness that occurs in mystical union. There is a surrender of being that is the necessary catalyst for the expansion of creativity, and divine-human intimacy. If the person maintains a balance between his or her cloistered space and intimate partners, spiritual energies are not necessarily dissipated and can, in fact, become enhanced. Every relationship is a journey in consciousness—of mind, body, and spirit—that draws lovers deeper into the mystery of each other. Remember the essential element: In the divine, total love is never in question. Therefore, intimacy between two people also involves an emerging expression of love—a growing, deepening process.

Love involves many things. It involves commitment. It involves faithfulness and fidelity. It involves desire for the other as he or she truly is. The Divine never demands, "I want you to be something you are not," "I want you to be less than you are," or "I want you to be something I have decided you should be, but I know you never can be." The Divine embraces us as we are.

This is why mystical intimacy is so liberating: because you do not have to be anything you are not. You are free to be your true self. In that sense, celibacy—as physical abstinence, energetic state, or spiritual metaphor—is very important. It reminds us to ask, "Who am I in myself? Who am I without the need to be attractive, to encourage or motivate my partner to be interested in me?"

This issue of love founded in love helps us understand how sexual intimacy mirrors mystical intimacy and becomes, in life, a horizon toward which we progress. Love has the potential to pull us forward toward the ever-increasing depth of our relationships. Although we know we can never reach perfection in this life, our desire and capacity to participate in physical joy, leads the way toward wholeness. The cosmos joins with us in this exploration, this experiment.

Sexual union is a mystery. It entails a journey of hearts, a timeless expanse of energy embedded in the wonder of physicality, forging a path of generative creativity in the body. When we envision ourselves as very sensitive, very intimate with all life, we understand what sexuality truly is.

Sexuality as Mystical Openness

IN THE MUTUAL LOVE and interpersonal relationship of sexuality, we participate in another type of intimacy. Although the two are not identical states of being, sexual union is similar to the ontological generosity that occurs in uniting with or cleaving to God. The last stage before the soul enters the chamber of its beloved is the dissolution of the ego or soul identity. As the ego is emptied, recognizing in a positive way that it is going to come back in again, the physical sensations occurring in the sexual act reflect the ecstasy of mystical union. This is why sexuality figures so largely in people's lives, and why it is such a compelling event.

The loss of ego is perhaps one of the profound ways in which sexuality has the potential to embody the mystical relationship. If you have a willful ego identity, then you cannot listen to the beloved. You cannot really participate in the reciprocity of love because your willfulness is stronger than your longing to *be* with another. When both people are strongly willful, it may be difficult to travel together through the adversity that couples normally navigate at some point in their relationship. Afraid to let go, each partner develops defenses as a way of warding off emotional closeness or truth.

Because organic life exists in a state of homeostasis—or equilibrium between interdependent elements—our physical bodies express "oneness" and possess the actual bio-spiritual capacity to experience it. In fact, I hold that the living universe dwells in various states of oneness, and reject the view—held by various religions and cultures—of the inferiority of the natural world as inadequate and faulty. The continuum of matter-spirit-divinity is so intrinsic to life that the differences among them are one of degree and not ontology. The world, in a very real sense, *is* the body of God.

Because of this inherent continuum and homeostasis, what we consider the height of passion—whether physical orgasm or ecstatic experience—does not fully take place in the organs of the body. Although the entirety of our physical makeup is involved, sexual relations also tap into spiritual and psychic levels of consciousness. When people concentrate only on bodily organs, or orgasm as the goal of sexual intercourse, they lose sight of this other dimension. In fact, that focus may take away from the full spiritual experience. If we can understand sexuality as an act of radical openness between two people—an act of love—and concentrate on and lose our fear of uniting with another, then the ecstasy of two becoming one can be experienced, whether or not physical orgasm occurs.

As reciprocity of being, sexuality has the potential to be healing and profound. On the other hand, it also can be damaging or scary for the person who fears drawing close to the center of being. As one of the most intimate experiences human beings tend to share, sexuality deserves to have its sacral dimensions affirmed. For some people, the body is just "a piece of flesh," or "a piece of matter," something to be used or abused for any purpose. When the body is denigrated, then instead of communion, one person objectifies another, which leads to injury and pain. At one time or another, each of us has experienced some such overt or subtle objectification. If sexuality does not at least try to move in the direction of integration, it risks descent into devaluing the body and its vital energies. Our union will not be a true union. It will not be intimacy. There will be overtones, subtle or overt, of domination, control, or rejection.

If you are in a relationship and try to segregate spirituality from sexuality, your spiritual life eventually will reach an impasse. When you believe, "What my partner and I do in bed is purely about the body, purely physical," and reject the deeper implications of intimate sharing, your heart will suffer and ultimately you may fail to build a holistic relationship. Coming to terms with the impact of sexuality and spirituality in your life is crucial to being fully human, even if you later decide to become celibate within a marriage or partnership.

At times our consciousness has difficulty holding in body, mind, and spirit what it means to be intimate with another person, even for a split second. Similarly, we often have trouble sustaining intimacy with the divine. If, for whatever reason, you cannot bear these moments of radical openness, then affirm that truth for yourself. Do not use it as an excuse to punish or to hurt yourself or others. You may not feel comfortable being very open. You may have been injured growing up. Nevertheless, it is important to realize that we have the capacity of openness, of continually pouring our hearts out into the world.

Historically, religious traditions have confined sexuality, from a moral point of view, to reproduction. The reproductive capacity of humans reflects—whether or not one procreates—the giving of oneself on the most embodied level, and is mirrored in the higher state of spiritual exchange in which the capacity for openness is in fact infinite. How can we help but be amazed when we look at our bodies and our personal lives in a mystical context? The mystery of being human is that we exist at the crossroads of infinitude and finitude.

Because we are both infinite and finite, the creative force within us is tied to the limitation of human bodies and the boundaries that finitude demands. The wisdom and challenge of sexuality are such that partners have to sustain their desire to give within the context of their need to retain boundaries, even if that need is unconscious. This is why celibacy and sexuality work as complementary energies. One implies aloneness and enclosure and the other, vulnerability and surrender. This complementarity maintains a healthy balance between the eternal and temporal aspects of being.

In my experience, many people—particularly those who are deeply spiritual—are more comfortable with giving than receiving. Our fear about or resistance to sexual intimacy may arise from the inability to maintain personal space, or a failure to form healthy boundaries. If we never learn how to preserve an inner enclosure, and our intention is toward giving away of self, then it is difficult to restore balance. We see this frequently with people—young and old—who experience love as an overwhelming passion, a desire to be everything for the other person, but without the balance of a strong center.

A challenge to the naturally giving person is that he or she over-gives, or is in an unequal relationship of giving. Oftentimes, one partner of a couple is a giver and the other partner is a taker, yet this imbalance is not understood. Spiritually, when giving is unequal, there is some kind of control, maybe possessiveness, and not a true sharing of selves. One of the trials of love is that it can veer into the realm of habitual desire, and the person becomes attached to his or her lover in an unhealthy way. When this behavior becomes obsessive or habitual it debases both parties, and causes suffering and pain.

There are times when, to truly be present with another person, we must turn away from the body's desires and seek the other in the spirit. In other words, withdrawing into a space of inner aloneness helps us to be available to our beloveds at a different level of consciousness, without the sexual connection. A relationship constantly directed toward materiality will suffer. Relationship needs the freedom of solitude, honoring each other's spiritual right to be alone. The pouring out of self complements the restoration of being, and the withdrawing of self in the mystical enclosure. Everyone has the capacity to return to one's center and temporarily close the door to outside energies.

Today, one of the exciting and positive results of the new monastic movement is the varied ways people and communities are experimenting with how to integrate the commitment to solitude in partner and sexual relationships, redefining the scope and function of the monk. We, too, can benefit from this integration. As contemplative life is deepened, we simultaneously thrive alone in our interior sanctuary and are generous in relationship. The more we embrace inner solitude, the more we acquire the strength for communion with others, and the less we are disturbed by the world's noise.

For many people, relationship demands have dominated their entire life. Often marriage or partnership problems—emotional, sexual, and physical—hinge on this issue: a lack of the sense of self, alone. Unconsciously, we crave time apart without the intrusion of other energies. We need permission to love solitude. Most likely we never learned self-love when we needed it. We learned through difficult experience and pain, but no one reminded us, "If you practice inner solitude, your life will be easier and more peaceful."

The capacity to withstand aloneness with the divine provides strength of being. At times we can become compulsive, craving an ecstatic experience we believe we can only have with one other person. However, mystical solitude helps us to develop an inner state of consciousness that can be as profound as any physical intimacy. In a sexually active marriage or partnership we also experience what radical openness is: the singularity of the divine-human relationship. Here, both types of generosity are taking place—in solitude with God and in communion with one's beloved—because they are complementary realities that relate to different dimensions of the person. Solitude is inside openness and openness is within solitude.

Because inner peace is difficult to sustain during the round of activities required on a daily basis, a practice of centering is of critical importance. We think we can bounce from one relationship to another and don't realize the impact that the frenzy of work or interpersonal conflict has on our souls. We tend to be hard on ourselves. Sometimes, we fail to see clearly how sacred everything is.

The value of centering practices is especially helpful for the person who has experienced violation of the body, mind, or spirit, which can affect his or her faith in the ability to have an honest, caring association with others. Physical and emotional abuses seep into consciousness, causing survivors to believe they are no longer pure of being. Sexual violation is particularly harmful, since sexuality in its natural expression is a self-gift. When intimate violence occurs, the person is often left with a lifelong soul injury. The more extreme the violation, the more deeply the psyche is affected. Such acts damage human dignity, which can cause the person to falsely believe that they are corrupted, impure.

The importance of solitude rests on its affirmation, over and again, of the untouchable and undefiled inner life of the soul. It is the cloister of your own being, and only you and God can enter there. This explains why returning to the hermitage within is healing and liberating, while sometimes difficult when a violation has occurred.

As you become conscious of the power of creativity, you are able to honor, preserve, and protect your sexuality integrity, which is also the integrity of body, heart, and soul. If you do not feel pure of heart, pray to be free of whatever shame, fear, or violation you have carried regarding sexuality. In monastic terms, one abstains from sex in order to give one's body to God. But, sexual relations also express the giving of oneself to

God. True love is the mutuality of giving and accepting. If a relationship has these elements, then it is on the path of mystical love.

The Complementarity of Love

EXPERIENTIALLY, love is always simultaneously embodied and universal, just as sexuality is simultaneously cloistered and relational. Personal love reflects the journey of the soul toward its beloved, in the singularity of the interpersonal bond. The cherishing of reciprocal love is so important in sexuality because it preserves each other from objectification, and enhances the couple's physical and spiritual bond.

We can realize the difficulty of participating in the mutuality of divine and human love. We can be gentle and kind with each other, recognizing that, imperfection aside, daily life is a heroic striving toward compassion and courage. Rainer Maria Rilke expresses it wonderfully in *Letters to a Young Poet*:

> And those who come together in the night and are entwined in rocking delight perform a solemn task and gather sweetness, depth, and strength for the song of some future poet, who will appear in order to say ecstasies that are unsayable. And they call forth the future; and even if they have made a mistake and embrace blindly, the future comes anyway, a new human being arises, and on the foundation of the accident that seems to be accomplished here, there awakens the law by which a strong, determined seed forces its way through to the egg cell that openly advances to meet it. Don't be confused by surfaces; in the depths everything becomes law.[2]

Monastic wisdom and practices assist in the development of sexual awareness because they advocate for the choice to be countercultural. In the contemplative life, we have the freedom to examine our societal options and to ask if they benefit or thwart the expansion of love. We can follow certain shared norms, but our decision should be the result of self-knowledge. We can choose for ourselves what is necessary to maintain an interior sanctuary in the midst of an active life. Our attempts, however imperfect or impeded, are in the service of the holiness of creation. If we maintain a sacred outlook on daily relations, including sexual ones, we will join in the process of making our time on Earth beneficial to peace and holy hope.

TWENTY-SIX

Rule of Life

INTRINSIC TO MONASTIC COMMUNITY is a rule of life, or code of conduct by which the adherents live out their vows, grow in spiritual depth, and preserve the community. Generally, codes or precepts governing a monastic lifeform develop organically, from the illuminated spiritual intent of those seeking the narrow path. Over time, like other human endeavors, they are susceptible to becoming bogged down in legalistic interpretation and strict adherence. Then a community or practice can lose its spiritual life force, become rigid and suffer from a lack of creativity.

A monastic rule is designed to transform lifelong habits that take us away from true happiness, and to provide a guideline or anchor to what is more real, more essential. For the monk, temporal goods of whatever kind are not permanent representations of happiness. Many people have expressed these concerns: "I purchased this thing, it's nice but now I want something new." Or, "Now I have a certain spiritual understanding but it's not taking me anywhere. I still feel unsettled, I still feel fragmented. I need to try something else."

Spiritually, these mental menaces indicate two things: 1) happiness is not fulfilled by temporal pleasures or material objects, and 2) something deeper is needed, even beyond spiritual knowledge. Liberation or enlightenment, or even simple contentment is not sustained by accomplishing everything you ever hoped for. Something within is drawing you toward a deeper kind of happiness, one that comes only from the sacred.

Thus, monasteries promote creative monotony that structures a monk's life around activities of prayer, charity, meditation, solitude, ritual, asceticism, silence, and obedience. This daily repetition is intended to reconnect monks with simplicity of heart, and teach them how to live in the rhythm of sacral time.

The monk's vocation, if you will, is to challenge the prediction that you will never know your true self, and that you always will be separate from your Source. Monasticism—taking of vows, living a rule of life—is radical. It reminds us over and over again that this world is both a veil obscuring and a window into the realm of the holy. For this reason, monastic life requires audacity and courage, and the full surrender of one's heart. It is a way of being that seeks the triumph of freedom.

If vows are the means by which we live out our love of the divine, the monastic rule assists us on the journey. It is the map we follow to become more grateful, receptive, and humble. Monastic rules also are described as codes of conduct, ideals, or standards of behavior to ensure the stability of the community. The variety and scope of monastic wisdom eludes facile summary; rather, in the following pages I include selected themes from several rules of life.

Code of Ascetics—Laws of Manu (*Manu-smriti*)

THIS SANSKRIT TEXT (c. 200 BCE) is held to be the most authoritative of the books of the Hindu code of conduct in India. It prescribes the obligations or *dharma* of each member of the four social classes (*varnas*) in each of the four stages of life (*ashramas*). The following rules—which represent only a portion of the precepts—are derived from Chapter 6, on the Proper Conduct of an Ascetic (sannyāsi).

1. A sannyāsi must relinquish all property.
2. A sannyāsi must give a promise of safety to all beings—whatever being comes to the sannyāsi for refuge, he is under an obligation to give it.

3. A sannyāsi must abstain from injuring creatures; he should not cause the slightest fear to any being.

4. A sannyāsi must practice restraint of the senses, he must entirely abstain from any form of sensual enjoyment—any form of luxury is forbidden. Traditionally in India a sannyāsi must always sleep on the ground and never use a bed because the majority of the common people sleep on the floor.

5. A sannyāsi must politely reject all forms of enjoyments that may be offered.

6. A sannyāsi must relinquish love and hatred. He must not bear affection toward favorable people or malice toward unfavorable people.

7. A sannyāsi must be equal-minded toward all sentient beings. He should not be partial to devotees nor impartial and hostile to any others.

8. A sannyāsi must regularly practice the vow of noble silence (*mauna*). At regular times the sannyāsi should observe the vow of silence and not speak any words whatsoever.

9. A sannyāsi must patiently bear harsh words that are spoken against him without retaliating. He must never intentionally insult anybody. Against an angry man let him not in return show anger, let him bless when he is cursed, and let him never say anything that is devoid of truth.

10. A sannyāsi must speak only the truth—he should not comment on anything that he does not personally know nor speak about things without knowing the established facts.1

Restraint: Buddhist *Vinaya*

THE DISCIPLINARY RULES of the Buddhist monk are called the *Vinaya*, a code of behavior conducive to the arising of wisdom and mindfulness, and leading to the cessation of suffering. In Theravada and Mahayana Buddhism, the *vinaya* generally consists of 227 rules for ordained monks (*bhikkhus*) and 311 for nuns (*bhikkhunis*). Often, these are distilled into ten precepts, or moral codes:

1. I undertake the precept to refrain from destroying living creatures.
2. I undertake the precept to refrain from taking that which is not given.
3. I undertake the precept to refrain from sexual activity.
4. I undertake the precept to refrain from incorrect speech.
5. I undertake the precept to refrain from intoxicating drinks and drugs which lead to carelessness.
6. I undertake the precept to refrain from eating at the forbidden time (i.e., after noon).
7. I undertake the precept to refrain from dancing, singing, music, going to see entertainments.
8. I undertake the precept to refrain from wearing garlands, using perfumes, and beautifying the body with cosmetics.
9. I undertake the precept to refrain from lying on a high or luxurious sleeping place.
10. I undertake the precept to refrain from accepting gold and silver (money).[2]

The aim of the precepts is twofold: to preserve the reputation of the Sangha, and to train individual monks. "If the Sangha," writes Vietnamese monk Thich Nhat Hahn, "loses its reputation and is not respected, it will be destroyed and people will not have the opportunity to practice as monks and nuns. . . . The second aim of the precepts is to protect and train individual monks and nuns, so that they have happiness and freedom."[3] Buddhist codes of conduct enhance the spiritual quest of the Sangha and the practice of monks and nuns, and are understood in their deeper implications and not solely as outer forms of behavior.

Dhamma-Vinaya (Truth-Discipline) was the Buddha's own name for the religion he founded. He pointed out how to release the self from suffering, and articulated the behavior of his followers who quest for absolute liberation. The connection between discipline and release recurs several times in the Pali Canon, the collected scriptures of Theravada Buddhism:

> Discipline is for the sake of restraint, restraint for the sake of freedom from remorse, freedom from remorse for the sake of joy, joy for the sake of rapture, rapture for the sake of tranquility, tranquility for the

sake of pleasure, pleasure for the sake of concentration, concentration for the sake of knowledge and vision of things as they have come to be, knowledge and vision of things as they have come to be for the sake of disenchantment, disenchantment for the sake of dispassion, dispassion for the sake of release, release for the sake of knowledge and vision of release, knowledge and vision of release for the sake of total unbinding through non-clinging.[4]

Humility: St. Benedict's Rule

DURING THE DECLINE of the Roman Empire, St. Benedict of Nursia (c. 480–543 CE) wrote a code of conduct that addresses how to live in a monastic community, especially regarding the right schedule and lifestyle proper to a monk. This treasured Christian monastic code—The Rule of Benedict—is direct and simple to read, and deals with a way of life and an attitude of heart rather than obscure metaphysical principles. It, thus, has served well the spiritual yearnings of generations of monks for more than 1,500 years.

Especially relevant is Chapter Seven of the Rule, where Benedict develops twelve steps of humility, using the image of a ladder, like the one Jacob saw in his dream (Gen. 28.12) of angels climbing up and down in a constant exchange between Heaven and Earth. "This ladder, then," writes Benedict, "will symbolize for each of us our life in this world during which we aspire to be lifted up to heaven by the Lord, if only we can learn humility in our hearts. . . . It is just such an exchange that we need to establish in our own lives, but with this difference for us: our proud attempts at upward climbing will bring us down, whereas to step downwards in humility is the way to lift our spirit up towards God."[5]

The first step of humility is "to cherish at all times the sense of awe with which we should turn to God." Drive away your forgetfulness. Be alive to the beauty of the world, and to God's commandments. Notice how Benedict categorizes awe as the first degree of humility. Being conscious of God in every aspect of your life is essential to ignite the flame of devotion within. It's not enough to be without sin; you must be steeped in the mind of God.

The second is not to love having your way or to delight in your desires. This injunction reminds us to love God, the monastic heart. This great spiritual teacher shows the subtlety of monastic life. One of the reasons that Benedict's Rule has survived for centuries is because it is both universal and particular. It is not strident in a particularistic way; it is not micromanaging the heart. Rather, the Rule is a broad expression of the way the human mind, body, and spirit are diverted from the pursuit of truth. It displays great intelligence and the ability to see into the heart of others.

The third step of humility is to submit your self out of love of God to the obedience of your superior. This is a very important principle. It doesn't mean that your conscience will agree with everything that your superior says or orders you to do. And there are other parts of the rule where Benedict discusses the requirements of the superior that are quite stringent, even more stringent than the obligation of monks. But still, the rule is to submit your self, to surrender, out of love of God. This provides an operating principle that you work from. You are listening to God's voice in order to measure and understand what the superior asks of you. It is not just rote, knee-jerk obedience.

There are many stories over the ages of sickly and pathological abbots, gurus, roshis, and bishops who abuse their power. Also, few people with a monastic temperament actually live in a formal community and have a spiritual guide directing their lives. Thus the admonishment to "submit oneself out of love of God to the obedience of your superior" could be understood as "Seek the help of others of like spiritual mind and with great diligence and critical awareness, pray to discern God's path for you, and always be obedient *to the call.*"

The fourth step is to accept patiently and in silence, enduring all things that you might not agree with or may believe are false. There is a Zen story that illustrates the fourth degree of humility. A Zen monk is accused of fathering a child, vilified by the community, and treated like a pariah. Although he did not father the child, he takes the child into his home and raises him without a word. He makes no attempt to defend himself or to dissuade the villagers from hatred toward him. Later, the parents admit that the monk did not sire the child, and he gives the child back without comment. The monk practices the perfection of acceptance.

The fifth is to not cover up your faults, but to humbly confess the sinful thoughts and evil deeds you have committed in secret. I can't tell you how many people refuse to acknowledge that they have made a mistake or resist releasing their interpretation of reality. For example, a woman in spiritual direction told me, "In meditation I got the idea that I should leave my family and join a monastery. I did that and I'm in terrible turmoil now." I asked, "Did you pray about this; did you think about your decision with spiritual guidance?"

Her response revealed not her regret about the decision, or about leaving her family inappropriately. The real difficulty was her ego, her pride. Because she had made the decision, it had to be true. She couldn't let go of attachment to the idea that the decision had to be right because it came from her. If *this* decision isn't true, then she held that every decision, everything she had done, was wrong.

Benedict wants the monk to uncover these hidden points of pride. Don't cover them up, he says. Let them go, be willing to admit what you're still holding as a buffer to protect your ego.

The sixth step of humility is to accept without complaint all conditions. I've noticed a very interesting example of humility at the monasteries I've visited. Most monks are intelligent and perceptive. They are trained to address grievances and seek change from a place of respect and gratitude for their situation. When Benedict instructs monks to accept without complaint all conditions, he doesn't mean situations that are against your true self. He means to avoid the murmuring, complaining level and instead go directly to the heart of the problem. The sixth degree is not passive. It's true, active transformation.

The seventh step is to speak of yourself as "of less importance and less worthy than others"—not with "a mere phrase" on your lips but with belief in your heart. In other words, constantly making the self less, not more, is the road toward true devotion. In much of the world's religious literature, humility is related to diminishing one's privilege or status. Of course, humility must be understood in its different contexts. For example, in a society where women are systematically oppressed, humility may be used to enforce a pathological diminishment of females. Thus, true humility refers to a healthy state of wholeness and ego development that is attuned to the mystical practice of inner poverty.

The eighth step of humility is to do nothing that goes beyond the common rule of the monastery and the example set by the prioress or abbot. In Benedict's case, this is the established rule of a residential monastery. For contemporary monks in the world, I would say: Do nothing that violates your primary commitment, which is your commitment to love God with all your heart. This step also tells us to learn from the wisdom of our ancestors, to value the truths taught by other holy people, and to find a wise teacher so that we do not make the mistake of becoming our own guides.

The ninth is to refrain from unnecessary speech and to guard your silence. One of the most essential elements in monastic traditions is silence. Benedict felt that silence is an outward expression of inner humility. By guarding silence, the monk is preserving mystery and is not constantly analyzing and dissecting reality with his or her friends or community. In a genuine monastic setting, the physical enclosure—absent extraneous noise and busyness—can be tangibly felt. Here you encounter what *is*, preserved by silence.

"The tenth step of humility teaches that we should not be given to empty laughter on every least occasion." Benedict is not critiquing humor, but the shallow kind of laughter that puts others at risk. True humor uplifts the heart and eases the soul. The humble person never uses speech to diminish another person. The humble person becomes a safe harbor for others, and handles human failings with delicate hands.

The eleventh is to always speak gently and seriously. I hear in Benedict's injunction the Buddhist notion of right speech. Humility walks tenderly upon the earth, and values the solitude of others. Accord to others their space, and share with each what is meaningful. Don't speak with empty words and judgmental hearts.

"The twelfth step of humility is concerned with the external impression conveyed by those dedicated to monastic life [and this] humility of heart should be" practiced in the oratory, the monastery or the garden, or a journey in the field, or anywhere else. Humility of heart should be apparent to all those who enter the monastery, as the monks should be free of pride or arrogance. Thus the humble person guards against excess approval or excess guilt.

Humility is the ability to know ourselves as God knows us. It is the foundation of all relations.

Holy Poverty: St. Clare of Assisi

UNDER THE GUIDANCE of St. Francis, Clare of Assisi (1194–1253) professed monastic vows on March 19, 1212, forming a community of nuns in the convent of San Damiano, the church property Francis restored with his own hands, outside the village walls of Assisi, Italy. It was not until the end of her life that Clare's monastic rule was granted by papal approval in 1252. Brought to Clare on her deathbed, she kissed the document several times and was buried clutching it, as a sign of her faithful efforts to place radical poverty at the heart of her vocation.[6]

Of the twelve chapters in this papal document, some historians believe that Chapters Six through Ten represent Clare's original text. The first five chapters deal with the canonical structure, including the name of the order, reception of candidates, fasting and confession, election of abbess, and silence. Chapters Six through Ten are more autobiographical, described in the first person, and address her conversion to absolute poverty, and how this commitment "frames their work (chapter 7), begging and alms (chapter 8), penance and those who serve outside the monastery (chapter 9), the admonition and correction of the sisters (chapter 10), the enclosure (chapter 11), and the visitator, chaplain, and cardinal protector (chapter 12)."[7]

In the Rule and "The Testament of Saint Clare," she emphasizes the "immense gifts" God has bestowed upon her community to practice radical poverty while "still living among the vanities of the world." Clare's commitment to the least, and her admonition to never take more than is necessary, includes the sisters' observance not to covet any possessions or property, including nature's right to remain "untouched and undeveloped."

From the Rule of Saint Clare:[8]

And just as I, together with my sisters, have been ever solicitous to safeguard the holy poverty which we have promised the Lord God and the Blessed Francis, too, the Abbesses who shall succeed me in office and all the sisters are bound to observe it inviolably to the end: that is to say, they are not to receive or hold onto any possessions or property [acquired] through an intermediary . . . except as much land as necessity requires for the integrity and the proper seclusion of the monastery; and this land is not to be cultivated except as a garden for the needs of the sisters. (Chapter Six)

The sisters shall not acquire anything as their own, neither a house nor a place nor anything at all; instead, as pilgrims and strangers in this world who serve the Lord in poverty and humility, let them send confidently for alms. Nor should they feel ashamed, since the Lord made Himself poor for us in this world. This is that summit of highest poverty which has established you, my dearest sisters, as heirs and queens of the kingdom of heaven; it has made you poor in the things [of this world] but has exalted you in virtue. (Chapter Six)

Regarding the sisters who are ill, the Abbess is strictly bound to inquire with all solicitude by herself and through other sisters what [these sick sisters] may need . . . [This is to be done] because all are obliged to serve and provide for their sisters who are ill just as they would wish to be served themselves . . . For if a mother loves and nourishes her daughter according to the flesh, how much more lovingly must a sister love and nourish her sister according to the Spirit! (Chapter Eight)

I admonish and exhort in the Lord Jesus Christ that the sisters be on their guard against all pride, vainglory, envy, greed, worldly care and anxiety, detraction and murmuring, dissension and division. Let them be ever zealous to preserve among themselves the unity of mutual love, which is the bond of perfection. Let them devote themselves to what they must desire to have above all else: the Spirit of the Lord and His holy manner of working, to pray always to Him with a pure heart, and to have humility, patience in difficulty and weakness, and to love those who persecute, blame and accuse us; for the Lord says: Blessed are they who suffer persecution for justice's sake, for theirs is the kingdom of heaven (Mt 5:10). But he who shall have persevered to the end will be saved (Mt 10:22). (Chapter Ten)

From "The Testament of Saint Clare":[9]

If these sisters should ever leave this place and go elsewhere, after my death, wherever they may be, they are bound nonetheless to observe the form of poverty which we have promised God and our most blessed Father Francis. Nonetheless, let both the sister who is in office and the other sisters exercise such care and farsightedness that they do not acquire or receive more land around the place than strict necessity requires for a vegetable garden. But if, for the integrity and privacy of the monastery, it becomes necessary to have more land beyond the limits of the garden, no more should be acquired than strict necessity demands. This land should not be cultivated or planted but always remain untouched and undeveloped.

From the above examples, we can see that these rules of life have stood up to the test of time because they are practical and are directed to the development of spiritual awareness in every situation. They are ethical codes of conduct that reconfigure the relationship between body and spirit, affecting decision-making, emotions, time management, and psychological health. The rule, adhered to daily and over many years, is its own spiritual practice, which leads the seeker ever more profoundly into the inseparable unity of divine-human-cosmos.

TWENTY-SEVEN

All Life is Prayer

PLANTS, ANIMALS, AND STARS participate in a symphony of devotion, each yearning toward its Source. The daily activity of butterflies and ants, sea urchins and manatees, wolves and deer are distinctive prayer forms. A family gathering for a festive meal becomes a collective prayer, celebrating the bounty of the Fall harvest. The sheer variety and magnificence of the prayers of sentient beings alter whatever narrow view of prayer we hold. Realizing that every life form is a cadence of prayer underscores the value of all possible utterances.

All life is prayer. From the moment of birth, until death stills our breath, each human heart, each soul, recites a ceaseless prayer, the very existence of our spirit in physical form an invocation toward the divine.

Prayer is the language of the spirit. It is our first language. In a sense, prayer precedes language. It certainly precedes theology. Much of the world's scriptures are written as prayer forms, such as this passage from the Katha Upanishad, on the nature of the true self:

> Heaven, formless is the Person.
> He is without and within, unborn,
> Breathless, mindless, pure,
> Higher than the high Imperishable....
> Fire is His head; His eyes, the moon and sun;

The regions of space, His ears; His voice,
the revealed Vedas;
Wind, His breath; His heart, the whole
World. Out of His
Feet, The earth. Truly, He is the Inner Self
(*Atman*) of all.[1]

The language of prayer, which is often desiccated in contemporary culture, yearns for resuscitation, to become again the speech from within. Prayer is not merely linguistic or intellectual, but is a living river of devotion bringing divine energies into the world. All forms of speech and types of action have the potential to be a prayer. A Hassidic story asks, "How does one study with a Rebbe?" Well, you watch him tie his shoes. Because if he is a true Rebbe—a true master—then there is going to be some form of prayer in his tying of shoes. In each act, however small, is prayer.

The commitments that guide monastic life—vows, rules, rituals, etc.—are designed to liberate prayer from our hearts, and to allow the divine sweetness to permeate our entire being. The monk's desire to be close to God creates a spontaneous eruption of longing, a dynamic communion of love. Thus, prayer is not only the culmination of a lifetime spent in its practice, but also the natural outcome of the soul's wish.

As the pure overflow of grace, prayer arises from humility, which transforms mere material renunciation. Physical pleasures are renounced not because they are inherently wrong, but because they are so compelling and distracting. The seeker hones and forges his or her life in the direction of the one deepest desire. To put it another way, we renounce material things in order to devote our whole being to the divine desire. It is a practical decision. How many things can we do at once? Can we really commune with God if we are so busy that there is no time to pray or meditate?

The practice of prayer is important because it trains us to carry the sacred into everything we do. In the midst of a tumultuous day, it is still possible to yoke our being to the divine being. It is often through life's trials that we are tested and turn to prayer. For many people, especially when they suffer through difficult times, the correlation between what is going on in their lives and their ability to pray is little understood, as if prayer and life events are two separate categories. It is here that our spiritual traditions can provide guidance and techniques to reconnect us with the soul's need.

The monk reminds us that daily existence is a form of prayer, and if our lives are disruptive or disassociated, our well-being on every level is affected. Awareness of the harmony or disharmony between one's prayer life and one's daily action is an important tool of discernment. If we live in such a way that our actions are out of sync with the deep self, we should realize that behavior is not separate from prayer. Life and prayer are integrated, and that is the great wisdom of the monastic traditions.

Ceaseless Prayer

FOR THE MONK, the entire occupation of each day *is* prayer. Prayer is not an activity that competes with other activities; it is the basis of every activity. Work is prayer. Writing is prayer. Gardening is prayer.

Since the intention of prayer or meditation practice is to come face to face with Mystery, the unity of prayer and action is essential. Prayer purifies intentions. With prayer, no other teacher is needed. Prayer is your teacher. The inner monastery of the heart protects the silence and solitude necessary to listen for God's direct speech. This is prayer: being led into the silence, where God speaks, filling you with love, unfiltered.

The monk advocates various forms of ceaseless prayer and meditation as necessary to the mystical growth of the soul. The order of the monastic day is built to harness the monk's divergent interests into an outpouring of devotion. The main purpose for living this way is to allow one's whole being to be transfigured by the Divine. Prayer can be thought of as the method the monk uses to consent to be transfigured, because prayer becomes, in essence, a vow: "I vow to be with you, always. I consent to be transfigured in you."

In prayer, your self is offered; your words are offered to God. Each syllable has power, as your being transfigures into the divine being and you become wholly engulfed, possessed, and impressed with prayer. An inner correlation between your words and your deep self takes place. Vocal or silent prayer raises the vibration of the cells of the body, and the entire mind-body-spirit complex, literally transforming structures of consciousness. In these special moments of divine communion, it is not just emotional and physical levels that are altered, but also the energy frequency of the whole person.

Across religious traditions, the vibratory changes that lead to inner transformation are intrinsic to meditation and prayer practices. The Jewish mystic Abraham Abulafia (1240–1291), for example, is renowned in Kabbalistic circles for his precise meditative techniques. "When your consciousness," writes Abulafia, "cleaves to His consciousness . . . according to His honorable and awesome Name," the recitation of the vowels of the Divine Name in particular sequences can induce mystical experience and raise consciousness to an ecstatic level. Similarly, Athanasius of Alexandria, a fourth-century Christian theologian, said, "God became man [or woman] so that man [or woman] could become God." Athanasius' theological insight is the foundation of *theosis*, to become divine-like, and the impetus behind the Jesus (Hesychast) Prayer. The Eastern Orthodox monk is exhorted to ceaselessly pray: "Lord Jesus Christ, Son of God, have mercy on me, a sinner," until every inhalation and exhalation is a spontaneous participation in divine unity.

The goal of monastic prayer is not to seek extraordinary experiences, but to bring you closer to the full experience of divine indwelling. In ceaseless prayer, your being is infused with radiant light. For the monk who submits to prayer throughout a lifetime, prayer itself is a divine teaching. The monk is transfigured into a living prayer.

The spiritual power of prayer does not guarantee that you will achieve the outcome you desire, because Mystery is more comprehensive than the human mind can grasp. Nonetheless, prayer has the potential to lift the soul to higher levels. The result of prayer may not be what you wanted, but it will be what the Spirit gives, something that touches your heart and soul, and something that would not have happened without your prayer reaching out to the cosmos. Prayer and the outcome of one's prayers are not causative. If you don't pray, that doesn't mean bad things will happen; and if you do pray, that doesn't mean things will go as you hope.

Prayer is the soul's mirror, reflecting inner harmony or disquiet. For example, in certain stages of spiritual growth, old prayer forms may be painful to recite, or no longer have meaning. The capacity to pray may be non-existent or weak, and you can feel abandoned and lost. Thus, your relationship to prayer can be a guide for understanding your inner experience. What is the quality of your life at this moment? Is praying easy for you, or do you struggle in prayer? Does your prayer feel fractured? Are you working frenetically, are you scattered, do you have little time for quiet? If you feel selfish, angry, rebellious, or irritable, each of these emotions relates to your capacity to release prayer from your heart.

The idea of *releasing* prayer is important. Prayer is not an ideal outside the self; nor is it one more obligation that must be added to the pile of commitments already on your calendar. Prayer is released, uncovered, from within. Each person, when given time for silence, or the peace of a retreat, at some point finds prayer spontaneously flowing from the heart. The release may happen immediately or it can take weeks, but prayer will overflow, whether it is heartfelt thanks for the day, an expression of wonder at a sunset, or long-held grief.

If you are dissatisfied with your prayer life, use these feelings to uncover some of the conditions behind this present state. Monastic communities structure the day to create time and place for peace, so the monk performs a daily rhythm that fosters the flow of prayer. Follow their wisdom and structure your day in such a way that you also cultivate periods of silence and solitude, honoring your need to follow a holy pattern of prayer.

In all this, it is important to recognize that another's life should never be judged by the quality of prayer in a particular moment. Without the context of a person's entire life, there is little understanding. One person might have ecstatic visions, while another might be experiencing a period of no prayer. Yet the person struggling with prayer may be further along his or her spiritual path than the person with visions. You have to question the whole life. What is happening in this life? What is the movement of the prayer life? Why is prayer now barren or now fertile?

Creating a structured prayer schedule can be difficult for new monks in the world. Life intervenes, and it is easy to become tired or in the wrong mood. I suggest that you counter your resistance by imaging a scene. Let's say you have a child at home. Imagine how much your child would prefer to have even a minute of your time and attention than none. As your child runs out the door to school, you hug and kiss your child goodbye. These moments mean everything.

This is how you can approach prayer: even one moment of communion or silence is meaningful. Commitment to prayer is designed to support love and intimacy with divinity. It is not supposed to be an external imposition. People tend to think of monastic commitment to prayer as conscription, even punishment: you must pray five times a day, or sit zazen eight hours a day. But, there is the possibility that if you commit yourself to a schedule of prayer, you will be happier, you will have permission to alter your life in positive ways. The contemporary monastic lifestyle is not about imposing prayer into a prayer-less life, but to give you permission to release the prayer that is already within you.

How to Pray

A QUESTION I am frequently asked: How am I to pray? This is a common concern and one that frustrates and weighs on those who pursue a spiritual practice. People tend to associate prayer with rote recitation of formal and authorized prayer forms taught in churches, synagogues, sanghas, or other religious communities. While some people do find benefit in traditional religious practices—reciting the rosary, vipassana meditation, contemplative prayer, etc.—others are confused about what constitutes a prayer life on a practical level. It is as if a link is missing that can take a person from distress with formalized prayers to the discovery of the rich prayers that exist within his or her heart.

Teresa of Avila describes mental (contemplative) prayer as, "nothing else than an intimate sharing between friends; it means taking time frequently to be alone with Him who we know loves us."[2] We can imagine God as our intimate friend, with whom we share everything. We can talk to the Divine about our needs, complaints, and difficulties. We can ask for advice, offer thanksgiving, and make acts of faith or reparation for our sins. We can seek guidance for our children, or shed tears about illness and death.

Quite frequently, the most efficacious pray is found in darkness, emptiness. When we find ourselves simply open to the vast mystery surrounding us, when we center our hearts on an obscure faith, and are absorbed into the divine Presence. This is the contemplation of night, when darkness quiets the soul, and we surrender to unknowing. Thomas Merton prays:

> Your brightness is my darkness. I know nothing of You and, by myself, I cannot even imagine how to go about knowing You. If I imagine You, I am mistaken. If I understand You, I am deluded. If I am conscious and certain I know You, I am crazy. The darkness is enough.[3]

Prayer also is advanced by arranging a place, and a set amount of time, each day. An hour or more is best, but even ten minutes spent in prayer or meditation is beneficial. The daily repetition of an established prayer schedule will develop into a visceral rhythm that will compel you to cherish those moments apart from the world. Should you be the type of person who finds switching gears difficult, reading passages from a spiritual book can be a prompt that leads to contemplation. If sitting quietly agitates, prayer can be active: walking prayer, bicycling prayer, carpentry or pottery prayer.

How do I pray? I find the simple contemplation of silence is the best. This is a state of offering myself to the One who is without image, who is unnamed, and who is beyond my mind or comprehension. In this prayer that is no-prayer, subject and object dissolve, liberating my longing.

When I do pray with words, I use those that are direct and honest: I love you, Holy One. Please help me to overcome anger. Please teach me forgiveness. I want to be made empty. O, Divine Mystery, I long to be one with you.

Prayer is my language, the way I speak when I say what I truly feel. It gives permission for passion—to prostrate on the Earth and ask for guidance, to kneel in front of an icon or a majestic mountain and allow grace to work in the soul, to cry out in anguish, and to plead for the ability to remember God's gift. I believe that our prayers are heard, the cosmos listens to our vibrations, and God's ears are receptive to our words. At night, when I am falling asleep, words from a prayer I wrote slip into my mind: *O, Mother of Compassion, Blessed is Your Heart of Pure Love.*

Walking in the hills, I hear quail whispering peace prayers. I watch nature praying: the falcon making circles in the air, a heron strolling through a vineyard, and the song of the Blue Oak's leaves rustling in the wind. Prayer is everywhere. And, I bring it everywhere with me. Sometimes, I voice it; sometimes, I am content to watch it be. It is an energy that flows into and out of my soul with each breath, curling and somersaulting in spirals, until letters settle in my mind, and then, caught up in the torrential waters of spirit soon become a rain of words. I cling to these lofty sounds, riding the wave of awe, straight back into the Divine Heart.

So, lie down on the Earth, feel the soil pulsing, the ants humming, the gophers digging. Are these not prayers? So, too, are the kettle on the stove, and the casserole in the oven, the dishes being washed, and the dog being fed.

Give us all your prayers, O Holy Life!! We want to absorb them into our souls, to unite with creation's extreme audacity of devotion. Even when we do not know we are praying, the universe is praying in us.

Why I am a Universal Monk

(To be read singly or in community)

In light of the intense suffering of our planet
    in the illumination of the mystical oneness of life
I need to express the depth of my feeling for Divine Mystery
    suffusing my soul with longing and devotion.
I offer myself to God in a gesture of complete gift
    in response to the unconditional gift I have been given.
I wish to reveal the intensity of my passion for the mysterious
    energy that loves me without motive or design.
I vow to uphold the dignity of all beings
    to prepare myself to be an oasis of compassion.
I affirm the solitary basis of existence and communion with
    the Alone,
    who gives meaning to my every breath.

The monastic vocation draws me into the cave of the heart
    centering me in *The Center*,
    detaching me from the noise and digressions of the world.
The monastic heart is a lover of the cosmos
    and yearns to be in service of the Holy.
Pulled into the chamber of solitude, I am married to silence
    and taught in secret of a reality with no name.
Here I find my greatest happiness as my whole being
    is enflamed by love of the sacred.

From my earliest youth I have been a monk without a habit,
a contemplative without a home, living between realms.
Transfigured by an understanding of a new spiritual life,
my soul suffers the divisions that wound the radiant Oneness.
If my heart were not open to the gift of divine benevolence,
my vows would be naught.

I am a universal monk, an interspiritual, global monk,
embracing the fullness of humanity's spiritual quest,
even as I live my own unique version.
For in the monastic heart that precedes every religious name,
the contemplative vow is uttered.
This is a state of consciousness that touches the original blueprint,
the wombing place of archetypes and forms.

I am a universal monk because I was called in the beginning
to experience suffering over our separation and exclusion.
Commanded by Love to embrace every religion and spiritual path,
I am not allowed to privilege one over another.

I am a universal monk because I strive to live each day
by the vows and commandments given to me,
offering to others the freedom and hope that I myself
am granted.

I am a universal monk, a global monk, because my monkhood
    extends beyond myself to embrace
    all the inhabitants of Earth and cosmos.

I am a universal monk because I have offered my soul
    as a site of unity and a home for the homeless
    in silence, in solitude flourishing with love of the world
    for its own sake
    for love alone.

I am a universal monk who would be bereft
    without the steady force that guides me
    without the community that shares my heart's desire
    for a planet of peace and happiness.

I am a monk who stands in protest to the agreement
    we humans make
    and the violence we humans inflict on the holy.

I commit myself and my soul
    to the transformation of our hearts
    to an ideal more noble and more compassionate.

I am a monk because I was called and I answered,
    Yes.

Acknowledgements

I am grateful for the work of the scholars and monastics I have cited in this text and for the encouragement of the many participants and students who gather year after year to share in a journey of the heart.

I am thankful for the members of the Community of a New Monastic Way for their interest in and support of my work during more than forty years. Their commitment to a monastic life in the world and their generous transcription of my audio recordings has been singularly important in bringing the book to print.

In particular, I would like to thank (in alphabetical order) those who have transcribed and/or edited many of the lectures that form the body of this work: Betty Bernstein, Neema Caughran, Suzy Elmiger, Susan Gallegos, Cathy Grigsby, Janna Kane (deceased), Nelson Kane, Patricia Kilcullen (deceased), Maya Lanzetta, Shana Lanzetta, Corinne Martin, Lily Oster, Margaret Riordan, Sarah Stein, and Joan Uraneck.

I thank Laurie Gibson who has guided the text into its present form through her insightful and generous copy-editing of each chapter, and to Tessa Avila for creation of the index. I thank my daughter, Shana Lanzetta, for creating and maintaining my website and posting my weekly meditations. I am indebted to my friend, Nelson Kane, who has patiently guided this book into print. A gifted graphic designer, it is Nelson's exceptional appreciation of the relationship between visual text and spiritual meaning that enriches the book's content and fosters a contemplative reading environment.

And, as always, I am forever grateful for my family who are the source of unending love, strength, and support.

Notes

CHAPTER 1 • Longing for Solitude

1. Beverly Lanzetta, *Emerging Heart: Global Spirituality and the Sacred* (Minneapolis: Fortress Press, 2007); idem, *Nine Jewels of Night: One Soul's Journey into God* (San Diego: Blue Sapphire Books, 2014).

CHAPTER 2 • The New Monk

1. Raimundo Panikkar, *Blessed Simplicity: The Monk as Universal Archetype* (New York: The Seabury Press, 1982),

2. Ibid. 20, 28.

3. Ibid. 7–8.

4. Ibid.

5. Ibid. 8–9.

6. Raimon Panikkar, "The New Monk," *Monastic Interreligious Dialogue Bulletin* 72, May 2004.

7. Francis Tiso, "Raimundo Panikkar on the Monk as 'Archetype,'" William Skudlarek, ed. *Dilatato Corde*. Volume 1, numbers 1 and 2: January-December 2011 (Brooklyn, NY: Lantern Books, 2012), 284. This article also can be found at *Dialogue Interreligieux Monastique/Monastic Interreligious Dialogue*, http://www.dimmid.org/index. asp?Type=B_BASIC&SEC=%7B383FB138-0B7E-4BB4-9629-665574E6B40C%7D

8. *Blessed Simplicity*, 11–12.

9. Bernadette Flanagan, *Embracing Solitude: Women and New Monasticism* (Eugene, OR: Cascade Books, 2014), 16.

10. Francis Tiso, "Raimundo Panikkar on the Monk as 'Archetype,'" 277–278.

11. Ibid. 294.

12. Ibid. 273.

13. Sandra M. Schneiders, I.H.M., *Selling All: Commitment, Consecrated Celibacy, and Community in Catholic Religious Life* (New York: Paulist Press, 2001), 117.

14. *Blessed Simplicity*, 27.

15. Ibid.

16. Ibid. 10.

17. Ibid. 6.

18. Ibid. 292–293.

19. Louis Komjathy, *Daoism: A Guide for the Perplexed* (New York: Bloomsbury Academic: 2014), 41.

20. Cited in Mayeul de Dreuille, *From East to West: A History of Monasticism* (New York: The Crossroad Publishing Company, 1999), 65.

21. Ibid. 68.

22. Ibid. 23. "But there is no proof," writes Mayeul de Dreuille, "of any direct influence from the religions of Asia on Christian monasticism and it seems, besides, that the latter sprang spontaneously from the Gospels. The similarities thus bear witness to man's fundamental desire to surrender himself completely to the search for the Absolute."

23. Cited in Thomas Merton, *The Wisdom of the Desert* (New York: New Directions, 1960), 30.

24. Laura Swan, *The Forgotten Desert Mothers* (New York: Paulist Press, 2001), 64–65.

25. Ibid. 58.

26. See Diarmuid O'Murchu, *Religious Life in the 21st Century: The Prospect of Refounding* (Maryknoll, NY: Orbis Books, 2017); Columba Stewart, "The Origins and Fate of Monasticism," *Spiritus: The Journal of Christian Spirituality* 10 (2010).

27. Norman R. Davies, "Dedicated Jewish Contemplatives: A Jewish Monastic Option?" http://zeek.forward.com/articles/117011/ Also, https://citydesert.wordpress.com/2014/01/05/a-jewish-contemplative/

28. Mohammad Ali Shomali and William Skudlarek, eds. *Monks and Muslims: Monastic and Shi'a Spirituality in Dialogue* (Collegeville, MN: Liturgical Press, 2012), ix.

29. Columba Stewart, "The Origins and Fate of Monasticism," 263.

30. The paragraphs on Monastic Interreligious Dialogue are adapted from Beverly Lanzetta, *Emerging Heart: Global Spirituality and the Sacred* (Minneapolis: Fortress Press, 2007), 93–95.

31. Paul Elie, *The Life You Save May Be Your Own: An American Pilgrimage* (New York: Farrar, Straus, Giroux, 2003), 416.

32. Tiso, "Raimundo Panikkar," 270.

33. Consult the MID (http://monasticinterreligiousdialogue.com/) and DIM-MID (https://dimmid.org/) websites.

34. Stewart, "The Origins and Fate of Monasticism," 263, 257.

35. Wayne Teasdale, "The Interspiritual Age: Global Spirituality in the Third Millennium," in Wayne Teasdale and George Cairns, eds. *The Community of Religions: Voices and Images of the Parliament of the World's Religions* (New York: Continuum, 1996), 209.

36. Panikkar, *Blessed Simplicity*, 28.

37. Bede Griffiths, *The New Creation in Christ*. Ed. by Robert Kiely and Laurence Freeman, OSB (Springfield, IL: Templegate Publishers, 1994), 89.

38. Bede Griffiths, *The Golden String: An Autobiography* (Springfield, IL: Templegate Publishers, 1980), 146.

39. de Dreuille, *From East to West*, 127.

CHAPTER 3 • Contemplation and the New Monk

1. Dionysius the Areopagite, *The Ecclesiastical Hierarchy*, VI.1.3, cited in William Skudlarek, *Demythologizing Celibacy: Practical Wisdom from Christian and Buddhist Monasticism* (Collegeville, MN: Liturgical Press, 2008), 11.

2. Ibid.

3. Dionysius the Areopagite, *The Mystical Theology, in Dionysius the Areopagite*, C.E. Rolt, translator (London: SPCK, 1983), 191.

4. Bernard McGinn, *The Foundations of Mysticism*, vol. 1, *The Presence of God: A History of Western Christian Mysticism* (New York: Crossroad, 1992), 24.

5. Richard of St. Victor, *Richard of St. Victor: The Twelve Patriarchs, The Mystical Ark, Book Three of the Trinity*, Grover A. Zinn, translator (New York: Paulist Press, 1979), 156.

6. Shirley du Boulay, *Beyond the Darkness: A Biography of Bede Griffiths* (Winchester, UK: O Books, 2003), 253.

7. Pat Hawk, *Pathless Path Newsletter*, vol. 1 no. 4 (2002), 3.

8. Paragraphs in this section, "Mystical Foundation of New Monasticism," have been adapted from passages in Beverly Lanzetta, *Radical Wisdom: A Feminist Mystical Theology* (Minneapolis: Fortress Press, 2005), 28-34.

9. See Wayne Teasdale, "Spirituality as a Primary Resource in Promoting Peace," *Interreligious Insight: A Journal of Dialogue and Engagement, (April 2006)*, available at http://www.interreligiousinsight.org/April2006/TeasdaleEssay.html

10. Teresa of Avila, *The Interior Castle, in The Collected Works of St. Teresa of Avila*, translated by Kieran Kavanaugh and Otilio Rodriguez (Washington, DC: Institute of Carmelite Studies, 1980), 4.1.4, p. 318 and 4.2.4, p. 324.

11. Thomas Merton, *New Seeds of Contemplation* (New York: New Directions, 1972), 3.

12. Ibid. 13.

CHAPTER 4 • The Desert Spirituality of New Monasticism

1. Meister Eckhart, in *Meister Eckhart: Sermons & Treatises*, 3 vols. M. O'C. Walshe, trans. (Longmead, Great Britain: Element Books, 1987), vol. 1, Sermon 8: 74 and 76.

2. Douglas Christie, "The Birth of the Word in the Soul," delivered to the General Assembly of the Dominicans, September 17, 2004. Personal copy.

3. Meister Eckhart: *Sermons & Treatises*, vol. 1, Sermon 3: 33.

4. Brought into Latin Christianity by John Scotus Eriugena and other ninth-century translators of Dionysius, the positive and negative ways are transposed from Greek into the Latin terms *via positiva* (positive way, way of affirmation) and *via negativa* (negative way, way of negation).

5. The Pseudo-Dionysius places apophatic theology in a culminating position with respect to the soul's return to its Source: "Now we must wholly distinguish this negative method from that of positive statements. For when we were making positive statements we began with the most universal statements, and then through intermediate terms we came at last to particular titles, but now ascending upwards from

particular to universal conceptions we strip off all qualities in order that we may attain a naked knowledge of that Unknowing which in all existent things is enwrapped by all objects of knowledge, and that we may begin to see that superessential Darkness which is hidden by all the light that is in existent things." *Dionysius the Areopagite: The Divine Names and the Mystical Theology*, translated by C.E. Rolt (London: SPCK, 1983), 195–196. See also Harvey Egan, "Christian Apophatic and Kataphatic Mysticisms," *Theological Studies* 39 (1978): 399–426.

6. See Ewert H. Cousins, "Kataphatic and Apophatic Theology: Symbols of the Journey," *Horizons*, 1985.

7. *Pseudo-Dionysius: The Complete Works*, Colm Luibheid, trans. (New York: Paulist Press, 1987), 136.

8. *Meister Eckhart: Sermons & Treatises*, vol. 1, Sermon 19: 157–158.

9. Ibid. Sermon 9: 83–85.

10. Ibid. vol. 2, Sermon 60: 105.

11. Ibid. vol. 1, Sermon 2: 20.

12. Ibid. vol. 1, Sermon 4: 40–41.

13. Ibid. vol. 1, Sermon 13(b): 117.

14. Ibid. *On Detachment*, vol. 3: 292.

15. Ibid. vol. 1, *Sermon 9*: 84.

16. The phrase "atman is Brahman" captures the primary view of ultimate reality in the Vedanta school of Hindu thought. Here, "atman"—eternal, immortal individual soul—is "Brahman," the world soul and primal reality of all being and existence. In our deepest selves, we are divine. In Zen, when the adherent is enlightened by the extinguishing of all desire—nirvana—then liberation is apparent in the cycle of existence (samsara).

CHAPTER 5 · *Via Feminina*: The Mystical Path of the Feminine

1. Beverly J. Lanzetta, *Radical Wisdom: A Feminist Mystical Theology* (Minneapolis: Fortress Press, 2005).

2. In addition to original writings of women mystics and monks, recent books specifically address women's contribution to monasticism and the feminine: Bernadette Flanagan, *Embracing Solitude: Women and New Monasticism* (Eugene, OR: Cascade Books, 2014); Diarmuid O'Murchu, *Religious Life in the 21st Century* (Maryknoll, NY: Orbis Books, 2017); Laura Swan, *The Forgotten Desert Mothers* (New York: Paulist Press, 2013); Steven Venderputten, *Dark Age Nunneries: The Ambiguous Identity of Female Monasticism, 800-1500* (Ithaca, NY: Cornell University Press, 2018); Christine Toomey, *In Search of Buddha's Daughters: The Hidden Lives and Fearless Work of Buddhist Nuns* (New York: The Experiment, 2015); Judith Simmer-Brown, *Dakini's Warm Breath: The Feminine Principle in Tibetan Buddhism* (New York: Penguin, 2002).

3. Thomas Merton, "Hagia Sophia," in *A Thomas Merton Reader*, Thomas P. McDonnell, ed. (New York: Doubleday, 1989), 506.

4. Christopher Pramuk, *Sophia: The Hidden Christ of Thomas Merton* (Collegeville, MN: Liturgical Press, 2009), 275.

5. Peter Schafer, "Daughter, Sister, Bride, and Mother: Images of the Femininity

of God in the Early Kabbala," *Journal of the American Academy of Religion* June 2000 Vol. 68, No. 2: 233.

6. Citation from Gershom Scholem, *On the Mystical Shape of the Godhead* (New York: Schocken Books, 1991), 148.

7. Peter Schafer, "Daughter, Sister, Bride, and Mother," 228 and 225.

8. Ibid. 228.

9. Ibid. 230–231.

10. Ibn al'Arabi, *The Bezels of Wisdom*, R.W.J. Austin, trans. (New York: Paulist Press, 1980), 275.

11. David Kinsley, *Hindu Goddesses: Visions of the Divine Feminine in the Hindu Religious Tradition* (Berkeley: University of California Press, 1988), 30.

12. Ibid.

13. Paula Gunn Allen, *The Sacred Hoop: Recovering the Feminine in American Indian Traditions* (New York: Open Road, 1992), location 285, Kindle Edition.

14. Paragraphs in this section, "Personification of the Divine Feminine," have been adapted from passages in Beverly Lanzetta, *Radical Wisdom: A Feminist Mystical Theology* (Minneapolis: Fortress Press, 2005), 28-34.

15. Meister Eckhart, Sermon 12. *Meister Eckhart: Teacher and Preacher*, Bernard McGinn, ed. (New York: Paulist Press, 1986), 270.

16. Liz Herbert McAvoy, "'The Moders Service': Motherhood as Matrix in Julian of Norwich," *Mystics Quarterly* 24 (1998) 4: 192.

CHAPTER 6 • Four Dimensions of *Via Feminina*

1. Abraham Joshua Heschel, *Holiness in Words: Abraham Joshua Heschel's Poetics of Piety*, Edward K. Kaplan, ed. (Albany: State University of New York Press, 1996), 66.

2. Abraham J. Heschel, *The Prophets: An Introduction* (New York: Harper & Row, 1955), 26.

3. Constance FitzGerald, "Impasse and Dark Night," in *Women's Spirituality: Resources for Christian Development.* 2nd ed., Joanne Wolski Conn, ed. (New York: Paulist Press, 1996), 427.

4. Teresa of Avila, *The Interior Castle, The Collected Worlds of St. Teresa of Avila*, Kieran Kavanaugh and Otilio Rodriquez, trans. (Washington, D.C.: Institute of Carmelite Studies, 1980), 6.9.18, 418.

CHAPTER 7 • The Dark Night of the Feminine

1. Constance FitzGerald, "Impasse and Dark Night," in *Women's Spirituality: Resources for Christian Development*, Joann Wolski Conn, ed. (New York: Paulist Press, 1996), 411.

2. Raimon Panikkar, "Some Words Instead of a Response," *Cross Currents* 29 (Summer 1979): 196.

3. Abhishiktananda, *Ascent to the depth of the Heart: The Spiritual Diary (1948-73) of Swami Abhishiktananda (Dom Henri Le Saux)*, trans. David Fleming (Kashmere Gate, Delhi: ISPCK, 1998), 213.

4. Henri Corbin, *Alone with the Alone: The Creative Imagination in Ibn 'Arabi*. 118.

5. Ibid. 168.

6. Ibid. 159-60.

7. Constance FitzGerald, "Impasse and Dark Night," 429.

CHAPTER 8 · Embodied Spirituality of Benevolence

1. Jorge N. Ferrer, *Participation and the Mystery: Transpersonal Essays in Psychology, Education, and Religion* (Albany, NY: State University of New York Press, 2017), 74. Ferrer's work is especially groundbreaking in this area. See Chapter Three, "Toward A Fully Embodied Spiritual Life". Idem. *Revisioning transpersonal theory: A participatory vision of human spirituality* (Albany, NY: State University of New York Press, 2002). Also consult: *Perceiving the Divine Through the Human Body: Mystical Sensuality*, Thomas Cattoi and June McDaniel, eds. (New York: Palgrave Macmillan, 2011); Lisa Isherwood and Elisabeth Stuart, *Introducing Body Theology* (Sheffield, U.K.: Pilgrim Press, 1998); M. T. Romero and R. V. Albareda. 2001, "Born on Earth: Sexuality, spirituality, and human evolution," *ReVision*, 24(2), 5–14.

2. Pierre Teilhard de Chardin, *Science and Christ* (New York: Harper & Row, 1968), 12–13.

CHAPTER 9 · A Theology of Intimacy

1. Grace M. Jantzen, "Flourishing: Towards an Ethic of Natality," Feminist Theory, 2 (2001): 219-32. Jantzen uses the term, "moral imaginary."

2. Nanci Hogan, "The Implications of a Politics of Natality for Transnational Feminist Advocacy: Transforming the Human Rights Moral Imaginary," *Grace Jantzen: Redeeming the Present*, edited by Elaine L. Graham (Surrey, England: Ashgate Publishing Limited, 2009), 228-229. Hogan, in reference to Jantzen's usage of the moral imaginary, writes: "It includes the norms, assumptions, prejudices, and prejudgements which give content to our dispositions to act and think and 'determine what is actually morally thinkable.'"

3. Jalal-ud-Din Rumi, cited in Andrew Harvey, *The Way of Passion: A Celebration of Rumi* (New York: Jeremy P. Tarcher/Putnam, 2001), 5.

4. This paragraph is adapted, with minor revision, from Beverly J. Lanzetta, *The Other Side of Nothingness: Toward a Theology of Radical Openness* (Albany, NY: State University of New York Press, 2001), 128–129.

5. Thomas Merton cited in *A Thomas Merton Reader*, ed. Thomas P. McDonnell (New York: Image Books, 1989), 510.

CHAPTER 10 · Love and Emptiness

1. *The Wisdom of the Desert Fathers*, Benedicta Ward, trans. (Oxford: SLG Press, 1975), 24. Translation slightly modified.

2. Jalal al-Din Rumi, *Fihi ma fihi (Discourses of Rumi)*. Cited in William C. Chittick, *The Sufi Path of Love: The Spiritual Teachings of Rumi* (Albany, NY: State University of New York Press, 1983), 201.

3. Anonymous, *The Cloud of Unknowing and The Book of Privy Counseling*, William Johnston, ed. (New York: Image Books, 1973), 102.

4. Thomas Merton, *Contemplation in a World of Action* (New York: Image Books, 1973), 36.

CHAPTER 13 • Purity of Heart

1. Cassian also traveled to Constantinople, where he met Eastern Orthodox mystics, including St. John Chrysostom, and then to Rome, where Pope Leo ordained him into the priesthood. Later, he moved to Marseilles, France, where he founded the Abbey of St. Victor, a complex of monasteries for both men and women. Cassian's writings on monastic principles became foundational to the development of Christian monasticism, from which St. Benedict adopted his monastic rule.

2. Martyrius, *The Book of Perfection*, Cited in *Purity of Heart*, 42.

3. Cited in *Purity of Heart in Early Ascetic and Monastic Literature*, Harriet A. Luckman and Linda Kulzer, eds. (Collegeville: MN: The Liturgical Press, 1999), 41.

4. Ibid. 136.

5. Ibid. 100.

6. See Henry Corbin, *Alone with the Alone: Creative Imagination in the Sufism of Ibn 'Arabi* (New Jersey: Princeton University Press, 1969), 221–222.

7. Ibid. 250-251.

8. Stephen Hirtenstein, "The Mystic's Ka'ba: The Cubic Wisdom of the Heart According to Ibn 'Arabi." *Journal of the Muhyiddin Ibn 'Arabi Society*, Volume 48, 2010; http://www.ibnarabisociety.org/articles/mystics-kaba.html

9. Ibn al'Arabi, *The Bezels of Wisdom*, R.W.J. Austin, trans. (New York: Paulist Press, 1980), 149.

10. Ibid. 153.

11. Hirtenstein, "The Mystic's Ka'ba," http://www.ibnarabisociety.org/articles/mystics-kaba.html

12. Augustine, *Commentary on the Lord's Sermon on the Mount with Seventeen Related Sermons*, Book II, translated by D.J. Kavanagh (Washington, D.C.: The Catholic University of America Press, 2001), 110.

13. *Purity of Heart*, 178-79.

14. Ibid. 181.

15. Ibid. 181–82.

CHAPTER 14 • Treasures of the Monk's Journey

1. Bernadette Flanagan, *Embracing Solitude: Women and New Monasticism* (Eugene, OR: Cascade Books, 2014), 3.

2. Thomas Merton, *The Silent Life* (New York: Farrar, Straus, & Giroux, 1957), 33–34.

3. Ibid. 24.

CHAPTER 15 • The Monastic Personality

1. Thomas Merton, *Conjectures of a Guilty Bystander* (New York: Image Classics, 1968), 155–6.

2. Anonymous, *The Book of the Book in Spirit: By a Friend of God. A Guide to Rhineland Mysticism*, C.F. Kelley, trans. (New York: Harper & Brothers, no date), 236.

3. Rainer Maria Rilke, *Letters to a Young Poet*, Stephen Mitchell, trans. (New York: Vintage Books, 1987), 78.

4. *Black Elk Speaks: Being the Life Story of a Holy Man of the Oglala Sioux*, as told through John G. Neihardt (Lincoln, Nebraska: University of Nebraska Press, 1988), 48–49.

5. Abraham Joshua Heschel, *The Sabbath* (New York: Farrar, Straus, and Giroux, 1979), 13–15.

CHAPTER 18 • St. Teresa on Prayer

1. Teresa of Avila, *The Interior Castle*, in *The Collected Works of Teresa of Avila*, Volume Two, translation by Kieran Kavanaugh and Otilio Rodriquez (Washington, D.C.: Institute of Carmelite Studies, 1980), Prologue.1, 281.

2. Ibid. 1.1.1, 283.

3. Ibid.

4. Ibid. Epilogue, no. 3, 452.

5. Ibid. 7.1.3, 428.

6. Ibid. 1.2.14, 294.

7. Ibid. Introduction, 271.

8. Ibid.

9. Ibid. 4.1.7, 319.

10. Ibid. 5.1.9, 339.

11. Ibid. 7.2.4, 434.

12. Ibid.

13. Ibid. 4.1.9, 320.

14. Ibid. 11.8, 113.

15. Teresa of Avila, *The Book of Her Life*, in *The Collected Works of Teresa of Avila*, Volume One, translation by Kieran Kavanaugh and Otilio Rodriquez (Washington, D.C.: Institute of Carmelite Studies, 1976), 11.6, 113.

16. Ibid. 14.2, 133.

17. Ibid. 16.1, 147.

18. Ibid. 17.4, 153-154.

19. 16.2, 148.

20. 18.1, 157.

21. *The Interior Castle*, 6.7.11, 42.

CHAPTER 19 • St. Augustine's Spiritual Journey

1. Evelyn Underhill, *Mysticism: A Study in the Nature and Development of Man's Spiritual Consciousness* (New York: New American Library, 1974), 168-169.

2. Ibid. 168.

3. A description of Manichaeism is found in John Ryan's introduction to *The Confessions of St. Augustine*, John K. Ryan, trans. (New York: Image Books, 1960), 20–21. "The Manichean religion took its name from Mani, its founder, a Babylonian who lived from 215 to 277. Mani claimed to have had various revelations, including one in which he learned that he was the Holy Spirit . . . His religion derived from many sources, but its chief characteristics may be summed up as follows. It was gnostic, that is, it claimed to have a special knowledge that led to salvation; it was a form of extreme metaphysical and moral dualism, in that it held for the reality and power of evil as well as of good; it had its sacred literature, which it stressed rather than ritual; it rejected the Old Testament and subjected it to detailed attack; it likewise attacked the New Testament, although not rejecting it completely; it looked upon the body as evil and advocated a spurious asceticism; it claimed to appeal to reason and to offer a rational solution to the problems of life; it was a missionary religion and held that it was universal, not only in providing salvation for all men, but also in having spread over the whole civilized world."

4. Translation taken from *The Confessions of St. Augustine*, John K. Ryan, 66–67. All citations from Augustine in this chapter are from the Ryan translation, and are documented by book, chapter, and verse.

5. Ibid. 2.10.18, 76.

CHAPTER 20 • Gandhi's Threefold Path

1. Mohandas K. Gandhi, *Prayer*, John Strohmeier, ed. (Berkeley: Berkeley Hills Books, 2000), 173.

2. Ibid. 41.

3. Mohandas K. Gandhi, *The Way to God*, M. S. Desphande, ed. (Berkeley: Berkeley Hills Books, 1999), 95.

4. *Prayer*, 16.

5. Mohandas K. Gandhi, *Book of Prayers*, John Strohmeier, ed. (Berkeley: Berkeley Hills Books, 1999), 39.

6. *The Way to God*, 21.

7. *Book of Prayers*, 41.

CHAPTER 21 • The Monk as Social Mystic

1. Alton B. Pollard, III, *Mysticism and Social Change: The Social Witness of Howard Thurman*. Martin Luther King, Jr. Memorial Studies in Religion, Culture, and Social Development (New York: Peter Lang, 1992), 1.

2. Pierre Teilhard de Chardin, *Toward the Future*, Rene Hague, trans. (New York: Harcourt Brace Jovanovich, 1975), 86-7.

3. Martin Luther King, Jr., "The Three Dimensions of a Complete Life," 11 December 1960. *The Papers of Martin Luther King, Jr.*, Vol. 5, Clayborne Carlson, ed. (Berkeley: University of California Press, 2000), 576.

4. Howard Thurman, "Mysticism and Social Action," cited in Alton B. Pollard III, *Mysticism and Social Change*, 65.

5. Howard Thurman, *With Head and Heart* (New York: Harcourt Brace & Company, 1979), 269.

6. Paragraphs about Dr. King on pages 267–268 and 276–277: Adapted from: *Revives My Soul Again: The Spirituality of Martin Luther King, Jr.*, Lewis V. Baldwin and Victor Anderson, eds. Copyright © 2018 Fortress Press to be published November 2018.

7. Anonymous, "How the Friend of God Suffers," in *The Book of the Poor in Spirit: By a Friend of God*, C.F. Kelley, ed. trans. (New York: Harper & Brothers), 229–51.

8. Thurman, *With Head and Heart*, 269.

9. Reiterated in Thomas Merton, *Conjectures of a Guilty Bystander* (New York, 1966), 156-57. For a realistic, compassionate understanding of this chapter in Merton's life, see Jim Forest, *Living with Wisdom: A Life of Thomas Merton* (Maryknoll, NY: Orbis Books, 1991), 121–38.

10. Thomas P. McDonnell, "An Interview with Thomas Merton," Motive 27 (1967): 32-41. Cited by George A. Kilcourse, Jr., "Thomas Merton's Contemplative Struggle: Bridging the Abyss to Freedom," *Crosscurrents*, Spring 1999. http://www.crosscurrents.org/essays.htm; http://findarticles.com/p/articles/mi_m2096/is_1_49/ai_54482239/, 3.

11. Abraham Joshua Heschel, *Israel: An Echo of God* (New York: Farrar, Straus, and Giroux, 1969), 224.

12. Catherine of Siena: *The Dialogue*, Suzanne Noffke, trans. (New York: Paulist Press, 1980), 35.

13. Ibid. 8–9.

14. Louis Fischer, *The Essential Gandhi: An Anthology of His Writings, Work and Ideas* (New York: Vintage Books, 1962), 216.

15. Dorothy Day, *The Long Loneliness* (San Francisco: HarperSanFrancisco, 1952), 78.

16. Thich Nhat Hanh, *Being Peace* (Berkeley: Parallax Press, 1987), 63–64.

17. King, "Letter from Birmingham Jail," *A Testament of Hope: The Essential Writings and Speeches of Martin Luther King, Jr.*, James M. Washington, ed. (San Francisco: HarperSanFrancisco, 1986), 290.

18. Mohandas K. Gandhi, *Harijan* (Ahmedabad: Navajivan Trust) 1946: 2–6, 167.

19. Mohandas K. Gandhi, *Autobiography: The Story of My Experiments with Truth* (New York: Dover Publications, 1983), xiii–ix.

20. Ibid. ix.

21. Ibid.

22. Martin Luther King, Jr., *Strength to Love* (Philadelphia: Fortress Press, 1981), 13.

23. King, *A Testament of Hope: The Essential Writings and Speeches of Martin Luther King, Jr.* James M. Washington, ed. (San Francisco: HarperSanFrancisco, 1986), 447.

24. Mary Elizabeth King, "Mohandas K. Gandhi and Martin Luther King, Jr.'s Bequest: Nonviolent Civil Resistance in a Globalized World," in *In An Inescapable Network of Mutuality: Martin Luther King, R. and the Globalization of an Ethical Ideal*, Lewis K. Baldwin and Paul R. Dekar, eds. (Eugene: OR: Cascade Books, 2013), 156.

25. King, "Beyond Vietnam: A Time to Break Silence," in *The Radical King*, Cornel

West, ed. (Boston: Beacon Press, 2015), 216.

26. "All the Great Religions of the World," Redbook magazine, November 5, 1964, in *The Radical King*, 98-99.

27. Fischer, *The Essential Gandhi*, 74.

28. Mohandas K. Gandhi, *All Men Are Brothers: Autobiographical Reflections*, Krishna Kripalani, ed. (New York: Continuum, 1984), 65.

29. Ibid. 78.

30. Ibid. 256–257.

31. Thich Nhat Hanh, "In Search of the Enemy of Man (addressed to (the Rev.) Martin Luther King)." http://www.aavw.org/special_features/letters_thich_abstract02.html

32. George A. Kilcourse, Jr., "Thomas Merton's Contemplative Struggle: Bridging the Abyss to Freedom," *Crosscurrents*, Spring 1999. http://www.crosscurrents.org/essays.htm; http://findarticles.com/p/articles/mi_m2096/is_1_49/ai_54482239/pg_5.

33. William Apel, *Signs of Peace: The Interfaith Letters of Thomas Merton* (Maryknoll: Orbis Books, 2006), 175.

34. Thomas Merton, *The Other Side of the Mountain: The End of the Journey* (San Francisco: HarperSanFrancisco, 1998), 135.

35. Thomas Merton, *Courage for Truth*, Christine M. Bochen, ed. (New York: Farrar, Straus, Giroux, 1993), 54–55. Also consult, Robert Inchausti, *Thomas Merton's American Prophecy* (New York: State University of New York, 1988), Chapter 10, "The Third Position of Integrity."

36. Thomas Merton, *Faith and Violence* (Notre Dame, IN: University of Notre Dame Press, 1994) 109–110.

37. Thomas Merton, The Wisdom of the Desert (New York: New Directions, 1960), 18.

CHAPTER 22 • The Wisdom of Vows

1. Benedictine monks, for example, retain the same elements as the three standard vows, but with additional meaning as prescribed by St. Benedict in the fifty-eighth chapter of his rule. These are: vow of obedience; vow of stability, remaining in one monastery for life; and vow of conversatio morum, to strive for conversion in one's own personal behavior and to faithfully persevere in the monastic observance as it is lived within the monastery.

2. Sandra M. Schneiders, *Selling All: Commitment, Consecrated Celibacy, and Community in Catholic Religious Life; Religious Life in the New Millennium*, Volume Two (New York: Paulist Press, 2001), 80.

3. Ibid. 108.

4. William Skudlarek, *Demythologizing Celibacy: Practical Wisdom from Christian and Buddhist Monasticism* (Collegeville, Minnesota: Liturgical Press, 2008), 1–2.

5. *Selling All*, 106–107.

6. Ibid. 2–3.

7. Ibid. 15.

8. See *School(s) for Conversion: 12 Marks of a New Monasticism*, The Rutba House, ed. (Eugene, OR: Cascade Books, 2005), xii–xiii.

9. See Mohandas K. Gandhi, *Vows and Observances*, John Strohmeier, ed. (Berkeley, CA: Berkeley Hills Books, 1999), especially "The Eleven Observances," and "The Ashram Vows," 29–48.

10. Martin Luther King Jr., available online at http://teachingamericanhistory. org/library/document/commitment-card/

11. These vows are based on Wayne Teasdale's nine elements of spiritual maturity, found in his book, *The Mystic Heart* (Novato, CA: New World Library, 1999) and developed from them by Rev. Diane Berke. Cited in Rory McEntee and Adam Bucko, *The New Monasticism: An Interspiritual Manifesto for Contemplative Living* (Maryknoll, NY: Orbis Books, 2015), xxxv–xxxvi.

CHAPTER 23 • Gandhi on Vows

1. Mohandas K. Gandhi, *Constructive Programme: Its Meaning and Place. The Collected Works of Mahatma Gandhi*, 75 (New Delhi: Publication Division, Ministry of Information and Broadcasting, 1958–1994), 155.

2. Mohandas K. Gandhi, *Gandhi on Women: Collection of Mahatma Gandhi's Writings and Speeches on Women*, Pushpa Joshi, ed. (Ahmedabad, India: Navajivan Publishing House, Centre for Women's Development Studies, New Delhi, 1988), 379.

3. Richard L. Johnson, ed. *Gandhi's Experiments with Truth: Essential Writings by and about Mahatma Gandhi* (New York: Lexington Books, 2006), 150.

4. Mahatma Gandhi, *All Men Are Brothers: Autobiographical Reflections*, Krishna Kripalani, ed. (New York: Continuum Publishing, 1984), 119.

5. Ibid.

6. *The Essential Gandhi: An Anthology of His Life, Work and Ideas*, Louis Fischer, ed. (New York: Vintage Books, 1962), 4.

7. *All Men Are Brothers*, 66.

CHAPTER 24 • Mystical Celibacy: Divine-Human Intimacy

1. Meister Eckhart, *Meister Eckhart: The Essential Sermons, Commentaries, Treatises, and Defense*, Edmund Colledge and Bernard McGinn, trans. (New York: Paulist Press, 1981), 178.

2. Ibid.

3. Pierre Teilhard de Chardin, *Toward the Future*, Rene Hague, trans. (New York: Harcourt Brace Jovanovich, 1975), 77.

CHAPTER 25 • Sexuality and Mystical Openness

1. Jorge N. Ferrer, *Participation and the Mystery: Transpersonal Essays in Psychology, Education, and Religion* (Albany, NY: State University of New York Press, 2017), 75.

2. Rainer Maria Rilke, *Letters to a Young Poet*, Stephen Mitchell, trans. (New York: Vintage Books, 1987), 39.

CHAPTER 26 • Rule of Life

1. U.Ve Sri Rama Ramanuja Achari, http://www.australiancouncilofhinduclergy. com/uploads/5/5/4/9/5549439/the_hindu_monastic_code.pdf

2. https://www.accesstoinsight.org/ptf/dhamma/sila/dasasila.html

3. Thich Nhat Hanh, *Freedom Wherever We Go: A Buddhist Monastic Code for the Twenty-First Century* (Berkeley: Parallax Press, 2004), 25–6.

4. *The Buddhist Monastic Code I: The Patimokkha Rules*, Thanissaro, trans. (Valley Center, CA: Metta Forest Monastery, revised third edition, 2013), 11.

5. *St. Benedict's Rule: A New Translation for Today*, Patrick Barry, OSB (UK: Ampleforth Abbey Press, 1997), 21. Subsequent citations in this section on humility are from this translation.

6. Mary Beth Ingham, "The Logic of the Gift: Clare of Assisi and Franciscan Evangelical Life," *Greek Orthodox Theological Review* 60: 1–2 (2015), 132.

7. Ibid. 135.

8. *Francis and Clare: The Complete Works*, Regis J. Armstrong and Ignatius C. Brady, trans. (New York: Paulist Press, 1982), 218–223.

9. Ibid. 230–231.

CHAPTER 27 • All Life is Prayer

1. Katha Upanishad II. 1-5, cited in Kenneth Kramer, *World Scriptures: An Introduction to Comparative Religions* (New York: Paulist Press, 1986), 42.

2. Teresa of Avila, *The Book of Her Life*, 8.5 in *The Collected Works of St. Teresa of Avila Volume One*, Kieran Kavanaugh and Otilio Rodriguez, trans. (Washington, D.C.: Institute of Carmelite Studies, 1987), 96.

3. Thomas Merton, "Thou Art Not How I Have Conceived Thee," *Dialogues with Silence: Prayers and Drawings*, edited by Jonathan Montaldo (New York: HarperSanFrancisco, 2001), 5.

Monastic Bibliography

Abhishiktananda. *Ascent to the Depth of the Heart: The Spiritual Diary (1948–73) of Swami Abhishiktananda (Dom Henri Le Saux).* Raimon Panikkar, ed. Kashmere Gate, Delhi: ISPCK, 1986.

——— *Prayer.* London: Canterbury Press Norwich, 2006.

——— *The Secret of Arunachala: A Christian Hermit on Shiva's Holy Mountain.* Kashmere Gate, Delhi: ISPCK, 1988.

Aiken, Robert. *Taking the Path of Zen.* San Francisco: North Point Press, 1982.

Ali Shomali, Mohammad, and William Skudlarek, eds. *Monks and Muslims: Monastic and Shi'a Spirituality in Dialogue.* Collegeville, MN: Liturgical Press, 1989.

Anonymous. *Silence: A Series of Conferences Given by a Camaldolese Hermit.* Bloomingdale, OH: Ercam Editions, 2011.

Anonymous. *The Cloud of Unknowing and the Book of Privy Counseling.* William Johnston, ed. New York: Image Books, 1973.

Bankei, Yotaku. *The Unborn: The Life and Teachings of Zen Master Bankei 1622–1693.* Norman Waddell, trans. San Francisco: North Point Press, 1982.

Barnhart, Bruno, and Joseph Wong. *Purity of Heart and Contemplation: A Monastic Dialogue between Christian and Asian Traditions.* New York: Continuum, 2001.

Benedict, Saint. *The Rule of Saint Benedict.* Timothy Fry, ed. New York: Vintage Books, 1998.

Bielecki, Tessa. *Holy Daring: An Outrageous Gift to Modern Spirituality from Saint Teresa, the Grand Wild Woman of Avila.* Rockport, MA: Element, 1994.

Cameron, Averil et al. *Desert Mothers: Women Ascetics in Early Christian Egypt.* New York: Edwin Mellen Press, 1993.

Carretto, Carlo. *I, Francis.* Robert R. Barr, trans. Maryknoll, NY: Orbis Books, 1982.

Cattoi, Thomas, and June McDaniel. *Perceiving the Divine Through the Human Body: Mystical Sensuality.* New York: Palgrave Macmillan, 2011.

Casey, Michael. *A Guide to Living in the Truth: Saint Benedict's Teaching on Humility.* Ligouri, MO: Ligouri Publications, 2001.

——— *Strangers to the City: Reflections on the Beliefs and Values of the Rule of Saint Benedict.* Brewster, MA: Paraclete Press, 2013.

——— *The Road to Eternal Life: Reflections on the Prologue of Benedict's Rule.* Collegeville, MN: Liturgical Press, 2010.

—— *The Undivided Heart: The Western Monastic Approach to Contemplation.* Petersham, MA: St. Bede's Publications, 1994.

Chittister, Joan. *Called to Question: A Spiritual Memoir.* New York: Sheed and Ward, 2004.

—— *Illuminated Life: Monastic Wisdom for Seekers of Light.* Maryknoll, NY: Orbis Books, 2000.

—— *The Rule of Benedict: Insight for the Ages.* New York: The Crossroad Publishing Co., 1996.

—— *Wisdom Distilled from the Daily: Living the Rule of St. Benedict Today.* San Francisco: Harper Collins, 1991.

Christie, Douglas E. *The Blue Sapphire of the Mind: Notes for a Contemplative Ecology.* New York: Oxford University Press, 2013.

—— *The Word in the Desert: Scripture and the Quest for Holiness in Early Christian Monasticism.* New York: Oxford University Press, 1993.

Corbin, Henry. *Alone with the Alone: Creative Imagination in the Sufism of Ibn 'Arabi.* Princeton: Princeton University Press, 1969.

Cottai, Thomas, and June McDaniel, eds. *Perceiving the Divine through the Human Body: Mystical Sensuality.* New York: Palgrave Macmillan, 2011.

Cozzens, Donald. *Freeing Celibacy.* Collegeville, MN: Liturgical Press, 2006.

Creel, Austin B. and Vasudha Narayanan. *Monastic Life in the Christian and Hindu Traditions: A Comparative Study.* Lewiston, NY: The Edwin Mellon Press, 1990.

Cummings, Charles. *Monastic Practices.* Kalamazoo, MI: Cistercien Publications, 1986.

De Bethune, Pierre-François. *By Faith and Hospitality: The Monastic Tradition as a Model for Interreligious Encounter.* Dame Mary Groves, trans. Herefordshire, UK: Gracewing, 2002.

De Caussade, Jean-Pierre. *The Fire of Divine Love: Readings from Jean-Pierre de Caussade.* Liguori, MO: Triumph Books, 1995.

De Dreuille, Mayeul. *From East to West: A History of Monasticism.* Herefordshire, UK: Gracewing, 1999.

Dekar, Paul R. *Community of the Transfiguration: The Journey of a New Monastic Community.* Eugene, OR: Cascade Books, 2008.

Despeux, Catherine, and Livia Kohn. *Women in Daoism.* Cambridge, MA: Three Pines Press, 2003.

Dogen, Eihei. *Moon in a Dewdrop: Writings of Zen Master Dogen.* Kazuaki Tanahashi, ed. San Francisco: North Point Press, 1985.

Du Boulay, Shirley. *Beyond the Darkness: A Biography of Bede Griffiths.* New York: O Books, 2003.

—— *The Cave of the Heart: The Life of Swami Abhishiktananda.* Maryknoll, NY: Orbis Books, 2005.

—— *Interreligious Hospitality: The Fulfillment of Dialogue.* Collegeville, MN: Liturgical Press, 2010.

Earle, Mary C. *The Desert Mothers: Spiritual Practices from the Women of the Wilderness.* New York: Moorhouse Publishing, 2007.

Ferrer, Jorge. *Participation and the Mystery: Transpersonal Essays in Psychology, Education, and Religion.* Albany: State University of New York Press, 2017.

Flanagan, Bernadette. *Embracing Solitude: Women and New Monasticism.* Eugene, OR: Cascade Books, 2014.

Flinders, Carol Lee. *At the Roots of this Longing: Reconciling a Spiritual Hunger and a Feminist Thirst.* San Francisco: HarperCollins, 1998.

—— *Enduring Grace: Living Portraits of Seven Women Mystics.* San Francisco: HarperCollins, 1993.

—— *Enduring Lives: Portraits of Women and Faith in Action.* New York: Jeremy P. Tarcher/Penguin, 2006.

Gandhi, Mohandas K. *Book of Prayers.* John Strohmeier, ed. Berkeley: Berkeley Hills Books, 1999.

—— *Prayer.* John Strohmeier, ed. Berkeley: Berkeley Hills Books, 2000.

—— *The Way to God.* M. S. Desphande, ed. Berkley: Berkeley Hills Books, 1999.

—— *The Bhagavad Gita According to Gandhi.* John Strohmeier, ed. Berkeley: Berkeley Hills Books, 2000.

—— *Vows and Observances.* John Strohmeier, ed. Berkeley: Berkeley Hills Books, 1999.

Glassman, Bernie. *Bearing Witness: A Zen Master's Lessons in Making Peace.* New York: Bell Tower, 1998.

—— and Rick Fields. *Instructions to the Cook: A Zen Master's Lessons in Living a Life that Matters.* New York: Bell Tower, 1996.

Griffiths, Bede. *Bede Griffiths: Essential Writings.* Thomas Matus, ed. New York: Orbis Books, 2004.

—— *The Golden String: An Autobiography.* Springfield, IL: Templegate Publishers, 1980.

—— *The Marriage of East and West.* Springfield, IL: Templegate Publishers, 1982.

Gyatso, Palden. *The Autobiography of a Tibetan Monk.* New York: Grove Press, 1997.

Hanh, Thich Nhat. *Chanting from the Heart: Buddhist Ceremonies and Daily Practices.* Berkeley: Parallax Press, 2007.

—— *Love in Action: Writings on Nonviolent Social Change.* Berkeley: Parallax Press, 1993.

—— *The Miracle of Mindfulness: An Introduction to the Practice of Meditation.* Boston: Beacon Press, 1975.

—— *Stepping into Freedom: An Introduction to Buddhist Monastic Training.* Berkeley: Parallax Press, 1997.

Harmless, William. *Desert Christians: An Introduction to the Literature of Early Monasticism.* New York: Oxford University Press, 2004.

Hart, Patrick. *A Monastic Vision for the 21st Century: Where Do We Go From Here?* Kalamazoo, MI: Cistercian Publications, 2006.

Hays, Edward. *The Passionate Troubadour: A Medieval Novel about St. Francis of Assisi.* Notre Dame, IN: Forest of Peace, 2004.

Henry, Patrick, ed. *Benedict's Dharma: Buddhists Reflect on the Rule of Saint Benedict.* New York: Riverhead Books, 2001.

Henry, Patrick G., and Donald K. Swearer, eds. *For the Sake of the World: The Spirit of Buddhist and Christian Monasticism.* Minneapolis: Fortress Press, 1989.

Herrou, Adeline. *A World of Their Own: Daoist Monks and Their Community in Contemporary China.* St. Petersburg, FL: Three Pines Press, 2013.

Heschel, Abraham Joshua. *The Sabbath: Its Meaning for Modern Man.* New York: Farrar, Straus and Giroux, 1951, 2005.

Isaac of Syria (also known as Isaac of Nineveh). *Daily Readings with St. Isaac of Syria.* A. M. Allchin, ed. Springfield, IL: Templegate Publishers, 1990.

—— *On Ascetical Life.* Crestwood, NY: St. Vladimir's Seminary Press, 1989.

—— *The Ascetical Homilies of Saint Isaac the Syrian.* Boston: Holy Transfiguration Monastery, 2011.

—— *The Wisdom of St. Isaac of Nineveh.* Sebastian P. Brock, trans. Piscataway, NJ: Gorgias Press, 2006.

Kaplan, Aryeh. *Meditation and Kabbalah.* San Francisco: Weiser Books, 1985.

Keating, Thomas. *Intimacy with God.* New York: The Crossroad Publishing Company, 2001.

—— *Open Mind, Open Heart: The Contemplative Dimension of the Gospel.* Rockport, MA: Element Books, 1991.

—— *Reflections on the Unknowable.* New York: Lantern Books, 2014.

—— *The Heart of the World: An Introduction to Contemplative Christianity.* New York: The Crossroad Publishing Company, 1999.

Komjathy, Louis. *Daoism: A Guide for the Perplexed.* London and New York: Bloomsbury Academic, 2014.

—— "The Daoist Mystical Body." In *Perceiving the Divine through the Human Body: Mystical Sensuality.* Thomas Cottai and June McDaniel, eds. New York: Palgrave Macmillan, 2011, 67–103.

—— *The Daoist Tradition: An Introduction.* London and New York: Bloomsbury Academic, 2013.

Kohn, Livia. *Monastic Life in Medieval Daoism.* Honolulu: University of Hawaii Press, 2003.

—— and Harold Roth, eds. *Daoist Identity: History, Lineage, and Ritual.* Honolulu: University of Hawaii Press, 2002.

Lane, Belden. *The Solace of Fierce Landscapes: Exploring Desert and Mountain Spirituality.* New York: Oxford University Press, 1998.

Lanzetta, Beverly. *Emerging Heart: Global Spirituality and the Sacred.* Minneapolis: Fortress Press, 2007.

—— *Nine Jewels of Night: One Soul's Journey into God.* San Diego: Blue Sapphire Books, 2014.

—— *Path of the Heart.* San Diego: Blue Sapphire Books, 2014.

—— *Radical Wisdom: A Feminist Mystical Theology.* Minneapolis: Fortress Press, 2005.

Luibheid, Colin, trans. *John Cassian: Conferences.* New York: Paulist Press, 1985.

Khan, Hazrat Inayat. *The Inner Life.* Boston: Shambhala, 1997.

Merkle, Judith A. *A Different Touch: A Study of Vows in Religious Life*. Collegeville, MN: Liturgical Press, 1998.

Merton, Thomas. *Contemplation in a World of Action*. Notre Dame, IN: University of Notre Dame Press, 1998.

—— *Entering the Silence: Becoming a Monk and Writer*. The Journals of Thomas Merton, Vol. 2 1941–1952. Jonathon Montaldo, ed. San Francisco: HarperCollins, 1996.

—— *The Inner Experience: Notes on Contemplation*. William H. Shannon, ed. San Francisco: HarperCollins, 2003.

—— *The Monastic Journey*. Patrick Hart, ed. Kansas City: Sheed Andrews and McMeel, Inc., 1977.

—— *Thoughts in Solitude*. New York: Farrar, Straus and Giroux, 1956.

——, trans. *The Wisdom of the Desert: Sayings from the Desert Fathers of the Fourth Century*. New York: New Directions, 1960.

McEntee, Rory, and Adam Bucko. *The New Monasticism: An Interspiritual Manifesto for Contemplative Living*. Maryknoll, NY: Orbis Books, 2015.

Mitchell, Donald W., and James Wiseman, eds. *The Gethsemani Encounter: A Dialogue on the Spiritual Life by Buddhist and Christian Monastics*. New York: Continuum, 1999.

Muller, Wayne. *How Then Shall We Live? Four Simple Questions That Reveal the Beauty and Meaning of Our Lives*. New York: Bantam, 1996.

—— *Sabbath: Restoring the Sacred Rhythm of Rest*. New York: Bantam Books, 1999.

Norris, Kathleen. *Acedia and Me: A Marriage, Monks, and A Writer's Life*. New York: Riverhead Books, 2008.

—— *The Cloister Walk*. New York: Riverhead Books, 1997.

O'Halloran, Maura. *Pure Heart, Enlightened Mind: The Zen Journals and Letters of Maura "Soshin" O'Halloran*. Boston: Charles E. Tuttle Co., Inc., 1994.

O'Murchu, Diarmuid. *Poverty, Celibacy and Obedience: A Radical Option for Life*. New York: A Crossroad Book, 1999.

—— *Religious Life in the 21st Century: The Prospect of Refounding*. Maryknoll, NY: Orbis Books, 2017.

Panikkar, Raimon. *Blessed Simplicity: The Monk as Universal Archetype*. New York: The Seabury Press, 1982.

—— *Mysticism and Spirituality. Part One: Mysticism, Fullness of Life*. Milena Carrara Pavan, ed. Maryknoll, NY: Orbis Books, 2014.

—— *Mysticism and Spirituality. Part Two: Spirituality: The Way of Life*. Milena Carrara Pavan, ed. Maryknoll, NY: Orbis Books, 2014.

—— *The Intra-religious Dialogue*. New York: Paulist Press, 1999.

—— *The Unknown Christ of Hinduism*. Maryknoll, NY: Orbis, 1981.

Paul, Diana. *Women in Buddhism: Images of the Feminine in the Mahayana Tradition*. Berkeley: University of California Press, 1985.

Pennington, Basil M. *A Place Apart: Monastic Prayer and Practice for Everyone*. New York: Doubleday, 1983.

—— *Centering Prayer: Renewing an Ancient Christian Prayer Form*. New York: Image Books, 1980.

Perron, Gregory. "Dwelling in the Heart of the Desert: On the Dialogue of Religious Experience and Monastic Interreligious Dialogue." In *Dilatato Corde*, Vol. 2:1 (January–June, 2012); see www.dimmid.org/index. asp?Type=B_BASIC&SEC={89DEECoD-25FA-49DE-BBA4-14B6F11C5886}.

—— "Entering the Heart of Our Heart: A Reflection on the Why of Catholic Monastic Celibacy." *Bulletin of Monastic Interreligious Dialogue*, No: 78 (October 2006); see www.monasticdialogue.org.

—— "The Significance of the Gethsemani Encounters and Monastic Interreligious Dialogue." *Bulletin of Monastic Interreligious Dialogue*, No: 78 (January 2007); see www.monasticdialogue.org.

—— "'To Go Where Heaven Urges Us': A Review of Bernard de Give's *A Trappist Meeting Monks from Tibet*" (Gracewing, 2010). In *Dilatato Corde*, Vol. 1:1 (January–June, 2011); see www.dimmid.org/index. asp?Type=B_BASIC&SEC={940AFF93-BF7F-47B5-92BB-0C8DE82D09E6}.

Peters, Greg. *The Story of Monasticism: Retrieving an Ancient Tradition for Contemporary Spirituality*. Grand Rapids, MI: Baker Academic, 2015.

Porter, Bill. *Road to Heaven: Encounters with Chinese Hermits*. San Francisco: Mercury House, 1993.

Pramuk, Christopher. *Sophia: The Hidden Christ of Thomas Merton*. Collegeville, MN: Liturgical Press, 2009.

Raasch, Joanna, and Harriet Luckman. *Purity of Heart in Early Ascetic and Monastic Literature: Essays in Honor of Juana Raasch, O.S.B.* Collegeville, MN: Liturgical Press, 1999.

Regnault, Lucien. *The Day-to-Day Life of the Desert Fathers in Fourth-Century Egypt*. Petersham, MA: St. Bede's Publications, 1999.

Sardello, Robert. *Silence: The Mystery of Wholeness*. Berkeley: North Atlantic Books, 2006.

Saso, Michael. *The Teachings of Daoist Master Zhuang*, 3rd rev. ed. Los Angeles: Oracle Bones Press, 2012.

Schneiders, Sandra M. *Buying the Field: Catholic Religious Life in Mission to the World*. New York: Paulist Press, 2013.

—— *Finding the Treasure: Locating Catholic Religious Life in a New Ecclesial and Cultural Context*. New York: Paulist Press, 2000.

—— *Selling All: Commitment, Consecrated Celibacy, and Community in Catholic Religious Life*. New York: Paulist Press, 2001.

Schmitt, Miriam, and Linda Kulzer, eds. *Medieval Women Monastics: Wisdom's Wellsprings*. Collegeville, MN: Liturgical Press, 1996.

Sellner, Edward C. *Finding the Monk Within: Great Monastic Values for Today*. Mahwah, NJ: HiddenSpring, 2008.

Skudlarek, William. *Demythologizing Celibacy: Practical Wisdom from Christian and Buddhist Monasticism*. Collegeville, MN: Liturgical Press, 2008.

——, ed. *Dilatato Corde*. Brooklyn: Lantern Books, 2012.

———, ed. *God's Harp String: The Life and Legacy of the Benedictine Monk Swami Abhishiktananda*. Brooklyn: Lantern Books, 2010.

——— and Bettina Baumer, eds. *Witness to the Fullness of the Light: The Vision and Relevance of the Benedictine Monk Swami Abhishiktananda*. Brooklyn: Lantern Books, 2011.

Silvers, Brock. *The Taoist Manual: Applying Taoism to Daily Life*. Nederland, CO: Sacred Mountain Press, 2005.

Simmer-Brown, Judith. *Dakini's Warm Breath: The Feminine Principle in Tibetan Buddhism*. Boston: Shambhala Publications, 2001.

Simpson, Ray. *High Street Monasteries: Fresh Expressions of Committed Christianity*. Suffolk, UK: Kevin Mayhew Ltd., 2009.

Sinetar, Marsha. *Ordinary People as Monks and Mystics: Lifestyles for Self-Discovery*. New York: Paulist Press, 1986.

Stewart, Columba. *Cassian the Monk*. New York: Oxford University Press, 1998.

——— "Evagrius Ponticus on Prayer and Anger." In *Religions of Late Antiquity in Practice*, Richard Valantasis, ed. Princeton: Princeton University Press, 2000: 65–83.

——— *Prayer and Community: The Benedictine Tradition*. Maryknoll, NY: Orbis Books, 1998.

——— "The Desert Fathers on Radical Self-Honesty." In *Vox Benedictina: A Journal of Translations from Monastic Sources*. Saskatoon, Canada: Peregrina Publishers, 8/1 (1991): 7–54.

——— "The Origins and Fate of Monasticism." In *Spiritus: The Journal of Christian Spirituality*. Baltimore: The Johns Hopkins University Press, 10 (2010): 257–264.

Swan, Laura. *The Forgotten Desert Mothers: Sayings, Lives, and Stories of Early Christian Women*. New York: Paulist Press, 2001.

Teasdale, Wayne. *A Monk in the World: Cultivating a Spiritual Life*. Novato, CA: New World Library, 2002.

——— *Bede Griffiths: An Introduction to His Interspiritual Thought*. Woodstock, VT: SkyLight Paths Publishing, 2003.

——— *The Mystic Heart: Discovering a Universal Spirituality in the World's Religions*. Novato, CA: New World Library, 1999.

Tiso, Francis. "Raimundo Panikkar on the Monk as 'Archetype,'" *Dilatato Corde*. Volume 1, numbers 1 and 2: January–December 2011.

The Rutba House, ed. *School(s) for Conversion: Twelve Marks of the New Monasticism*. Eugene, OR: Cascade Books, 2005.

Waddell, Helen. *The Desert Fathers*. New York: Vintage Books, 1998.

Ward, Benedicta. *The Lives of the Desert Fathers*. Kalamazoo, MI: Cistercian Publications, 1981.

Wilson-Hartgrove, Jonathan. *New Monasticism: What It Has To Say To Today's Church*. Grand Rapids, MI: Brazos Press, 2008.

Index

M

O

obedience, 261

    abuse of power and, 342

    monastic life and, 293–294

O'Murchu, Diarmuid, 362n26, 364n2

One Spirit Learning Alliance and Interfaith Seminary, 300. *see also* Berke, Diane

origins, of various religions, 139

P

Pali Canon (scriptures of Theravada Buddhism), 340–341

Panikkar, Raimon

    on the archetype of the monk, 24–32

    Blessed Simplicity: The Monk as Universal Archetype, 24–25

    dark night of the feminine and, 105

    early life, 25–26

paradox. *see* contradiction

passion

    defined, 321

    mystical celibacy and, 320–321

passive contemplation

    in the monastic ideal, 217

    v. active contemplation, 54–56, 199

patriarchal spirituality, 106–107

"permeable soul," as a personal quality, 203–204

personality

    in monastic life, 200–213

Philo of Alexandria, 34

Pignedoli, Cardinal Sergio, 38

"Please Call Me By My True Names" (Hanh), 272–273

Pledge of Nonviolence (King), 300

Pollard, Alton B., on social mysticism, 264–265

positive v. negative theology, 65

poverty

    Rule of St. Clare of Assisi, 345–347

    spiritual v. material, 294–295

Prajñaparamita (The Perfection of Wisdom in Eight Thousand Lines), 52, 85

Pramuk, Christopher, on "Hagia Sofia," 83

prayer

    Abraham Abulafia on, 351

    all life as, 348–355

    how to, 353–355

    in monastic life, 194

    practice of, 349–350

    release v. action, 352

Books by Beverly Lanzetta

Nine Jewels of Night:
One Soul's Journey into God
ISBN 978-0-9840616-1-7

Path of the Heart:
A Spiritual Guide to Divine Union
ISBN 978-0-9840616-2-4

Emerging Heart:
Global Spirituality and the Sacred
ISBN 978-0-8006-3893-1

40 Day Journey with Joan Chittister
ISBN 978-0-8066-8031-6

Radical Wisdom:
A Feminist Mystical Theology
ISBN 0-8006-3698-8

Foundations in Spiritual Direction:
Sharing the Sacred Across Traditions
ISBN 978-0-9840616-0-0

The Other Side of Nothingness:
Toward a Theology of Radical Openness
ISBN 0-7914-4950-5

BEVERLY LANZETTA is a theologian, spiritual teacher, and the author of many groundbreaking books on emerging global spirituality and new monasticism, including *Radical Wisdom: A Feminist Mystical Theology, Emerging Heart: Global Spirituality And the Sacred,* and *Nine Jewels of Night: One Soul's Journey into God.* Dedicated to a vision of theological openness and spiritual nonviolence, her work has won praise for its wisdom, eloquence, and mystical insight and is considered to be a major contribution to what theologian Ursula King called "a feminine mystical way for the 21st century". Beverly has taught theology at Villanova University, Prescott College, and Grinnell College and has started a number of religious and monastic initiatives including the Desert Interfaith Church, Interfaith Theological Seminary, Hesychia School of Spiritual Direction, and the Community of a New Monastic Way. She is a much-sought-after mentor for the new generation, including the "spiritual but not religious" and new monastics alike, as she brings with her forty years of experience as a guide to answering the universal call to contemplation.

Made in the USA
San Bernardino, CA
29 November 2019